THE LATE JAMES FIS

# THE LIFE AND TIMES

OF

# COL. JAMES FISK, JR.,

BEING

A FULL AND IMPARTIAL ACCOUNT OF THE REMARKABLE CAREER OF A MOST REMARKABLE MAN; TOGETHER WITH SKETCHES OF ALL THE IMPORTANT PERSONAGES WITH WHOM HE WAS THROWN IN CONTACT,

SUCH AS

*DREW, VANDERBILT, GOULD, TWEED, Etc., Etc.,*

AND A FINANCIAL HISTORY OF THE

COUNTRY FOR THE LAST THREE YEARS.

EMBRACING, ALSO, THE LIVES OF

HELEN JOSEPHINE MANSFIELD,
THE ENCHANTRESS,

AND

EDWARD S. STOKES,
THE ASSASSIN.

BY R. W. McALPINE,

A MEMBER OF THE NEW YORK PRESS.

*ILLUSTRATED.*

NEW YORK:
THE NEW YORK BOOK COMPANY, 145 NASSAU STREET;
B. R. STURGES, 81 WASHINGTON STREET, BOSTON;
SCHUYLER SMITH, LONDON, ONTARIO;
U. S. GENERAL SUBSCRIPTION AGENCY, PHILADELPHIA, PA.
DOBBS & McCOLLUM, TITUSVILLE, PA.; C. P. BRADWAY, DANVILLE, PA.
H. H. NATT & CO., CINCINNATI, O.; F. DEWING & CO., SAN FRANCISCO.

EDWARD S. STOKES.

# TABLE OF CONTENTS.

## CHAPTER XVII.



## CHAPTER XVIII.



## CHAPTER XIX.



## CHAPTER XX.



## CHAPTER XXI.



## CHAPTER XXII.



## CHAPTER XXIII.



## CHAPTER XXIV.



## CHAPTER XXV.



## CHAPTER XXVI.



## CHAPTER XXVII.



## CHAPTER XXVIII.

## CHAPTER XXIX.



## CHAPTER XXX.



## CHAPTER XXXI.



## CHAPTER XXXII.



## CHAPTER XXXIII.



## CHAPTER XXXIV.



## CHAPTER XXXV.



## CHAPTER XXXVI.



## CHAPTER XXXVII.



## CHAPTER XXXVIII.

## CHAPTER XXXIX.



## CHAPTER XL.



## CHAPTER XLI.



## ANECDOTES, Etc.



## BIOGRAPHICAL SKETCHES.

HELEN JOSEPHINE MANSFIELD.

# INTRODUCTION.

No apology for offering this book to the public is needed. The tragic occurrence on the 6th of January, 1872, which resulted in the death of Col. James Fisk, Jr., terminated the career of a most remarkable man, whose name had become familiar to nearly every reader in the world. For five years or more he and his deeds were always subjects of general interest; the boldness of his schemes, his seeming recklessness in every operation in which he engaged, the character of the associates with whom he was most intimately connected, made him at all times remarkable, and the reading public were never tired of discussing him. The manner of his taking off, and the singular circumstances leading to it, have only increased the desire to learn all that may be known of the man, and it is with the view of fully satisfying that desire that this book has been prepared. He was a man of unbounded ambition; full of generous impulses, though erratic and somewhat reckless. No enterprise was too vast for his ambition, or too difficult for his genius; and no giant of the money world could intimidate him when he had made up his mind to accomplish a given object. Everything he touched was a success. The drama, the opera, the railroad, the stock-market, and even our local marine found in him a ready capitalist and a shrewd leader. He did not hesitate to grapple with Vanderbilt, one of the financial monarchs of the age, and the astute and wily Daniel Drew was not loath to secure the aid of the young adventurer. His purse was ever open to the needy, yet his charities were rarely marked by ostentatious display. As the commander of a regiment, he lavished money in supporting his own organization, while he created a spirit of rivalry which infused new life into the whole of the National Guard of New York, and forced from many prominent military men what they had previously denied him, a hearty recognition of his enterprise and public spirit.

One of the most eccentric men that ever basked in the sunshine of prosperity, he was at the same time one of the most kindly. He was wayward, yet clear-headed; hot-tempered, yet easily won by a pleasant word; notoriously indifferent to the opinion of the world, but ever ready to alleviate humanity's sorrows. His faults were many, but now that he is dead, thousands of people who felt his quiet sympathy, and enjoyed his princely bounty, will forget the follies of the erring man, and remember only the tender solicitude of the benefactor and his prompt and hearty answer to appeals for aid. The world has not had time to forget his labors on behalf of the Chicago sufferers; and there are many who can recall that bright sunny Sabbath-day when the news of the battle of Antietam reached Boston, and when Fisk, then an obscure dry-goods salesman, by appeals to the clergy and the congregations of the city, induced them to devote the holy day to the preparation of needful supplies for the sick and wounded braves on that bloody field, and toiled throughout the day and night in superintending the transportation of the precious freight.

But James Fisk, Jr., must not be judged altogether on his merit as a good-hearted man. He was a power in the land. His audacity in speculation was fully matched by the success that attended his efforts to control the Legislature, and even the Judiciary, on nearly all occasions when their action was needed to advance his interests. For many years the bar of Europe and America strove in vain to loosen his grasp upon the Erie Road, and all to no apparent effect. The strongest attacks upon him resulted in nothing. The man seemed predestined to a life of unvarying success. His influence upon the financial history of the country for three or four years was greater than that of any hundred other men combined, for he dealt with Fortune with a perfect trust in her good-will to him, and his dealings were almost unparalleled in their magnitude. "The pistol-shot of a cyprian's champion," said the *Tribune*, on the morning after Fisk's death, "will have its echo in every exchange of the world."

The same journal, always the bitterest in its denunciations

of the singular man, thus sums up the salient points in his character, and comments upon his strange career:

"It is doubtful whether even in this age, so fruitful in phenomenal men and in sudden transitions, any more picturesque life than Fisk's can be recorded. His purposes were as insane as those of Train or Clootz, yet he accomplished them all. His morals were as loose as those of Casanova or Lauzun, yet in this reticent age he had no reserve or concealments. He was an adventurer as fantastic as Cagliostro, but never pretended to be anything more than what he was. 'If I were not Alexander,' said the Macedonian, 'I would be Diogenes.' This Yankee peddler was both—cynic and conqueror. Even fiction furnishes few personages more absurd in qualities and in fortune. Falstaff was not droller, more sensual, and more prudent. The list which Leporello made of his master's victims was scarcely more varied in race and name than that of this travesty of Don Juan. Even the story of Aladdin ceases to seem so impossible when we think of this illiterate Vermonter stepping almost without an interval from his cart of notions to take the reins of a great corporation, to purchase to-day a fleet and to-morrow a theater, to make to-day a panic and to-morrow a statute, to buy legislatures and prima donnas, to dazzle Wall street with the brilliancy of his thefts and Central Park with the splendor of his equipages; to complement Sardanapalus with Robert Macaire.

"It is not creditable to our society and our civilization that such careers are possible. But the public conscience, if not vigorous enough to prevent them, has still enough vitality to mark and to resist them. In the hight of his power Tweed knew no men but politicians. When Fisk was the most dreaded man in the business world, he had no social relations. His four-in-hand usually conveyed more spotted reputations than his own. His box in his own Opera House was shunned as if infected, by all who had any character to lose. The enormous diamonds he so delighted to wear only shed a stronger light upon the isolation in which he lived.

"His eccentricities marked him out for punishment. He lived so much in the public eye, his vanity and desire for admiration made him so grotesquely picturesque, that he became a sort of type of that spirit of lawless fraud and plunder which created him and by which he flourished. It was strong and vigorous in Wall street long before him. He was plucked and stripped by it when he first arrived here. He grappled with it, and at last forced it to serve him. There were worse men in the street than he could learn to be. When he is laid away in a grave where only a few will regret him, meaner and cooler rogues, who now join in condemning him, will go on cheating their friends and neighbors the same as before. But the public notice and reprobation was attracted by the magnitude, the audacity, and the marvelous luck of this man's ventures. His carriages, his gems, and his uniforms continually advertised him to the general indignation, as the plumage of a tropical bird betrays him to the hunter. His flashes of cynical and defiant humor furnished unfailing quotations to the haunters of the Clubs who imitated in silence the vices they affected to denounce. He was a predestined scape-goat, and so Wall street willingly loaded all its sins on his broad shoulders and sent him out into the wilderness of ill-repute.

"We know the worst of him. What there was good in him the world has had little chance to learn. He was no hypocrite—if that is any praise. When he devoured the widow's substance, he differed from many of his associates in refraining from the pretence of long prayers. In the household circle where he was known before he became the James Fisk, Jr., of history, he will be sincerely mourned and wept. Perhaps it is as well that we should leave his story as it is known to the world—a warning and a lesson. There would be little to regret in the close of his career, if the public reprobation which was so freely lavished upon him could be turned upon the system that produced him and the slyer transgressors he has left behind."

In this book the whole story of Fisk's remarkable career is told plainly and truthfully. No pains have been spared to make it what we hope the public will declare it to be, an impartial Life of James Fisk, Jr.

JAY GOULD.

# THE
# LIFE AND TIMES
## OF
# JAMES FISK, JR.

---

## CHAPTER I.

JAMES FISK, JR., one of the very many singular characters whom the New England States have produced, was born near the battle-field of Bennington, Vermont, on the 1st of April, 1835. His father was an old-fashioned country peddler, of a class now seldom met with except in regions far removed from railroad lines, although sometimes encountered even in districts which the iron horse traverses in all directions. He was a very plain, commonplace man, with no education, and imbued with very little more taste than that acquired in a life devoted to petty trade and in a country inhabited mainly by people more given to manual labor than to intellectual culture. His mother, the eldest daughter of a well-to-do farmer, was noted for her neatness and thrift, and her great devotion to her husband and family. She died when Jim was two years old, and shortly afterward the elder Fisk married again.

At the age of five, little Jim, a fat and mischievous urchin, whose great delight was in "making a trade" with some play-fellow, or in wandering away for miles in the country with a certainty of being soundly flogged on his return, was taken by his parents to Brattleboro, where his father established his head-quarters. Here Jim was sent to school, and was not long in making himself famous, not for proficiency in his studies, but, on the contrary, for his utter inability to appreciate the beauties of literal combination as set forth in Webster's old spelling-book, and his quaintly-expressed contempt for the syntax of his native tongue. Long after he had reached "three syllables" and had learned to write with some degree of skill, he continued to spell "busy" with two *z*s and an *i*, altogether ignoring the *u*, which he evidently believed to be out of place. One of his copy-books, used when he was about twelve years old, is still preserved by his step-mother at her home in Brattleboro, and to say that it is a literary curiosity is to do meagre justice to one of the most original of all the written results of school-boy labor ever examined by the critic. Hardly a page but shows the antipathy of the boy to everything like set forms, and hardly a line but bears evidence of his natural contempt for uniformity. The little book contains three or four compositions, one of which, entitled "A Piece about The Dog," is as unique as anything ever penned by Artemus Ward. The young writer says in his "Piece" (which had evidently been originally written "Peace"):

"A Dog is an animal with fore legs because he is a quad-rooped. I like large dogs best because they can run further and fight better than little dogs and they can also cetch rabits. A big dog aint worth much without hes got good breed into him. Then I had drather hev a littler one. They can also drag sleds some has been learned to cary sticks and baskets and seterer. The bulldog is the best fighting dog because most likely he was made for that purpus. A terrier goes mostly for rats but they can also fight. I think the newfoundland is the noblest dog, he saves children from drownding and they are sagasious. This is all for the present."

He was remarkably fond of dogs, horses and other animals, and had a special liking for little children, a trait that characterized him through life. One of his schoolmates says that Jim Fisk was ready to fight the largest boy at school whom he might detect in an act of cruelty or oppression toward anything weaker, whether child or beast.

Mr. Fisk, Sr., was very successful as a peddler, but like nearly all Vermonters he was ever ready to speculate outside of his legitimate business. He traded in live-stock to some extent, bought and sold real estate, and shortly after taking up his residence in Brattleboro built the Revere House, now the property of Mrs. Fisk. The hotel was much needed, but was not always well managed; so, when the elder Fisk became dissatisfied with a tenant, he would take charge of the house himself and leave his peddling business in the hands of trusted agents. For a long time young Jim served as a waiter in his father's hotel, and was always popular with the guests. His ready wit, his unfailing good nature, his promptness, and his strict honesty in rendering accounts and giving change, gave him a good name, which not even the reports of his later career can injure in the estimation of his numerous old customers, the honest farmers of Eastern Vermont. Jim was fond of reading the few papers that reached the village, and as his memory was good he always mastered their contents and could entertain a select company of travelers with an unfailing stream of news-items from all parts of the world, seasoned and spiced with his quaint comments. As his hearers were seldom great readers, Jim had a great advantage over them, and he was more than once credited with the authorship of witty things that he had gathered from the "serious column" of the papers and treasured in his mind for future use.

"I used to set with a lot of old fellows around the stove on cold winter nights," said Fisk to a friend, a few months before his death, "and spin yarns. I tell you, it was fun to watch the faces of them men. Most of them liked jokes best, but some had a pious preference for stories with a one-horse moral. Well, I knew lots of such stories; but, to save my life, I couldn't help running in a joke once in a while, and then you'd ought to seen the skeered looks of the sober-sided ones. Once I told a long story. It was about some Adolphus or other that killed his rival on account of jealousy. They were both courting the same lovely maiden, whose father was a deacon in a slab church with a skew gable and a square steeple, with one of these corn-twisted lightning-rods pinting up from the top of it like the stick of an umbrella. I described the lovely maid, with her amber hair and her striped calico gown and her soft blue eyes, and pictured her on the way to meetin', with Adolphus a little ahead of her, and the other fellow on the opposite side of the road. Then I got her into church, where she devoted in a most proper manner, with all the young men gazing upon her like head-lights on that curve up yonder at Carr's Rock. Then I escorted her home again, where the two rivals met at the garden gate, and indulged in profanity. This part of the tale I cut short, like a terrier's tail, of course. Then I told how the two infatuated young men fit at that garden gate, and how the lovely maid with the amber hair rushed out, and was just in time to see her favorite killed. Well, you see, I made a long story of it, but I finally got her and Adolphus in love, on account of the explanation he made when they had him in jail, where she had been to carry him tracts and home-made bread, and to gabble with him through the bars. Then

AS A TAVERN-BOY.

IN BUSINESS WITH HIS FATHER.

Adolphus was pardoned, you know, and the happy pair got married. Then I wound up by remarking that Virtue was its own reward some time or other, any how. When father heard that, and seen old Mr. Payson Godfrey open his eyes and start as if to go out, he said, 'Look here, Jim, you know well enough that that wasn't in the story. Go out to the barn, now, and bed them horses.' Well, I didn't recover from that expose for a good while. My reputation was jammed, like a passenger car with nary a bumper; for, you see, most of these old cusses thought that my stories and things was all original."

Fisk, Sr., was not long in discovering that his boy possessed a rare talent for trade, and that although he knew little of spelling and much less of grammar, he was a ready reckoner, and rarely made a mistake in any question of figures. He, therefore, began to take Jim with him on his peddling tours. The youngster at once proved the correctness of the father's impressions; for his general quickness, his strong intuitive knowledge of character, his retentive memory, and his natural Yankee acquaintance with the quality and value of all merchantable goods, combined to make him from the very start, at the age of thirteen, more useful than any man the peddler had ever employed. Wherever he traveled with the old-fashioned wagon, he was sure to be welcomed, for he was a general favorite. Business increased at a rate that Fisk, Sr., had never anticipated.

"I say Jim," said the father one day, after having returned to "headquarters" with an empty wagon and a full wallet, "suppose I give you a wagon?"

"That's a question I've been asking myself," replied young hopeful. "I don't much cal'late on working all my days for board and clothes, and I think, if you'll only give me a good set-out, we can make things siss."

A wagon was ordered from Bennington, and a fair bargain entered into between father and son. The two lines of travel more than doubled the business of the firm, and the country began to ring with the remarkable success of James Fisk & Son.

## CHAPTER II.

YOUNG FISK was now in his element. He was, to a certain extent, his own master; the business in which he was engaged exactly suited his disposition, and his popularity was daily increasing. But the elder Fisk was a constant restraint to the young enthusiast. He saw in his son strong evidence of a desire to shine by

> "showing a more swelling port
> Than his faint means would grant continuance,"

and soon learned that the youngster was much given to fine horses, and had an abiding faith in jaunty wagons most gaudily painted and elaborately adorned. He therefore tried to check the boy in his exhibitions of showy trappings, fast horses, and gaudy vehicles. Father and son could not agree. Their ideas touching the means to a successful end were entirely different. Young Fisk was a natural advertiser. He believed that nothing could help a business man half as much as to be talked about. Our great newspapers, our most successful merchants, our quacks and other humbugs, are all imbued with the same idea, but fortunately have better facilities for making themselves conspicuous. The two found that they could not work well together. One day at a breakfast table of a tavern where they chanced to meet on one of their trips, young James turned to his father in his impulsive way and astonished the old gentleman with the query:

"Say, Pop, what 'll you take for your share in this show?"

("Show" was always a favorite word with Fisk. He was very fond of shows of all kinds, and had at one time acted as an assistant to Van Amburgh, the great lion-king. His career in New York in connection with the Opera House and other places of amusement, and with Montaland, Silly, Aimée, and other "shows," is a sufficient evidence that he never lost the taste formed in his youth.)

"Well," said Fisk Sr., who, like most trading Vermonters, always answered a question *de more Scottice*—that is, by asking another; "Well, what 'll you give?"

Said James, promptly—he had already made a close calculation as to the value of the working stock of the firm—"I'll give you $3,000 for your share, jest as it stands, with your two old roans that ain't worth $100, the two bays, your old wagon, that I'll sell for lumber, and my wagon. We haven't $1,000 worth of goods left, and I think the offer is fair."

"But what 'll I do, Jim, if I give up?"

"Why, come and work with me. I'll give you $15 a week."

"Done," said Fisk, Sr.; and the transfer was made.

It was not long before the country side rang with the praises of Jim Fisk's new turn-outs. His new wagons were the most splendid affairs ever seen in New England. His horses were of the best breed, and such specimens of horseflesh as had certainly never been driven by peddlers before. His drivers and agents were all selected from among the shrewdest and most experienced itinerant merchants in the

State. Before starting out from Brattleboro' on his first grand tour in force, he organized his business thoroughly, showing the same tact, forethought and dash that ever afterward characterized the man in whatever he might be engaged. His stock of silks, satins, velvets, laces, jewelry, and the thousand and one little nothings that help so materially to make up the sum of the country girl's happiness, was immense. He was always selling out and always replenishing from Boston and New York, and for miles and miles through the country in which he dealt there were few people, either farmers or merchants, manufacturers or mechanics, who did not believe that James Fisk, Jr., was the heaviest dealer outside of "York;" and the matrons and maids from one end of his route to the other could never have been brought to admit that Jim Fisk was not the most captivating peddler, the most stylish driver, and the most princely traveler that ever measured silk, cracked whip, or settled tavern bill.

Long after the period here spoken of, when Fisk was a millionaire, when money kings feared him, when the press flattered him, when fortune seemed to promise never to withhold her favors, he was heard to say to a knot of friends collected in his cosy office in the Erie Building:

"Happy! By George, them was the happiest days of my life! I had everything I hankered after, money, friends, stock, trade, credit, and the best horses in New England. Besides, by —— I had a reputation. There wasn't no man that could throw dirt onto Jim Fisk. My word was good, my bills was paid prompt as the splash of a musk-rat. Look how it is now! Because I've been lucky, half these d—d papers call me a thief, and they even blackguard me because I've been a peddler. Happy! *You bet!* I was as proud on the top of that wagon, behind those four bays, as I am now; and I'll be busted if I didn't sleep a sight better. In them days I didn't know Delmonico. I didn't keep a French cook and other luxuries too numerous to mention, but I could eat my rations at any country tavern with a bully relish, and talk pious after supper a good deal more comfortable than I can now. By the Lord! If it wasn't for the excitement, and the Twelve Temptations, and a few other little things here that I couldn't have in Vermont, I'd rather be driving that wagon than managing the Erie Railway."

It is a great pity that he could not have remained among his native hills, where, in pursuit of a calling for which he was admirably adapted, he could have passed a long life of usefulness, with his name free from taint, and his reputation for honesty and morality untarnished. For it is well known among his friends that during his career as a peddler, when his transactions were on the largest scale, he was never accused of unjust dealing, although acknowledged to be, perhaps, the shrewdest trader in the State. His vices seem to have been contracted after his removal to New York, where he was thrown constantly in contact with men accustomed to the dissipations of city life.

After conducting his peddling business for a year or more with great success, Fisk accepted the offer of a position with Jordan, Marsh & Co., merchants of Boston, of whom he had purchased the greater part of his dry goods. They knew that he was prompt, honest and energetic; and had heard time and again of his great popularity and success as a trader. Fisk had been very extravagant in living, and no less extravagant in providing for the wants of others. His business, although large and remunerative, left him very little ahead of the world at the end of the year, and believing that there was a bright future before him, he gave up his wagons and horses, and went to Boston, where he entered the service of Jordan, Marsh & Co., as salesman.

"I tell you," said Fisk, when once relating his experience, "that was the most disagreeable position I ever tried to fill. I once drove team for a menagerie. I've been chief engineer of a peddler's caravan. I used to wait on table in a country tavern. I've speculated. I've run railroads and steamboats. I've had an Opera House on my hands, with a cantankerous, yawping set of Opera Buffers to quiet and to feed. I've been a'most anything and everything, but I'd rather be hired to drink panegyric by the week, or to track old Greeley, or even to run for the White House with Grant alongside of me, than to be salesman in a dry-goods shop. I don't mean a retail concern, for there'd be fun in that for me, but a wholesale shop, where they buy by the cargo and sell by the raft. Why, you've got to stand up alongside of a pile of goods and dicker with a man. I never liked to dicker. Then if you don't sell him you are below par, you see. When you hear of an arrival at a hotel, if you're drumming as well as selling, you must start off, find your man, interview him, like these reporters, treat him to the kind of pizen he likes best, and then lie to him like thunder. Now, if there's anything I hate worse than dickering, its lying. I never could bear to lie. Well, you come it over that man. You get him into your place. Then you try to make him believe that your firm sells cheaper and better goods than all the rest in the trade. He don't believe it, and you don't. He knows that you don't believe it, and you know that he don't believe it, but there you stand like a pair of virtuous owls, and maybe you sell him. If you don't, he goes to some other shop where truth is quoted at a high figure. He hears the same story from some other virtuous salesman, and maybe he comes back to you. He's a darned fool if he does; might save shoe-leather and hoof, you see, by stopping jest where he is. I don't like to run after trade. It's worse than lying—jest about as bad again. When I was in Vermont, it was beneath my dignity to run for it. People used to run for me. I've had a whole ambulance of orders many a time that I couldn't fill, and more a coming in. Never be a salesman, my son, is my advice. The poet says, 'Better to have lost and won than never to have played at all,' but unless nature has borned you with a dry-goods mark onto your back, don't be a salesman. Better be a nunnery."

At the end of six months his employers informed him that as a salesman he was a failure.

"I know that," said Fisk, "but suppose you try me at something else. You can't eat soup with a fork. Put me at something that I feel I can do. Let me go out into the world for you, and I'll make my light shine like a bushel of fire-bugs."

At this time his habits of extravagance were very marked, and while he was strictly temperate, and was not known to gamble, or to spend his time with improper characters, his funds were always low just after the first of the month, and Jim Fisk became known as a man very careless in money matters. This imputation, however, applied to him only in regard to his own money. His employers always regarded him, and still remember him, as one of the most accurate and conscientious clerks in Boston.

## CHAPTER III.

THE breaking out of the war was Fisk's first opportunity to display to any great extent his wonderful ability to take in at a glance the possibilities of a speculation, his boldness in taking the risk, and his perfect recklessness in carrying out his quickly formed plans.

Immediately after the calling out of the first 75,000 troops there was a great demand for supplies of cotton and woollen garments for the soldiers. Fisk was soon in the front rank of speculators in quest of contracts, and his success in securing them was as great as the means whereby he secured them were secret. It has always been shrewdly guessed that he paid liberally for the favors granted him, knowing that the profits on the transactions would be immense. And they were immense. Surprised and delighted at the genius of their salesman, the firm gave him full liberty to do as he pleased in the contract business, and furnished him with blank checks to be used at his discretion in defraying his enormous expenses. They had perfect confidence in the man—a confidence which was never for a moment shaken. His rooms at Washington, whither he went to deal with Government officers, were the finest at Willard's. They were open day and night, and the most generous hospitality was dispensed to all who choose to call upon him. His visitors comprised officers of all ranks, but he was particularly partial to members of the Quartermaster's Department, whom he had a powerful object in winning. It is unnecessary to say that his wines and cigars, his delicate lunches, his jokes, and, perhaps, a little of his money judiciously distributed, gained the point for which he had been striving.

He secured a heavy contract for the supply of cotton and woollen shirts and underclothing, which netted the firm a clear profit of $150,000; and in addition, disposed of hundreds of pairs of old blankets which had long cumbered the warehouse, and which his partners had despaired of ever selling. The samples which he had taken to Washington were approved on inspection, and after his full supply was exhausted he was awarded a contract to furnish thousands more at a large advance on cost. These he had made to order at mills in the vicinity of Boston, and so rapidly was the work done under the unceasing stimulus of his sharp "Hurry up!" sent daily over the wires, that the full supply was in camp and distributed days before the terms of the contract called for their delivery at Washington. His expenses at Willard's at this time were $1000 a day.

On one of his trips to the Capital, just before the close of the Fall Campaign of 1861, he was surrounded by a number of army officers stationed at Washington, many of whom were afterward suspected of having been at that time deeply interested in various contracts. The wine had flowed freely, the guests were hilarious, and Fisk himself, having that day effected a brilliant stroke, was brimming over with fun. But then, as ever afterward, there were moments, in the midst of the most uproarious mirth, when the undercurrent of feeling would come to the surface, and make itself known and felt in some quaint expression of sentiment, some earnest, tender word of pity, called forth by the sight of a suffering face, or the sound of a sorrowful voice. Even a careless remark about an act of wrong or injustice would often evoke from this rare compound of good and evil such expressions of honest anger as satisfied his hearers that he was not altogether the buffoon or the trickster.

The conversation, on the occasion referred to, was on the subject of contracts and supplies. Smith's successes and Jones's failures were canvassed with a boisterous hilarity that would do honor to the Stock Exchange on "Hat Day." It was told how Robinson outwitted Thompson, and the joke "made the circles of their eyes flow with distilled laughter;" how Johnson and Grimes played, each to get the better of the other; how West beat North; how North retaliated with a *coup* that made him master of the situation; and the merriment was unbounded.

"But did you hear," said one of the party during a lull—"did you hear how Brown, of Philadelphia, and Jones, of New York, managed to run their shoddy pants and their paper-soled shoes through the Quartermaster's Department, and how they got that fat contract?"

"Let's have the story!" cried a dozen or more; and the story was told, amid peals of laughter.

Jim Fisk, perhaps the most illiterate man present, the most uncultivated, seemingly the most reckless and sensual, did not join in the laugh, but sat silent, with his chair tipped back against the wall.

"Good, wasn't it, Fisk?" said a young adventurer, turning toward him as the story was brought to a close.

"Good? Yes, d——d good," said Fisk with emphasis. "Did they hang Brown? Did they shoot Jones? If they didn't they had ought to. D——d hounds! I tell you, gentlemen, it's one thing to trade and another thing to steal. It's one thing to make a good bargain and get a good profit, even when you deal with a poor man. But it jest strikes me like a trip-hammer onto a barnacle, that Jones and Brown was a mile ahead of felony in the first degree when they took their contracts and sent in their goods and got their money. Who paid for them shoddy pants and them soft-shelled shoes? Why, they were paid for by brave men with their blood, and, by G—d, I think they had ought to had a *quid pro quorum*, or something almighty close to it, for their outlay. The man that will take the upper hand of a soldier in the field, is worse than a thief—there's no sand in his craw—he's a d——d God-forsaken, pink-eyed, white-livered scoundrel, and his clothes don't fit him. The sooner he takes to gravel the better."

This vehement outburst was entirely unexpected. It was like the explosion of a shell in a quiet camp; and it is said that ever after the delivery of the Vermont speculator's impromptu speech, his guests were very careful not to broach "shoddy" again, except to speak of contractors of the Brown and Jones type in the most indignant and scornful terms.

## CHAPTER IV.

FISK'S wonderful success soon led to his being admitted as a member of the firm of Jordan, Marsh & Co., whom he had so faithfully served, and the way to fortune was at last opened to him. He continued to bid for and secure large contracts, to supply which it became necessary for the firm to purchase mills and manufacture for themselves. Their business increased so rapidly that even the purchased mills were unable to turn out the great quantities of goods called for; and as there were no more mills to buy, they erected several, and became leading manufacturers. This giant stride was made at the suggestion of their junior partner, whose word at this time was almost equivalent to law. They obtained the monopoly of certain kinds of goods by depleting the market, and by purchasing the only mill (that at Graysville, Vermont), which was then producing them. The mill was run for about two years at a tremendons profit, and when no longer needed, was sold to its former owner at a moderate advance on cost.

The war had now been in progress for some time, and communication with the South was practically closed. Cotton, which, in the Confederacy, was a drug at twelve cents a pound, was very scarce at the cotton centres of the North, where it sold readily at from $1.20 to $2.00 a pound. The manufacturers were beginning to suffer severely for the want of the raw material, and many mills, whose owners could not pay the market price, were either closed or converted into woolen mills.

Fisk, with his usual foresight, had laid in a large stock of the precious staple some time before it reached its maximum figure, and prudently refused to part with it on any terms when the dearth came. Every pound of it was needed for the consumption of his mills, and although the quantity stored was immense, he knew that the great demand for the goods made by the firm would exhaust the supply long before the Federal forces would be able to penetrate to the cotton region, release the thousands of bales there stored, and open an avenue for its transmission to the North. With the readiness of a veteran speculator, trained to watch, record, and seize the opportunities of the hour, he proposed that the firm should at once begin the business of running cotton through the lines from the Southern States. There was but little discussion on this point. Jim Fisk's plans had never failed. His projects, although sometimes wild, were always feasible. The profits of the cotton speculation, conducted as he designed, could not, if the cotton could be procured, prove other than enormous. None of the staple had as yet been forwarded to the north; the market was empty; the demand was great. His proposition to engineer the movement was accepted without a question, and in the month of February, 1862, Fisk began his operations. He first established amicable relations with government officials on either side, by means known only to himself and them. He sent down to Tennessee trusted agents, shrewd, bold, brave men, to whom danger weighed nothing in the balance against the prospect of splendid gains. At this time cotton was being destroyed all over the South. Lovell, in command at New Orleans, had ordered that all the cotton in his department should be given to the flames, for he knew that Farragut, then approaching the devoted city, would soon have the whole country under his control, and would consequently be able to furnish the factories of the North with millions of pounds which the Southerners were then unable to use. In Georgia, Alabama, South Carolina, Mississippi, and Tennessee, immense quantities had already been destroyed; but among the planters there were many shrewd enough to foresee that one day their crops would be worth more in greenbacks than in ashes, and these had prudently hidden their stock where the inspecting officers of the Confederate government were unable to find it. Their cupidity overcame their patriotism, and in time they found their reward for the choice they had made between principle and interest.

Among Fisk's most able adjutants in the cotton speculation was his father, who was the first agent sent to Tennessee to survey the position and report. A number of sharp Yankee dealers were placed under him, and in a short time the result of their boldness and skill was apparent.

The first boat-load of cotton from Tennessee to Pittsburg, during the war, arrived on the 22nd of April, 1862. This was a meagre cargo, and was forwarded under the care of United States officers and consigned to the Quartermaster's Department at Washington. Another and another followed. All at once the supply began to increase at a rapid rate. Hundreds and thousands of bags and bales came in, with which the government had nothing to do. These were consigned to Jordan, Marsh & Co., of Boston, who now became, for the time, the cotton kings of the country.

During the month of May, Fisk had run down to Memphis to expedite affairs. He found everything going on well, but his ambition to work wonders in the money world was now beginning to develope itself, and he resolved to redouble his efforts to make himself felt as a power in the land. He had gained the favor of the administration at Washington, and was supplied with unlimited facilities for passing to and from the Federal camps. His passes had been secured by Lottie Hough, an actress, and a beautiful and accomplished woman, whose skill and boldness were fully equal to the requirements of the business in which she proposed to engage. She entered into a regular partnership with Fisk, took charge of affairs at Memphis, Nashville, and Huntsville, divided the profits at the end of the war, and retired with a fortune. The agents under her were shrewd men and had been furnished with immense sums with which to make purchases of cotton. They bought largely, and thousands of bales were forwarded to the Boston firm. The risk of transportation was so great at this time that five per cent. was charged for insurance by companies at Boston and New York, nearly all of whom lost heavily, notwithstanding their extravagant charges.

New Orleans surrendered to Farragut on the 25th of April, 1862, and on the 1st of May General Butler took command of the city. He had not been long there before Fisk had his agents at work in the surrounding country. Lovell had destroyed large quantities of the cotton stored on the plantations of Louisiana, particularly those along the Mississippi, but there were thousands of bales safely stored where the Confederate officers had not been able to find them, and these were greedily bought up by the energetic speculators, who, favored by certain government officials high in authority, had but little difficulty, after reaching the Federal lines, in getting their stock fairly on the way to the markets of the North.

When the Red River expedition began operations, Fisk himself went down to New Orleans, and thence up the river to the cotton country in which Banks was at work. Before leaving the Crescent City he purchased the steamer *Joseph Peirce*, to be used as a cotton transport between the river country and the city. She had made several successful trips, when, one day, while at a wood-landing she was boarded by an army officer who demanded transportation for himself and a number of soldiers. The remonstrances of the captain proved of no avail, and the soldiers took possession of the steamer. They brought on board with them a large quantity of cartridges and other fixed ammunition. Hardly had the boat put out from the shore when there was a terrific explosion, and in less than half an hour she was a complete wreck. The survivors of the explosion reached the shore only after experiencing the greatest difficulties. At the close of the war Fisk entered a claim against the government for the value of the steamer and her cargo, but it was never allowed. The loss to the firm by this accident was nearly $350,000.

Jordan, Marsh & Co. were now shipping to New Orleans millions at a time for the purchase of cotton, and were honoring almost daily sight-drafts of from $100,000 to $500,000. Their receipts of cotton were immense, and their shipments to Europe were sufficiently liberal to keep many English factories from breaking up, and consequently thousands of operatives were continued in employment who otherwise would have been thrown upon the world to suffer for the necessaries of life.

Associated with Jordan, Marsh & Co., were William Dwight and Francis Skinner & Co., of Boston, all of whom cleared large sums for a long time. It was their custom to ship directly from New Orleans to Liverpool in order to create exchange, to pay for merchandise bought in Europe but they continued also to ship large quantities to the North, where there was always a good market. It is a notable fact, however, that when a settlement was made, there had been so much loss by fire and by fall in price, that the profits of the Red River Cotton Expedition were found to be next to nothing. The Memphis, Nashville and Huntsville speculations, on the contrary, were wonderfully remunerative.

Before Banks left the Red River country, Fisk, emboldened by his successes, became almost recklessly venturesome. His purchases of cotton sometimes reached $800,000 a day, many of the heaviest transactions being conducted either by himself or under his own eye. It is said that on one occasion, while outside the Federal lines, with a wallet containing $250,000 strapped to his shoulders, he was surprised by a squad of rebel soldiers, who appeared suddenly at the edge

IN BUSINESS FOR HIMSELF!

of a clearing over which he was about to pass. Fisk was already tired, and being a stout man and fearful that, encumbered as he was, he would fall into the enemy's hands before he "could heat an acre," he unstrapped his wallet, threw it down behind a tree, and ran for dear life. On the following day there was an advance of the Federal forces, and the spot on which the valuable deposit had been made, was under the old flag. Search was made for the wallet and the quarter of a million that it contained, but no trace of it could be found.

"Well," said Fisk, drawing a long breath, when all hope had fled, "I guess I'll sleep about as well to-night as if I had that darned wallet for a pillow. There ain't nothing the matter with *my* old tin stove."

This last expression was a very common one with the eccentric Fisk. He used it on all occasions when he desired to announce his perfect satisfaction with himself; and long afterward, when occupying his cosy quarters in the Erie building, he was accustomed to check any demonstration of ill-humor on the part of his *alter ego,* Jay Gould, by singing out, in a cheery voice, "Why, Gould, what'n thunder's the matter with *your* old tin stove?"

In the summer of 1862, Fisk, Sr., while actively engaged in cotton buying and forwarding in Tennessee, was sunstruck. For a long time his life was despaired of, but he recovered his physical health on his return to Boston, where his son and his daughter-in-law (for Fisk, Jr., was now a married man) were unremitting in their attention to the sufferer. As his wonted strength returned, it was discovered that his intellect had become much impaired, and following the advice of eminent physicians, his son placed him in an insane asylum, where, supplied with all that money could furnish, and cared for tenderly by his relatives, the old gentleman soon recovered. Fisk, Jr., employed two experienced nurses to wait upon his father, and spared no expense to make him comfortable and happy, and to insure his return to complete mental health.

On the Sunday following the battle of Antietam, in September, 1862, the news of that terrible conflict reached Boston. Thousands of wounded and dying men lay upon that bloody field, the force of surgeons was insufficient to attend to the pressing wants of the sufferers, rations were short, and medicines, bandages and luxuries for the victims of the fight were almost exhausted. The meagre dispatches that reached Boston on that bright Sabbath morning told the story of the battle, and the one line that announced the scarcity of needed food and clothing among the soldiers of both sides then lying within our lines about Sharpsburg, was an appeal that touched the heart of the erratic Fisk, and drew forth from him an expression of sympathy that deserves to honor his name forever.

He rushed to Jordan's house. The bells were ringing for church. The streets were thronged with people on their way to worship.

"Jordan," said he, impetuously, "can't nothing be done? Are them poor fellows to lay down there suffering while we people up here enjoy all the comforts of life and have lots to spare? What can we do to stir things up?"

"I don't know, indeed," said Jordan, pondering.

"Well, I *do* know," said Fisk, as he started for the door. "I'm going to see if the preachers of Boston can't be made to preach God in a new way to-day. It may be wrong for people to buy and sell on the Sabbath, and the making of goose bridles I know is a sin, but if you'll help me I'll have more pious Sabbath-breaking done here before sundown than all the angels can keep track of."

His plans were soon laid. Messengers were sent to all the churches with the request that, in the name of humanity and patriotism, the congregations should engage in the work of preparing lint, bandages, clothing, medicines and delicacies for the wounded on the banks of the Antietam, and in the hospitals in and around Sharpsburg.

To the honor of the Bostonians, be it said, this suggestion was eagerly acted upon. Nearly every man, woman and child that had anything to give, or could scrape lint or make and roll bandages, went into the work with spirit. Before night Tremont Temple was a vast store-house of goods contributed by the citizens; and there, with coat off and sleeves rolled up, with the perspiration streaming down his face, was Jim Fisk, giving orders here, helping to pack a box there, and everywhere in a minute, laboring as if for very life. And by common consent, every detail of the business was intrusted to him, and nobly did he perform the self-imposed duty. That night, car-loads of supplies were on their way to the front, and in a day or two, thousands of sufferers were soothed and gladdened by the timely distribution of the various comforts which had been collected through the efforts of the young dry-goods merchant.

Said a gentleman to the author about a month after Fisk's tragic death, when the conversation had turned upon this stirring period in our country's history: "I was with Fisk all that day and all that night, and never in my life have I seen any one throw his whole soul into his work as that man did. He seemed to do more in an hour than any three other men. He had an eye to everything, ordered everything, controlled everything. Everybody deferred to his judgment; in short, the movement was Jim Fisk's, and it was so recognized and acknowledged."

## CHAPTER V.

FISK'S speculations were not confined to cotton. In order to create exchange to pay for merchandise imported by the firm, he would purchase and ship to Europe anything which promised to yield a good return. His shipments of butter and cheese were sometimes very heavy, and once he sent out by one steamer no less than a thousand bales of hops, at that time in great demand on the other side of the water. His income from his business and from the various speculations in which he engaged was now quite large, but his style of living was very expensive, and his outlay in quiet charity almost reckless. From the time that Fortune began to smile upon him, he was in the habit of aiding old friends and acquaintances in his native State, in many instances bringing school-mates, playfellows and neighbors to Boston and providing them with situations or setting them up in business for themselves.

The firm of Jordan, Marsh & Co. was now one of the wealthiest in the country, and their wealth and influence were daily increasing. Not only were their transactions with the Government among the most gigantic; their trade with Europe was immense; their manufacturing facilities almost unequalled, and their power in the markets of the country second to that of none. All this they owed to Fisk, the junior partner, who at the beginning of his career with them as salesman had proved to be incompetent. His foresight, his knowledge of men, his remarkable tact, his reckless use of money in the prosecution of a rapidly-formed and cherished design, had done more for them than all their original capital, and they appreciated their colleague. But he was becoming too strong for them. In business there was no such thing as self-abnegation with Fisk. He recognized his own strength, and never failed to exercise it when he evolved a plan of operations and proposed it; he could not brook opposition, for he seemed to have a foreknowledge that his projects would be successes, and the event usually proved the accuracy of his judgment. Little by little he had gained such an ascendancy over his partners, that they acted upon his merest hints with a complete confidence, and rarely were they deceived. At last it came to be understood that he could enter into any negotiation in the name of the firm without going through the formality of a conference.

Shortly after becoming a member of the house of Jordan Marsh & Co., an unfortunate inventor called upon him and asked his assistance in pushing a patent. He described the invention, explained its uses and recited the story of his trials and his failures to secure for the patent the success that he knew it merited. Fisk examined the model. It was an instrument to be used in connection with woolen machinery, and the keen Vermonter at once saw that it was of real value.

"I tell you what I'll do with you, Goulding," said he, "if you can get Congress to pass a bill for your relief, and can get seven years time for this thing, I'll buy it."

A few months afterward he purchased Goulding's patent,

paying $75,000 for it and taking the risk of fighting for it in the courts. All the woolen manufacturers in the country were in a combination to break the patent and evade the payment of the royalty, but Fisk fought them from State to State and from court to court, spending no less than $400,000 in legal expenses before the firm realized one dollar on their investment. In this, as in nearly everything else that he undertook, he was successful, beating his opponents in every State except Pennsylvania, where the celebrated "Goulding Patent" case is still undecided.

The other partners were, of course, pleased with their success, for the Goulding patent proved to be a mine of wealth. But, as before remarked, Fisk was becoming too strong for them. He was overshadowing the firm, and bade fair to ignore his partners altogether. But what could be done to check him, or to force him into a proper recognition of the rights and claims of others? To remonstrate, to protest, to argue with him, they knew would result in nothing. A remonstrance would be answered with a joke, and surely an argument, however logical, would not destroy the man's individuality. They knew by this time that Fisk could not act a subordinate part; that in whatever he engaged, it was a requirement of his nature that he should direct, control, and command. Jordan and Marsh therefore agreed to offer Fisk a fair price for his share of the business, and much to their surprise the offer was accepted without a moment's hesitation, and Fisk with a fortune in his pocket withdrew from the firm.

But he did not remain idle. In the course of a few weeks he laid in a large stock of dry goods and began business by himself in a splendid store at the corner of Sumner and Chauncey streets, a short distance from his old stand, where he had during his four years' connection with Jordan, Marsh & Co. made name, fame and fortune. His new venture was a failure. The fates were against him. The prices of dry goods went down rapidly, and there was but little trade. The commercial and financial prospects of the country were gloomy. All business was unsettled, and the shrewdest financiers were preparing for a crash. So, after a few months, Fisk closed his store, paid all his obligations, and with the remnant of his capital entered upon an entirely new life, that of stock speculator in Wall street.

Fisk could never be content without making a display. He loved bright colors and elegant trappings, and from his early boyhood to the day of his death nothing suited him that was not the best of its kind. When he rented an office in Broad street he fitted it up in the most extravagant manner, giving *carte-blanche* to the artists and workmen employed to make it the most attractive den ever dreamed of by bear or bull. His rooms were crowded every day, and all day long, by the gamblers of the street, who drank his wine and enjoyed his jokes, and—won his money. With his customary boldness he plunged headlong into the dangerous speculations of the street, but soon found that he would require schooling in this branch of business before he could hope for success. He was mercilessly hugged by the bears, and unceremoniously tossed by the bulls, but with indomitable pluck and a blind trust in the possibilities of the future, he held his ground until the street had swallowed every dollar of his money and he was ruined.

"I'll be square with you yet," said he, as he shook the dust of Wall street from his feet and took passage back to Boston.

"What are you going to do now, Fisk?" said a friend who accompanied him.

"I'm going to dog Boston a little. Then I propose to come back to this den of iniquity and boss Wall street a little. Then I expect to pick my teeth and enjoy myself a little. But I've got to hurry up, for as my school-teacher used to tell us, 'Thecrastination is the proof of Time,' or something to that effect. I'll be back in Wall street inside of twenty days, and if I don't make things squirm I'll eat nothing but bone button soup till Judgment Day. Damn 'em! they'll learn to know Jim Fisk yet!"

Fisk's word was good in Boston. He had never violated a pledge, had never failed to meet every obligation, and although not personally respected by the staid and sober Puritans of the Hub, was universally esteemed in business circles as a safe man to deal with. He met his old friends and acquaintances, told the story of his discomfiture with many a pungent comment, and was soon in funds again. Before the month had expired, he was once more in Wall street, somewhat improved in experience, but no whit less bold and self-confident than when he first tried conclusions with the veterans of the stock market.

Fortune again smiled upon him. Nearly all his ventures were successful, and "Jim Fisk's luck" became the by-word of the street.

## CHAPTER VI.

AT this time Daniel Drew, the "King of the Bears," but better known as "Uncle Daniel," was casting about for capitalists to purchase his Bristol line of steamers. He had heard a great deal concerning the enterprise and shrewdness of Fisk, and determined to secure him if possible as his agent to negotiate the sale.

The two singular men met at Fisk's office, and interchanged views on the question of steamships, railroads, stocks and finance, and in the course of an hour or two struck up a friendship that promised to be lasting. The cunning old millionaire was carried away with admiration for his new acquaintance. He found him possessed of more than ordinary ability, with just the kind of dash to insure success in an emergency, and with a rollicking *bonhomie* perfectly irresistible.

"I think you'll do, Jeems," said Uncle Daniel. "Take right hold, make a good sale, and I'll take good keer of you."

"All right, old man," said Fisk, heartily, (they were now on the most intimate terms,) "all right. I've all along wanted to go in cohoot with a pious old cuss like you. I think it will do me good. How are your theologs out at Madison? If I was only a little younger I'd kick Wall street and take a short parson course out at your seminary."

"Now, Jeems," said Drew, screwing up his wrinkled face and speaking with his head on one side and his right eye half closed—"now, Jeems, don't crack jokes on an old man. I skeercely think you'd larn much at Madison. I think your spear is finance, and I rayther guess you are of that opinion yourself."

"You bet!" was Fisk's laconic but emphatic response.

No time was lost in arranging for the sale of the steamers. Fisk entered into a combination with Jay Gould and others, and on the day of the sale, when only two of the nine vessels composing the Bristol line were up, he had them knocked down to him at $1,300,000.

"What name?" said the auctioneer.

"Jim Fisk," was the reply.

The auctioneer knew no Jim Fisk at that time; but when the future "Admiral of the Sound Fleet" marched up to the desk and presented a certified check for $2,000,000, no other introduction or indorsement was needed, and the property in the two finest steamers of the Bristol line was duly made over. A short time afterward the remaining seven steamers of the line were purchased by the same parties for $1,000,000.

Daniel Drew was then the treasurer of the Erie Railway Company, a heavy stockholder in that and other vast enterprises, and altogether one of the most powerful and influential financiers in the country. He had formed a high estimate of Fisk's abilities, and the consummate skill with which he managed the sale of the Bristol steamers, and the tact he displayed in various other operations which Drew had suggested and endorsed, more than confirmed Uncle Daniel in his opinion. He made up his mind that he would start Fisk in a wide field in which his talent should have ample scope; and with this end in view he established the firm of Fisk & Belden, the latter name being that of one of his favorite brokers.

The young firm soon made their mark in Wall street. Prompted in nearly all their operations by Daniel Drew, than whom no shrewder and more cautious speculator ever handled scrip, they rarely failed to secure large returns for their investments, and besides adding largely to the capital of their patron, they increased their own store by working quietly on the points with which they were regularly furnished, and were not long in becoming noted as among the wisest stock gamblers on the street.

Some time in the beginning of 1866 Daniel Drew created

an intense excitement by his first great "bear" movement—that is, a systematic movement to depress certain stocks. The result was the ruin of a large number of operators not in the ring, and the enriching of those with whom Drew had shared the secrets of his plan. Among the latter were James Fisk, Jr., and his partner. Several of the leading operators had tried to foil the old man, but his plans had been too well laid, and when the day for final action arrived, he and his numerous aids achieved a most signal victory.

The slang of Wall street is a technical dialect, many words of which it will be necessary to use in the course of this narrative, and therefore a few words of explanation for the unsophisticated reader may not be out of place.

When an operator wishes to bring down the price of a given stock, he is said to "bear" it, and is called a "bear."

When he desires to advance the price of a stock, they say on the street that he "bulls" it, that is, tosses it up, as the taurine creature does little boys with his horns.

Smith, who has been dabbling in Squankum Railroad Stock, is strongly impressed with the belief that the price, now 100, is about to come down. Jones, on the other hand, is sure of a rise. Smith has disposed of all his stock, and Jones is anxious to get as much of it as he can. He calls upon Smith and bargains with him for 1000 shares at 100, to be delivered in a certain time. Smith is now said to be "short" of Squankum, because he has bound himself to sell at a certain time and a fixed price, an amount of the stock which he does not own; and Jones is "long," because he has agreed to take the stock at that price.

Now Smith must buy of some one who holds the stock, but, as it will not pay him to purchase at 100 and sell at the same price, he waits to see whether the stock will fall, and, of course, does all he can to bring about that fall. Suppose Squankum runs down to 75, Smith buys 1000 shares at 75 and turns them over to Jones at 100, receiving in cash for his profits, $25,000. If Squankum, on the contrary, goes up to 125, instead of falling to 75, Smith loses $25,000, for he must still deliver to Jones at 100 as per agreement.

When a heavy operator wishes to make a "corner" in stocks, he makes contracts with a number of brokers to deliver to him within a certain time, say 100,000 shares of stock at a certain price. Perhaps there are only 60,000 shares of that stock in the field. He goes to work quietly, buys all of that stock at the lowest possible figure, and locks it up. The "shorts" who have agreed to furnish him with 100,000 shares, are now at his mercy. Their agreement must be fulfilled or they must be dishonored. They therefore seek the operator at the end of the time which had been agreed upon for the delivery of the stock, and either pay him in cash what he demands, or make such other terms as he is willing to agree to.

The buying and selling of stocks or other securities, when done by professional dealers among themselves, does not require the transfer of money. The largest operations are conducted without the use of a dollar of cash. If Jones and Smith are accustomed to dealing together, they simply make memoranda of sale and purchase, and come to a settlement at any time most convenient to both.

If Robinson, a merchant, desires to purchase stock for speculation, he goes to Smith or Jones the broker, and pays him a small percentage on the cost of the stock. Suppose he orders 1000 shares of Rock Hill at 100. Instead of paying $100,000 cash, he deposits $5,000, $10,000 or $20,000, as the case may be—just enough to cover any probable fall in the price of Rock Hill within a given time. This deposit is called the "margin." The broker purchases the stock, charging his customer interest on the difference between the deposit and $100,000, holds the stock as security, and "carries" it until ordered to sell. If the price goes down the customer loses his margin. If it rises the broker pays him back the deposit together with the percentage on the investment.

## CHAPTER VII.

In the early part of 1866 Daniel Drew had provided himself with 58,000 shares of new Erie stock. It had been placed in his hands as collateral security for money furnished by Drew to the Erie Railway Company, the directors never dreaming that, crafty as they knew the old man to be, he would ever throw this stock upon the market. But he did. It was his sharpest weapon in the "bear" movement spoken of in the preceding chapter. After "bearing" Erie stock from 95 to 50, by flooding the market with the new issue, he bought his collateral back at 50, and held himself ready for another strike.

On the 8th of October, 1867, an election of officers of the Erie Railway Company was held. There were three parties in the field. The old officers headed by Daniel Drew, with whom James Fisk, Jr., was now thoroughly identified, had no intention to relinquish their power, and were determined by hook or by crook to secure a reëlection. Cornelius Vanderbilt, already owning and controlling three of the greatest roads in the country, was ambitious to take Erie also in his grasp, and thus become the railroad monarch of the United States, and he had a strong following. John S. Eldridge and Jay Gould, largely interested in the Boston, Hartford and Erie Railroad, then in a desperate struggle for existence, headed the third party. The Boston, Hartford and Erie road had its eastern terminus at Boston, and connected with a branch of the New York and Erie road at Fishkill, New York, and promised to become in time, if properly managed, one of the best paying roads in the country. On application to the Legislature of Massachusetts by the Directors of the road, that body had voted to give the company the sum of $3,000,000 provided the additional sum of $4,000,000 was raised elsewhere. The main incentive, then, of the Eldridge party, to secure a foothold in the Erie management was to obtain from this wealthy corporation the $4,000,000 so badly needed to float their own.

Eldridge, prompted by Jay Gould, then as now acknowledged to be one of the keenest diplomatists in business circles, approached Commodore Vanderbilt and proposed a coalition, to insure the downfall of the Drew party. The Commodore had not forgotten certain mortifications he had experienced on account of Uncle Daniel, and his love for the sanctimonious speculator was not of that double and twisted kind which precludes the possibility of wearing out.

"Damn the innocent face of that old hypocrite," roared the Commodore, as he brought his ponderous fist down upon his desk with a bang that shook the house, "I'll whip him if it costs me a leg."

The coalition was formed, and the factions were drawn out

in line of battle, each confident of victory. Numerical strength was on the Vanderbilt-Eldridge side, but the two leaders well knew that the enemy was shrewd and crafty, that he had traversed every inch of the ground, and that he was too fertile in resources to allow himself to be badly beaten without a lively fight, after bringing into play the full force of his wonderful strategic faculty. To block the favorite game of the wily Drew the opposition had preliminary affidavits and other papers prepared with the view to having an injunction issued enjoining Drew from using at the election any of the shares of stock not belonging to the already authorized capital stock of the Company.

It may be well to remark here that at the election the share-holders cast a vote for each share of stock held, and the majority of the stock would, of course, carry the election. In addition to his shares of the original stock of the Company, Daniel Drew held, as before mentioned, the 58,000 shares of the new issue, which he had received as collateral security for a loan, and on which he had already cleared a fortune. To prevent the use of this extra stock was the object of Vanderbilt and Eldridge in trying to obtain an injunction from the Courts.

Drew was not to be completely foiled. He soon learned of the movements and plans of his enemies, and on the Sunday preceding the election, after having engaged in his customary devotions at his favorite church, he paid a visit to the Commodore, who could not have been more surprised at the entrance of the ghost of his sloop Mary Jane under double reefed mainsail, than at the appearance of his wrinkled and stoop-shouldered opponent.

But the visitor was pleasantly received in the splendid parlors on Washington Square; for the Commodore, rough as he is in the marts of trade, is a thorough gentleman at home, and likes nothing better than to dispense hospitality with a liberal hand and a cheerful voice.

"Commodore," said Drew, with a whine, "I find that you and them Eldridge people are trying to kill me. Now, do you think it's fair to work a ring agin an old man like me?"

"Uncle Dan, you are no older than I am, and it strikes me that you cannot have forgotten the rings you have worked against me. You are even now trying to worry me out of Erie by one of your damned tricks."

"Don't swear, Commodore, don't swear. And don't lose your temper. Be cool, now, and let's talk this thing over."

"Sail on, Uncle Dan," said the Commodore.

"Well, you are agoing to get out an injunction agin me to prevent me from votin' on them 58,000 shares. You may be right, and then agin you may be wrong. We'll say nothin' about that. You sail your own boat. What I want to say is jest this here. You and me needn't be afeard of them Eldridge people—"

"What the hell do you mean?" said the Commodore. "*I* afraid of the Eldridge people! I think not, you old fool!"

"No, you don't understand me. To come to the pint. If we work together we can drive these fellows out into the cold. I can't afford to give up my position in the Erie management, and if I retain it I can help you in more ways than one."

An agreement was entered into. Drew pledged himself to unite with Vanderbilt in advancing Erie stock, and Vanderbilt promised to aid in keeping Drew in his position as treasurer and director of the Erie Company. This act of treachery to the Eldridge party brought down upon Vander-

DANIEL DREW.

bilt's head such torrents of wrath as only he could stem. Eldridge, with face

> "White as the lips of the cliff-chafed sea,
> Pale with its tidal passion,"

and Gould, boiling over with rage, called upon the Commodore when the tidings of the new combination were brought to them.

"Gentlemen," said the Commodore, mildly, "Uncle Dan and I have come to the conclusion that you had better haul in your horns. I am sorry that you were not here three hours ago to hear how piously the old man talked, and with what a hell-fired lot of Christian arguments he backed up his proposition. It would have done you good, gentlemen, it would have done you good. He was so mild and placid, so different from you, Eldridge. You ought to take lessons of the good old man. It would make you better. But suppose we go around and see Dan, and talk this thing over."

A carriage was called, and in a few minutes the trio were ushered into Drew's parlor, where the old man soon joined them, his face wreathed with smiles. He was so glad to see them!

"Now, Uncle Dan," said Vanderbilt, after the compliments of the day had been passed, "tell us about it. These young men want to hear from your own lips why in hell you have seduced me from my allegiance to the original combination. Tell them all about it."

"Gentlemen," said the placid old intriguer with a quiet smile, "self-preservation is the fust law of natur. I had no idee of getting beat, and I thought that in order to git the best of your combination I'd break your lines. Well, I done it, and that's all I have to say about it. I'm sorry for you, indeed I am. But (with a smile) it couldn't be helped, it couldn't be helped."

A long discussion ensued. Gould, the cautious, soon discovered that threats would avail nought against so fearless a veteran as Vanderbilt, and so crafty a trickster as Drew; so with a nod to Eldridge he "drew in his horns," and was followed at once by his companion. The Sunday's work was brought to a close at a late hour by a solemn agreement that there should be peace between the contending forces, that Drew was to continue in the Erie management, that Eldridge should be made the President of the Company, that Vanderbilt's orders should be obeyed in regard to the running of the road, that Eldridge's road, the Boston, Hartford and Erie, should have the $4,000,000 needed to secure the Massachusetts Legislature appropriations, that Erie stock should be advanced, and that Wall street should be made to bleed copiously for the support of these corporations and the honorable gentlemen who wielded them.

## CHAPTER VIII.

"THERE be quips and quirks, Artabal, among them which overmuch practyze deceite; and verily, they which do most boldly lie, when that their memorie is less in longnesse than their tongue, they do meete ofttimes with somedeal sorrowe. When thou thievest, Artabal, see that thou say no word to no man touching thy deed, till that the judge hath thee in bonds to pleade. Then lie thee black in the face. When that thou betrayest thy fellow, dig for him a deepe pit in the whiche he may fall, never more to come forth therefrom other than as dead; for truly, he being a liar, will, if he be lefte amongst the quicke, will betray thee, and lo, thou art done for!"—*Backet's Old Buckle.*

IN order to escape a great deal of unpleasantness, as well as to retain a place in the confidence of their constituency whom they had betrayed, the Eldridge men furthermore agreed at this remarkable meeting of Mammonites on that starry Sabbath eve, that they would support the nominees of the Ring, omitting the name of Daniel Drew; and that one of their directors, chosen at the election, should immediately resign, whereupon the other directors should at once fill the vacancy by electing Uncle Daniel.

The election was held. James Fisk, Jr., and Jay Gould were chosen as Directors, and so was Mr. Underwood, the gentleman selected by the Erie Ring to resign in favor of Daniel Drew, a duty which he performed with alacrity a few minutes after his election, and for the performance of which he no doubt "impetticosed a gratility" proportioned to the service he had rendered the pious speculator.

When Wall street heard that the great "King of the Bears" had been defeated, great was the excitement. The cubs of the street hung their heads and howled with anguish, but the bulls bellowed with delight, and up went Erie stock like a rocket. But in the next hour there came the tidings that Underwood, the pliant tool of the Ring, had resigned, and that Daniel Drew was again in power in the Erie management. The horns of the bulls were no longer exalted. The big bears and the young cubs of the street hugged each other and rubbed noses for very joy. Erie fell more than three per cent. that day, and more than one operator's fingers were scorched.

The Drew Ring, composed of a few choice spirits, now made preparations to "bull" the stock under the direction of Daniel Drew. To the old "bear" the whole business of mapping out the campaign and disposing of the forces, and fighting the battles, was confidingly intrusted. The conspirators bought largely at 70, believing, in their innocence, that Uncle Daniel could not fail to lead them to a fruitful victory.

Near the close of the year 1867, Drew's plans having been laid, everything was in readiness for the grand *coup*. Erie was bought in large quantities by those in the secret. Down went the stock, and then up again, and down again, for a month or more, in spasmodic vibrations, like the movements of a crazy pendulum. Uncle Daniel seemed bewildered.

"I never seen sich a queer performance in my life," said Uncle Daniel. "But keep on buying, boys, for it's sartain to raise. Don't be skeered."

Up went the stock again, and confidence was restored. The Ring became jubilant, and invested wildly. Down it fell again, and the consternation and alarm among the conspirators was intense. Their "long" contracts were nearly matured, and ruin stared many of them in the face. But they had Daniel Drew behind them. When money was needed to put up, Drew advanced it from the common fund, and the game went on. But the stock continued to fall. Suspicion at last fell upon the leader of the Ring, and after keen investigation the confederates were thunderstruck at the discovery that the stock they had been purchasing had been furnished by Drew's own brokers! The church founder had violated his solemn pledge, and had betrayed his fellows, by going back to his first love, and "bearing" the stock instead of "bulling" it.

The old man's point had been gained. He had bought heavily when the price was low; when it rose he had not only advanced money with which to purchase, but had even furnished the stock. He crammed the market till everybody held as much Erie as he could carry, and then when the price went down he bought again. James Fisk, Jr., and Jay Gould were the only operators in the secret except Drew himself and his own brokers.

When the truth became generally known, Drew called his confederates together.

"Gentlemen," said the old man, blandly, "I thought as how it mought be well for us to meet to-day in order to come to a settlement. Things is not quite so bad as many of you supposes. For sartain reasons of my own I found it necessary for to alter my original plan that was formed fust off, and to let you know nothing about it. I know that some of you has been worried, but you needn't worry any longer. I have made mighty good use of the fund, and am now able to make a fair division of the profits."

Vanderbilt had been badly sold. His quondam ally, who, with many whines and hand-wringings, had begged for his coöperation, had played the traitor. The "Railroad King" had met his match, and his strongest objurgations failed to express his anger, or to do justice to the various other unpleasant feelings that struggled for utterance. He vowed vengeance against Drew, and swore by everything good and bad, from Jupiter to the Furies, from Olympus to Hades, that he would not rest until Erie should be added to the string of railroad pearls that shone in his casket of gems.

His first move was a wretched failure. He dictated to the Board of Directors in regard to the management of the road, but the Bezonians had chosen their king, and Vanderbilt was not his name. They quietly snubbed the Commodore, and he was then forced to admit to himself that his power was broken.

It was not in his nature to remain in the condition of a defeated man. He had started in life as a boatman at the Whitehall stairs, had run a shilling ferry to Staten Island, and was now, perhaps, the wealthiest citizen of the United States, hale and hearty, although more than three score and ten, and with a will that nothing could subdue. He knew no fear, but held with the old poet, that,

> "When desperate ills demand a speedy cure,
> Distrust is treason, and forbearance, folly."

The Commodore lost no time. Having succeeded in winning Jay Gould over to him, he formed a new combination to send Erie stock up again. The work was begun without delay, and the stock rose rapidly. Daniel Drew was to all appearances more bewildered than during the season of his last "bearing" campaign, when Erie *would* go up in spite of his efforts to keep it down. But his bewilderment did not shake the old man's faith in himself. He went "short" on Erie with a recklessness that astounded the wildest dealers, and it soon became evident to Vanderbilt that his cunning enemy's bewilderment was only the outward and visible mask that covered an inward and devilish design to circumvent his foes by a new trick fished up from his exhaustless repository.

## CHAPTER IX.

DREW was now the holder of 58,000 shares of Erie stock, 28,000 of which were issued to him in May, 1866, together with $3,000,000 of bonds which he had converted into common stock at 60 cents on the dollar. With this, his collateral, and with the shares which he had obtained by converting $2,000,000 of bonds of the Buffalo, Bradford and Pittsburg Railroad into Erie stock,* he did not fear to cope with the Vanderbilt combination, of whose movements he was fully aware.

On the 17th of February, 1868, the celebrated case of Frank Work against Daniel Drew and others, was opened before Judge George G. Barnard, in Supreme Court Chambers, New York. The plaintiff, one of the Directors of the Erie Railway Company, sued Uncle Daniel, his co-director and the Company itself, to compel the former to return to the

* This road Drew and other Erie Directors had purchased for a song in 1866. They then issued its bonds for $2,000,000, and leased it to the Erie Company for a heavy sum. By taking from the Erie pocket the money with which to pay the lease, they cleared annually nearly 60 per cent. of their investment. The bonds of the B. B. and P. Railroad were turned in, Erie bonds issued for them, and these converted into Erie stock.

Company 58,000 shares of stock, and to prevent the latter from releasing the Company's claim on Drew.

The allegations of the complaint were, substantially, that in May, 1866, the duly issued stock of the Company was about $25,000,000, and that at that time they had the right to issue 28,000 shares more, merely for construction purposes; that at that time Drew, being then a Director, and a member of the Executive Committee, and being largely short of Erie, at from 96 to 70, (averaging about 90), got the Directors to issue to him these 28,000 shares and bonds for $3,000,000, convertible at pleasure into stock for 60 cents on the dollar, the money advanced to be payable in two years, with interest; that Drew at once converted his bonds into stock, thus getting immediate control of 58,000 shares to fill his short contracts, and to use in speculation; that he had, in using his bonds in this way, more than made the 60 per cent. advanced, with interest; and that, as the transaction was fraudulent, (he having been at the time a Director of the Company, and the contract having been made for his benefit,) Drew should account to the Company for all his profits on the transaction, and return the stock to the Company, to the end that the 30,000 shares, or $3,000,000 bonds, be destroyed, and the 28,000 shares be applied to their legitimate object.

On the sworn complaint, Judge Barnard granted the following injunction:

"It appearing to my satisfaction from the complaint in this action, and the affidavit thereto attached, that sufficient ground for this order exists, I do hereby order that the defendants in this action do absolutely desist and refrain from paying out of any of the funds of the Erie Railway Company to Daniel Drew any part of the principal or interest of certain moneys amounting to the sum of $3,450,000, or thereabouts, which were received by said Company at divers times, and during the year 1866, from the said Daniel Drew, as a loan or advance of 60 per cent. upon 28,000 shares of common stock, and $3,000,000 worth of convertible bonds of said Company; also from releasing, or in any manner discharging, or attempting to release or discharge the said Daniel Drew from any liability which he may have incurred to said Erie Railway Company, or from any cause of action which the said Company may have against him.

"And I do further order that such of the defendants herein as are members of the Executive Committee of the Board of Directors of said Company do absolutely desist and refrain from authorizing or consenting to any such payment or release, or any settlement of accounts between said Company and said Daniel Drew, or any compromise of any of the matters embraced in the complaint, or any disposition of the 58,000 shares obtained by said Drew from said Company, other than the delivery of the said shares to said Company; and I do further order that said Drew do in like manner desist and refrain from demanding or receiving from said Company the payment of the principal or interest of the said advances to said Company, or any part thereof, and from taking any proceedings at law or otherwise for the collection of said principal or interest, or any part thereof, or for the foreclosure of any lien which he may have, or claim to have, upon any stocks or bonds of said Company as security for said advances, until the account between him and the said Company of and concerning the dealings set forth in the complaint in this action shall have been judicially settled and the balance thereof ascertained.

"GEORGE G. BARNARD,

"*Justice Supreme Court.*"

This injunction was sued for by Frank Work; but it was a well known fact that the main-spring of the movement was the irate Commodore Vanderbilt.

On the 19th of February Judge Barnard issued a second order suspending Drew from the Erie Directory and from his office as Treasurer, and ordering him to appear and show cause why he should not be permanently removed.

The Courts were kept busy with the Drew case for some time, and many strenuous efforts were made by Uncle Daniel's counsel to have the injunction dissolved, but in vain. On the 28th of February, Frank Work gave additional facts in verification of the petition presented on the 19th, which may be thus briefly set forth:

"The last election of Directors of the Erie Railway Company was held on the 8th of October, 1867. Deponent was elected as one of the Directors, but Daniel Drew was not. Immediately after the election, and on the same day, Mr. Underwood, one of the newly elected Directors, resigned, and said Daniel Drew was elected by the Board of Directors to fill the vacancy occasioned by that resignation, and was also elected Treasurer of the Company. Deponent was present at that meeting of the Board. Deponent knows of said Drew's having obtained from the Company the 58,000 shares mentioned, from having frequently heard Drew speak of having obtained them. Deponent further says that he has seen the reports of the Directors of said Company to the stockholders for the years ending December 31, 1865, December 31, 1866, and September 30, 1867, which reports were published by authority of said Directors, and purported to exhibit all the outstanding stock of said Company, common and preferred; that in all of said reports the issue of said

58,000 shares of stock is wholly suppressed, and said reports contain no mention of said shares. Deponent further says, that it has been for a long time past, and is now matter of common notoriety among dealers in the New York Stock Market, that Daniel Drew is and has been largely 'short' of the stock of the Erie Railway Company; that the dealers who are in the habit of transacting his stock business have for a long time past been large sellers of that stock and large borrowers of the same for delivery; and from the knowledge which deponent has, and has for a long time past had, of the transactions in the New York Stock Exchange, in which deponent is a large dealer, deponent believes that the said Daniel Drew has not only sold and parted with the 58,000 shares so obtained from the said Company, but that he is 'short' a large amount in addition. Deponent further says, that he knows that Daniel Drew has been for a long time past in efforts to depress the market value of the stock of said Company; that he has circulated rumors disparaging to the credit of said Company, and has, for some months past, in deponent's presence, on various occasions, publicly proclaimed that the stock of said Company would sell at lower rates than those at which it was selling at the time of said declarations, and that it has been for some months past generally understood in the New York Stock Market that said Drew was 'bearing' the stock of said Company, which is a technical term signifying that he is speculating for a fall in the price thereof.

"Deponent further says, that early in February, 1868, it was reported in Wall street that the Erie Railway Company were issuing additional stock; that deponent, having attended every meeting of the Board of Directors since his election, and not having learned of any such issue, called upon

Daniel Drew at the office of D. Groesbeck & Co., brokers of said Drew, and then and there stated to said Drew the rumors which deponent had heard, and asked him for information on the subject; that Drew denied that any such issue had been made, or that any such issue was in contemplation, and stated to deponent that the Company had no authority to issue any stock except in exchange for the stock of railroads held under lease, and that no such change had been made, or was in contemplation. That some days afterward deponent was informed by Martin E. Green, who is a large operator in the same office with D. Groesbeck & Co., and who was in the room at the time of the conversation with Drew, that half an hour before said conversation, Drew had informed him, Green, that he, Drew, had converted more than a million of dollars of the securities of the Buffalo, Bradford and Pittsburg Railroad Company into stock of the Erie Railway Company, and that said stock was then in Groesbeck's box ready for delivery; that afterward, on February 18, 1868, deponent attended a meeting of the Directors of the Erie Railway Company, at which the said Drew was present, and deponent then and there stated to Drew the substance of deponent's interview with Green, deponent withholding only the name of the said Green; and deponent then charged Drew with having told him a falsehood, and Drew did not deny the charge."

The case was again up on the 4th of March, this time with the people as complainants. The new petition against Daniel Drew and the Company was substantially the same as that presented by Frank Work, but set forth in addition that "since the last election of Directors in October, 1867, several of the Directors elected, being more or less interested in the Boston, Hartford and Erie Railroad, the Erie Company had agreed to guarantee the payment of 7 per cent. interest on $4,000,000 of bonds on that railroad, part of which bonds with such guarantee, having been issued, and part remaining in the hands of Drew and Davis unsold."

Another injunction, following substantially the prayer of the petitioners, was granted by the Court..

The Erie litigation was now fairly launched, and bade fair to float for an indefinite period to the great delight of an army of lawyers. On the very day the above mentioned injunction was issued in New York against the Erie Railway Company, another was issued by Justice Ransom Balcom, of the Supreme Court, sitting in Broome County, restraining Frank Work and the people from prosecuting that Company. The plaintiffs in this case were the Company and James Fisk, Jr., the latter now appearing for the first time prominently in a case destined ere long to make his name known the world over.

Fisk was the first witness called. He testified that as a Director of the Erie Railway Company he had personal acquaintance with the facts and motions referred to in the complaint; was acquainted with Frank Work, and had sat with him as a co-director; was acquainted with the plans, policy, business, and resources and business condition of the Corporation, and with its relation to the Central line of New York; knew the facts connected with the issue of 28,000 shares of stock, the conversion and exchange of bonds, the Buffalo, Bradford, and Pittsburg Railroad, the contract with the Boston, Hartford and Erie Railway Company, and the extension of the broad gauge in Ohio.

Jay Gould testified that previous to the election of Directors in October, 1867, it was a matter of public notoriety in New York that those who controlled the Harlem and Hudson River Railroad would endeavor to get control of the New York Central; and to increase the business of the latter were making strong efforts to control the Board of Directors of the Erie Railway Company. Among those parties were Augustus Schell, Richard Schell, and Frank Work. The witness averred that the efforts made were for the purpose of putting the Erie road into the hands of those who had millions invested in a great rival line; that it was by getting proxies sent to himself or his agents that Work was elected a Director; that on the 17th of February, Work had a notice served on the Directors to prevent them from extending their broad gauge to Chicago. Witness further testified that Work came into the Erie Board as the representative of Cornelius Vanderbilt, the leading manager of the Harlem, Hudson River, and Central Railroads; and that, although Work knew of the circumstances relating to the loan by Drew on stock of the Company, he voted for Drew as a Director and also as Treasurer.

The injunction prayed for by the plaintiffs, and granted by Justice Balcom, reads as follows:

"Supreme Court, County of Broome. The Erie Railway Company and James Fisk, Jr., plaintiffs, agt. Marshall B. Champlain, Attorney-General of the State of New York, Josiah Bardwell, J. C. Bancroft Davis, Alexander S. Diven, Daniel Drew, John S. Eldridge, William Evans, Eben D. Jordan, Jay Gould, Dudley S. Gregory, George M. Groves, Frederick A. Lane, Homer Ramsdell, Wm. B. Skidmore, Henry Thompson, James S. Whitney, Frank Work, and the people of the State of New York, defendants. On the complaint herein, and on the affidavits of James Fisk, Jr., and Jay Gould, and on motion of Mr. Eaton, counsel for the plaintiffs, and it appearing to me that there is good cause therefor, and the proper undertaking having been executed, I do hereby order and require:

"That the defendant, Frank Work, and his attorneys, counsel and agents, do severally and wholly refrain from promoting, sustaining, or taking any part in the prosecution of the petition or either of the suits referred to in the complaint, and also that all proceedings therein be, and they are hereby stayed; that said Work do not, as a Director or otherwise, institude, promote, or take part in either suit in this complaint referred to, and do not promote or take part in any other suit or proceeding against the Erie Railway Company, or against any officer thereof, in respect to any action of the Board of Directors or Executive Committee, or in respect of the rights, duty, or authority of said Board, Committee, or Company, or concerning the records, proceedings, or books or papers of either said Company, Board, or Committee. That said Work do not appear at any meeting of said Board of Directors or Committee, or otherwise act or assume to act, or give any direction or advice as Director or officer of the Erie Railway Company.

"That the Attorney-General and his agents do refrain from proceeding under or upon the petition referred to in the complaint, and from taking any further proceeding in any suit in the complaint mentioned; and also that all proceedings in the suit in the complaint mentioned, in which the people of the State of New York are represented in the complaint therein as being plaintiffs, be stayed; and that said Attorney-General do not authorize or institute, in the name of the people or otherwise, any other suit or proceeding against the Erie Railway Company, in reference to any matters mentioned in the complaint therein.

"That said Work, on the complaint and affidavit herein

referred to, and on such further affidavits as may be served on him eight days before the term hereinafter named, show cause before a Special Term of this Court, to be held at Cortlandville, in the county of Cortland, on the 7th day of April, 1868, why he should not be suspended as Director of the Erie Railway Company."

## CHAPTER X.

BUT immediately after the issuing of Judge Barnard's order of the 17th of February, restraining him from using his 58,000 shares of stock, the ready-witted Drew, always fertile in resources, and now the head and front of the Erie Directory, prevailed upon the Board, without much difficulty, to issue $10,000,000 of new bonds "for construction purposes." The bonds were at once converted into stock, the cunning trick having been played in both its stages just in time, for at a later hour of the same day, Judge Barnard's second injunction was issued. Had the judge taken a little less sleep, indulged in a little less slumber, on that morning, many of the events recorded in this history would never have occurred.

The new stock, 100,000 shares, was issued in equal parts to Daniel Drew and James Fisk, Jr. Uncle Daniel distributed his shares among his brokers, but Fisk quietly held his, and waited for his veteran leader to move.

Commodore Vanderbilt was now ready to strike the market. His orders were issued, and his agents were as busy as

FISK AND GOULD GOING TO JERSEY.

bees purchasing Erie stock, and up it went with a bound. On the 29th of February, it was 68¾, and Vanderbilt seemed to have everything his own way, but

> "The best laid plans of mice and men
> Gang aft aglee."

Daniel Drew had his keen eyes upon the street, and his fingers upon the wires.

"Throw your stock," said he, to his merry men, one and all. "Don't wait a minute." And then to himself, "I'm raily sorry for Vanderbilt, but he oughtn't to be so rash. A man of his years ought to know better than to fly in the face of Providence. I pity him, indeed I do; and I hope this blessed day will be a lesson to him."

The stock held by Drew's brokers was thrown upon the market without a moment's delay, and every share was bought by Vanderbilt's retainers. All at once the character of the stock was discovered, and the bulls were amazed and terrified. Down went Erie to 65, and the hearts of the bears were made glad.

"It'll git to 60 afore long," said Uncle Daniel to one of his agents; "and I'm not afeard to venture that it'll go as low as 55 afore the day's over."

"Mr. Drew, Mr. Drew!" exclaimed one of Uncle Daniel's men, who just then rushed in from the street out of breath; "Erie's going up like the devil. Vanderbilt is buying every share of the stock he can get. What's to be done?"

Uncle Daniel was thunderstruck. He had thought to bring the Commodore to his knees, and, in the language of Job, make his enemy "to bite the dust;" but with more than $4,000,000 of Erie stock saddled upon him that day, and with a gloomy prospect before him, Vanderbilt was as firm as a rock. He bought every share of Erie that was offered, and the stock shot up to 70, and then to 72 and 73. Drew was more than puzzled; he was absolutely dismayed. Short contracts for millions remained uncovered, and they were fast reaching maturity. He saw that the superior pluck of the Commodore had carried him through the storm, and that to attempt to cripple, much less to kill him, would be next to impossible.

To add to the old man's trouble, Judge Barnard granted an injunction restraining him from acting as an officer of the Erie Company. This was done about the 1st of March. On the 10th of that month suit was brought by Richard Schell (in Vanderbilt's interest) against the Erie Company, Daniel Drew and others, on the complaint in which Judge Barnard had issued the injunction, enjoining the Directors from holding any meeting at which Frank Work was not permitted to take part; further enjoining the officers of the Company from doing any act by which the capital stock of the Company, not already duly issued to *bona fide* holders, should be issued or created; from increasing the stock, and from converting the Company's bonds into stock.

In this place it may be well to give a *résumé* of the causes which led to the great fight between Vanderbilt and the Erie people. The Erie road and the New York Central, the latter controlled by Cornelius Vanderbilt, lead from New York to the interior of the State—the Erie directly, and the Central through its connection with the Hudson River and Harlem roads. Unfortunately for the Erie road, its gauge, or the width between its rails, is so much broader than that of most of the roads connecting with it at its western terminus, that the cars containing freight coming from points beyond it, can not be run upon its track, and must therefore be sent over the Central road, the gauge of which is better suited to their wheels. To remedy this disadvantage, the Erie Company had projected two improvements—first, to lay a third rail on its own track, so as to accommodate narrow gauge cars; and second, to lay a similar rail on certain narrow gauge roads terminating at Chicago, so that its own cars could be run directly to that city. In addition to this, as the Central had control of some of those connecting roads this side of Chicago, they proposed to build a few miles of broad gauge road from a point where the broad guage terminated to the nearest point which they could reach beyond the influence of the Central. To do all this required money, and they made the necessary arrangements to raise it.

Here, however, Cornelius Vanderbilt stepped in, and endeavored to thwart the consummation of a scheme which, in his judgment, threatened the interests of the New York Central Railroad, and by resorting to legal proceedings through his agents, he for the time embarrassed the progress of the Erie improvements. The Erie people, headed by Daniel Drew, were not idle. Vanderbilt, through his friend, Frank Work, whom he had placed in the Erie Board for the purpose of keeping informed of its plans, had obtained an injunction suspending Drew from his office, and forbidding the borrowing of money which had been resolved upon; but Drew, through Fisk, had also obtained an injunction upon Frank Work, suspending him also, and forbidding him to prosecute his suit against Drew.

On the 10th of March, as before mentioned, Richard Schell obtained a counter injunction against Daniel Drew and his associates; and Mr. Belden, formerly the partner of James Fisk, Jr., obtained still another injunction, on the same day, against the whole Vanderbilt party, and even Judge Barnard himself, who granted the injunction against Daniel Drew. Then, on that day there were no fewer than six suits in full blast, with a fair prospect of more to come. The war was carried on by the use of means well known to the financiers of Wall street; and the violent fluctuations in the Erie stock simply indicated the predominance of one party or the other. At this period the friends of Erie were in the ascendant, and were sanguine of carrying out their purpose. There was then a strong feeling in the community against Vanderbilt. One of the daily papers in commenting upon the struggle, said:

"Now, if this contest affected only the gamblers in stocks, it would not much concern the public; but, as it appears to us, every citizen has the deepest interest in its being terminated as soon as possible by the discomfiture of Mr. Vanderbilt. What would be the result if he were to obtain the control of the Erie, as he has of the Central road, may be judged by the policy he has adopted since the latter fell into his possession. He has so raised the price of freights from this city to the various towns along its line, that it costs as much to carry goods from here to Syracuse, Rochester, and other such places, as it does to carry them to Cleveland, Detroit, and Chicago. Let him once get the Erie road into his power likewise, and the tariff of freights along its whole length will be raised in the same manner, and not only that, but the freights on all the Western roads connecting with the two.

"The consummation of the Vanderbilt project is not likely to be effected. The Courts, in the first place, will, as soon as the case can be properly presented to them, dissolve the injunctions obtained against Mr. Drew, and the rest of the Erie Directors; and besides, a Committee appointed by the

State Senate is now investigating the whole affair with a view to prevent by legislation the anticipated injury to the City and State."

## CHAPTER XI.

THE Erie case was now one of the main topics of the day. On Tuesday, the 10th of March, there were rumors of a fresh injunction against Erie, Vanderbilt, and others, and the movements and counter movements, injunctions and counter injunctions, were bringing the matter to such a pass that it was almost impossible to do, or even to say anything, without running the risk of going to jail for contempt of Court. At this time the following was the condition of affairs in this remarkable case.

Two suits and a proceeding in the interest of Frank Work (Vanderbilt) against Daniel Drew.

A counter suit enjoining Frank Work from acting as a Director of Erie, and staying all proceedings in the preceding suits.

A suit by Schell, one of Vanderbilt's attorneys, restraining the last suit, and restraining the Erie Company from acting without the consent of Frank Work.

Then came rumors of an action against Vanderbilt, Schell and Work, restraining them from doing anything at all.

The last rumors were correct, a suit having been commenced in Kings County, and an injunction issued by Judge Gilbert. This suit brought in as parties, Judge Barnard and

Commodore Vanderbilt. As a matter of interest the papers on which the injunction was granted, and the injunction itself are here appended:

"Supreme Court, County of Kings.—William Belden *agt.* Cornelius Vanderbilt, Wm. H. Vanderbilt, Richard Schell, Augustus Schell, James H. Banker, George G. Barnard, Frank Work, Josiah Bardwell, J. C. Bancroft Davis, Alexander S. Diven, Daniel Drew, John S. Eldridge, William Evans, Eben D. Jordan, Jay Gould, Dudley S. Gregory, George M. Groves, Frederick A. Lane, Homer Ramsdell, William B. Skidmore, Henry Thompson, James S. Whitney, James Fisk, Jr., the Erie Railway Company, and Marshall B. Champlain, Attorney-General of the State of New York. William Belden, plaintiff, on behalf of himself and all other stock holders and other creditors of the Erie Railway Company, complains and alleges:

"1. That the Erie Railway Company is a Corporation organized under certain acts of the Legislature, etc.

"2. That the plaintiff is the owner of one thousand shares of the stock of the said Erie Railway Company, of which a part is standing to his name on its books; and he is also the owner and holder of a bond of the Company for the sum of $1000 payable October 1, 1880.

"3. That the defendants, Work, Fisk, Ramsdell and others, are Directors of the said Erie Railway Company.

"4. That the said Erie Railway Company maintains and operates a railway extending from the City of New York, through the States of New Jersey, Pennsylvania and New York, to Dunkirk and Buffalo; such railway having a broader gauge than most other railways in the country, and its cars being for that reason unable to pass over most of the roads connected with it.

"5. That the business and profits of the Company would be very largely increased by the opening of railways of an equal gauge connected with said railway, and leading to the West, so that cars might pass over the same from New York to all the principal Western cities, without change.

"6. That another line of railway between the cities of New York and Buffalo is formed by certain lines known as the Hudson River Railroad, and Harlem Railroad, and the Central Railroad, all having a narrow gauge, uniform with that adopted by most railroads in this country.

"7. That the Corporations owning these three roads are all controlled by the defendant, Cornelius Vanderbilt, who is a Director in each of them, and a majority of stock in each such Corporation is owned by him or by persons acting for his interest, and in uniform coöperation with him.

"8. That the business of the said Erie Railway Company is carried on in constant competition with the said three roads, which have a common interest in opposition to that of said Company.

"9. That the said Company has for some time past endeavored to complete its connection with the West by securing the opening of railways with a track of equally broad gauge with its own, and as the plaintiff is informed and believes, its Directors had nearly completed such arrangements as would accomplish this result, when the proceedings hereinafter mentioned were commenced.

"10. That, as the plaintiff is informed and believes, a combination was entered into some time during the month of February, 1868, between the defendants, Cornelius Vanderbilt, Wm. H. Vanderbilt, Frank Work, Richard Schell . . . . to speculate in the stock of the said Erie Railway Company, and to use the process of the Courts for the purpose of aiding their speculations, for which purpose they had various consultations together, in which it was agreed that the said Work, as agent for the said conspirators, should bring actions and other proceedings in the Courts, whereby the said Company should be restrained from carrying out its plans for extending its connections with the West, and from fulfilling its contracts for the issue of stock, and whereby its Directors, or some of them, should be suspended or removed, and a receiver of its property should be appointed.

"11. That in pursuance of the said conspiracy, the said Work commenced an action against the said Company on or about the 17th day of February, 1868, for the purpose of preventing said Company from paying a large sum of money lawfully owing by it to the defendant Daniel Drew. On the 19th of February, 1868, he caused a petition to be filed in the name of the people of the State of New York, for the removal of the said Drew from his office as Director and Treasurer of said Company; and on the 2d of March, 1868, he caused an action to be commenced in the name of the said people against the said Erie Railway Company, and eleven only of the seventeen Directors, for the purpose of restraining it from completing the arrangements previously entered into for the extension of a broad gauge track connecting its road with the West.

"12. That in the two actions above mentioned, the said Work obtained injunctions to restrain said Company from paying its said debt to Daniel Drew and from fulfilling its contracts for the extension of connecting lines to the West; and in the petition above mentioned, an order was granted suspending said Drew from his said offices, and requiring him to show cause, within two days, why he should not be removed therefrom.

"13. That, although the petition aforesaid, and the summons and complaint in the last action, purport to be signed by the Attorney-General, the plaintiff is informed and believes that all these proceedings are originated and exclusively prosecuted by attorneys employed by the said Work, acting as agents for the said conspirators.

"14. That in none of the said proceedings have any of the stockholders of the said Company other than the eleven Directors aforesaid, been made parties or had any opportunity to be heard, although such proceedings affect the interests of the said stockholders more than those of the Directors.

"15. That the defendant, Frank Work, as the plaintiff is informed and believes, is an agent of the defendant, Cornelius Vanderbilt; and ever since his election as a Director of the said Erie Railway Company, he has acted in bad faith, for the interest of said Vanderbilt and the competing lines, and instituted all the said proceedings in bad faith, for the like interest, and for the interest of the conspirators aforesaid.

"16. That the acts and proceedings aforesaid are intended by the parties concerned to prevent said Erie Railway Company from successfully competing with the said Central, Hudson River, and Harlem Railroads, and to embarrass the business of said Company, and to prevent it from securing its fair share of traffic from the West, and that they are well adapted to accomplish that purpose, and unless restrained by this Court, they will cause irreparable injury to the said Company, its stockholders and creditors.

"17. That the issues raised by the complaints in the two actions above mentioned are in good part the same; and as the plaintiff is informed and believes, the whole controversy might have been determined in a single suit; and these various proceedings have been multiplied in bad faith, and for the purpose of annoying and injuring the said Company, its officers and stockholders.

"18. That in order to complete and operate the railroad of said Company, and especially to lay a double track, put down steel rails, and purchase cars, engines and other necessary equipments, it has been necessary for said Corporation to borrow large sums of money, and it will be necessary hereafter to borrow large sums; and in order to borrow said moneys it has been and will continue to be necessary for such Company to issue bonds, as provided by law, coupled with the right to convert the same into stock.

"19. That a large number of such bonds so legally issued, are now outstanding in the hands of *bona fide* holders for value, who claim the right to convert the same into stock, as provided by the tenor of said bonds; and if the Company refuse to comply with their said contract, they will become responsible for very heavy damages in case of depreciation in the stock; and that the injunction in the last mentioned suit restrains the Corporation from converting said bonds now outstanding into stock, and from issuing any new stock, or any convertible bonds, which injunction was artfully contrived in order to cripple the Corporation as aforesaid, wherefore the plaintiff demands judgment:

"1. That the defendants, Cornelius Vanderbilt, Wm. H. Vanderbilt, George G. Barnard, and others, be restrained by injunction from advising, inciting, commencing, prosecuting, maintaining, or carrying on, any suit, action, petition, or proceeding having for its object in whole or in part the removal or suspension of the Directors or officers of the Erie Railway Company, or any of them, or the procurement of a receiver of the property of the said Company, or any part thereof, or the disposal in any way of such profits or any part thereof, or the restraining of the said Company from carrying out any agreement heretofore made by its Directors, and from continuing or helping to continue any such action, etc.

"2. That the defendant, Frank Work, be restrained by injunction from acting as Director or other officer of the said Erie Railway Company.

"3. That the defendant, the Erie Railway Company, be required to issue stock in accordance with the terms of its convertible bonds upon demand of the holders of such bonds, and

"4. That the said Directors, other than the said Work, be required to continue in the performance of their proper functions as such.

"5. That all the parties to the proceedings mentioned in the complaint be required to submit their claims to the decision of the Court in this action.

"THOMAS G. SHEARMAN,
"*Plaintiff's Attorney.*"

"William Belden being sworn, testified: 1. A large speculation of an extraordinary character and amount has been progressing in Erie Railway stock for three weeks past. 2. I am a banker and broker. Stock brokers with whom I am in daily intercourse, who are engaged in buying and selling said stock, have informed me that among the persons engaged in said speculation are Cornelius Vanderbilt, Richard Schell, Augustus Schell, James H. Banker, George G. Barnard, and Frank Work. 3. The said Barnard is in the constant habit of resorting to Broad street, where said transactions are going on, and frequenting the office of one of the principal firms of brokers who are engaged in buying said stock, and who, as deponent is informed and believes, carry on said transactions for the person aforesaid."

Henry N. Smith testified to the same facts; whereupon Judge Gilbert issued the following injunction:

"It appearing satisfactory to me by the affidavits of the plaintiff and Henry N. Smith, and the complaint duly verified by the plaintiff, that sufficient grounds for an order of injunction exist, I do hereby order:

"1. That the defendants, Cornelius Vanderbilt, Wm. H. Vanderbilt, Richard Schell, Augustus Schell, James H. Banker, George G. Barnard, Frank Work, and Marshall B. Champlain, their agents and servants, refrain from advising, inciting, or commencing any action, suit, petition, or proceeding, having for its object, in whole or in part, the removal or suspension of the Directors or officers of the Erie Railway Company or any of them, or the procurement of a receiver of the property of the said Company, or the disposal in any way of such property, or the restraining of the said Company from carrying out any agreement heretofore made by its Directors, or doing any act in furtherance of said conspiracy.

"2. That the defendant, Frank Work, refrain from acting as a Director or other officer of the said Erie Railway Company.

"3. That the defendant, the Erie Railway Company, be enjoined and restrained from refusing or neglecting to issue stock in according with the terms of its convertible bonds, upon the demand of the *bona fide* holders of such bonds, and

"4. That the said Directors, other than the said Work, be enjoined and restrained from refusing or neglecting to continue in the performance of their proper functions as such, until the further order of this Court; and in case of disobedience to this order, they will be liable to the punishment therefor prescribed by law. But this injunction is not intended to interfere with the judicial functions of said George G. Barnard. And I do further order that the said defendants show cause before me, at special term, to be held at the Court House of the City of Brooklyn, on Wednesday, March 18th, at 10 o'clock A.M., why said injunction should not be continued.

"J. W. GILBERT,

"March 9, 1868. "*Justice Supreme Court.*"

On the same day the Vanderbilt party brought still another suit in the name of John Bloodgood; and in this suit, brought against Daniel Drew and the other defendants named in the Schell suit, an injunction was granted by Judge Cardozo.

On the 13th of March, 1868, one of the New York daily papers contained the following leading editorial written by one of the best legal writers of the age:

"To decide a cause without hearing it, is a despotic exercise of authority worthy of the court of Judge Lynch. The granting of injunctions by a single judge, on the *ex parte* application of one of the parties to an anticipated controversy, bears a close resemblance to the summary judgments of that famous tribunal. One familiar with the genius of the common law, its jealous regard for private rights, its eagerness to afford every man an open trial, face to face with his accusers, would infer that such an authority was entirely abnegated, or, if used at all, would be invoked only in extraordinary cases at rare intervals. Such was once the practice. But a power which judges in early times never dared to exercise, and which, at a later era, they used only when it was impossible by other means to prevent the sacrifice of precious rights, has in our day become almost as common a proceeding as the issuing of a summons by a justice of the peace. To restrain a party, without notice or trial, from executing his official functions, or selling or using his property, or doing any other matter or thing which he has ordinarily a right to perform, unless he is forbidden so to do by the final judgment of a competent tribunal after a fair trial upon the merits of the controversy, is an arbitrary exercise of power which a Court in extraordinary exigencies may feel restrained to put in requisition, but which is so liable to abuse that it will be 'more honored in the breach than in the observance.'

"This despotic power has no enviable parentage. It arose in the English Court of Chancery in a dark and superstitious age, when that ambitious prelate, Cardinal Wolsey, held the great seal of that arbitrary prince, Henry VIII. A sheer usurpation at the outset, it not having been sanctioned by act of Parliament, it was an ecclesiastical assault upon the common-law courts, where private rights had found some slight shelter from the oppressions of the grasping minister and his greedy master. Like all usurpations of authority, it grew by what it fed upon, till, after a long resistance from commoners, lawyers, and clients, it was recognized as a legitimate function of the Chancellor, and ultimately, through rivalry, it stealthily crept into the courts of common law. Being closely watched, it was cautiously and rarely exercised. The offspring of usurpation came to America with other judicial relics, some precious, some worthless, of our English ancestors. Down to a recent period our judges called it into use only in great emergencies, which would not brook delay, and where the ordinary course of proceedings afforded no adequate remedy for the emergency.

"The practice of issuing *ex parte* injunctions, arbitrary in its essence, and invariably prejudicial, and sometimes ruinous to private rights, has degenerated into an abuse that deserves rebuke and demands correction. As oppressive as the Star Chamber, it is worse in one particular than that odious tribunal; for it tries a party in his absence, without giving him previous warning; or, rather, it condemns him without trying him at all. The usual mode of obtaining this process is short, sharp, and summary. A lawyer appears before some judge sitting in a dark alcove of the court-house, or perhaps literally in his *chambers*, armed with an artful affidavit of some vindictive John Doe, and the auxiliary bond of some James Straw, and procures an order against some unsuspecting Richard Roe, who happens to be president of a bank or treasurer of a railway, enjoining Roe and everybody who is, or who might, could, would, or should be connected with him in business, from doing anything whatever, on pain of fine and imprisonment; and thereupon, quick as thought, the affairs of a great banking house or railway company are thrown into ruinous confusion. In course of time other lawyers are called in; and intrenched behind reams of affidavits and piles of law books, a fusilade of 'wise saws and modern instances' begins—the jaws of the judicial alligator, however, never for a moment relinquishing their grip upon the victim. After a war as interminable as that of the Roses, the umpire yawns through the complications of a controversy which he took up at the wrong end, and comes to the conclusion that Doe never had any case at all, and so he dissolves the injunction, and Roe creeps out of the alligator's jaws a triumphant and a ruined man, while the bank or railway with which he was innocently connected, has suffered a loss of hundreds of thousands of dollars. The fleeced parties, bail bond in hand, now start out to find Straw. It is a bootless undertaking; for he is either *non est*, or, if found, proves to be what he always was, not worth a dime.

"We are compelled to make these general comments on this subject by the controversy now going on in our Courts respecting the Erie Railway and the Rock Island Railroad. We refrain from discussing the merits of these cases. They may afford amusement to stock-jobbers and fat fees to lawyers, but they doubtless seem to the shareholders and bondholders of these corporations something more serious than a burlesque on judicial proceedings. If there be grounds for suits between these litigants, let them be commenced and carried on in the usual way. When Demetrius moved for an injunction against Paul for preaching at Ephesus, the bulls and bears and barristers of that idolatrous city came to

DIRECTORS' ROOM AT TAYLOR'S HOTEL.

their senses on being reminded by the clerk that the law was open, and that there were deputies, and that they could implead one another in a regular and decorous manner."

During the session of this year a committee was appointed in the New York Senate to investigate certain charges of mismanagement against the Erie Railway Company. The principal ground of the complaint was the resolution passed on the 19th of February of that year, for the issue of bonds to the amount of $10,000,000, convertible into stock of the Company, and the conversion of the bonds into stock for purposes of private speculation. Two reports on this matter were submitted. The majority of the committee arrived at the conclusion that the issue of bonds had been obtained by Daniel Drew, to be used for his personal gain, "utterly regardless of the interests" of other stockholders in the Company, and that Eldridge, the President, and James Fisk, Jr., and Jay Gould, Directors, were concerned, and probably interested with Daniel Drew, in these "corrupt proceedings." The report closed with the following resolution:

"*Resolved*, That the fraudulent abuses developed by the investigation of the management of the present Directors and officers of the New York and Erie Railway Company demand that increased penalties for such offences shall be imposed for the protection of stockholders and the community, and the special committee conducting such investigation be, and they are hereby instructed to report a bill making it a felonious offence for any Director or officer to fraudulently issue stock of the Company in which he holds such trust, or to convert to his own purposes the proceeds of any stock or bonds; or to fraudulently take or carry away to another State, or with like intent, keep or retain them to evade legal process in this State, the moneys or effects of such Company."

6

A minority report was submitted, which commended the general management of the Erie Railroad, and declared that there was uncontradicted evidence that the right of the Board of Directors to pass the resolution of February 19th was not doubted or questioned either in the Executive Board or Board of Directors, and was therefore not a willful violation of the law. It then recommended that an act be passed legalizing the issue of $10,000,000 of stock, as well as various other acts of the Directors which had been complained of as illegal. The action recommended by the minority of the committee was favored in the Senate.

In the Assembly, on the occasion of the adoption of a committee report adverse to a bill which had been framed in the interest of the Erie Railway Company, the following communication was submitted to the House:

"ASSEMBLY CHAMBER, April 1, 1868.

"*To the Hon. Speaker of the Assembly:*

"I, E. M. K. Glenn, a member of this House, from my seat in this House, do charge as follows:

"1. I charge that the report on the Erie Railroad Bill was bought.

"2. I charge that a portion of the vote on this floor, in adopting the said report, was bought.

"3. I charge that the members of this House were engaged in buying their fellow members.

"4. I charge that a portion of the vote on the Harlem Milk Bill was bought.

"5. I charge that some of the Committees of this House charge for reports.

"6. I charge corruption, deep, dark, and damning, on a portion of this House. I ask the adoption of the following:

"*Resolved*, That the Speaker appoint a committee of five to investigate the foregoing charges, that three of the committee be taken from that portion of the House that voted no on the Erie Railroad Report, and two from that portion that voted aye, and that the committee have power to employ counsel and send for persons and papers; the committee to sit in this Chamber during the recess of the Legislature. The committee may employ a clerk."

Mr. Glenn's motives in making these charges having been called in question, he declared that he made them in behalf of no Company or Corporation. He had been offered $500 for his vote, and knew a member who had been offered $1200. He claimed that in the name of justice this matter should be probed to the bottom.

A committee was appointed to investigate these grave charges, but Mr. Glenn refused to serve on it because of the feeble state of his health. He asked, however, that he might be represented by counsel in supporting the accusations he had made. This privilege was not allowed, but a committee was appointed to carry out the investigation.

Mr. Glenn, on being summoned before the committee, was unwilling to give his testimony, because it would implicate one of the men before whom he was required to testify; and on the following day he accused that member of the committee, by name, of having offered him $500 for his vote. He then asked to be relieved from taking any part in the investigations. The committee decided that there was no ground for the charges against either the gentlemen named, or any other member of the House, whereupon Mr. Glenn sent in his resignation in a long letter, in which he reiterated the charges already made. It was decided not to receive this document, as the House had nothing to do with the resignation of members if they saw fit to vacate their places. In the discussion on this subject the opinion was very generally expressed that the member who was so indignant at the offer of $500 for his vote must be out of his head.

## CHAPTER XIII.

DREW had been ordered to appear before Judge Barnard on the 10th of March, to show cause why he should not be permanently removed from the Erie Directory, but the counter injunction, fulminated against not only the Vanderbilt party, but against Judge Barnard himself, came as a welcome relief to Uncle Daniel, and gave him the right to disobey Judge Barnard to his heart's content until the granting of another injunction.

The accommodation of the Brooklyn judge was granted on the 9th. On the morning of that day, the market was feverish. Erie, under the steady but powerful pressure applied by Commodore Vanderbilt and his agents, had run up to 78, and notwithstanding the favorable action of Judge Gilbert, Daniel Drew was unhappy. His short contracts for millions were fast reaching maturity, and Erie was up to a ruinous figure already, with a fair prospect of advancing still further.

On the morning of the 10th, the stock was at 79 and firm. Vanderbilt's trained men were hard at work with orders from their chief to keep the market strong. Fisk had not yet acted, and Drew began to fear that his young *protégé* was about to betray him. Orders were issued to all his brokers to buy Erie before another jump, so that he could fill his contracts. All at once Fisk's 50,000 shares came in showers upon the market. By this time, Vanderbilt buying to ruin Drew, and Drew purchasing to save himself, the stock had reached 83. Every share of Fisk's stock was greedily taken, but before the day closed the street was wild at the discovery of the character of the material which he had thrown on it in such vast quantities. It was too late. Down went Erie to 71, and dozens of adventurers were ruined in an hour.

Vanderbilt stood like a rock in the storm. Foiled again, and this time by a *parvenu* whose name he hardly recognized. But he did not flinch. His agents were ordered to keep on buying as long as a share of stock remained, and by the power of this one man's will the panic was stayed. He had lost $10,000,000.

On the 14th of March several issues of the Erie controversy came before Judge Barnard in the Supreme Court Chambers. The court-room was crowded with spectators interested in the matter, and the proceedings were of a lively and somewhat exciting character. Mr. Fullerton called the attention of the Court to the Erie case, stating that orders of attachment had been issued against various Directors of the Erie Railway, and that he had understood that one or more of these Directors were in the custody of the Sheriff. He then demanded that the return of the Sheriff be read.

Mr. Field, for the respondent, called the attention of the Court to the fact that any application for an attachment was a violation of Judge Gilbert's injunction, and therefore any attachment in it must be dismissed.

Mr. Fullerton claimed that the proceeding by attachment

was an entirely new proceeding not within the injunction of Judge Gilbert.

Mr. Field read the affidavits to show that this contempt proceeding was a proceeding in the old suits.

Mr. Justice Barnard was of the opinion that this was a new proceeding to see whether there had been a violation of orders of the Court.

Mr. Field.—Not initiated by the Court, I hope.

Judge Barnard.—Certainly not. This Court would be only too glad to get rid of it.

Mr. Field.—I understand then, that your Honor decides that this case must go on; and I most respectfully, and with all due consideration for your Honor, claim that this matter cannot go on before your Honor. It is on record that your Honor is interested in this suit, and before your Honor can go on you must decide that you are not interested in it, and that decision your Honor should not make. With the utmost respect for your Honor, I claim that this matter should not go on before you.

Judge Barnard.—Before I granted this attachment I was fearful that I might violate this injunction that was granted by Mr. Justice Gilbert, and Mr. Justice Balcom; but I became satisfied on examination that they did not intend to tie up the proceedings that were occurring subsequent to the filing of the injunction. This contempt of the Court, therefore, occurring afterward, they could not have intended to prevent that which they could not foresee would take place, and I do not see any reason for changing the opinion that I then had.

Mr. Field.—Then your Honor's idea is that they did not intend to stop future proceedings, but past proceedings for contempt?

The Court.—Not for a contempt. That is an independent proceeding which they could not foresee would take place.

Mr. Field.—But the injunction is positive and explicit that they refrain from taking any further proceedings.

Mr. Fullerton.—In what?

Mr. Field.—In all the proceedings mentioned in the order.

Mr. Fullerton.—Against the Erie Railway Company?.

The Court.—As far as Mr. Drew is concerned.

Mr. Field.—The gentleman is very bold, but he is mistaken. (Mr. Field then read from the order, "in any suit in any complaint.")

The Court.—I do not think it is necessary to discuss this, because neither Mr. Drew, nor Mr. Work, nor the Attorney-General has anything to do with this proceeding, which is entirely new.

The names of all the parties against whom proceedings were issued were then called by the Sheriff, and Messrs. Lane and Skidmore answered.

Mr. Fullerton asked that the parties answering be compelled to plead. Mr. Field said that there was a proper course to pursue, and the other side should know it.

The Court held that counsel for the parties attached declining to answer, the matters must proceed on regular interrogatories. Meanwhile Messrs. Lane and Skidmore were served in court.

The Court then put the matter over to Monday the 23d of March, to permit the attached parties to answer the interrogatories, and meanwhile held Mr. Diven in $100 bail, and Messrs. Lane and Skidmore in like amounts, stating that he would hold the parties who had not appeared in $500,000 each.

A dispute then arose on the settlement of the order, Mr.

Field claiming that their objection and Judge Barnard's statement (given in the order which follows) should be included in the order of the Court; and the Vanderbilt party, represented by Mr. Rapallo, insisting that no such order should be made. It was ultimately settled that the decision of the Court should be entered in an order, and that Mr. Field should also enter an order including that order, as follows:

"The People, etc., against Diven. The plaintiffs moving this day to proceed upon the attachment issued against the defendant for an alleged violation of an injunction, it was objected that the motion for an attachment was made in violation of another injunction of this Court, and therefore that no further proceedings should be had, which objections were overruled. It was then objected that the judge now sitting could not hear and decide on the questions upon an attachment, because he was a party to another suit, being part of this general litigation, and was interested therein; the judge disclaiming that he ever had any interest in this litigation, or that he was ever interested in the slightest degree, either directly or indirectly, remotely or contingently, in the Erie or any other stock, or ever had any; which objection the Court also overruled, and thereupon made an order, of which the following is a copy:

"The defendant being charged with contempt of court in violating an injunction issued in an action in the Supreme Court, wherein the People of the State of New York are plaintiffs, and the Erie Railway Company and others, Directors of said Company, are defendants, on the 3rd of March, 1868, and a writ of attachment having been issued against him for such contempt directed to the Sheriff of the City and County of New York, returnable on the 14th of March instant, whereupon the said Sheriff has returned that he did attach the said defendant, Diven, and had him in custody before the Court, and the said Diven, on being, by virtue of said attachment brought personally before the Court, and denying that he is guilty of the misconduct charged as aforesaid against him; now it is, on motion of Marshall B. Champlain, Attorney-General of the State of New York, on behalf of the people, ordered that the said plaintiffs do, on or before the 18th March, 1868, forthwith file in the office of the Clerk of this Court interrogatories specifying the facts and circumstances alleged against the said defendant, Diven, and that they serve a copy thereof upon the said defendant or his counsel; and that the said defendant do put in written answers to said interrogatories, upon oath, and file the same with the said Clerk, on or before the 21st inst.; and it is further ordered that the said defendant appear before this Court on the 23rd inst., at 10 A.M., to which the further proceedings are adjourned; and that meantime the defendant be discharged on giving bail in the sum of $100, to appear on the said 23rd of March, and then and there abide and perform the order of the Court in the premises.

"GEORGE G. BARNARD."

This having been settled, Mr. H. F. Clark stated that plaintiffs' counsel had nothing to present to the Court in the matter postponed to that day. They desired to have this question of contempt settled first. This, therefore, if the other side were willing, they would ask should go over to Monday, the 23d inst., when the attachment matter was to come up. But they had a new proceeding. The order of the Court had been clearly violated in the issue of $10,000,000 of new stock. They (the plaintiffs) had prepared a new complaint to reach the proceeds of this stock. They had been unable to serve the defendants, but three of them, Diven, Skidmore and Lane were in court. It would, perhaps, be hardly fair to compel them to answer immediately; but he would ask that they be directed to show cause on Monday why a receiver should not be appointed.

Judge Barnard said he did not see why it should be delayed. The matter might be disposed of at once.

The order was then taken to show cause forthwith.

Mr. Skidmore was at once served, but Messrs. Diven and Lane had left the room.

Mr. Field held that the matter was entirely *ex parte*, and declared that he would not argue if the other side dared to proceed on such a service.

The Court then appointed George A. Osgood receiver of the proceeds of the new stock, directing him to give security in $1,000,000, and to deposit the proceeds whenever they should amount to $500,000 in the Union Trust Company.

This action of Judge Barnard was severely criticised, some of the papers almost exhausting the vocabulary of abuse in dealing with him. From a large number of leading editorials written on this subject, the following from the *Sun* is selected because of its seeming fairness and its moderate tone:

"Cornelius Vanderbilt is the President of the New York Central Railroad, and largely interested in the Western lines of narrow gauge roads. These interests require that he should destroy or control the Erie Railway. This is a wide gauge road, and is about to enter upon arrangements with certain Western roads, by which it is supposed that the business power and influence of Mr. Vanderbilt will be seriously impaired. George Osgood is a well-known Wall street man, and the son-in-law of Mr. Vanderbilt.

"The Supreme Court is a tribunal having peculiar control over the operations of corporations and their officers; among other things it has power, upon proper cause shown, to remove an officer, to dissolve corporations, and to appoint receivers of their property. George G. Barnard is a Justice of that Court, and not unknown to a certain kind of fame.

"The struggle for ascendancy in the kingdom of railroads had grown to gigantic proportions in Wall street; millions of dollars were involved, and the courts of justice were appealed to. The legal proceedings were inaugurated some time since by the regular attorneys of Mr. Vanderbilt, who appeared before Judge Barnard, and acting ostensibly for the Attorney-General of the State, procured *ex parte*, that is, privately and without notice, an order suspending the Treasurer of the Erie road from his office; and about the same time the other Directors were enjoined from holding meetings and acting as Directors. The order suspending the Treasurer was appealed from, and an effort made to procure an immediate hearing by the General Term of the Court, upon the ground stated by counsel that the order was of so startling a character, and, if admitted as a precedent, so threatening to every vested right of property, that all former proceedings on appeal ought to be suspended, and an instantaneous rehearing had. This application failed, the judges, Justice Barnard presiding, deciding that the General Term could not, without the consent of parties, suspend the rules of proceeding, and the senior justice (Judge Ingraham) declaring significantly that there need be no fear that *such proceedings* would pass into precedent.

"In the mean time, in another suit, Cornelius Vanderbilt,

George G. Barnard and others were on oath charged with conspiring to accomplish certain purposes touching the Erie Railway and its management; and therefore an injunction was issued by Mr. Justice Gilbert, of the Second Judicial District, restraining the parties charged from proceeding further in the suit mentioned, and especially from prosecuting or maintaining any proceedings to procure a receiver of any part of the property.

"The charge as of the Erie Railway Company and against Judge Barnard has been so widely promulgated, that doubtless every citizen has heard of it, and probably every one has formed some opinion upon it. Under these circumstances it is due to public decency, and Judge Barnard owes it to himself, that he should bear himself with dignity and circumspection.

"On Saturday, as we learn from our law reporters, Mr. Horace F. Clark, a son-in-law of Mr. Vanderbilt, acting ostensibly as counsel for the Attorney-General, applied to Judge Barnard for an order returnable to-day, requiring the Erie Directors to show cause why a receiver should not be appointed for a certain $8,000,000. The startling audacity of such a demand by counsel need not to be commented upon. In an application of such import, it would seem that one day, and that Sunday, would be a short time to prepare to fully enlighten the Court and secure the ends of justice. The rule of law in all cases of notice, however trivial the application, requires eight days' notice. It was understood that on Monday Judge Barnard would not be holding the branch of the Court in which this application would be heard, and that it would come before another Justice of the Court.

"According to the report of the scene, Mr. Justice Barnard, upon reading the order, inquired why it was not made returnable forthwith and before him; and with his own hand so changed the application, and then pointed out a Director of the Erie road sitting in court, on whom the order might be served, and who was required to show cause upon the moment why the order should not be granted. No such cause was shown; and upon the spot Justice Barnard, a co-defendant in an action charging him with complicity with Cornelius Vanderbilt in his schemes to ruin the Erie Railroad, upon the motion of Horace F. Clark, son-in-law of Cornelius Vanderbilt, appointed George A. Osgood, another son-in-law of Cornelius Vanderbilt, receiver of eight millions of dollars, being, it is likely, all the money belonging to the Erie Railway Company. However, the process of Justice Barnard does not run into the State of New Jersey, where it is said the fund in question is.

"The Constitutution of the State provides but one way for the relief of the bench and the public in certain cases, which is by impeachment. The term of Justice Barnard expires on the 1st of January next, and it is stated that he will be a candidate for re-election.

"The seriousness of this condition of things cannot be over-estimated, and it seems to us that the press, the bar, and every enlightened and conservative element of society owes a duty to the whole, and that a united and courageous effort ought to be made to secure at least the observance of a decent decorum in the courts of law."

## CHAPTER XIV.

THE proceedings in Judge Barnard's Court on the 14th of March, gave but little uneasiness to the Erie Directors whom the deputy sheriffs had failed to serve with writs. James Fisk, Jr., Jay Gould, John S. Eldridge, and Uncle Daniel Drew, were safely ensconced in cosy quarters at Taylor's Hotel, Jersey City, where, with the Company's books at hand, and with a fire-proof safe containing $8,000,000 in greenbacks, they proposed to establish the offices of the Erie Railway Company, and bid defiance to Judge Barnard and his injunctions. They had flitted to New Jersey on the 11th, immediately after learning from their "guerillas" that the Philistines were upon them—that the officers of the law were out in force anxiously searching for the inaccessible Directors, whom they desired to serve with sundry unpleasant documents issued from Judge Barnard's Court.

They had been but a short time in New Jersey when they succeeded in having a bill passed through the Legislature of that State in a very short space of time, giving the Erie Railway Company all the rights, titles and privileges of a New Jersey corporation. They made a division of the profits of the recent transactions in Wall street, and set about laying plans for another campaign at an early day.

The Erie Railway War assumed a new and most exciting phase on the night of March 16th, in the attempt of an organized gang of forty well-known New York ruffians to kidnap Daniel Drew, James Fisk, Jr., Jay Gould, and their associates in exile; but the nefarious design failed of accomplishment. A morning paper of the 17th gave the following report of the affair:

"It was generally understood that yesterday Mr. Drew and his companions would transfer their head-quarters to the Erie Railway building at the Long Dock, but from timely intimations received from their agents, the project was abandoned.

"In the forenoon yesterday Mr. Masterson, chief detective of the Erie Railway force, was informed that something was to be done, but what it was he was unable to learn. He therefore took precautions to prevent any demonstration that might be made. Nothing however occurred until about four o'clock, when it was observed that a number of suspicious looking characters, who came across the Pavonia ferry, were congregating about the depot and lounging around the restaurant, until after the arrival of several boats, the crowd now having increased to about forty men.

"Soon these began to make inquiries for Mr. Archer, contractor with the Company for receiving and delivering freight. When they could not find Mr. Archer, they asked for Mr. Drew, then for Mr. Fisk, Mr. Eldridge, President of the road, and others of the Directors. Being told that none of these gentlemen were about the depot, the gang dispersed, some returning to New York by way of the Hoboken ferry; some by the Pavonia; while others made a reconnoissance at Taylor's Hotel, Jersey City, where the Erie Railway Directors were quartered, and then disappeared.

"While the gang were at the depot, Chief Masterson, Robert E. Danbers, one of his assistants, together with Detectives McWilliams and Nugent, of the Jersey City police, recognized among them such well-known characters as Cusick,

Jim Elliott, Jack Connelly, Pete Roche, Mike Welch, George Dorson, Pete Elliott, and others. The new chief of police, N. Fowler, who was formerly a dealer in Washington market, was present in citizen's dress, and recognized among the crowd a number of ex-Washington-market butchers, who are now well-known sporting characters.

"These men being known as the very worst kind of desperadoes, and not likely to relinquish a project, especially as it was reported they were to receive $50,000 for their services, Mr. Drew and the other gentlemen were naturally very much alarmed for their personal safety. It was believed that the ruffians would return to Jersey City late at night, and watching the opportunity, when but few people were about, would, pistol in hand, make a dash on Taylor's Hotel, overpower the employés, and then seize Mr. Drew and his associates, and convey them away before any opposition could be offered.

"Under these circumstances it was deemed advisable to call upon the police for protection.

"Chief-of-Police Fowler was therefore sent for, and a consultation held, when Mr. Fowler readily consented to afford the desired protection. Accordingly at nine o'clock roll-call a number of the men were selected and ordered to remain, while the entire force sent out on duty were notified, the moment they saw rockets sent up, to hasten with all speed to Taylor's Hotel. The men who had been detained were then directed to arm themselves, and subsequently they were quietly admitted to the hotel, one by one, and took up their quarters in a large room on the second floor, ready for any emergency. The railway detectives and other of the employés of the road were also present to render assistance. Patrols were sent out, the ferries watched, and every precau-

THE GUARD ROOM AT TAYLOR'S HOTEL.

tion taken to prevent a surprise should the ruffians attempt a raid. Up to midnight everything passed off as usual, but as the hotel is kept open all night, it was thought that they might act some time between midnight and morning."

On the same day, on the other side of the Hudson River, a scene fully as exciting, but of a different character, was enacted. Monday, March 16th, had been fixed by Judge Barnard as the day for the settlement of his order appointing George A. Osgood receiver of Erie's eight millions. Some time between Saturday and Monday, Richard Schell, acting for the Drew party, had invoked the power of Mr. Justice Clerke, and an order was granted by him enjoining the settling of that appointment order, and staying all proceedings thereon.

Judge Barnard opened the proceedings of his court at 11 o'clock by announcing, to the evident astonishment and dismay of the Vanderbilt party, that he had been served with an order staying all proceedings in the matter, and directing parties to show cause on the 1st of April why the order for a receiver should not be vacated.

Mr. Clark.—Is this an ordinary exercise of the Court's power?

Judge Barnard.—The order was served on me by Messrs Field and Burrill; the papers on which it was granted were not served on me. I understood that they had been served on Mr. Vanderbilt.

After a complete silence of nearly half an hour, Judge Barnard suggested that the matter should stand over to Tuesday, and the court adjourned. But on Tuesday the case was again postponed to Thursday, the 19th, Judge Barnard remarking that "he hoped some Judge of the

Supreme Court would see the error of his ways and reverse his action."

The money market at this period was assuming a character of great stringency, which was attributed to the action of speculators in locking up greenbacks, and also to the fact that the discredit thrown upon railroads by the attacks upon Erie, had caused many loans upon railroad stocks to be called in. To add to the distress of those who had bought stocks and borrowed money, government was selling gold and buying greenbacks, and this had the effect of increasing the exactions of money lenders.

## CHAPTER XV.

THE proceedings in the Erie case before Judge Barnard on the 19th of March, were of a most extraordinary character. The Justices of the Supreme Court, as well as some of the lawyers engaged in the litigation, had now become parties to the quarrel, and injunctions and counter injunctions and stays of proceedings, and other legal obstacles in the way of justice, were as plenty as Bible House tracts.

At half-past 11 o'clock the first gun was fired by Horace F. Clark calling up the motion for a receivership of the Erie money. He recapitulated the many facts connected with the early history of the war on Erie, and at last brought the story down to the 9th of March.

"There had not till then," said Mr. Clark, "been any interference with your Honor's ordinary jurisdiction by any of your colleagues. On the 9th of March, William Belden, a partner of Mr. Fisk, went with a complaint to a judge of an adjoining district, and procured an injunction in his suit. At this point your Honor was made a party. No application had been made to you, accessible at all times; no application was made to modify, alter or change your injunction. For the first time in the history of the State and County was the Court itself made a party on a false charge.

"The complaint presented to Justice Gilbert was full of false statements and fraudulent concealments. It was intended to drive your Honor from the consideration of the cause, and to bring it before some more supple and less fearless judge. (He then read the 10th section of Belden's complaint, and continued.) Here is Mr. Belden, the partner of Mr. Fisk, charging your Honor with fraud, he having already sold the stock short to depress it for his partner, and making his own partner defendant. Justice Gilbert stated yesterday, that when he granted this injunction he was lying on a sick-bed, and that when he granted it he did not intend to authorize the issue of any stock. When it was before him he stated that the fact of the injunction was unknown to him, and that had he known of such an injunction, he would not have granted his own order. He had granted the order, not designing to cripple this court in its ordinary jurisdiction."

He then read Judge Barnard's affidavit read before Judge Gilbert. This denied, in the broadest and fullest terms, that he had anything to do with Erie speculations, or that he had any interest whatever in the result of the litigation.

After Mr. Clark had read the order issued by Judge Clerke, restraining Vanderbilt, Schell, Barnard and others, Judge Barnard said:

"You will draw up an order to show cause, returnable forthwith, and serve it forthwith on Mr. Eaton, the Attorney of the Company, why this injunction should not be vacated."

Mr. Rapallo.—Your Honor is aware that the venue in this action is laid in Steuben County.

Judge Barnard.—That makes no difference—the order was made here.

Mr. Fullerton.—One word to disabuse the minds of any who have listened to the tirade of this morning as to the propriety of this action. This injunction is but an ordinary exercise of the jurisdiction of the Court of Equity *to prevent the multiplicity of suits*, and to bring into one single suit all the litigations which have arisen, or can be anticipated, growing out of one transaction. .... The same question arises as in the New Haven suit. On the one side it is claimed that the issue of certain stock was unauthorized. On the other the Company and their counsel believed that issue to be legal. So with the guaranty of bonds which are made part of the litigation. They should all be included in one suit. We have included every person as a party who has, or is believed to have an interest. We submit that this is a proper and respectful proceeding.

The injunction is not extraordinary, except so far as a justice of this court being a party can be considered so. But judges are, after all, men, and may be made parties to a suit. It is not such a wonderful thing that parties should be enjoined from suing. In the Amidon suit there were four hundred and fifty defendants, all retained from suing. When a receiver is appointed all suits are stopped. Our duty is done when we have produced to the Court a legal stay of proceedings; whoever violates that order violates the law; and in a court of law that should be enough.

Judge Barnard.—In regard to the last order of Justice Clerke, I have been informed by a majority of my colleagues that as far as it restrains my action it is invalid. As far as concerns my own interest in the matter, any one who reads these proceedings will see that the charge is entirely false.

I shall vacate Judge Clerke's order granted on the 16th instant, and at once perfect the order appointing Mr. Osgood receiver, and approve the sureties when offered."

At four o'clock this order was settled, after a debate over technical points, and was entered with Mr. McKean, the regular Clerk of the Court having been enjoined from acting.

Mr. Field then moved, on an affidavit of D. B. Eaton, that the Erie Railway Company intended in good faith to appeal, and asked for a stay of proceedings.

Judge Barnard (sternly). The defendants are in gross contempt, and their proceedings have been such as in the opinion of the presiding justice, are not warranted by the position of the case. The motion is denied.

Mr. Field (excitedly, but with great dignity).—I shall take the liberty to apply to any other judge of this Court for this order.

Judge Barnard (slowly and with emphasis). *And I to vacate such order.*

Mr. Field.—I shall endeavor to obtain justice in the case.

This joust between Judge Barnard and David Dudley Field, one of the recognized leaders of the New York bar, created a great deal of discussion during the day among the legal fraternity, and on the following morning the papers were almost unanimous in their denunciation of Judge Barnard's singular action.

Before night, another startling story came across from "Fort Taylor," as the Erie head-quarters in Jersey City were now called. Another attempt to kidnap the mild and placid Uncle Daniel, the rollicking Fisk, the keen-eyed and reticent Gould, and their fellow exiles! For a while it was believed that an effort was about to be made to take the State of New Jersey *vi et armis*, but with the saloons, halls, staircases, lobbies, corridors, steps, pavements, cellars, garrets, and roof of Taylor's Hotel packed with armed men furnished by the authorities, and drawn from the Erie shops, the good people of Jersey City lost their fear, and went to bed that night fully satisfied that their commonwealth was safe from the assaults of any foreign enemy. Poor Uncle Daniel was terribly frightened, but Fisk looked upon the reported attempt of the roughs as a very good joke, and while he plied his garrison with champagne and cigars, and distributed liberal supplies of greenbacks among them, he lost no opportunity to play upon Drew's fears and make him the common butt of ridicule. But the attacking party did not appear, and "Fort Taylor" was intact.

## CHAPTER XVI.

On the 20th of March the Erie War broke out at Albany before the Assembly Committee on Railroads, and waxed hotter and hotter as the day wore on. It had now assumed the proportions of a contest in which the opposing lines of battle were long drawn out, and in which the sound of the fray on the right could hardly be heard by the forces on the left, miles and miles away. It was a warm fight, but although the foemen were at close quarters, and "as fire answered fire, and through their paly flames, each battle saw the other's umbered face," there was little damage done. The Committee met for the purpose of hearing arguments with reference to the bill to legalize stock issued by the Erie Railway Company. John Ganson, John H. Reynolds, Samuel Hand, and Hamilton Harris, all distinguished lawyers, appeared for the bill; and Charles O'Conor, Horace F. Clark, Sandford E. Church, James C. Spencer, and C. M. Depew, equally well known, against it. Mr. Ganson argued that the stock was issued for the purpose of improving and equipping the road, and making further Western connections, and that it was the duty of the Legislature to protect the Company in its efforts to accommodate the public.

Mr. Clark, representing the Vanderbilt interest, opened an argument in reply, but was obliged to stop on account of indisposition.

Charles O'Conor held that the Company was liable for all the stock issued, and asserted that the greater part of it was held by opponents of the bill.

On the 23d the arguments were continued, Charles O'Conor opening in a scathing denunciation of the bill. He was followed by John Ganson and De Witt C. Littlejohn, whose arguments in favor of the bill may be thus briefly summed up:

They claimed that the friends of the bill legalizing the acts of the Directors had nothing to do with stock-jobbing operations, and it was not passed with the view of giving them facilities as speculators. If frauds had been committed, or parties had been guilty of a breach of trust, the courts were open for redress, and nothing contained in the bill would affect such action. The Erie Company had not appeared before the Committee at their own instance, but because the Committee of Investigation had been raised in the Senate, thus throwing doubt upon the action of the Company. The true nature of the war waged in Wall street, in the Supreme Court, and before the Legislature, upon the Directors of the Erie Company, was not thoroughly understood. It was looked upon as a contest affecting the interests of the stockholders alone, and since large dividends were promised by the Vanderbilt party, while the policy of Eldridge and his associciates was to expend the earnings of the road, as well as the proceeds of loans and new stock, in improving the track, extending the Western connections, and generally increasing their ability to carry freight and passengers, great sympathy was expressed for the former. In the eyes of many, a railroad is a mere money-making machine, and the only way in which they judge whether its management is good or bad, is by measuring its annual profits. Mr. Eldridge could not make as much money as Mr. Vanderbilt claimed he could; therefore, it was said, let the concern be handed over to Mr. Vanderbilt. This was the line of argument adopted by Mr.

Vanderbilt's counsel. But those who were misled by this kind of reasoning forget that Mr. Vanderbilt could pay more money over to the Erie stockholders, in the shape of dividends, only by taking more than was then taken out of the pockets of the people who depended upon the road for passage and freight. If he added to the gross receipts, he must add to the fares and the rates of freight. If he diminished expenses, it would be by stopping the outlay for new cars, locomotives, iron and buildings, and thus diminishing the usefulness of the road. It was not pretended that he and his sons and sons-in-law were any more honest than Mr. Eldridge and the Board of Directors. The accusation against them was that they were running the road at too low figures, or were spending its earnings in permanent improvements, instead of dividing them among the stockholders. If Mr. Vanderbilt should gain control of the road, he would endeavor to increase fares and freights, thereby oppressing the public for the benefit of stockholders.

The general feeling seemed to be in favor of the Erie bill, and the following extract from the editorial columns of a leading New York paper gives fair expression to the prevailing sentiment:

"Any one who remembers how Vanderbilt used to manage his steamboats in the days when he owned steamboats, or who looks at the miserable cars, worn-out tracks, and scanty train accommodations which now characterize the Hudson River, Harlem, and New York Central railroads, under his administration, can judge what the fate of the traveling and freight-sending public would be, if the sole obstacle to the full gratification of his economical propensities presented by the competition of the Erie road were removed. The stockholders might or might not get greater dividends, but the citizens of New York and the farmers of the West would be squeezed for their benefit; and for every dollar they received, we should lose ten from the interference with business which would be caused by the Vanderbilt policy. On general principles, too, apart from the special circumstances of the contest to which we now refer, the public ought to resolutely discountenance the system of railroad combinations and monopolies which is getting to be so much the fashion. Sitting by and idly or approvingly witnessing the consummation of schemes which can have no other result, if carried out, than to levy tribute upon every passenger and every pound of freight passing between this city and the West is the hight of folly. This metropolis derives all its prosperity and all its greatness from the cheapness and facility with which goods and passengers can be carried to and from it in every direction. The avenues of communication with it being now in rival hands, competition tends to produce lower prices and increased accommodations. Let, however, this rivalry and this competition be stopped by a consolidation of interests, and we shall find ourselves at the mercy of a gigantic monopoly, whose only merit will be the doubling and trebling of its dividends at the public expense. Legislation will be powerless before the corruption of the monopolizers, and the people will be pillaged by them without defense. In view of such considerations, we have done what we could to awaken the attention of our readers to a sense of the peril which threatens them, and we trust that our efforts have not been in vain. Already the Legislature has under consideration a bill for the protection of the Erie Railroad, and we are informed that another bill looking to the conversion of the Erie Canal tow-path into a public line of rails, is soon to be reported. These measures will effectually defeat the Vanderbilt schemes, and we trust they may be at once adopted."

## CHAPTER XVII.

UNCLE DANIEL grew tired of life in barracks. He did not like Jersey City. He missed the cheering outlook upon Wall street during a storm, and longed to be where he could aid in raising one.

Sunday being a *dies non* in law, the exiles ran no risk in passing that day in New York; so, promptly at 12 o'clock on Saturday night, the eager band filed down from the fort to the ferry-house, and within a few minutes were on the old stamping ground, safe from the officers of the law for twenty-four good hours. This they did regularly while they remained in exile.

Gould, Fisk and Eldridge, of course, opined that the pious Uncle Daniel was in the habit of spending the Sabbath with his family, and at his favorite church in Fourth Avenue, where he delighted to exhibit pride in his humility, by passing the money-plate.

An accident aroused suspicion against the old man. Fisk sent for his best detective.

" Sam," said he, "I have a lingering notion that hypocrisy is a disease that all the sulphur in the other place can't drive out of a man's system, and I've always thought that old Drew had it bad. He 's playing points on us, and I want you to watch him. When we trot off next Saturday night to prepare for worship on Sunday in New York, keep your eye on Uncle Dan. Shadow him till he gets right here again. Find out where he goes, and report to me."

Saturday night came. Uncle Dan disappeared after the party reached the New York side, and, taking a carriage, drove to his home. The detective was close behind him, accompanied by a trusty assistant, who watched the Drew mansion for the rest of the night. In the morning Sam relieved him, and stood "on post," patiently awaiting developments. At about ten o'clock he had the satisfaction of seeing the venerable object of his anxiety emerge from his front door. In a moment a carriage drove up, and Uncle Daniel entered it.

"Oh," said Sam to himself, "the old coon's going to church, I guess."

Detectives sometimes guess wrong. The shrewd Sam did in this case. Daniel Drew saw not the inside of any holy place that blessed day.

The carriage, closely followed by Sam in a light cab, which he had kept near at hand, drove to the city residence of Commodore Vanderbilt. Uncle Daniel alighted, walked slowly up the steps, rang the bell, and in a moment was out of Sam's range of vision.

The detective hastened back to Jersey City, and made his report. He found Fisk in a frenzy. It had just been discovered that the wily Drew had "conveyed" the funds of the Company; and the information that he was in consultation with their enemy, Vanderbilt, only confirmed the exiles in their belief that they were in a close place, and that all their ingenuity and boldness would be required to extricate them.

All day Monday, Drew was absent. He was playing a

shrewd game; but one of his intended victims was too wide awake to be cheated. Fisk, knowing that Drew had deposited a very heavy amount of his private funds in a Jersey City bank, sued out an attachment, and had the money placed beyond Drew's reach.

On Tuesday, Uncle Daniel returned. He met his colleagues with many smiles, and gave plausible excuses for his absence.

"Never mind that, Uncle Daniel," said Fisk, with a gay laugh; "we're all so glad to see you back. You have n't any idea how anxious we were about you. 'Fraid the sheriff had put his unholy hands upon your person, and that you would never meet our gaze again. But," added he, in a different tone, as he fixed his eyes upon Drew's, and spoke with a peculiar emphasis, "how did you leave the Commodore?"

Drew was startled. How did that secret leak out? Was it possible that Fisk could have followed him?

"And what have you done with our money, you damned old hypocrite?" continued Fisk, while Gould and Eldridge sat by in silence, enjoying the consternation of the aged trickster, and anticipating a richer scene when he should learn how his pupil had outwitted him.

"Why, Jeems, ain't I Treasurer of the Company?"

"That's all right," replied Fisk; "but we want to know what the Treasurer has done with our money."

"Well, it was n't safe here; so I tuck it to York," whined Uncle Daniel.

"That won't hold water, Daniel Drew," said Fisk, twitching his moustache; "but I've no doubt it's all right, since you say so. We all know you would n't lie—O, no; you *could n't* if you tried, you damned sanctimonious old goosy gander. But, Daniel, when you try to bamboozle us, to throw dust into our eyes, to play points, or to circumvent us, and try to be best dog in the fight *all* the time, why, then, you must stay over in Jersey, and breathe the invigorating air of the Flats. I was afraid *your* money was n't safe, Daniel, so I had it attached, for fear, you know, that some unauthorized cuss might get hold of it, and squander it in riotous living."

Drew's astonishment, chagrin and rage knew no bounds. How blind he had been, not to know that his pupil had studied with an object in view the many lessons he himself had set him! The old man walked up and down the room with hands crossed behind his back, and eyes cast down. For two minutes there was perfect silence.

Suddenly Drew came to a full stop. Turning to Fisk with a smile on his face intended to be winning, he said:

"Well, Jeems, you are about as keen as you need to be. How kin we compromise this?"

"Bring back our money," said Fisk.

The next day the Erie funds were again in the safe, and the attachment on Drew's bank funds removed.

But Daniel's clandestine visits to Commodore Vanderbilt continued, and his companions in exile kept their own counsel in regard to their knowledge of the fact, never by a word allowing Drew to think that he was even suspected.

## CHAPTER XVIII.

THE secret meetings between Vanderbilt and Drew were regularly kept up, and at last resulted in giving the Commodore an assurance that he would have no trouble in bringing Erie ultimately into his hands. He learned from Drew, who was uncommonly communicative, that no more stock should be issued, and this was the point which he most desired to gain. He redoubled his efforts to control the action of the Legislature in the railroad matter, and with the power of immense wealth to back him he succeeded in having the Erie bill killed on the 27th of March by a vote of 83 to 32.

Two days previous to this decisive action of the Albany Legislature, Jay Gould made public some singular facts which were embodied in the following affidavit, and some of which have been already given in a preceding chapter:

"*State of New Jersey, County of Hudson:* Jay Gould being duly sworn, deposes and says: That he is acquainted with the various parties on both sides of the Erie litigations, including Messrs. Cornelius Vanderbilt and Daniel Drew; that previous to the last annual election of Directors of the Erie Railway Company, deponent had a large interest in the stock of the company, and took an active part in the canvass which resulted in a change of management; and while said canvass was progressing, deponent came in contact with said Cornelius Vanderbilt, Richard Schell, Frank Work and Daniel Drew. The canvass was made against said Drew on the part of deponent and associates; shortly after deponent had enlisted in the aforesaid contest, at the request of Richard Schell and C. C. Norvell, the financial editor of the New York *Times*, who gave the deponent a letter of introduction, deponent called upon Charles A. Rapallo, who was engaged in drawing up a complaint against Daniel Drew concerning his alleged contracts with the Erie Railway Company and substantially the same suit recently instituted before Judge Barnard, in which Frank Work is plaintiff. At this interview Mr. Rapallo read deponent the complaint as far as completed, and stated that he had spent most of the previous Sunday with the Commodore at his house, going over and correcting the complaint. Mr. Rapallo wished to procure certain facts and information, which deponent procured or aided him in procuring, and the complaint was accordingly perfected. And deponent further says, that during the said canvass, deponent counted as with him a block of about ten thousand shares, standing in the name of Work, Davis, and Barton; this had been promised verbally, and deponent had in consideration given Mr. Vanderbilt an agreement to put said Frank Work in said Board as his representative. As the canvass was drawing to a close, deponent called upon Mr. Work for the proxy, in accordance with the verbal agreement above stated. Mr. Work then informed deponent that he could not give the proxy without the consent of Mr. Vanderbilt; that evening deponent met Mr. Vanderbilt, Richard Schell and Frank Work at the Manhattan Club. Mr. Vanderbilt at first said he would not consent to give the proxy, because he feared he would join hands with Daniel Drew. It was finally arranged that I should give a bond with certain penalty, the bond to be void if we defeated Drew; but good if he were elected. This bond deponent

IN CENTRAL PARK.

RELIEF FOR CHICAGO.

signed. After it was done, Mr. Work gave deponent his proxy upon said 10,000 shares of stock. The reason stated to deponent why Mr. Vanderbilt was anxious to defeat Mr. Drew was that Mr. Drew was bearing stocks, and was finally instrumental in producing the money stringency, which took place just previous; that Drew had several millions on deposit, and knowing that Mr. Vanderbilt and his friends were carrying a large amount of stock, never offered them any assistance. And deponent further says, that on the Sunday previous to the election, Mr. Drew, then knowing his defeat to be certain, went to see Mr. Vanderbilt; that at that interview Mr. Vanderbilt read over the complaint and injunction in the Frank Work suit to Drew; the result of that interview was that Vanderbilt and Drew struck hands together, and Drew agreed to go in with Vanderbilt and his friends and bull Erie with them. Schell then came to see deponent and Eldridge, and invited us to meet the Commodore at his house that evening. We went accordingly, Vanderbilt, Schell, Eldridge and myself, to Mr. Vanderbilt's house. Mr. Vanderbilt had a programme arranged as follows:

"1. New Board to guarantee the $4,000,000 of Boston, Hartford and Erie Railway bonds.

"2. All expenses attending the canvass were to be paid. (Mr. Vanderbilt said we could come there after the election and get the check through him and Mr. Gould's bond was to be cancelled.)

"3. The following to be the Board: C. Vanderbilt, Daniel Drew, Horace Clark, James H. Banker, Augustus Schell, William H. Vanderbilt, John S. Eldridge, Henry Thompson, Jay Gould, J. C. Bancroft Davis, General Diven, and others whose names deponent cannot now recollect. To the proposition No. 1, all assented, Schell, Eldridge, Vanderbilt and myself. To the second and third, we replied, that we had gone through the canvass anti-Drew men; that we could not honorably change front. Mr. Vanderbilt insisted that Drew should go upon the ticket. Some rather plain talk ensued, and we left without, of course, assenting to the said third proposition. We gave as a reason that the combination between him and Mr. Drew had taken us by surprise, and we wanted time to think of it. After leaving Vanderbilt's, and on my way up-town, deponent called on Mr. Drew; a few moments after, Mr. Vanderbilt came in and Mr. Drew saw him in the back room, his dining-room. Deponent wished to get some light or explanation in regard to the sudden alliance between Vanderbilt and Drew. Drew afterward informed deponent that at that interview Vanderbilt asked him if Diven could be depended upon to take responsibilities, and proposed that the election be adjourned, and no election had; thus leaving the old Board to hold over; and deponent further says that in order to conciliate Mr. Vanderbilt, it was afterwards arranged that after the election a vacancy should be made in the Board and Mr. Drew substituted to fill the vacancy; but the other names mentioned by Mr. Vanderbilt were not upon the ticket, and deponent further says that subsequently a 'pool,' as it is called in Wall street, was formed to buy $9,000,000 of Erie stock. Among the parties interested in such combination were Vanderbilt, Drew, Richard Schell, John Steward, James H. Banker; and that all of the said parties were operating together in said 'pool' until about the last of January last, when it was closed up, the stock sold and profits divided; that after said 'pool' was closed up the said Schell was very much dissatisfied with the said deponent, and said to said deponent that Drew had cheated the 'pool,' and that he should follow him on his contract with the Company.

He said to deponent that he had no fight with any other Director excepting Drew, and with him because, as he alleged, he had cheated in the 'pool;' and deponent is informed and believes that after the suits were brought said Schell went to General Diven and offered to withdraw them if Mr. Drew would take the 5,500 shares of stock off his hands at 75, or pay $20,000 to the poor of New York; but said proposition was declined. The suits referred to are those in the name of Frank Work, which said suits he assumed to control; the suit in which said Schell was plaintiff was subsequently commenced; and deponent further says that he was induced to vote for the guarantee of the $4,000,000 of the B. H. & E. Railroad bonds, partly because Messrs Schell and Vanderbilt approved of it at a meeting heretofore referred to, on a Sunday evening at Vanderbilt's house; and partly because the old Board had agreed to it. That deponent was never interested in the bonds or stock of said Company, his sole interest being the Erie Railway Company; but deponent has been since informed and believes that said Schell was in the interest of the B. H. & E. Railway Company, and actually received 1000 shares of the stock of that Company as a consideration for his influence in aiding to secure the passage of the resolution authorizing the guarantee of said $4,000,000 of bonds against which he now complains.

"(Signed) JAY GOULD.

"Subscribed and sworn March 25, 1868.

"CHARLES C. MARTINDALE,

"*Notary Public.*"

On the same day the following statement was made by the President and Treasurer of the Erie Railway Company, contradicting the charge that the $10,000,000 new stock was issued without the surrender of an equal amount of bonds, etc.

"OFFICE OF THE ERIE RAILWAY COMPANY,
"JERSEY CITY, *March*, 25, 1868.

"TO THE PUBLIC.—The report in some of the morning papers said to have originated in Albany, that the 100,000 shares of new stock of the Erie Railway Company were issued, without the surrender of an equal amount of convertible bonds previously issued, and that the proceeds of the bonds so issued were not paid into the treasury, is entirely without foundation.

"The truth is, that the whole amount of convertible bonds ($10,000,000) was issued (as we believe legally) and sold, and the proceeds were paid into the treasury of the Company, and not a dollar of the stock has been issued except upon the surrender of an equal amount of convertible bonds."

On the 30th, after a long consultation between the defeated and chagrined Directors, now known as the "Exiles of Erie," Jay Gould ran up to Albany with a full pocket-book and with *carte blanche* to use as much money as might be found necessary to change the sentiment (or the votes) of the law-makers; and to give them in his own clear, terse, and vigorous language, good reasons why they should repent of their error and lend a helping hand to the Company which he so well represented. His rooms at the best hotel in Albany became at once the favorite resort of a large number of the people's servants, all "Honorables" by virtue of their office, but honorable only in title.

Affairs were moving along pleasantly, when to Mr. Gould's intense disgust there appeared to him one morning a deputy sheriff, armed with a summons issued by Judge George G. Barnard, ordering him to appear before him, the said Judge, immediately, or to give bail in $500,000 to appear on the following Saturday. The required bail was given, and Mr. Gould, with mind now at ease, was ready to proceed with the delicate business he had in hand.

## CHAPTER XIX.

Jay Gould appeared before Judge Barnard on the day named in his bond, and immediately returned to Albany, only to discover after a few days that he had been badly sold by the very legislators whom he had bought at high prices. The report of the investigating committee of the Legislature was favorable to the Vanderbilt interest. To say the least, the action of the lawmakers was inconsistent and illogical. The new stock issued by the Erie Directors was either legal or illegal. If legal, then the committee stultified themselves by reporting against it. If illegal, they were none the less wanting in judgment when they acted for the encouragement of Vanderbilt, who at the very time he was laboring to have the stock branded as counterfeit or worthless, had bought no less than $8,000,000 of it. The money paid for the stock was now under lock and key in the Erie Railway office at Fort Taylor in Jersey City, and thus withdrawn from the money market. The buyers on the street were necessarily borrowers, and had drained the banks to carry their heavy loads. The effect was telling upon the general community, and merchants of the best credit found it difficult to procure accommodation. It was evident that if this state of things continued, the most serious results would be experienced at an early day.

The situation was a peculiar one at this stage of the war. Vanderbilt seemed to be working to depreciate the property for which he had paid millions; and the reading and thinking public were not slow to believe that motives other than those which appeared, must have occasioned so strange a reversal of all experience among owners of valuable property. The people argued that if the stock sold to Vanderbilt was unlawful stock, he could recover his money at any time by due process of law; but what was wanted was the money in circulation, and the improved railway accommodations it would provide. Vanderbilt's plan of discrediting the Directors of the Erie Company could only result in locking up the money indefinitely and in giving him a doubtful cause of action, at best, against the Directors as individuals. The public interest demanded that Vanderbilt should be protected in his investments and that the stock which he had purchased should be declared valid; and this the Legislature had power to do. The action of the Legislature in reporting against the Erie Directors met with almost universal condemnation.

March 27th was an exciting day in the Legislature. The Erie bill was the main question before the Assembly, and after a sharp fight it was defeated. A telegraphic dispatch to the New York press briefly announced the fact and closed thus:

"The Erie managers abandoned the contest last evening, and the chief of them took French leave, to the great disappointment of the lobby and many of the members, who had reckoned on a severe struggle to-day to overcome the report of the committee, which it was known was to be adverse.

The air is full of rumors as to the means by which the triumph of the Vanderbilt party was secured, *but it will not do to repeat them.*"

On the 1st of April the Committee appointed to investigate the affairs of the Erie Railway Company presented the following report, through Mr. Pierce, of the majority:

"The conclusions of the majority are that the evidence must satisfy any fair-minded man that the issue of the $10,000,000 bonds subsequently converted into stock, was procured by Drew to be used by himself for private speculation, and utterly regardless of the interests of those whom he was bound to respect. It is believed that Eldridge, the President, and Fisk and Gould, Directors, were concerned, and probably interested with Drew in these corrupt proceedings. These men, to escape process of our courts, whose mandates they have violated, have sought shelter in New Jersey. Your Committee caused these men to be personally notified for examination, but they refused to trust themselves within the jurisdiction of the State. Your Committee is informed that they have applied to the Legislature of New Jersey for protection, but cannot believe that the authorities of that State will interfere with the chartered powers of a corporation created by this State, or attempt to shield officers from the merited responsibilities of their conduct. There are other transactions involving the dealing of the Directors with the Company, of a highly reprehensible character, the particulars of which will be found in the evidence submitted. The Company has guaranteed a large amount of coupons of the bonds of a contemplated railway from Boston to the Hudson River, of which Company the said Eldridge is President; and the Company has also entered into obligations to build a railroad from Akron to Toledo, Ohio. These acts have been done without consulting the stockholders, and without authority of law.

"Your Committee infer from the evidence that the persons named have very little, if any interest in the stock or securities of said Company, and are quite satisfied that they have taken advantage of their position and influence for purposes of private gain and emolument.

"Your Committee believe that within the principles established by the Court of Appeals in the Schuyler case, the stock improperly created and fraudulently put into circulation, is nevertheless valid and binding against the Company in the hands of *bona fide* holders, but as between those who have been injured by the above mentioned wrongful acts, and the persons who committed them, the former have legal remedies in the courts. The Committee have considered what, if any, legislation should be adopted in the premises. Although the franchises and privileges granted by the State have been used for corrupt purposes, yet it must be remembered that this has been done by unfaithful agents, and not by meritorious agents.

"Justice demands that these agents should be removed, but as the courts have ample power over them, the Committee have not deemed it necessary to introduce a bill for that purpose.

"JAMES F. PIERCE,
"JOHN J. BRADLEY,
"A. C. MATTOON."

The following is the substance of the minority report:

After commending the action of the Erie Directors, in regard to the arrangements with the Boston, Hartford, and Erie, and with the Michigan Southern, and Northern Indiana Railroad Companies, the minority say:

"The Erie is a competing line with the New York Central, which has direct connection with the Eastern and Western States, and without the connections sought to be made would soon become a mere tributary to its great central rival. It would be a self-evident proposition, that almost the very existence of the Erie Railway as a leading corporation, depends upon its having a broad-gauge connection with Chicago. That in the leasing and conversion of the stock of the Buffalo, Bradford and Pittsburgh Railroads, while it is possible that injustice may have been done the stockholders of that road and the Erie, the evidence before the Committee does not establish it, and the public are not interested in it; that in the loan of Daniel Drew to the amount of $3,480,000, the undersigned see no clear reasons in the contracts, or in the evidence bearing upon the same, for charging the Directors with injustice or negligence; but as to the resolutions passed by the Directors, February 19th, authorizing the issue of $10,000,000 convertible bonds, the undersigned say that they have the uncontradicted evidence of Mr. Diven and Mr. Davis that the right of the Board to pass such a resolution was not doubted or questioned either in the Executive Board or Board of Directors; that the act had been previously done repeatedly, and referred to the stockholders, and reported to the Legislature without challenge or comment. We have the sworn statement of Davis and the testimony of Diven, that the power has been exercised by the Central, Hudson River and other railroads in the State.

"As a Board of Directors, therefore, they are not chargeable, in passing that resolution, with a willful violation of the law; and the undersigned believe that, had it not been that outside parties were interested in obtaining control of said Erie Railroad, no question would ever have been made as to the right to pass such a resolution, or issue the convertible bonds in accordance therewith. As to whether certain persons, acting in their individual capacity, not officially as Directors, have perpetrated a wrong on other persons, or whether they have made improper use of the knowledge they gained exclusively as such Directors, in affecting the price of stock in Wall street, or whether the stock, after being innocently signed by the proper officers, was improperly used, or thrown upon the market by individuals acting not in their official capacity, or whether they, as individuals, made an improper use of the money thus obtained, or whether the injunction had been improperly violated by individuals, the undersigned do not stop to consider, because these questions belong to the courts. The undersigned think an act should be passed legalizing the ten millions of dollars of stock, and the contracts with the Boston, Hartford and Erie, and the Michigan Southern, and the Northern Indiana Railroad Companies, prohibiting a director or officer of the Erie Company from being a director in the Central, Harlem, or Hudson River Railroad Company, and *vice versa;* prohibiting any future contract tending to consolidation between the Central, Harlem, and Hudson River Railroads, and making any sale or contract to sell in this State any stock of any railroad on a future day null and void, unless said stock shall, at time of such sale or contract to sell, be and continue until the day specified in such contract or sale, in the possession of the party so selling or contracting to sell.

"G. W. CHAPMAN,
"W. J. HUMPHREY."

## CHAPTER XX.

VANDERBILT stock was now on the rise, and Erie's prospects dark indeed. But the ready-witted, cool, calculating and indomitable Jay Gould was not cast down. He filled his wallet again, and with a surgeon's certificate of disability in his pocket, (to secure him from forced attendance at Court,) he opened another campaign. On the 4th of April, he had appeared before Judge Barnard and given a bond in $50,000 to appear on the 8th, and his trial for violating Judge Barnard's injunction was begun. The time of the Court was taken up with the examination of John B. Haskin by James T. Brady, mainly on the subject of the alleged corruption of the Judge by the witness. On the following day the case was again up, but Gould, having secured his physician's certificate, had gone back to Albany. The proceedings were very interesting, but of no importance to the contesting parties or to the public. Judge Barnard, when asked what disposition should be made of the testimony taken the day before, replied, with much feeling:

"The testimony of Judge Haskin yesterday, to use the language of a gentleman I have just left, was outrageous and scandalous, and should be stricken out at once as a mark of respect to the Court. That part which is not scandalous the Court will receive."

Mr. Brady (excitedly): We want the testimony to stand as it does stand, and as it will stand, and as nobody can prevent it from standing forever.

The case was adjourned for a week.

On this day there were no fewer than four several proceedings in the courts in the Erie case. The first was before the Common Pleas, in the matter of the *habeas corpus* of Jay Gould. In the Supreme Court, General Term, the second form in which the case came up, was the continuance of the argument in the General Term on the appeal from the order appointing a receiver. The third was set for the Supreme Court Chambers, in three motions to dissolve injunctions; and the fourth was the proceedings in the attachment, before Judge Barnard. The fights between the railroad giants were thus far productive of good only to the army of lawyers employed.

Well, as related before, Jay Gould was soon busy again at Albany. How much money he spent in his efforts to convince the members of the Legislature of their grievous error in opposing the Erie, no one will ever know; but it is beyond question that $500,000 would not cover the outlay. His arguments, backed as they were, were eminently successful, and although the Investigating Committee of the Assembly were then trying the charges of bribery and corruption brought by Mr. Glenn against Mr. Alexander Frear and others, (mention of which is made in a preceding chapter,) a number of the members showed an earnest desire to share Mr. Gould's funds, and were at once treated with a liberality that took even the greediest by surprise.

He had been summoned to appear before Judge Barrett on the 11th of April, but when the Court Officer, James Oliver, came for him, he refused to go to New York, slammed and locked the door of his room, and directed his counsel, Hamilton Harris, to say to the officer that he would take all the responsibility. Judge Barrett immediately issued an order setting forth these facts, and requiring Hamilton Harris and Jay Gould to show cause on the 14th of April why they should not be punished for the misconduct and contempt alleged in James Oliver's affidavit. Mr. Harris appeared and purged himself of the charge, but Gould was represented as being too sick to travel, and the case was postponed.

His ailment was very peculiar. It incapacitated him from obeying the order of a Supreme Court Judge; but, in its very worst stage, seemed to quicken his wit and to strengthen in a remarkable degree his executive faculties, and his power to act upon the feelings and consciences of men whom he desired to control. While suffering from one of his severe attacks of his disease, (for which there is no name in any of the medical books, and which, having no symptoms, could not be diagnosed,) he drew up another Erie Bill, which, with the amendments afterward made in the Legislature, reads as follows:

"Section 1. It shall not be lawful for the Erie Railway Company to use any money realized from the convertible bonds issued by said Company on the 19th day of February, 1868, and under the 3rd day of March, 1868, the said bonds amounting in all to $10,000,000, except for the purpose of completing, furthering, and operating its railroads, and for no other purpose. No clause in this section contained shall affect any right of action of any person against any officer or agent of the Erie Railway Company; nor shall it affect any action or proceeding now pending, save as herein provided; nor shall anything herein contained be held or construed to affect any liability, civil or criminal, of any officer or agent of the said Erie Railway Company, or of any other person. The use of the moneys in this section mentioned, by any officer or agent of said Railway Company for any other purpose than is herein mentioned, shall be a felony, punishable upon conviction thereof by imprisonment in a State Prison for not less than two, nor more than five, years.

"Section 2. The future guaranteeing by the Erie Railway Company of any other railway corporation necessary and proper to secure a connection of said Erie Railway with other railroads, so as to form a continued line of communication between New York and Chicago, for the purpose of securing better facilities for the traffic of said Erie Railway Company, and contracts hereafter made for that purpose, shall be deemed and taken to be within the powers of said Company; nor shall any stockholder, director, officer, or agent of the Hudson River, Harlem, or New York Central Railroad Company, enter into any agreement with any stockholder, director, officer, or agent of the Erie Railway Company, to fix the price for carrying freight or passengers through, or to or from, any point in this State; any stockholder, etc., or other person authorized, aiding or abetting to such an agreement, shall be deemed guilty of misdemeanor, and, upon conviction thereof, shall be punished by fine or imprisonment, or both, in the discretion of the court.

"Section 3. No stockholder, etc., in either the New York Central, Hudson River, or Harlem Railroad Company shall be a director or officer of the Erie Railway Company, and no stockholder, etc., of the latter Company shall be a director of either of the three first-named Companies.

"Section 4. It shall not be lawful for the Erie Railway Company to consolidate its stock or any part thereof, to divide its earnings or any part thereof, with the New York Central, the Hudson River, or the Harlem Railroad Company; and any contract made between the Erie Railway

Company and either of the three above Companies for such consolidation or division shall be void.

"Section 5. This act shall take effect immediately."

The bill came up for the final reading on the 18th, and was passed by a vote of 17 to 12. The yeas were: Banks, Beach, Chapman, Folger, Graham, Hubbard, Humphrey, Mattoon, Morgan, Morris, Nichols, Nicks, O'Donnell, Parker, Stanford, Van Petten, Williams.

The nays were: Bradley, Cauldwell, Creamer, Crowley, Edwards, Kennedy, Murphy, Norton, Palmer, Pierce, Thayer, Tweed.

Mr. Mattoon, who had fought the bill in committee, was now one of Erie's strongest friends. His conversion was due to the cogency of Gould's arguments at his rooms in the Delavan House, where he lay a martyr to an anomalous disease, from which he did not recover until the successful passage of the Erie Bill, and its endorsement by Governor Fenton on the evening of the 21st.

## CHAPTER XXI.

THE announcement of the defeat of Vanderbilt in the Legislature produced but little effect in Wall street, as the decision had long been determined in the minds of the operators. Central held at about 113, and Erie at 66¾, but later in the afternoon of April 21st, Central jumped to 119¾ and Erie to 70½. This movement was puzzling to the wisest dealers, but in two or three days the cause was made apparent. Uncle Daniel's visits to Vanderbilt had resulted in an agreement to compromise matters. The Commodore was to discontinue all his suits against the Directors, and allow the "Exiles of Erie" to return to their accustomed haunts. He was to receive from them for 50,000 shares of Erie $2,500,000 in cash, $1,250,000 in bonds of the Boston, Hartford and Erie Railroad at 80, and $1,000,000 cash additional for the "option" of taking 50,000 shares more of Erie at any time within four months, at the price at which he had agreed to sell. He was also to have the nomination of two new Directors. Eldridge was to receive for $5,000,000 of Boston, Hartford and Erie bonds at 80, $4,000,000 of Erie acceptances. Drew was to hold fast to what he had made by speculating in Erie in his peculiar way, but was to pay into the treasury of the Company $540,000 to settle what claims the Company might have against him. Fisk and Gould were not considered in this arrangement; but to conquer their hostility to the terms of the compromise their

AT LONGBRANCH

associates agreed that Drew, Eldridge and some others should resign from the Board.

The "Fort Taylor" garrison returned to New York on the 22nd, and on the 25th of April, Wall street was in a flutter. The leading Vanderbilt stocks began to show increased signs of activity, and advanced in price. On the 27th Central closed at 127, and Erie at 71¼.

A few days previous to this Judge Barrett had discharged the *habeas corpus* proceedings against Gould, and as it appeared to the Court that Gould had intended no disrespect in disobeying the order served by James Oliver at Albany, the contempt proceedings were also discharged. But the cases for contempt against Gould, Fisk and other Directors, for violating Judge Barnard's injunction were not allowed to drop, although the bail in Fisk's case was reduced from $50,000 to $11,000.

After Drew and Eldridge retired from the Erie Board the new management passed through a severe ordeal of criticism, but along in September there seemed to be a change in public opinion in their favor. The principal managers had now left the street and its speculations, with which they had been so long connected, and were devoting their energies to the recuperation of the Erie road by controlling all its natural resources for freight and passengers, and forming new combinations designed to increase business. They leased the Paterson and Newark Railroad, thus securing for the Erie road a large Western traffic hitherto diverted from it, opened new connections with the coal fields of Pennsylvania, added to their fleet of Sound steamers, and provided for a growth of their grain trade by building warehouses and elevators wherever needed. Erie stock was now down to 46.

But unfortunately this "change in Peter's life" was not for

long. On Saturday, November 14, Erie then at 37, there was a sharp decline, and Erie fell to 35, rising subsequently to 37⅛. The cause of the break was due to the fact that 40,000 shares of it were pressed for sale, the stock having declined to 22½ at the London Stock Exchange, causing a rumored panic in Lombard street. Wall street was much agitated, and on the 16th the excitement was on the increase. Anxious buyers crowded the Long-Room each jostling the other for place and power to purchase. Quickly the price of Erie advanced to 61, and almost as quickly fell to 48½. Millions of dollars changed owners on this occasion. It transpired that for several weeks Fisk, Gould, and the other Directors of the Erie had been secretly issuing millions of new stock and selling it for any price they could get. A number of other stock gamblers had been buying the stock with a view to obtain control of the Company and put their own men in as Directors. As, however, the new issues kept coming on the market the price kept sinking lower and lower. The buying party, in the meantime, many of them being Englishmen, had sent their purchased stock to England as fast as they could; but their friends there, when they found that there was no limit to the quantity manufactured by the printing press, became alarmed, and telegraphed to their brokers here to sell at any price, shipping the stock back at the same time by steamer. The brokers on this side, thinking to help themselves, and knowing that they would receive plenty of the stock in ten days, the period required for the steamer's passage, undertook to sell ahead, borrowing meanwhile to make their deliveries. But suddenly the speculators who had been selling the new stock, having plenty of money, turned about and bought up all the stock actually here; and as the steamer could not arrive within a week, they had compelled the foolish brokers who had made sales at 40 and thereabouts, to buy in at 55 and 60 to meet their contracts.

On the 18th another chapter in the seemingly interminable Erie Railway War was commenced. August Belmont and Ernst B. Lucke, joint owners of 4000 shares of Erie common stock, sued before Judge Sutherland to set aside the Board of Directors and to appoint a receiver. They represented in their complaint that unauthorized stock to the amount of $60,000,000 had been issued,—$20,000,000 of it since the settlement of the former suit in the Spring. An injunction was applied for, and granted by Judge Sutherland, restraining the Company from any further increase of the number of its shares. But Fisk and Gould had not been asleep. Nearly a week before the suit was brought they had sought the aid of Judge Barnard, who had kindly appointed Jay Gould receiver of the Company, thus anticipating the action of Mr. Belmont.

Another suit was commenced on the following day by Charles McIntosh, who held 200 shares of Erie, and another injunction granted; and in Judge Barnard's court an amendment was made to the order appointing Jay Gould as receiver, which allowed him to purchase 200,000 shares recently issued with the funds of the Company (now about $15,000,000), and as only that amount was supposed to be in the market, a panic was imminent.

In the Belmont suit James Fisk, Jr. was a witness. His testimony was given in the following affidavit:

"..... On Sunday morning, November 15, 1868, Mr. Daniel Drew unexpectedly called upon me; he said he had come to make a clean breast of it, and to throw himself upon our mercy; that he was short of Erie stock 30,000 shares. I told him I knew that, and that was not half of it; and that he was short in addition 40,000 'calls.' He complained bitterly of his position; he then entered into an explanation as to certain proceedings that he said were being got up by parties who were to attack us in the courts; he said he had been in the enemy's camp, and all that he cared about was to look out for number one; and if we were willing to help him he would make a clean breast of it. I told him that his disposition and his nature were so vacillating, that I should not trust him unless he made a clean breast of it to begin with. (Much merriment was provoked in the court-room when this part of the affidavit was read.) He finally, after much hesitation, said he would tell me that Work, Schell, Lane, and Thompson were embarked in a scheme with him; he refused to tell me in whose name the proceedings were to be instituted; upon inquiring closely of him whether the case was taken up on its merits, or as a mere stock operation, he admitted that I was to relieve those who were short of the stock. I presented the idea to him as to what the others would do, and he said he could take the ringleaders with him if they were also provided for, and that he would break up the whole scheme. He begged and entreated that I should go and bring Mr. Gould, saying he knew that if he could see Gould he could benefit his position, and would tell us who were to be the plaintiffs in the suit. I tried to convince him that this was one of his old tricks, and that he should be the last man to whine at any position he had put himself in with regard to Erie. Finally I consented to go and get Gould, and I did so. I was not present at the entire interview between Gould and Drew, but such portion of the conversation as I heard was of the same nature as that held with me. He also used many arguments upon Mr. Gould and myself to induce us to help him with regard to the stock. He stated to us that it was within our power to protect ourselves, and urged us to issue some convertible bonds, saying that nobody could know anything about it. This Mr. Gould and I refused to accede to.

"At this time he told us that a suit was to be brought in the name of August Belmont; that he was present at a meeting they had held last night, and heard the papers read. We told him over and over again that we could not help him. He would not leave us, but insisted on remaining, and Mr. Gould and myself finally, unable to get rid of him in any other way, told him that we would meet him again at 10 o'clock that evening. We then parted. Subsequently, about 11 o'clock, I found Mr. Drew waiting for us. At that time Mr. Gould was not present, and I again told him that nothing could be done. He said, 'Then, if you put this stock up, I am a ruined man.' He harped upon the fact that he was willing to pay a large amount of money for the use of 30,000 or 40,000 shares of stock for fifteen days, and offered me as high as three per cent., which would amount to nearly $100,000 for the use of it for that time. Finding that he could not induce me to accede to his wishes, he took another tack, saying that there was a conspiracy against us, that they would ruin us if they could, and that they would have the stock down at all hazards; and that if I would not agree to anything with him, he would give his affidavit to the other side, having before stated that he would not give his affidavit if I would come to his rescue. He said: 'You know that during the whole of all our other fights I objected to ever giving my affidavit, but I swear I will do you all the harm I can, if you do not help me in this time of my great need.' He also said, 'You can loan me the stock,' and added, 'I will give you three per cent. for it. You have the power to issue more convertible bonds, and I will buy the bonds from you with the understanding that I shall not pay for them unless you are caught.' I positively and unequivocally declined the proposition, as I had done before.

"After talking in this strain for more than an hour, I adhering to my decision that nothing could be done, he, at about 1 o'clock, Monday morning, said, 'I will bid you good night,' and went away.

"JAMES FISK, JR."

Drew kept his promise. He and other sufferers from large "short" sales and "puts" on Erie, organized a combination for the purpose of embarrassing the Erie clique and depreciating the value of the stock. To effect this purpose and temporarily block transactions in Erie shares, they circulated a form of agreement for signature among brokers and bankers, which pledged the signers against dealing in Erie stock, until the Company should deposit its transfer books in the hands of some respectable banker or financial institution for the reference of stockholders. At the same time a movement was initiated to induce both Boards of Brokers to strike Erie stock from their lists until the Directors should take such action. Erie was now at about 41.

In course of time the injunctions granted by Judge Barnard in the McIntosh suit were vacated, and ex-Judge Henry E. Davies made receiver in the Belmont suit. But things had again reached such a pass that a Supreme Court judge's order was hardly worth the paper on which it was written. The day after Judge Sutherland's appointment of ex-Judge Davies as receiver, Judge Barnard removed the cause (Belmont *vs.* Erie) so far as it affected James Fisk, into the United

States Circuit Court, staying all proceedings in the action in the State Courts against Fisk. The effect of this was to leave Fisk in possession of the road as a Director, free from the control of Receiver Davies. Judge Barnard also granted a stay of proceedings in the matter of the receivership in the Belmont suit, pending an appeal by the defendants; and on the same day Judge Sutherland granted an order to show cause why Judge Barnard's stay of proceedings should not be vacated. Next morning the order for receiver in the Belmont suit was settled, and Judge Sutherland vacated Judge Barnard's stay of proceedings and placed ex-Judge Davies in possession of the property of the Erie Company.

In commenting upon the existing state of affairs, a morn ing paper used this language:

"The Erie war has now become a scandal and a crime. The robes of the judiciary are rumpled and stained by being dragged into this foul controversy, The hand of justice has proved impotent in this exigency, and has only entangled and tightened the knots it has failed to untie. The management of the Erie Railway ought to be radically changed. If there be found virtue enough in the new Legislature, it should be invoked to annul its present charter, and bestow upon it a revised one; and either through its own sovereign power select the officers of the Company, or devise some mode of appointment by which it can be delivered out of the hands which long since ruined its stock, and will soon render a large portion of its bonds worthless, and ultimately whelm the corporation in irretrievable bankruptcy."

There were now two receivers of the Erie Company's property—Jay Gould, appointed by Judge Blatchford; and ex-Judge Henry E. Davies, appointed by Judge Sutherland.

On the 26th of November a motion to have Judge Blatchford's order vacated was made before another judge.

A few days later the contest was invested with new interest by the proceedings in the United States Circuit Court. The affidavits were numerous and extended, and the day was spent in reading them. The main interest attached to the affidavit of Jay Gould, which gave to the world for the first time the secret of the compromise between Vanderbilt and the Erie exiles. This was on the 1st of December, on which date also the business community were startled at the news that Gould and Fisk had absconded on the night before with all the funds belonging to the Erie Company. Fisk had left the city, it is true, but he had simply run to Binghamton to obtain certain signatures to documents relating to the business of the Company, and was back on the following morning attending to business, and enjoying heartily the graphic accounts of his midnight flight as contained in the morning papers.

Now appeared a new difficulty to supplement the series already existing between the judges of the Supreme Court. Judge Sutherland and Judge Cardozo were brought in conflict by the granting of an order by the latter which vacated the order previously granted by the former, and there seemed to be no prospect of ever reaching the limit of the judicial game of cross-purposes.

But fortunately, Judge Balcom of the Supreme Court, sitting in Broome County, now stepped in and attempted to bring order out of chaos. On the motion of the Attorney-General, he granted an order whose first effect was to set aside all the proceedings had in New York City with the conflicting orders of Judges Barnard and Sutherland. It nullified the appointment of a receiver which had been made by Judge Sutherland. Substantially, too, it obviated the order of Judge Blatchford of the United States District Court, appointing Jay Gould receiver of a certain portion of the funds of the Company, and, pending the investigation, leaving the Directors in charge of the business as before. By this order the Hon. Giles W. Hotchkiss, of Binghamton, was appointed to examine into the affairs of the Company, to ascertain all the facts in the operation of the Directors and the condition of the corporation, and to report the result of his investigation, as a basis of a final disposition of the whole subject.

## CHAPTER XXII.

AFTER indulging in much hilarious merriment over the mistaken zeal of the newspaper reporters, who had sent him away from the city with from six to eight millions of funds belonging to other people, Fisk bethought him that he could create a genuine sensation by putting some of the journals to trouble by suing them for libel. He began with the *Tribune*, laying his damages at $100,000, and then opened upon the *Springfield Republican* with a demand for $50,000; and the property of the latter was attached for that amount on the 3d of December. The *canard* had affected Erie stock four per cent., and had injured his reputation as an honest man.

The Directors of the Erie Railway Company had been on the defensive for a long time. They now determined to attack their enemies and rout them. They began by suing out an injunction restraining the New York Central Railroad Company from issuing more stock; then, as a preliminary to an action which they proposed to commence against Commodore Vanderbilt for the recovery of the $5,000,000 "extorted" from the Company in July, James Fisk, Jr., with his counsel, Thomas G. Shearman, Esq., on Saturday afternoon, December 5th, called upon the Commodore at his office in Fourth street, to make formal tender of the stock "forced" upon the Company in settlement of the old suits, and to demand the return of the money alleged to have been paid as a bonus to effect their withdrawal. A reporter gave the following account of what occurred:

"About 2 P. M., a carriage drove up to the Commodore's office, and the two gentlemen alighted, bearing between them an enormous black carpet-bag. This bag, which bore a remarkable resemblance to those mysterious receptacles carried years ago in this city by the rebel hotel-burners, contained 50,000 shares of Erie stock, representing at 70, the price for which they were said to have been returned from the Commodore, three and a half millions of dollars, together with cancelled checks amounting to a million dollars more. Bearing this immense package between them, the gentlemen staggered up to the office door and rang the bell. An attendant promptly admitted them, when they found the Commodore seated in his easy chair near his private telegraph instrument, quietly puffing a prime Partaga and reading the dispatches from the Stock Exchange. He had just received the announcement, "Erie, thirty-six," when the burly Mr. Fisk, approaching him, remarked:

"How are you, Commodore? I've come to see you on very important business—unusually important business."

Commodore.—Glad to see you, Jim. How de do; let's hear your business.

Fisk.—Well, Commodore, I've come on behalf of the stockholders of the Erie Railway Company to collect from you the four millions and a half of dollars which they were forced to pay over to you last July to have these suits discontinued. [Opening the bag.] Here are 50,000 shares of Erie, which you made us take off your hands at 70, which, I calculate, is $3,500,000. We want you to take this stock, and draw your check immediately, with interest from July 11th; and furthermore, we want another million from you, which was paid for no consideration; and please to make out your check for that amount also, with interest from the same date.

Commodore (slightly taken aback).—I haven't had anything to do with this business, and don't know anything about it.

Fisk.—O, now, that's all gammon, Commodore. We mean business, you know. We're after that money, and mean to have it. We don't want to be hard with you, and if you settle up without further trouble, why, we may let up on the interest. But, if you don't draw your check rightaway, suits will be commenced for the recovery of the funds thus wrongfully obtained, and we shall attach your property for the amount.

Commodore (angrily).—I ain't sold no stock to the Erie Company, nor received any million bonus, so I sha'n't pay the money.

Fisk.—Well, Commodore, we have come to make you a formal tender of the securities. Here is the stock which you forced on the Company, and the cancelled checks for the bonus. If you won't pay up, why, we shall have to sue you. Good-day.

Commodore (excitedly).—Good-day, Jim; you can sue and be ———.

[The remainder of the sentence was lost in the noise occasioned by the sudden departure of Mr. Fisk and his counsel, with the mysterious black bag between them.]

Fisk's threat was executed in due time, and suit was commenced against Vanderbilt on the 11th of December.

His threat against the *Tribune* was carried no further than the threshold of a suit for libel; but toward the *Springfield Republican* he showed a determination to wreak his bitterest revenge. On the night of the 22nd of December, Samuel Bowles, well-known as the editor and proprietor of the *Republican*, was at the Fifth Avenue Hotel, with his invalid wife. At about nine o'clock, while conversing with Murat Halstead, of the *Cincinnati Commercial*, and William Bond, Esq., President of the New Almaden Quicksilver Company, he was approached by two sheriff's officers, who, after exhibiting a warrant for his arrest, took him in custody and conveyed him in a carriage to Ludlow Street Jail. The officers were evidently in a great hurry to get their captive away, and his friends had no opportunity to exchange a word with him. Charles A. Dana, of the *Sun*, hearing of the arrest, hurried to the Fifth Avenue, and, accompanied by Messrs. Bond and Halstead, at once sallied out to obtain legal advice, but finding that it was too late to secure the release of their friend by giving bail, the three drove to the jail to see that every possible arrangement should be made for his comfort. Here they found several indignant members of the Union League Club, all of whom had been refused permission to see Mr. Bowles, and to whom the unwelcome information had been given that the prisoner would be obliged to remain in durance all night. The apartment prepared for him was a small room on the ground floor, and the accommodations about as good as the building afforded. For the comforts and luxuries supplied him that night, Mr. Bowles was required to pay $19.50.

During the evening of Mr. Bowles' incarceration, several friends of his learned that at a reception given to A. Oakey Hall, Mayor elect, at the residence of Augustus L. Brown, Sheriff O'Brien was present. Murat Halstead and Colonel Bliss hurried to Mr. Brown's, and there found the Sheriff, Judge McCunn, the committing magistrate, and James Fisk, Jr., the prosecutor. "Approaching the Sheriff," wrote a careful reporter, "they proposed then and there to give bail for the prisoner. To this the Sheriff made some objection about office hours, which was, however, quickly overcome, when he requested the gentlemen to wait a few minutes, until he consulted his legal adviser. After waiting about an hour, they ascertained that the Sheriff had gone away, leaving a verbal message for them to the effect that he could do nothing until office hours the next day, thus strengthening the impression that already prevailed, that the purpose was to keep the respondent in confinement for the night at all hazards."

Mr. Bowles' arrest and incarceration in Ludlow Street Jail excited an intense degree of feeling throughout the city, particularly in literary circles. The manner of the arrest and the malicious motives that prompted it, were commented upon freely by the reading and thinking community, and nowhere did they seem to inspire very favorable remark toward James Fisk, the prosecutor.

The following editorial, clipped from the columns of one of the many journals that commented very freely upon the affair, embodies the sentiment that universally prevailed. It was printed on the morning after Mr. Bowles was released, on giving $50,000 bail:

"Mr. Bowles, of the *Springfield Republican*, whose arrest and incarceration in Ludlow Street Jail, at the instance of James Fisk, Jr., we reported yesterday, was released early in the day. Bail in the amount of fifty thousand dollars was given for him by Mr. Cyrus W. Field and Mr. A. A. Selover. The annoyance of confinement for a single night in jail, Mr. Bowles endured with good humor, as a novel enterprise in life; so that the purpose of Mr. Fisk, to cause him extreme annoyance and inconvenience, was not accomplished. The only very unpleasant circumstance in the case was that Mrs. Bowles, who is an invalid, was in town at the time, and could not but suffer considerably from the unexpected and rather alarming absence of her husband. Possibly the gratification which Mr. Fisk may derive from having inflicted intense pain upon a most estimable lady, whose nerves had been brought by sickness to a condition of peculiar sensitiveness, may make up for the failure to work the desired degree of torture upon her husband.

"There is something truly contemptible in the feeling that dictated the manner of this arrest. That Mr. Fisk should be aggrieved by Mr. Bowles' comments upon himself in connection with the recent transactions of the Erie Railway Company, is not surprising. If he desired to procure redress by means of a suit for damages, it was perfectly proper to do so As a libel suit differs from an ordinary prosecution in alleging an injury to character, the law allows the arrest of the defendant, and his confinement until he has given security for his appearance at the trial. It was then perfectly in order for Mr. Fisk to have Mr. Bowles arrested, and to compel him to furnish bail; and had nothing more been done in this case, it would have excited no unusual attention. But the sort of arrangement into which Mr. Fisk seems to have entered with the Sheriff's officers, to seize his enemy at a disadvantage, and to immure him so that for twelve hours at least his rescue would be impossible, was a base and petty proceeding, which a gentleman might possibly be led into under the influence of extreme anger, but which he would afterward be heartily ashamed of, and endeavor to apologize for by every means in his power."

The following is Fisk's affidavit, on which the warrant for Mr. Bowles was issued by Judge McCunn, at a night session of his court, as a special favor to Fisk:

"James Fisk, Jr., being duly sworn, deposes and says that he is the plaintiff in the above entitled action; that on the 28th day of November, 1868, the defendant, Samuel Bowles, being the principal editor, or editor-in-chief, of certain newspapers published by the said Samuel Bowles & Co., in the City of Springfield and State of Massachusetts, known and described as 'The Daily Springfield *Republican*' and 'The Semi-Weekly Springfield *Republican*,' did compose and publish of and concerning this deponent, plaintiff aforesaid, the following false, malicious, scandalous and defamatory matter, to wit: 'But Fisk has probably destroyed the credit of the railroad, (meaning the Erie Railway Company,) while piling up a fortune for himself. The multiplication of its stock has been fearful. From thirty millions of nominal capital a year ago, it has been raised to sixty or seventy millions, and what there is to show for the difference beyond some worthless securities of the Hartford & Erie Railroad and a million or two of real estate, it is now impossible to say. The issue of new shares seems to have been wanton, and to no purpose in great part but to gamble in Wall street with. Nothing so audacious, nothing more gigantic in the way of swindling has ever been perpetrated in this country, and yet it may be that Mr. Fisk and his associates have done nothing that they cannot legally justify, at least in New York courts, several of which they (meaning deponent, Fisk, and others) seem wholly to own. Fisk's operations are said to be under the legal guidance of both David Dudley Field and Charles O'Conor, and now both Judge Barnard of the State and Judge Blatchford of the United States Court, back up and help on his proceedings. . . . . Many even of his friends predict for him the state prison or the lunatic asylum.'

"Deponent further says that the same matter as last above recited as having been published in the said 'Daily and Semi-Weekly Springfield *Republican*,' was republished in 'The Weekly Springfield *Republican*,' also published by the above named defendants, on the 5th day of December, A. D. 1868. Deponent further says that an action was commenced in this court by this deponent on the 21st day of December, 1868, for libel for the above recited false, malicious, scandalous and defamatory matter, as above stated, published by the defendants against the above named plaintiff, claiming damages in the sum of $50,000.

"Deponent further says that the said newspapers, published by the defendants, have a wide and extensive circulation in the City and County of New York and elsewhere, and that by reason of said publication this deponent has been damaged and injured in his character and reputation, and his usefulness and efficiency as a director and manager of the vast interests intrusted to his care as Managing Director of the Erie Railway Company seriously and wantonly injured and damaged—this as well for the stockholders in said Company at large as for this deponent. JAMES FISK, JR."

WITH U.S. GRANT.

It is more than probable that the following paragraph from the editorial in the *Springfield Republican* had as much to do in exasperating Fisk as the extracts he saw fit to use in his affidavit. He had been as roughly handled by the *Tribune* and other papers, which did not hesitate to class him among swindlers and thieves; but none had gone so far as to cast ridicule upon his person, any more than to question his possession of more than ordinary mental ability:

"The appellation of 'fat, fair and forty,' so often applied to well preserved women, belongs peculiarly to him. He is almost as broad as he is high, and so round that he rolls rather than walks. But his nervous energy is stimulated rather than deadened by his fat, which gives, indeed, a momentum to his mental movement and his personal influence."

A day or two after Mr. Bowles' release, Fisk, while in Boston, rushed into print with the following:

"To the Editor of the *Boston Evening Gazette*:—On the 28th of November last, 'Samuel Bowles, Esq., of Springfield, Mass.,' published an editorial, headed 'The New Hero of Wall Street.' It was devoted to a bitter, abusive, untruthful and unprovoked attack on my origin, vocation, habits, personal appearance and family afflictions. For example, with a reckless disregard of truth and railroad possibilities, 'Samuel Bowles, Esq., of Springfield, Mass.,' said: 'But Fisk has probably destroyed the credit of the railroad, while piling up a fortune for himself. The multiplication of its stock has been fearful. From thirty millions of nominal capital a year ago it has been raised to sixty or seventy millions, and what there is to show for the difference beyond some worthless securities of the Hartford & Erie Railroad and a million or two of real estate, it is now impossible to say.' Were it not inconsistent with my well-known good nature and forgiving disposition, I should unhesitatingly pronounce 'Samuel Bowles, Esq., of Springfield, Mass.,' an abandoned falsifier and a fool on that single statement. Further on, the *Springfield Republican* has asserted its capacity for wholesale slander by the following astounding calumny on the Bench and Bar of New York: 'Nothing so audacious, nothing more gigantic in the way of swindling, has ever been perpetrated in this country, and yet it may be that Mr. Fisk and his associates have done nothing that they cannot legally justify, at least in the New York courts, several of which they seem wholly to own. Fisk's operations are said to be under the legal guidance of both David Dudley Field and Charles O'Conor, and now both Judge Barnard of the State and Judge Blatchford of the United States Court back up and help on his proceedings.'

"The alleged indifference of the New York city authorities to the incarceration of 'Samuel Bowles, Esq., of Springfield, Mass.,' was not, you will see, entirely unjustifiable. Culpable as I am in selling 'silks, poplins and velvets by the yard,' the generous nature of 'Samuel Bowles, Esq., of Springfield, Mass.,' is not finally and utterly turned against me until he has ascertained that I am guilty of having a father who is unhappily an inmate of a lunatic asylum. This sours all the milk of human kindness in the breast of the Springfield journalist, and he prophetically consigns me to a 'mad-house or state prison.' Under the circumstances, Messrs. Editors, don't you think I had cause to feel vexed with 'Samuel Bowles, Esq., of Springfield, Mass.'? In order to protect my rights, I appealed to the law, which is the highest expression of human wisdom for the good government of mankind. If any error has been committed, those who made the law committed it. I regret that the wife of 'Samuel Bowles, Esq., of Springfield, Mass.,' was disturbed or even annoyed by her husband's temporary absence. As for the sympathy of the sycophantic horde of office-seekers and small-beer editors, who clamored around the jail gates for their comrade's release, their abuse I expected and am indifferent to. Mr. Bowles proposed the game himself, and I bowled him over the first innings. I think it will be generally conceded that I have as much right to defend my personal character as *any* newspaper has to attack it. At all events, I shall do so with the most unflinching determination, until it is proven to the contrary. Mr. Bowles need not fear but that I will bring him to trial before a judicial tribunal, and then 'let justice be done though the heavens fall;' and these are a few of the reasons, Messrs. Editors, why I arrested and locked up 'Samuel Bowles, Esq., of Springfield, Mass.'

"Your obedient servant,

"JAMES FISK, JR.

"AT HOME, BOSTON, MASS.,

"*Christmas-Day.*"

## CHAPTER XXIII.

FISK'S strong feeling against Bowles had an earlier origin than in the scurrilous paragraph in the *Republican* concerning his personal appearance, or in those which referred to his trickery and dishonesty as an Erie Director. At the time Fisk was sustaining the Goulding Patent, to which reference has been already made, and maintaining in the courts of the country, at an enormous expense, his right to hold and use it, one of his strongest opponents was Samuel Bowles, then heavily interested in the manufacture of cotton and woolen cloth by means of machinery to which the Goulding instrument was applicable. Bowles opposed the payment of the royalty to Fisk, and hence the birth of a bitterness on the part of the "Vermont peddler," which needed only the stimulant of a personal insult to increase to deadly hatred.

Mr. Bowles' own story of his adventure in New York was told in the *Springfield Republican* two or three days after Christmas, and as his account of life in Ludlow Street Jail is extremely interesting and spicy it is here reproduced:

"If I owned a patent medicine, or were a candidate for office, or even an itinerant peddler of sleazy silks and scented soaps, money could not buy of me the experience in Ludlow Street Jail, which those representatives of business and political sensations and swindlings, Fisk and Butler,* and their

* George Butler, now (1872) Consul-General to Egypt, a nephew of General Benjamin F. Butler, and a son of Colonel Butler, who accompanied the general to New Orleans. Mr. Bowles had been conspicuous in the opposition to General Butler in Massachusetts, and the nephew took vengeance upon him by pointing him out to the officers on the night of the arrest.

allied representatives of what they call law and justice in New York—Judge McCunn, Counsellor Vanderpoel, and Sheriff Jimmy O'Brien—persuaded me into last week. Being a simple country printer and editor, and the accidental author of one book, the pecuniary profit of the transaction is not so clear; though it is a fact that a shrewd Yankee publisher offered the next day 'to go a thousand better' for a new book—which suggested $1,000—$19.50 for lodging and breakfast=$980.50 possible net gain. But not foreseeing then how famous my enemies were making me, and how infamous themselves, by this little bon-bon joke for their evening's entertainment at Mr. Augustus L. Brown's, Fifth Avenue, I thought first and chiefly of the fine philosophy of the Frenchman, that experience is all that life can give us, and that whosoever offers a fresh bit of that is a real if unconscious philanthropist. Here truly was something rare and original in that line, and after the first surprise was over, I looked about to make the most of it.

"All the outward events of the taking-off, the revelations of the 'ring' at Mr. Brown's, the scenes around the jail, night and morning, have been sufficiently described. The officials exhibited only just as much severity as was necessary to represent the meanness and brutality which they were charged to execute. The purpose was to give me all the letter and none of the liberty of the law, all its cruelty, none of its courtesy; to prevent my friends knowing for what I was arrested, or where I had been taken; to insure beyond peradventure my confinement for the night; and all the persons engaged in the transaction, from lawyers and judges, down to the jail scullions, certainly earned extra pay for the fidelity with which they stuck to this purpose of their *employers. Whatever of failure they met with was none of* their fault. That which other persons had through the night was strictly denied, or cunningly prevented me; and soon discovering this, I philosophically accepted the goods the gods had provided. One of these was the finalest edition of the *Evening Express*. For the first time in my life I mastered the mysteries of its 'make-up.' I claim almost the right of original discovery, and henceforth can begin at the beginning and go through its dancing and discordant columns without missing an item of news.

"After the 10 o'clock bombardment by my friends, the jailer, who is really a good-natured little Irishman, began to smile through the deep small-pox pockets of his face. Mr. Blunt's denunciation of him as 'a vagabond,' and Mr. Halstead's query as to what his old office might be worth in greenbacks, both seemed to tickle his vanity, and remarking that I seemed to have some pretty earnest and influential friends, he proceeded to make me as comfortable as the prison-house would permit, with a strict eye, however, to both the law and the profits.

"I could have a bed in the room, half room, half cell, of another gentleman, Mr. John Livingston, an old New York lawyer, and editor of the *Law Magazine*, who had been clapped in only an hour or two before I was, and on a similar process to mine—his offence being the writing of a letter about a person who he said was a rascal—for which, with board, the price was $15 a week, half a week to be paid any way. But, saying I would have the best he had under the rules of the prison, he showed me a room on the ground floor, leading out of the general dining-room, now piled up with furniture, which he partially cleared away, and placed it at my disposal at the rate of $35 a week, 'half down.' There was a general shabbiness, or rather untidiness, about the whole premises, and no bed-room furniture in the room but two small hard beds, a carpet, and chairs in abundance; but my door was not locked, and I had in fact the run of the whole floor, of which, indeed, I seemed to be the sole occupant, office, dining-room, kitchen, and closets, which were kept brilliantly lighted for the whole night.

"But I had not yet mastered the fascinating problem of the five o'clock edition of the *Express*. And from the moment of entrance I had seen that here was what I had not supposed existed in America, a miniature Marshalsea, and Dickens' charming story of 'Little Dorrit' came up before me in all its details. What would n't I have given for Mr. Houghton's large-print household edition of it for the night's reading and comparison! So I went back to the office where more or less of my fellow-prisoners were playing cards, reading, and talking, while in the hall above others were enjoying a game of billiards.

"Ludlow Street Jail is devoted to prisoners under civil suits—for libels, for slanders, for that class of debts not yet expunged from jail offences, for breaches of trust, and all that description of constructive offences or suspicion that, under the old common law, border on crime, yet do not touch it; also for criminals under Federal laws, counterfeiters, smugglers, post-office robbers, murderers on the high seas, etc. These latter are confined in cells in the upper part of the building, and have no consort with the former, who have the privilege (?) of paying for their board and lodging and a wide range of liberties together within the house. But Dickens describes it better: 'Itself a close and confined prison of debtors, it combined within itself a much closer and confined jail for smugglers. Offenders against the revenue laws, and defaulters against the excise or customs, who had incurred fines they were unable to pay, were supposed to be incarcerated behind an iron-plated door closing up a second prison, consisting of a strong cell or two, and a blind alley some yard and a half wide which formed the mysterious termination of the very limited skittle-ground in which the Marshalsea debtors bowled down their troubles.'

"The old residents—prisoners for days, weeks, and months, as most of them were, reconciled, contented, jolly—treated me with a tender inattention which was most exquisite. They neither stared at nor asked questions of me, but kept on with their play, talk, or reading. Only the newest comer explained his case and asked mine. The others soon seemed to know all about my affairs—how, I can hardly tell; but, certainly, I never met more delicate politeness than the indirect and secret manner in which they satisfied their curiosity. I thought with a shudder how different it would have been if this Marshalsea recognized the rights of women to imprisonment.

"Late as it was, few seemed to have gone to bed, and callers were still admitted—except to me. Our 'Father of the Marshalsea' soon came down stairs—a tall, straight, gentlemanly old man dressed in black, with rich white hair and beard, and a benevolent, yet wise face; his would have been a marked appearance and manner in the United States Senate, or in the Supreme Court. All paid tribute to him as he moved about. Most of the others were younger men, and exhibited no sense of their condition, except in a certain manner of unrest, which led them from billiards to cards, from these to papers, and again back with unnatural frequency.

"There was suggestion of a game to see who should pay for the oysters, or a bottle of ale or cider; the jailer's assistants, over-grown, green boys, were asked to go out for this or that luxury; there was a good deal of chaffing about one another's impecuniosity; and sly, but successful appeals, at the last, for a 'night-cap' out of the jailer's private stores.

"Not until midnight was there any suggestion of discipline; then there was a rap and a call of 'bed-time!' from the second story; and I was soon left alone in the office. Wandering about the floor, I found a generous bathing-room, a large and well-appointed kitchen, a long and plainly furnished dining-room, apparently always ready for a meal, and open alike to the officers and the civil prisoners. The building was overheated with steam, and I was moved to beg, with success, for the window in my room to be opened for fresh air; and affairs were apparently more disorderly and untidy than usual, because the principal public room, a sort of sitting-room and library and reception-room for the civil suit inmates, was in process of repainting and frescoing, and could not be used.

"The bed did not invite sleep; I could not keep down the the sense of the humorousness of the situation; it disputed place with anxiety for my invalid wife, for whose care I had exposed myself to this petty persecution of my enemies, and with sympathy for the children to whom the jolly side of the experience would not suggest itself; and along with these, mixing with half sleep, came those nervous speculations that Dickens describes as possessing Arthur Clenman when he slept in the Marshalsea. The steam-pipes fizzed and fumed—suppose they should burst. Would it be easy to escape if one wanted to? Would this genteel scroll of iron work that guarded the lower windows in respect to the supposed superior social beings to whom the rooms were devoted, give way more easily than the plain cross-bars above? I could hear a stream of water coursing under the walls. Suppose it should get dammed up, and the building be flooded from the bottom, I should be the first victim. How about fire, which these floods of gas suggested? Where was the man who had the key?—and would he rather let us burn up than have us go free? I got up once, as I used to when in camp among the mountains, and strolled about to accustom myself to the novelty of the place. The night-watchman was eating a hearty lunch in the dining-room; all else was silent and dead within the house; and without, the city was at its quietest. At long intervals the heavy horse-car went rattling by. Then I went back and slept, and dreamed of Fisk's young and romantic days when I used to meet him among the Green Mountain towns, with his gay horses, and his richly painted wagon, with his wife's pretty face in vivid colors on its side, and her pretty person by his side under a huge caleche on top of the wagon. That was before Boston had invited, and New York had tempted; before he became the Prince of Hartford and Erie, and the King of Erie; before other seductions than those of power and wealth had entered in and possessed him.

"It was but a limited toilet that I could make in the morning. There was plenty of fresh water and clean towels, and an older inmate who came down in velvet and beaded slippers, and genteel morning jacket, and well furnished dressing case, offered me his soap, more cleanly than that provided by the city and county of New York; but with a delicacy of self-respect, as well as of respect for me, which I am sure Fisk could never appreciate, he forbore to tender me any other of the contents of his toilet box. To your true resident of Marshalsea, there are limits to generosity, and to the use of things in common. He observes the usages of the best society, that expects every gentleman to have a hair-brush and tooth-brush of his own. Then we gathered in the office, and sent out for a news-boy, who came again and again to supply the extra demand. We were curious to see how the busy outside world looks in at the quiet, self-composed, self-contained life of the prison-house, and even I could not fail to catch at once the feeling of contempt with which these inside eyes of bodies confined, but spirits free, looked out upon the hot unrest and wrangling life of free materialities, but enslaved souls.

"Soon the morning calls began, and the door-bell was continually ringing. A daughter to see a father, a wife to see her husband, a lawyer to find his client, a brother to help a brother; some for 'our set,' more for the less cheerful prisoners above. We could see the procession file in from the office; a poor woman in rags, with a baby folded in among them, hurrying up-stairs to find the criminal husband and father, and cheer his despairing heart, and report the state of the children without; here, too, an unmistakable Fanny Dorrit dropped in for a morning call upon her Sparkler—no tears, no tenderness, 'no bigod nonsense' as Dickens has it, trigly and daintily dressed, chaffing gaily with her husband and his companions, her hard, bright eyes flashing. It was sad indeed to witness the degree of their induration to the experience; but again, a sweet-faced and sad-voiced daughter appeared, and held close counsel with her father in the corner, restoring one's faith in the best and truest side of human nature. But my friends began to pour in so fast now that I had no time to watch those of the others. From now till the hour of release, their carriages rolled up every few minutes.

"First came that indefatigable son of Springfield, the friend of my youth and of my manhood, George Bliss, Jr., who had spent the night in proving the disloyalty of the Sheriff, and the close affiliations of the Ring that connived at my imprisonment, and who soon put in train the formalities necessary to both make and break the bonds. Then Springfield men and Berkshire men, who happened to be in town; members of Congress; old Californians, whom I had not seen since the Fremont campaign; brother editors; real estate owners; millionaires; dear Mr. Clark, of the Brevoort, I could see through the windows unfolding himself out of his carriage; the spirit and the person that laid the Atlantic cable, impapatient of every moment's delay; prominent lawyers, whose manliness and friendship for me Fisk's money could not subsidize;—all indignant at the meanness of the outrage, hearty in sympathy, abounding in proffers of assistance,—not one, happily, brought by enmity to my persecutors, but all by personal friendship or righteous indignation at the perversion of law to the use of a spiteful revenge—all by the instinct of the Divine test, 'I was in prison and ye visited me!' Dr. Holland writes that if one wants to get acquainted with Americans, the simplest way is to go to Europe. I say, if you would know your friends, get imprisoned in a New York jail.

"The humor of the thing was gone now—the pathos had begun; what Fisk's night had utterly failed to accomplish, this morning's foray of friends most easily and sweetly did. There was a race of bail bonds; Mr. Seward, taking the real-estate along in his carriage, came in ahead of Colonel Bliss, who had to go after his; and after paying the jailer $17.50 for my room and breakfast—most excellent tea and toast, I am bound to say—and $2 for jail fees, my prison doors swung open, and my night in jail was ended. There are a good many hotels in New York at which one can pay a great deal of money for very small accomodations; but the Ludlow Street Jail seems to me to surpass them all in that regard. With such elements of generous income, it can hardly be excusable for the Republican Legislature at Albany this winter to swell Sheriff O'Brien's fees, and carry his income up from its present $120,000 to its desired $150,000. What cost me $19.50 has probably cost him $25,000; and judging from the tendencies of public opinion, others in the circle of conspirators against a country editor's liberties will pay dearly for this little whistle. Their fun culminated at Mr. Augustus L. Brown's party the night before—mine is apparently not likely ever to cease. For, such experience as this, with its humor and its pathos, its study of a rare phase of human life, its wealth of friendly feeling, will be an unending source of pleasure and of profit. . . . . . As between my enemy in this case and myself, the triumph is mine, the loss his. He sought to disgrace me, foolishly thinking that one man can disgrace another. Had he been wiser, or had wiser counsel, he would have known that no man can be disgraced but by himself."

## CHAPTER XXIV.

FISK committed a great blunder in speaking of Samuel Bowles in terms of contempt. He was held in high esteem by the best people in the country; as an editor he was widely known and respected, and his journal had few equals. It was always bold and fearless in the promulgation of truth and in the defense of honest principles. It is to be regretted, however, that while believing it necessary and right to attack James Fisk in his official capacity as Director of Erie, he stepped aside to ridicule the man as an individual. The questions which the article was intended to discuss were of too serious a character to be associated in any way with strictly personal allusions, and those of a most offensive character. If any further evidence were required of the esteem in which Mr. Bowles was held, it might be found in the names of the gentlemen who invited him to a public dinner immediately after his release from Ludlow Street Jail. The invitation was signed by Governor Bullock, Governor Claflin, General N. P. Banks, J. L. Motley, the historian, Peter Harvey, George S. Hilliard, Chas. G. Green, Josiah Quincy, General Charles Devens, R. H. Dana,—in short, by fifty of the most prominent citizens of Boston, including men of every shade of political opinion. In his reply declining the dinner, Mr. Bowles spoke of the functions of the press in the following language:

"The corruptions in politics, and the corruptions in business affairs, have become offensive and startling within the last few years; and the moral sense of the community seems at times to have become blunted by the successful display and repetition of practices that violate every principle of fair dealing and integrity, and put the control of government, and the value of many kinds of property at the mercy of political adventurers and ruthless stock-gamblers. The press really seems to be the best, if not the only instrument with which honest men can fight these enemies of order and integrity in government and security in property. I know it is often crude in its reports, and wanton and cruel in its comments; these evils must and will be corrected with its growth,—and, compared with its future, American journalism is now but in its feeble infancy;—but we have more to fear at present from its good nature, from its subserviency, from its indifference, from its fear to encounter prosecution and loss of patronage by the exposure of the wrong and the exposition of the right. A courageous independence and integrity of purpose, coupled with a fearless expression of truth as to all public individuals, corporations and parties, are the features in its character to be most encouraged now. We can be patient with crudeness, even with a degree of recklessness, if we can have these other and necessary qualities in vigorous exercise. The press of to-day should be what Russell Lowell describes it, 'a dreadful mastiff with a scent so keen for sheep in wolves' clothing, and for certain other animals in lion's skins,' rather than the crouching spaniel, begging for food from every quarter, licking the hand that disgraces it, and only mildly protesting against outrages upon itself and the community it is set to guard.

"My own observation is, that the press rarely does injustice to a thoroughly honest man or cause. It may be deceived with regard to a private individual, and misrepresent him for a time; but with reference to public men and measures, its knowledge is more intimate and complete than that of any other agency can be, and I know that it withholds unjustly to the public one hundred times, where it speaks wrongly once of the individual."

Before Fisk had returned to New York from Boston, he was thus comically berated by a newspaper writer:

"Mr. James Fisk, Jr., who had Mr. Bowles arrested for libel, is himself a libeller. He has grossly libelled two of our most prominent business men, Commodore Vanderbilt and Daniel Drew; and we can see no good reason why, when he next visits this city, he should not be arrested at the suit of one or both of them, and imprisoned in the Ludlow Street Jail, at an expense of nineteen dollars and fifty cents a night.

"Commodore Vanderbilt is the greatest railroad man in the country, and Mr. Drew is the greatest founder of a religious seminary in the country, besides being as much of a railroad man as Mr. Fisk; and we do not propose to look on contentedly and see these great New Yorkers abused. Mr. Drew is not only the founder of an excellent seminary, at which the best of morals are taught and young men are fitted for the ministry, but he also knows how to keep a hotel, and formerly kept the Bull's Head; and if Mr. Fisk ever stopped there when he drove his peddler's wagon, we dare say he fared better than he is likely to in his libel suit.

"The airs which Mr. Fisk puts on toward Mr. Vanderbilt and Mr. Drew are certainly calculated to afford these gentlemen and the public at large some amusement. Mr. Fisk considers it libellous to associate his name with theirs, and to compare him with them. Oh! the aristocracy, the exclusiveness of peddlers who have once reached the dignity of driving four-in-hand!

THE INTRODUCTION.

"The derogatory remarks of Mr. Fisk about our distinguished fellow-citizens are contained in his proceedings in the case against Mr. Bowles. The defendant having demanded of plaintiff's attorney a bill of particulars, one was served accordingly, containing a copy of the entire article published in the *Republican*, and assigning the following as one of the reasons for considering it libellous: 'And the said Cornelius Vanderbilt and Daniel Drew, also named in said libel, are persons who, having been largely intrusted with the direction of sundry railroad corporations, are commonly reported to have made use of the power and authority intrusted to them, for the promotion of their own sinister and private ends, rather than in the due discharge of their respective trusts.'

"That will do for Mr. Fisk."

## CHAPTER XXV.

THE suit, commenced by Fisk against Vanderbilt, to recover the $5,000,000 "extorted" from the Erie Directors in exchange for 50,000 shares of stock, and to force the Commodore to take back the stock, was again before Judge Barnard in January, 1869. The main interest of the great crowd that thronged the court-room seemed to centre in James Fisk, Jr., whose eccentricities were now widely known, and whose every move was as keenly watched by the public as if he were another thaumaturgic Cagliostro.

When it came his turn to be examined in the case, Fisk

responded briskly to the call, and took the stand with a jaunty alacrity which satisfied the spectators that he would not fail to give them a rare treat. Nor were they disappointed. The quaint, queer humor of the man, combined with his uncommon shrewdness, gave a character to everything he said that required nothing more than his self-satisfied air and manner, and his assumption of boyish simplicity, to make his testimony as interesting and laughable as the funniest scene in the best comedy. The examination occupied some hours, but only so much of it is here given as may best show the peculiar "twist" of the ex-peddler's wit and wisdom:

Question.—When did you first meet Commodore Vanderbilt on business connected with the matters contained in this suit?

Fisk.—I had one interview with the Commodore some time last summer. It was pretty warm—not the interview, but the weather. I remember that well, because the Commodore was a little profane about it. (Laughter.) I can't exactly fix the date of the first interview, but I know that it was after my return from Jersey. I had been absent in Jersey for a short lapse of time, (laughter all over the court-room, even the judge relaxing into a broad smile,) and when I got back, I thought I would make the Commodore a friendly call. (Laughter.)

Q.—Did you call on Mr. Vanderbilt?

Fisk.—I think I did. (Laughter.)

Q.—Do you know that you did?

Fisk.—Most undoubtedly. (Laughter.) The recollection thereof is vivid and the memory green. (Laughter.)

Q.—What passed at the interview between you and Commodore Vanderbilt?

Fisk.—Well, the Commodore received me with the most distinguished courtesy, and overwhelmed me with a perfect ambulance of good wishes for my health. When we sat down and got fairly quiet, we came plump up to the matter that was uppermost, and then we had it out. From the beginnning I saw that Vanderbilt would try the gum game—

Q.—What do you mean by the gum game, Mr. Fisk?

Fisk.—Well, it would take a long time to explain that. You see, it's a game that so many can play at (laughter); and every man has his own peculiar way in dealing and cutting and working for points. What I mean is, that I saw that Vanderbilt was cunning—not half as cunning as Drew, though—and I thought that pr'aps I would n't stand much chance with him. He has the advantage of years on his side, and a good deal of promiscuous experience. Well, he told me that several of the Directors were trying to make a trade with him, and he would like to know who was the best man to trade with. "Why," said I, "if the trade is a good, honest one, you'd better trade with me." (Laughter.) Then he said that old man Drew was no better than a batter pudding, (laughter,) or words to that effect; that Eldridge was demoralized, and that our concern was without head or tail. (Laughter.) This was n't overly complimentary; but, after thinking a minute, I said I thought so, too. (Laughter, in which the court was forced to join.) Then he became very earnest, and said he had got his blood-hounds on us, and would pursue us until we took that damned stock off his hands—he'd be damned if he would keep it. I was grieved to hear him swear so, (laughter,) but being obliged to say something, I remarked quietly that I'd be damned if we'd take it back, (great laughter,) and that we'd sell him stock jest as long as he'd stand up and take it. (Great laughter.)

Well, when I made this observation, the Commodore mellowed down a little, (laughter,) and said he thought it would be a great deal better for us to get together and arrange this matter. Then he began to tell tales. (Laughter.) He told me that Daniel Drew, when we were suffering in exile over in Jersey, (laughter,) used to slip off to New York at night, whenever he could get away from our vigilance; that Drew would come to his house—the Commodore's—and let out our little secrets. Then he wanted to know if a trade with Drew and Eldridge could be slipped through our Board, adding in a sort of a seductive way, that if it could, we should all be landed safe in the haven of peace and harmony. (Pause.)

Q.—Well, what then, Mr. Fisk?

Fisk (with a look of virtuous determination.)—Of course, I told him I would not agree to anything of the kind; that I would not submit to a robbery of the road under any circumstances; and that I was dumbfounded, actually thunderstruck, to think that our Directors, whom I had always esteemed as honorable men, (great laughter,) would have anything to do with such outrageous proceedings.

Q.—Is that all that was said?

Fisk.—I rather think not. (Laughter.) We talked about half an hour, and I think I could say a great deal more than that in half an hour. (Laughter.)

Q.—Can you repeat anything more that was said?

Fisk.—I don't remember what more was said. I remember that the Commodore put on his other shoe. (Laughter.) I remember the shoe on account of the buckles. (Laughter.) You see, there were four buckles on that shoe. (Laughter.) I had n't ever seen any of that kind before, and I remember it passed through my mind that if such men wore that kind of shoe, I must get me a pair. (Great laughter.) This passed through my mind, but I did n't speak of it to the Commodore. I was very civil to him. (Laughter.)

Q.—Where was Gould all this time?

Fisk.—He was in the front room—I suppose. I left him there and found him there, but I don't know where he may have been in the meantime. (Laughter).

Q.—Where was your next interview with Mr. Vanderbilt?

Fisk.—The next interview was at the house of Mr. Pierrepont. Gould and I had an appointment with Eldridge at Fifth Avenue Hotel, and as we did not find him there, we went out to see if we could find him.

Q.—Can you give the date of that meeting?

Fisk.—No, sir.

Q.—Can you give the week?

Fisk.—No, sir.

Q.—Can you give the month?

Fisk.—No, sir.

Q.—Can you give the year?

Fisk.—No, sir. Not without reference. (This reply was accompanied by such a quizzical expression of face that everybody was forced to laugh.)

Q.—What reference do you want?

Fisk.—Well, I shall have to refer back to the various events of my life to see just where that day comes in, and the almighty robbery committed by this man Vanderbilt against the Erie Railway was the most impressive event in my life. (Laughter.) The meeting at Pierrepont's was a week or ten days after the first interview with Vanderbilt. Gould and I went there about 9 o'clock. We stepped into the hall together. We asked if Mr. Pierrepont was in. The servant said he would see. When the servant went into the drawing-room, I was very careful to keep on a line with the door, so I could see in. (Laughter.) Presently Mr. Pierrepont stepped into the hall, resembling a man who wasn't in *much*. (Laughter.) I asked him if our president was there. After some thoughtfulness on his part, he said he thought he was. (Laughter.) During this time I had moved along toward the drawing-room door, Mr. Pierrepont having neglected to invite us in. (Laughter.)

Q.—Where was Gould?

Fisk.—Oh, he was just behind me; he's always right behind at such times, (laughter,) and while he entertained Pierrepont I opened the door and stepped in, (laughter,) and found most of our Directors there. I stepped up to Mr. Eldridge and told him we had been to the Fifth Avenue Hotel and did not find him. He said he knew he was not there. (Laughter.) I asked what was going on, and everybody seemed to wait for some one else to answer. (Laughter.) Being better acquainted with Drew than any of the rest of them, though perhaps having less confidence in him, (laughter,) I asked him what under heavens was up. He said they were arranging the suits. I told him they ought to adopt a very different manner of doing it than being there in the night—that no settlement could be made without requiring the money of the Corporation. He begun to picture his miseries to me, told me how he had suffered during his pilgrimage, saying he was worn and thrown away from his family, and wanted to settle matters up; that he had done everything he could, and saw no other way out either for himself or the Company. I told him I guessed he was more particular about himself than the Company, and he said, well, he was; (laughter;) that he was an old man and wanted to get out of the fight and his troubles; that he was much older in such affairs than we were—I was very glad to hear him say that—(laughter) and that it was no uncommon thing for great corporations to make arrangements of this sort. I told him if that was the case I thought our state prison ought to be enlarged. (Laughter.) Then Eldridge, he took hold of me. He talked about his great exertions, what he had done and consummated, that there were only two dissenting voices in the Board—Gould and myself—and that if we came into the matter to-morrow the Company would be free and clear of litigation and everything would be all right, as he had got the Commodore and Work and Schell to settle on a price. I told him I couldn't see it. I had fought that position for seven months, night and day, and for seven weeks in Jersey I had hardly taken off my clothes, fighting to keep the money of the Company from being robbed; and I could see no reason why we should not fight it on still. He said he didn't want to go into it, but had tried to do the best he could with Gould and myself, and could do nothing, and now an arrangement had been made with Vanderbilt, and it was all right and must go through that night. I said I did not believe it was legal; these lawyers were all on one side, and I wanted to see my lawyer. He said that was no good. (Laughter.) Then Mr. Pierrepont argued with me. He said he did not think there was any one present who was not going to derive benefit from it. Rapallo was writing at a table. Schell was buzzing around, (laughter,) interested in getting his share of the plunder. Work was sitting on a sofa. I had nothing to say to him, (laughter,) as we were not on very good terms, Gould and I had a conversation together, and not till 12 o'clock at night did we give our consent. I told him I did not believe the proceedings were legal; that we had no lawyers; that the lawyers there were sold to Eldridge—hook, line and sinker. (Laughter.) Gould said Eldridge had paid Evarts $10,000 for an opinion that it was all right, and Dorman Eaton had been paid $15,000 for an opinion, and said it was legal. I told him I thought it a queer way of classifying opinions. (Laughter.) Gould consented first. He said he had made up his mind to do so as the best way to get out of the matter. I told him I would consent if he did. Drew came to me with tears in his eyes and asked me to consent, and I consented. Then there was some paper drawn up and passed around for us to sign. I don't know what it contained. I didn't read it. I don't think I noticed a word of it. I don't know the contents, and have always been glad I didn't. (Laughter.) I have thought of it a thousand times. I don't know what other documents I signed—signed everything that was put before me. (Laughter.) After the devil once got hold of me I kept on signing. (Laughter.) Didn't read any of them, and have no idea what they were. Don't know how many I signed—kept no account after the first. I went with the robbers then and have been with them ever since. (Laughter.) After signing all the papers I took my hat and left at once in disgust. (Laughter.) I don't know whether we sat down or not. I know we didn't have anything to eat. (Laughter.)

Q.—Didn't you have a glass of wine or something of that sort?

Fisk.—I don't remember.

Q.—Wouldn't that have made an impression upon you? (Laughter.)

Fisk.—No, sir! I never drink. (Laughter.) I think I left at once as soon as I had done signing. As we went out I said to Gould we had sold ourselves to the devil. (Laughter.) He agreed to that and said he thought so too. (Laughter.) I remember Mr. White, the cashier, coming in with the check-book under his arm, and as he came in I said to him that he was bearing in the balance of the remains of our Corporation to put into Vanderbilt's tomb. (Laughter.)

Q.—When was the next interview?

Fisk.—The next interview with Vanderbilt was several days after.

Q.—Was Gould with you?

Fisk.—Yes, sir! We never parted during that war. (Laughter.) We went to his office one morning and found his man Friday in the front room. (Laughter.) Don't know his name. It was the same man I had seen a hundred times before when I had been there with Drew. We found the Commodore in the back room. I asked him how he was getting on. He said, "First-rate" (laughter); that he had got the thing all arranged, and the only question now was whether it could be slipped through our Board. I told him that after what I had seen the other night, I thought anything could be slipped through. (Laughter.) He said we would have to manage it carefully. I told him I didn't think so—that they would be careful to go it blind. (Laughter.) He said the trade had been consummated at Pierrepont's house. I said I had no doubt of it. He said it ought not to have been carried out; that Schell had got the lion's share, and some of the lawyers on the other side might have to go hungry. (Laughter.) He asked if we were conversant with the rest of the trade. I said I had no doubt the whole thing had been cooked up in such a manner that it could be put through. (Laughter.) He spoke about putting Banker and Stewart into our Board, and said it would help both him and us carry our stock, as people would say we had amalgamated, and Vanderbilt's men coming into the Erie Board would strengthen the market. That was admitted, but it worked rather different from what we expected. (Laughter.) I next saw him a day or two before the prosecution was closed up. Gould thought the Commodore's losses had not been so large as represented, and asked to see his broker's account. The Commodore said he never showed anything, and we must take his word. He reiterated his losses, and said they were so large because, when they had got him to give his order to sustain the market, the skunks had run and sold out on him. (Laughter.) As we were coming away he said, "Boys, you are young, and if you carry out this settlement there will be peace and harmony between the roads." Previous to commencing this suit, I made a tender of 50,000 shares of Erie stock to Vanderbilt. I went up to his house in company with T. G. Shearman. I received the certificates of shares from Gould and put them in a black satchel. (Laughter.) It was a bad, stormy day, so we got into a carriage and I held the satchel tight between my legs, (laughter,) knowing they were valuable. (Laughter.) I told Shearman not much reliance could be placed on him if we were attacked, he was such a little fellow. (Laughter, in which Mr. Shearman joined.) We concurred in the opinion that it was dangerous property to travel with—(laughter)—might blow up. (Laughter.) We rang the bell and went in. The gentleman came down and I said, "Good morning, Commodore. I have come to tender you fifty thousand shares of Erie stock, and demand back the securities and money." He said he had had no transactions with the Erie Railway Company, (laughter,) and would have to consult his counsel. I told him I also demanded a million of dollars paid him for losses he purported to have sustained. He said he had nothing to do with it, (laughter,) and I bade him good morning. (Laughter.)

Q.—When were you made a Director of the Company?

Fisk.—I became a Director in the Erie Railway on the 13th of October, 1867.

Q.—You remember that date?

Fisk.—I do, well! It forms an episode in my life.

Q.—What fixes it in your mind so well?

Fisk.—I had no gray hairs then. (Laughter.)

Q.—You have gray hairs now?

Fisk.—Plenty of them. And I saw more robbery during the next year than I ever dreamed of as possible.

Q.—You saw it, did you?

Fisk.—I didn't see it, but I knew it was going on. I am now a Director of the Erie Railway, and its Comptroller. My duty as Comptroller is to audit all the bills; as Director, to manage the affairs of the Corporation—honestly. (Laughter.)

As the witness was about leaving the stand, he turned to Judge Barnard and said, with a serio-comic expression of bashfulness and timidity upon his broad face:

"I would like to make an apology to the Court. This is the first time I've been on the stand, and I may overstep some of the rules. (Laughter.) If I do, it is wholly in ignorance. It is new business to me, and if I don't keep within the rules, I ask my counsel to guide me, for I don't know when I may be imposed on." (Laughter.)

"Oh," said one of the Vanderbilt counsel, "your lawyer will look out for you."

Fisk.—Don't give yourself any trouble about that. I am abundantly able, with the aid of his Honor, to look out for myself. (Laughter.)

"You seem to be a very frank, outspoken, straightforward witness, Mr. Fisk," said the lawyer. (Laughter.)

Fisk.—Well, you see, I am not much accustomed to you fellows. (Laughter.) I was never on the stand as a witness but once before.

"When was that, Mr. Fisk?"

Fisk.—That was up in Vermont when I was a boy. It was in a cow case. (Great laughter.)

This exhibition of good-natured audacity was the talk of the town the next day, and Fisk became more and more the lion of New York, and the cynosure of the quidnuncs' eyes.

## CHAPTER XXVI.

JANUARY 12TH, 1869, the opening of the Albany and Susquehanna Railroad took place, more than 5,000 persons taking part in the ceremonies. The fact is mentioned here merely because the new road was destined to figure very extensively in the history of Erie before the close of the year.

A month previous to the date above given, Jay Gould and James Fisk, Jr., purchased of S. N. Pike the splendid marble building on the north-east corner of Eighth Avenue and Twenty-third street, and after remodelling its interior, and fitting it up in a style of grandeur almost unsurpassed, they christened it the "Grand Opera House," and rented the greater part of the building to the Erie Railway Company for offices, at a yearly rental of $75,000, or about ten per cent. of its cost. Fisk, carrying out a design that he had long contemplated, refitted and refurnished the theatrė, which, under Pike's management, had been a failure, and with a fine Opera Bouffe troupe from Paris brought out in rapid succession a number of Offenbach's pieces.

Some two months before Gould and Fisk purchased the Grand Opera House, which was always a "Grand Opera House" without the grand opera, the former proprietor, Mr. Pike, had rented one of the large halls on the second floor to Dr. R. P. Perry, the leader and superintendent of the New York Sunday-School Union, for mission purposes. One day, about the middle of January, the teachers and pupils found the doors closed against them. A demand was made by the superintendent that he and his flock be allowed to enter, but this was refused, whereupon a meeting was organized upon the sidewalk, and the following resolutions unanimously adopted:

"*Resolved*, 1. That, holding as we do, a three years' lease of our hall, and having performed, and standing ready to perform, all obligations on our part as to rent or otherwise, there is no man, or corporation of men, that can rightfully or legally deprive us of the full enjoyment of our privileges under the said lease.

"2. That James Fisk, Jr., the representative of the Erie Railway Company, through whose instrumentality this unprecedented action has been taken, in thus designedly locking the doors of our hall against us, and in detaining our property, has deliberately attempted to destroy our organization, and interfere with the usefulness of a prosperous Sunday-school; that he has not, in fact, the faintest shadow of an excuse or palliation; and that he has been guilty of a high-handed offense against the rights of the community receiving the benefits of the school.

"3. That no reliance of the author or authors of this outrage upon influences to protect and shield them shall hinder or deter us from doing all in our power to recover our lost rights, and reëstablish ourselves in our Sunday-home."

In a day or two the other side of the story was told in the following letter, addressed to the editor of one of the morning papers, by Thomas G. Shearman, James Fisk's counsel:

"Sir,—Your journal contains resolutions, adopted by a Sunday-school, (recently meeting at Pike's Opera House,) denouncing Mr. James Fisk, Jr., by name, as having been guilty of a 'high-handed offense,' in excluding the school, without 'the faintest shadow of excuse or palliation.' These resolutions are simply the culmination of a prolonged and ingenious attempt to compel the present proprietors of Pike's Opera House to subscribe a large sum in support of Mr. Perry's Mission School. And as I have advised Mr. Fisk to pursue the course he has taken, I feel no hesitation in meeting the issue personally, and showing the character of the transaction, not merely upon my responsibility as counsel, but as a friend of Sunday-schools, and for many years a teacher myself.* Mr. S. N. Pike, with a liberality very creditable to him, gave Mr. Perry a so-called lease of a large room in the Opera House, for use on Sundays only, at $500 a year, the property being well worth $1,500. Almost immediately afterward, he sold the Opera House to Messrs. Fisk and Gould, and gave a deed warranting it free from all leases, it may be by mistake. Messrs. Fisk and Gould found it absolutely necessary to divide the room thus rented into smaller offices, if it was to be of any use to them during the

* Mr. Shearman has been for some years Superintendent of the Sunday-School attached to Mr. Beecher's (Plymouth) Church, in Brooklyn.

week. They, therefore, sent to Mr. Perry, explained the circumstances, and desired to make an amicable settlement. Mr. Perry asked that a new school-house should be built for his flock, at an expense of between $20,000 and $40,000, as a condition of their retirement. An estimable gentleman associated with Mr. Perry in the work, advised him to reduce his demand to $5,000 in cash, which he ultimately did; but a day or two afterward, he having employed a lawyer, the figure was raised to $6,000. Messrs. Fisk and Gould then offered to secure any one of several comfortable halls in the neighborhood, to furnish it with seats, and to pay the rent for three years, such rent being double that which the Sunday-school had agreed to pay. This offer was rejected, and they were told plainly that Mr. Perry would have cash, and nothing else. The rent was not paid or tendered when due, nor has it ever been paid. Messrs. Fisk and Gould, therefore, acting upon the advice given to them, took possession of their own. Yours obediently,

"THOMAS G. SHEARMAN."

The threat of Dr. Perry against the proprietors of the Opera House was never executed. It is said that Fisk and Gould generously forgave Dr. Perry his debt and in addition presented the Sunday-school with $1000.

The air was now full of rumors in regard to the proposed extension of old roads and the building of new ones. One of the most important was that in reference to the Erie Railway. It was said that they had completed their arrangements for broad-gauge connections with both St. Louis and Chicago. "To Cincinnati," said rumor, "they will operate the Atlantic and Great Western, which they have leased, and thence to St. Louis they have made a partnership ar rangement with the Ohio and Mississippi, so that its proposed change of gauge will be stopped, and it will be run on joint account with Erie. The connection with Chicago is to be made through the Columbus, Chicago and Indiana Central line, which crosses the Great Western at Urbana. The various roads leased of this Company are 715 miles long. One of them, extending to Indianapolis, is also to be laid with a broad-gauge, and the Erie people are bargaining for one of the lines that reach westward from that city." At Chicago there was also a report that the Erie Directors were negotiating for the Rock Island line, with a view to lay a third rail over its entire present and prospective length, in order to obtain a connection with the eastern terminus of the Union Pacific. There was an audacity and magnificence about these alleged plans which agreed well with the character and habits of the two leading spirits of Erie, and the public were hopeful that, in time, their projects would be carried out, and that the Erie, Atlantic and Great Western, Ohio and Mississippi, and Columbus, Chicago and Indiana Central, an aggregate already provided of 2,117 miles of broad-gauge railway would be operated substantially, if not actually, under one single management.

These various projected movements gave rise to much serious discussion among parties interested in railroads; but there was another class, the newspaper men, who, although supposed to know everything, were very much exercised to understand this subject at all. One of them, in despair, when called upon by the journal he represented to write an editorial embodying the facts, ground out for the *Cincinnati Times* the following lucid explanation:

"We are satisfied that the public are a good deal perplexed to understand all about the numerous railroad schemes, com-

THE FIGHT BETWEEN THE BULLS AND BEARS ON BLACK FRIDAY.

binations, etc., that have been going on during the past few weeks, and our readers, although the most intelligent portion of the public, are no doubt greatly mystified about it also. We candidly acknowledge that we were a little in doubt ourself, until we made a determined and thorough examination of the subject; but now it is all as clear as mud to us. We know all about it, and are enabled to make our readers understand it, too.

"You see, the Atlantic and Great Pan-Handle Railroad Company, having leased the Sharpsburg cut-off, together with its connections—including, of course, its uncles, aunts, cousins, and their connections—so as to control the traffic over the Harrison Pike, it became necessary for the Chicago, Fort Wayne and Pittsburgh Railroad to buy up the capital stock of the Hamilton, Indianapolis Central and Little Miami, if they could hope to expect to maintain their hold upon the trade of Licking River and Duck Creek. Another object was to get into the Cleveland Union Depot at St. Paul in advance of Alexander Hamilton's stages.

"Then the New York Central (Park) Company, holding a majority of the stock in the Pennsylvania Southern and Northern Alaska Railroad, executed a flank movement by leasing the stockholders of the Susquehanna and Chesapeake Canal, *thereby securing a direct broad-gauge route from the Isle of St. Thomas to the foot of Fifth Street.* This, of course, necessitates the buying up of the Fifth Street Ferry Dock property, or the construction of a bridge connecting the Union Base-ball Grounds with Eden Park—a harmonious blending of the East and West interests.

"Vanderbilt, who wants to be considered the Colossus of Rhodes—that is to say, of rail-roads—is determined to cut off the Pennsylvania Central from the Northwest. He sent a man up there yesterday to cut it off, but at this writing the result is not known.

"The Pennsylvania Central immediately turned about and gobbled up the Jack Noble Dughill Railroad, and then effected a lease of the old reliable Corduroy Road, by which move they cunningly monopolize the commerce of Cheviot, forming the only direct line between that flourishing section and the principal markets of Europe.

"There was considerable excitement at the sale of the Dughill Road, which took place yesterday. More stockholders voted than were on the books of the company, and, on examination, it was discovered that one was a whip-stock holder; (a low stage-driver;) another held no stock except an old-fashioned one he wore around his neck; another kept a stock-yard; while a fourth was simply a holder of old stock ale—the heaviest stockholder in the lot. This latter individual was detected when it was proposed to 'water the stock,' when he howled dismally.

"All that is now needed to complete our brilliant combinations is a railroad starting at the Little Miami elevator and running up Deer Creek, along the Eggleston Avenue, to intersect with the affluent pipe and the Mill-Creek Improvements; thence along Western Avenue to the Lunatic Asylum, which will, unquestionably, be a grand Union depot—at least for all railroad men, and those others who attempt to comprehend their gigantic railroad schemes."

## CHAPTER XXVII.

ALMOST from the day it was opened, the Albany and Susquehanna Railroad had been a bone of contention between two rival cliques. James Ramsey, who was in reality the builder of the road, having labored almost against hope for seventeen years to secure its completion, was the President of the Company. The Board of Directors were divided, about half of them being strongly opposed to Ramsey. James Fisk, Jr., and Jay Gould had long had their eyes upon the Albany and Susquehanna. It connected with the Erie at Binghamton, and commanded the trade of one of the most fertile regions in New York State. If made a part of the Erie road it would render Erie at once the real rival of the Central for through business between New England and the Western States, and would afford the coal interests of Northern Pennsylvania direct communication with the Eastern markets. Fisk and Gould determined to secure control of the new road. They struck hands with the anti-Ramsey Directors, and the war began. In a very interesting article from the pen of the Hon. Jerry S. Black, Attorney-General under President Buchanan, the full history of the war is given. It is condensed from the March number of the *Galaxy*, a wide-awake magazine for the times, and herewith reproduced:

"In the years 1869 and 1870 there occurred a contest for the control of the Albany and Susquehanna Railroad which, in some of its features, is among the most remarkable that this generation has known. It concerned vast material interests, and, from peculiar circumstances, engaged an amount of public attention not often bestowed on such subjects. It produced a long series of litigations, angry, complicated, and multifarious. The judicial authorities were wholly unequal to the task of settling the dispute; for, instead of composing the strife, their intervention only intensified it, until at last the parties, mutually scared by the cross-fire of conflicting injunctions which the courts were launching at all alike, sought relief in the more peaceful arbitration of pike and gun. When this was stopped by the Executive, the newspapers took up the war, and, going over the whole ground again, they not only canvassed the rights and wrongs of the parties, but assailed counsel and judges with most unlimited censure. . . .

"Mr. Adams* is an hereditary bondsman to the truth; by his blood and birth he owes service to the right, and if he flies from it we have a warrant to reclaim him as a fugitive. We do not believe that he would lend the authority of his great historical name to a willful misstatement, or that he would even take up an evil report against his neighbor and help to propagate it for the mere purpose of gratifying anybody's malevolence. But his intense dislike of James Fisk, Jr., seems to have unbalanced his judgment upon every subject with which Fisk has the remotest connection. This is the one masterless passion which sways him in all the moods and tenses of his thought. Fisk is his *bête noir*. His enmity to Fisk is extended not merely to Jay Gould, Fisk's partner in business, but it embraces all Fisk's associates in the manage-

* Charles Francis Adams, Jr., who had written "Chapters of Erie," taking ground against the Directors of that Company. Mr. Black's article is largely taken up with a criticism on the essays.

ment of the Erie Railroad, and takes in every lawyer who has ever defended his rights and every judge who has ever allowed him to use the legal process of his court. The moral sense of Mr. Adams has been offended, perhaps very justly, by something he has seen in Fisk's conduct or character; and his indignation has become so preternaturally excited that he likes or loathes all other men as they happen to be for Fisk or against him in any of his contests whether right or wrong. . . .

"It was not necessary for Mr. Curtis* to tell us that he had no personal knowledge of, or association with Mr. James Fisk, Jr., or his partner Jay Gould. Nobody would have suspected that grave and learned gentleman of any close companionship with a man so *outré*, irregular, and eccentric in his tastes and habits as Mr. Fisk. If ignorance of Fisk and all that Fisk inherits be a virtue, then we can claim to be as virtuous as anybody. But we make no pretensions whatever to that outrageous and extravagant righteousness which prompts Mr. Adams not only to denounce Fisk himself, but to assail every man that does him justice, and heap laudations without measure on all who try to swindle him or his associates.

"Most of our readers will altogether fail to understand the merits of the controversy or the incidents which attended it, unless they make themselves acquainted, at least to some little extent, with the singularities of New York jurisprudence, produced partly by what is called a reform in the Code of Procedure, and partly by a most anomalous and extraordinary organization of the judicial system. A moment's attention to this will explain our meaning, and show that the confusion, misapprehension, and total failure of justice which

* George Ticknor Curtis, author of "An Inquiry into the Albany and Susquehanna Litigation, etc."

took place in these cases, while they could not possibly have happened in any other country, could scarcely have been avoided in New York. . . .

"In New York the revolutionary party did itself honor by accepting the leadership of the ablest and most distinguished jurists of the State. A full Code, as comprehensive as that of Napoleon, and as minute in its details as that of Livingston, was the work of their hands. They laid it at the feet of the Legislature, and that body adopted the Code of Procedure, but rejected all else that was proposed. They put into operation just enough of it to abolish the distinction between law and equity, without preventing the possible abuses of either; to confound all remedies by mixing them together and making one form of action serve against every species of wrong; and to banish every trace of science from pleading. What might have been the success of this empirical raid on the Common Law if the whole Code had been adopted, it is impossible to say; but the experiment as actually made is not merely a failure—it is a disastrous visitation upon the people of the State. Instead of the cheapness, certainty, and promptness which the reformers no doubt intended to promote, the unlucky suitor is vexed with endless delay, impoverished by enormous costs, and at every turn is liable to be tricked and deluded to his ruin. The new Code encourages ignorance, rapacity, and fraud, by inviting everybody to practice it who cannot live at any other trade, and gives a large share in the administration of justice to a class of men for whom the English language had no name until a new epithet of contempt was added to the vocabulary. . .

"But under the Code, the wall of partition between law and equity is completely broken down; the law judges are all chancellors, and, *vicè versa*, all chancellors are law judges, and they administer both equity and law in forms so exactly alike that the judges themselves do not know, and are not bound to know, which is which. There is, therefore, no possible excuse for employing more than one tribunal in the same cause. Nevertheless, the frequent and allowed practice is, for the defendant, instead of answering a complaint, to file a counter complaint against his adversary. An injunction is the favorite weapon in all contests. Its simplicity commends it to the professional mind, as the simplicity of the knout and the bastinado makes them dear to the heart of the Muscovite and the Turk. It can always be got for the asking, if the request be accompanied with an affidavit that somebody wants it 'to the best of his information and belief.' It is granted of course, *ex debito justitiæ*, without examination and without notice to the opposite party; it is granted privately; it is not put on record; it is not placed in the hands of a public officer to be served or executed, but the judge gives it to the complainant himself or his attorney, who keeps it a secret if he pleases, until he catches his victim at a disadvantage, and then springs it upon him from his pocket. Unfortunately, however, this is a game that two or a dozen can play at as well as one. The party enjoined by one judge can go to another judge, equally facile, and get an injunction against his adversary, commanding that the order of the first shall be disobeyed. Or a third person may seek a third judge, who will readily throw his force against either or both. There are thirty-three judges in the State, of equal grade and coördinate power, elected in eight districts, and residing in different regions, to whose jurisdiction there are no territorial limits except the lines of the State. Each one of these claims the right, and exercises it, of enjoining whom he pleases, without regard to the cognizance which may have been previously taken of the subject or the parties by one or more of his brethren; and his process, orders, or decrees are equally potential in every part of the State. A man enjoined by a judge in New York city to do a thing may be ordered by a Buffalo judge *not to do it;* and a Brooklyn judge who has commanded one of his constituents to refrain from a particular act, may be met the next day by a counter order from Rochester in which the same party is solemnly directed to *refrain from refraining.* These injunctions are not mere *brutum fulmen;* the judicial guns on either side are loaded to the muzzle with the heaviest metal they can ram down. Each judge demands implicit obedience to his own order, and the penalty of disobedience cannot be escaped by showing that the parties are under conflicting orders from another quarter; for the learned magistrates who administer the Code act on the principle of that ultra democracy which insists that one man is not only as good as another, but a great deal better. It happens thus that, in a case involving numerous and complicated interests of great value, all persons concerned get hemmed in with injunctions from various parts of the State, commanding them, by authority which they dare not question, to do everything, and at the same time to do nothing. They can neither move nor stand still without incurring a penalty somewhat like that of outlawry in feudal times. Their cause may be pending in a score of courts at once; a party who prosecutes or defends in any one of them is guilty of contempt, and if he fails, a decree is pronounced against him by default. His condition is like that ascribed by Lorenzo Dow to a predestined reprobate under the creed of Calvin:

> You shall and you shan't—you will and you won't;
> You're condemned if you do, and you're cursed if you don't.

"When all the parties are bound hand and foot, so that justice, or even an investigation in the courts, has become a thing of impossible attainment, the case is considered about ready for trial in the newspapers, where the suitors, the counsel and the judges, are plastered with praise or covered with odious imputations, according to the various interests and tastes of those who engage in the discussion. We venture, though with some diffidence, to pronounce this rather a poor substitute for the trial by battle which would have been accorded in the Middle Ages. So thought the parties in the Susquehanna and Albany suits; for they actually loosened the deadlock of the courts by physical force. It is true that the champions did not go out on the open plain, and, after taking an oath against witchcraft, beat each other with sand-bags to show whose cause was holiest in the sight of God; but they did try whose judges had made the most righteous injunctions by rushing against one another with colliding locomotives.

"It is due to the framers and original supporters of the Code to say that they never contemplated the frightful perversions which it has been made to undergo, nor are they at all responsible for the absurd arrangement of the judicial department which causes these scandalous conflicts of jurisdiction.

"We devoutly believe that a fair consideration of the Albany and Susquehanna litigations will throw the blame of them on shoulders which have heretofore not borne their proper share. We will briefly present the most important of the facts pertaining to this *cause célèbre*, and leave the public to judge whether the attacks on the long-established fame of Mr. Field and his patrons have any foundation in truth. The same public may determine, if it can, 'by what conjuration and most mighty magic' the Ramsey party have managed to invest their leader with the reputation of a persecuted saint. If we happen to have any readers who feel an interest in the most important of all worldly concerns—the distribution of justice among the people of a great State—some of them may be led to inquire if the system of judicial procedure, which produces such intolerable evils, cannot be amended, or, if change be impossible, what amount of passive fortitude is required to bear it as it is;

> How end this dire calamity;
> What reinforcement may be gained from hope;
> If not, what resolution from despair.

"The Albany and Susquehanna Railway Company was incorporated in 1852, and began work in 1853, but the line was not opened for traffic until January, 1869. It stretches a distance of one hundred and forty miles from Binghamton, where it connects with the Erie, to Albany, whence its freights may be carried by direct routes to divers parts of New England. The Erie had previously sent its branches into the anthracite deposits of Pennsylvania, and needed the use of the Albany and Susquehanna as a means of getting the coal it brought to Binghamton as far as Albany on its way to the New England market; and it was, of course, the interest of the new road to take all the business it could get in that way. Its track had been laid on the exceptional broad-gauge of the Erie, which shows that its projectors had, from the beginning, contemplated that it would support and be supported by that line. It would, undoubtedly, have been improper for the great company to take control of the smaller one, or to appropriate its earnings; but their geographical relations, the similarity of their structure, their duty to the public, and the mutual interests of their proprietors, all required a cordial coöperation in business. Nevertheless, there was no special arrangement to that end, and no proposition to make one, until the stockholders of the Albany and Susquehanna solicited the aid of the Erie to rid them of the dangerous dishonesty which had crept into the management of their own internal affairs.

"It was the great misfortune of the Albany and Susquehanna corporation to have trusted one Joseph H. Ramsey as its President and financial manager. He did not prove himself faithful. The bargains by which he raised money at usurious rates were not only disapproved by his constituents; they were indefensible on the score of common prudence. When his own interests were in conflict with the duties of his trust, he showed a lack of qualities even more important than sound judgment. He paid himself, on one occasion, $16,000, for services which he alleged he had rendered the company as its attorney. He made the bill and settled it, absolutely refusing to let the Finance Committee pass upon it. He made a contract on behalf of his corporation with an express company, in which he ruinously sacrificed the interests of the party he professed to represent; it turned out afterward that he was a partner in the express company. Mr. Adams has proudly claimed for him, as a great merit, that he went to the Legislature 'in behalf of the enterprise.' Of such are the Albany rings. He ran for Congress once, and while he was a candidate he issued three thousand free passes over the road to as many electors, whose favor he sought to win at the expense of the company. At the time of his suspension from office, he owed the company $20,000, which he had taken from its funds for his own purposes, on his own terms, and by his own leave. Whether he subsequently disgorged this money, does not appear.

"It was manifest to the stockholders that these practices could not be continued without ruin to their prosperity, and infamy to the character of their corporation; and they determined to stop them. But, like many other reformers, they committed the fatal mistake of adopting half-way measures. Instead of turning Ramsey out neck and heels, they reëlected him; but, by a very decided vote, chose a majority of Directors, strong enough as they thought, and true enough, to control his action and compel him to be honest. Seeing their forbearance, and probably mistaking it for timidity, he was hardy enough to tell them to their faces that he would permit no such oversight of his conduct as they proposed; that he would not belong to a divided direction; that at the next election either he or his opponents must go out. The stockholders accepted the issue thus tendered to them, and to maintain that issue was the object of all their subsequent struggles. Thus the corporators were hopelessly divided into two hostile factions. One of them, known through the legal proceedings as the Church party, and holding a large majority of the stock, was bent on having officers whose fidelity they could trust; and the other, led by Ramsey, wished to subordinate all the interests of the company severely and constantly to his own.

"The next election was to take place in September, 1869, and the parties began without delay to look around them for the material of the contest. The authorized capital of the company was $4,000,000, divided into 40,000 shares of $100 each. Of these 40,000 shares 17,238 were outstanding in the hands of *bona fide* holders, who had paid full price for them, and whose right to vote on them could not be disputed. The Church party were thoroughly satisfied that they and others opposed to the existing management held a clear majority of the legal and honest shares. On the other hand, Ramsey was not without expedients by which he hoped to win. About 2,400 shares had been forfeited by the failure of the original subscribers to pay for them. These were re-issued by Ramsey to one David Groesbeck for twenty-five cents on the dollar, in direct violation of a general law which forbade any railroad company to sell its stock for less than par. Groesbeck was not only unscrupulous enough to become a party to this fraudulent over-issue, by which the honest stock would be watered, but he was entirely willing to vote it as Ramsey, his partner in the fraud, might desire. When the latter gentleman discovered that he could not balance the real stockholders in that way, he resorted to another trick, which was, if possible, baser as well as bolder. He got together certain of his confederates secretly at his own house, and distributed among them certificates for 9,500 shares of stock, for which they had not paid, and did not mean to pay, a single cent. It was necessary that something should appear to have been paid, but the recipients of the shares could not or would not furnish any money for that purpose. Ramsey himself had no cash of his own to advance, but he went to the company's safe, of which he had the key, took out bonds, the property of the company, amounting to $150,000, pawned them to the same Groesbeck who had taken his former over-issue, and thus raised enough to pay ten per cent. on the 9,500 shares. It is not easy to conceive a transaction more thoroughly iniquitous than this. It was a double fraud; it was intended to stuff the ballot-box with bogus votes, and make the stockholders pay the expenses of the cheat upon themselves out of their own funds. That it might want no aggravating circumstance, it was planned and executed by a trustee whose solemn duty it was, in law and conscience, to protect and defend the rights of the injured parties against the knavery of others—not make them the victims of his own.

"In the meantime, the Church party, not knowing of these things, and unable to foresee what Ramsey might do, thought it prudent to reinforce themselves by getting as many of the *bona fide* shares into their hands as possible, and thus make their majority large enough to balance any fraud which he could carry out. A considerable amount of the stock was held by towns along the line of the road, and it could not be got for less than par. In these circumstances, they applied to the Erie managers for assistance, in money, to buy the shares which might be needed. The request was acceeded to. There was no lawless intrusion of Erie, or of Fisk and Gould, into the affairs of the Albany and Susquehanna; no volunteering in the dispute between Ramsey and his constituents; no compact for any undue share in the control of the road. The men of the Church party desired to save their corporation alive out of the hands of Ramsey, and the Erie managers knew, that by assisting them, they would promote the true interests of every honest stockholder in both companies. Where motives so fair, and wise, and obvious, exist, for one party to make, and the other to accept, a business proposition, it is not necessary, but it is shameful, to allege corruptions which there is nothing to prove, or even to suggest.

"When the assistance of the Erie men was assured to them, David Wilber and others, of the Church party, proceeded, by the authority of Mr. Gould, and with money furnished by him, to buy Albany and Susquehanna stock wherever they could get it; and they secured a considerable number of shares, mainly from the towns, paying full price for them. By the 3rd of August, the Church party, and the friends of the company who acted with them, had 11,400 shares of the undisputed stock, leaving only 6,139 in other hands. Assuming that Ramsey might get all these, he must be beaten nearly two to one. Even if his friend and fellow-sinner, Groesbeck, should vote the 2,400 fraudulent shares held by him, the Church men would still have a majority of 2,864. Judge Barnard, at the instance of Mr. Bush, a member of the Church party, put Groesbeck *hors de combat* by an injunction which commanded him to deliver up his stock into the hands of Mr. W. J. A. Fuller, who was appointed to hold it as receiver, so that Groesbeck could not vote it unless he would come forward and show that he had a title, which, of course, he did not attempt to do, knowing very well that he could not. The 9,500 false shares mentioned above had not yet been fabricated, nor had the corporation safe been robbed to pay for them at the time we now speak of.

"Ramsey did not confine his operations to mere aggressive frauds upon his constituents; he was a master of defense as well as offense. 'Fitz James's blade was sword and shield.' When he saw the heavy purchases his opponents were making, he instantly directed the Treasurer to make no more transfers upon the books of the company to the Church party. Accordingly, Phelps, the Treasurer, refused to make official note of the transfer from the town of Oneonta, although there was no appearance of illegality about the sale, and the commissioners were personally present to affirm its perfect regularity.

"To strengthen himself in his false position, he got an Albany judge to make an injunction forbidding the transfer. This was, and could be, nothing but a mere sham. It was in effect, though not in form, a suit by himself against himself, to restrain himself from performing a duty which he had predetermined not to do anyhow. The Church party not only got his Albany injunction dissolved, but fulminated another upon him from New York, which commanded him to refrain from his refusal to make the transfer.

"But Ramsey defeated the object of this last injunction, by an outrage which has no parallel even in the history of his own iniquities. He furtively took the books of the company, carried them away, and hid them, part of the time in a tomb in the Albany grave-yard, and part of the time in other lonely places, where they were beyond the reach of judicial process, out of the stockholders' sight or knowledge, and accessible only to himself and a few of his trusted accomplices. By this *conveyance*, as Pistol would call it, of the record, he not only prevented all transfers to *bona fide* purchasers, but put it into his power to fabricate, without detection, as much bogus stock as he might need for his own purposes. In point of fact, it was on the same night signalized by the disappearance of the books that he manufactured the 9,500 shares, which he pretended to pay for with the proceeds of the company's bonds.

"It was very plain by this time that the stockholders needed the help of judicial authority to save their rights from the most atrocious violation; and it will be seen hereafter that judicial authority, as administered in New York, was very far from being effective to that end. However, the war of injunctions had already commenced. The next gun was a heavy one. It was an order obtained *ex parte* from Judge Barnard, in New York City, suspending Ramsey from office, and restraining the issue of any more stock, unless under a resolution of the Directors, after public notice, and upon payment of its par value. This order was made at the instance of David Wilber, a stockholder, a director, and an

active supporter of the Church party. The complaint charged Ramsey (and, no doubt, charged him truly) with divers misdemeanors, which showed that he was wholly unfit for his trust, or indeed for any other. The proceeding was justifiable in this particular case, not only because the law allowed it and the Court awarded it, but because the special end it aimed at was just and proper.

"But it is not easy to defend on general principles the wisdom of the law which permits even a guilty man to be scourged before he is condemned. It is true that Ramsey was offered a chance of being heard in his own defense *after* he was deposed; but this reverses the inflexible rule of the Common Law, which in all cases and under all circumstances requires the hearing to *precede* the punishment. Indeed, the New York Code has in this respect but one example to keep it in countenance, and that is found in the hard ruling (according to Virgil's report) of the judge who presided in what may literally be called 'the court below:'

> Gnosius hic Rhadamanthus habet durissima regna,
> Castigatque, auditque dolos, subigitque fateri.

"Sir Edward Coke, quoting these lines, says: 'The philosophic poet doth notably describe the damnable and damned proceedings of the Judge of Hell. First he punisheth, and then he heareth, and, lastly, he compelleth to confess. But good judges and justices abhor these courses.'

"Ramsey and his advisers not only learned the lesson their opponents taught them, but they bettered the instructions. They were quick enough to see that, under a law which struck without hearing, a false accusation was just as good as a true one. Ramsey, therefore, did not close his eyes to sleep before he trumped up a series of charges against Mr.

Herrick, the Vice-President, and four of the Directors, that they were in a conspiracy with the Managers of Erie, for a surrender of their line to that corporation, which was corruptly managed by Gould, Fisk, and others, for their private ends. On this complaint, a judge of the Supreme Court at Albany promptly, and without the least hesitation or demur, granted an injunction to restrain the Vice-President and Directors from exercising their functions. This swept the board clean, and left the Albany and Susquehanna Railway Company, with millions of dollars' worth of property, in a most critical situation, and without a soul who could legally take charge of it.

"The judges of New York were as rapid in their movements as the old courts of Pie Poudre.* Ramsey got his injunction to stop transfers on the 2d of August. On the 3d he was enjoined to make the transfers. On the 4th Wilber's injunction deposed him; he was notified of it on the morning of the 5th, and on that same day he made his counter complaint; in the course of the night he carried off the books and fabricated the false stock; on the next morning he served his order upon the Vice-President, and the corporation was broken to fragments.

"Thus far Ramsey was the winner. With the records of the corporation in his exclusive possession, a treasurer at his elbow, to whom his word was law, and numerous active confederates to do his bidding, he was master of the situation. To be sure, his enemies had deposed him, but he had also deposed *them*, and put their property in peril of extreme and ruinous loss; 'which, if not victory, was at least revenge.'

* "An ancient Court of Record in England, incident to every fair and market, of which the steward of him who owns or has the toll is the judge. It has now fallen into disuse."—*Blackstone*. French, *Pied-poudreux*, dusty foot.

"Things had come to a crisis in the affairs of the Company where the stockholders could do but one thing, and that was to have receivers appointed who would keep the road running until its regular management could somehow be restored. The Church party, who owned by far the larger part of the stock, and who had paid not only fair but high prices for it, could not look upon their condition with calm indifference. They were constrained to act promptly. Accordingly, on the evening of the 6th of August, they applied to Judge Barnard, and got him to appoint two receivers, Charles Courter and James Fisk, Jr. The appointment of Mr. Fisk provoked a torrent of vituperation. It has been considered a sufficient reason for charging the judge, the counsel, and all others concerned in it, with gross corruption. Without stopping to inquire whether Mr. Fisk was or was not as proper a person as any other for such a trust, we note two facts which should stop this outburst of calumnious accusation. In the first place, the authority given the receivers was joint, and Fisk could do no act, good, bad, or indifferent, without the approbation of his colleague, who was and is a gentleman not only of very large estate, but of most unblemished character; and secondly, the appointment was made with the consent, expressed in writing, of seven Directors representing an undoubted majority of the stockholders. The order was privately signed by the judge, after the manner of New York judges; but if this was law and custom in all cases, as it undoubtedly was, why should there be an outcry about the observance of it on this occasion? It becomes especially absurd when we find that another judge, acting in Ramsey's interest and at his request, was doing the very same thing at Albany on the same night and at about the same hour.

"Yes, Ramsey had countermined the Church party again. Before Messrs. Courter and Fisk could reach Albany with Judge Barnard's warrant to take possession of the trust, Judge Peckham had privately, in the office of his son, invested a Mr. Pruyn with the same powers, and Mr. Pruyn had possession of the Company's office and the road at that end of it. Messrs. Courter and Fisk, by their agents, got hold of the Binghamton end, and that was all they could do. This brought the parties to close quarters. The conflict between opposing receivers, holding their authority from courts of equal jurisdiction, and acting under irreconcilable orders which each party claimed to be of superior obligation, presented in a practical shape the ancient problem of an immovable body encountered by an irresistible force. Judge Peckham's receiver determined to hold fast, and the magistrate who made him did not suffer him to languish for lack of helpful process and reinforcing decrees. Judge Barnard, not to be behind his brother Peckham in pluck and energy, provided *his* receivers with writs of assistance and all the other weapons they asked for out of his judicial arsenal. Everybody was in contempt, and everybody was in default. The sheriff, whose duty it was to execute the conflicting orders was utterly bewildered. He was required to call out the *posse comitatus* to support each party against the other. He could not perform the functions of his office unless he would 'divide himself and go to buffets with the pieces.' A great battle was impending, and as the sheriff with his *power of the county* was to be on both sides, the result could not possibly be foretold. Hostile bodies of workmen were drawn out, armed with pistols and bludgeons, and locomotives got up steam and ran into one another. The scene would be an odd one in any civilized country outside of the State where it occurred; for all parties were fighting under the ensign of public authority. It was judicial power subverting order and breaking the peace; it was law on a rampage; it was justice bedevilled; in one word, it was the New York Code in full operation.

"The Governor, it seems, had been watching the current of this heady fight; he thought it might be his duty to interpose the militia between the combatants, and conquer a peace by making a war upon both of them. The opposing receivers, 'to stop the effusion of blood,' were persuaded to unite in a petition to the Governor to take possession of the road and operate it by a superintendent of his own choosing. The Governor thereupon appointed Colonel Banks, stipulating that his custody should end as soon as the rights of the contesting parties could be ascertained and settled. This peaceable adjustment was effected by the exertions of Mr. D. Dudley Field, who, though his partners had previously been concerned for the Church party, now first appeared as an active participant in the controversy. His wisdom, good temper, and sound sense discerned what was not seen by others—the incapacity of the judicial department to manage such a business, and the necessity of putting it under executive arbitration.

"The property of the Company being now safe from destruction, the stockholders had nothing to do but watch and pray that Ramsey might not by any stratagem defeat their right to choose an honest Board of Directors. The election day came round in the fullness of time; the majority proceeded to business and cast their votes; but Ramsey pronounced their organization illegal, retired with his confederates to an adjoining room, opened a poll, and declared himself and others in his interest duly elected. He did not vote the 3,000 shares sold to Groesbeck, nor the 9,500 fabricated on the 5th of August; but he and his friends held some undisputed shares which they did vote at their own poll, and by ignoring the majority he was able to count himself in without difficulty. Both Boards claimed to be duly elected, and they organized by choosing Messrs. Church and Ramsey their respective Presidents. Both demanded the surrender of the corporate franchises into their hands, but the Governor did not think himself authorized to decide between them.

"Two or three circumstances connected with the election, though unimportant in themselves, require to be noticed here, because they have been much commented on elsewhere.

"The fraudulent asportation of the records was accomplished on the 5th of August. The election was on the 7th of September. On the night of the 6th, Phelps and a son of Ramsey secretly carried the books to the rear of the building and hoisted them up to the window of the Treasurer's room in a basket, with a rope tied to its handle. Nobody but Ramsey and his little band of confederates knew of this midnight restitution of the books until they were produced at the stockholders' meeting next day. In the mean time the Church party, seeing the election approach and feeling the necessity of having the ledgers and stock-lists for inspection, and having failed in various efforts to get even a sight of them, resolved upon taking a legal remedy. They brought suit in the Supreme Court for the City of New York against Ramsey, Phelps, Pruyn, and Smith, charging them with carrying away the books and concealing them from the stockholders. By the Code the defendants in such a case are liable to personal arrest, and bail was accordingly demanded in $25,000. The process was issued on the 6th of September, and the parties were arrested (and bail taken immediately) on the morning of the 7th (the election day), the sheriff having chosen his own time to execute the process. We have entirely failed to comprehend what the meaning of the men can be who vilify Messrs. Field and Shearman and their clients for bringing this suit. Of all the measures taken by either of the parties against the other, throughout the contest, this seems to us the most unquestionably just and proper. It is mere nonsense to call it harsh or oppressive. It was meant to redress a most atrocious wrong, for which the perpetrators, by the law of any other Christian country, would have been condemned as criminals to heavy fines and long imprisonment, without bail or mainprise. . . . .

"The presence of what has been called 'a congregation of roughs' in the room was subsequently talked of very freely. It is doubtless true that on both sides of the apartment there crowded a considerable number of men not clothed in purple and fine linen, nor having much the appearance of heavy capitalists. It happened thus: The inspectors under whose auspices Ramsey designed to hold the election, were disqualified for their office by reason of not being stockholders. To restrain them from acting, the Church party of course betook themselves to the everlasting injunction, and on the morning of the election got out one of those convenient engines to neutralize the illegal authority which Ramsey wished to bestow and probably to abuse. This would leave the inspectors to be chosen *viva voce*, and the impressiveness of assent or dissent might depend on the number of throats and strength of lungs employed in expressing it. Probably both parties anticipated this or something like it. It is certain that both improvised a force of courageous and muscular gentlemen, and, by putting a proxy in the hands of each one, they gave them all a technical right to be present and to swell the volume of the *ayes* and *noes* with their 'most sweet voices.' But there was no actual disorder, no intimidation, no violence or threat of violence.

"Another thing: Groesbeck had been enjoined, and his 2,400 fraudulent shares had been put into the hands of a receiver to be held so that Groesbeck could not vote them. The Ramsey men, on the morning of the election, undertook to trump this injunction by getting from Judge Clute, of the Albany County Court, another injunction which forbade the inspectors to receive *any votes of the Church party* unless the *holders* of the fraudulent stock should first vote on that. Fuller, the receiver, happened to be present. No doubt he was puzzled. He *held* the stock, and, by legal intendment, Judge Clute's order applied to him if it applied to anybody. He could not give it back to Groesbeck without defeating the purpose for which he held it, and exposing himself to the danger of being laid by the heels. If he refused to vote it or let it be voted, a large majority of *bona fide* stockholders, with rights to vote otherwise undisputed, would be totally disfranchised. He took the advice of counsel and untied the knot by literally obeying the Clute injunction and voting himself. Ramsey and his men were fairly infuriated by the failure of their shallow and impudent trick. He and his counsel and his judge had made the blunder of supposing that Groesbeck was in law the holder, and they got an injunction which they fancied would reinstate his fraudulent possession or else defeat the clear right of all their opponents. But they got one which in fact and in law defeated themselves. Mr. Ramsey is not the first engineer that was hoist by his own petard.

"The Governor naturally desired to get rid of the perplexing and anomalous trust imposed upon him by the agreement of the parties. Perceiving that the election was an abortion, and seeing that the judiciary had completely failed to settle anything in any of the numerous suits pending between the parties, he directed the Attorney-General to commence another in the name of the people *against both parties together*. This was not a *quo warranto*, nor a *mandamus*, nor a *bill in equity*, nor an action in *case* or *trespass;* these terms belong to 'the jargon of the Common Law,' and the Code does not condescend even to pronounce them. It was a proceeding against the corporation itself which the Governor had under his care, and against forty-nine individuals, of two fierce parties, contending against one another for its management. The complaint does not charge them with any offense against the plaintiff, but with mutual injuries committed by one set of the defendants against the others; and these wrongs consisted mainly in bringing suits for what they respectively averred to be their rights, a course of conduct which the Governor (truly enough, perhaps) thought would result in no good to anybody.

"Of course the defendants could not make up an issue either of law or fact between themselves, no matter how they might sever in their answers to the plaintiff. In the dark days of Kent and Livingston and Spencer it was thought morally impossible to introduce evidence until there was an issue to which it might have some kind of application. But here the defendants were called in and permitted to fight one another to their hearts' content, without pleadings or proofs, and the judge was wholly emancipated from that barbarous bondage which in past times would have compelled him to pronounce his decree *secundum allegata et probata*.

The proceeding seemed sufficiently free from 'technicalities. It was apparently not fashioned, like the injunction, on the principle of the bastinado, but rather modelled after that other form of Turkish justice in which the Sultan, when he finds a cause too difficult to be otherwise dealt with, sews up the stubborn disputants in the same sack and casts them into the Bosphorus to go down the tide together—which they generally do with a most edifying disregard for the rules of navigation.

"This curious cause came on for hearing (which, in the nomenclature of the Code, is called a *trial*) at Rochester, before Judge E. Darwin Smith, without a jury. It was argued by Mr. D. Dudley Field for one portion of the defendants and by Mr. Henry Smith for the other, the plaintiff apparently taking no part whatever; and it was decided in December, 1869. Probably nothing more severe has been said, or could be conceived, of Mr. Justice Smith's judgment than the laudatory words bestowed upon it by Mr. Adams. We quote them:

"'There are cases where a judge upon the bench is called upon to vindicate in no doubtful way the purity as well as the majesty of the law; cases in which the parties before the court should be made to feel that they are not equal, that fraud is fraud even in a court of law—that cavilling and technicalities and special pleading cannot blind the clear eye of equity. It is possible that even a judicial tone may be overdone or be out of place. There are occasions when the scales of justice become almost an encumbrance, and both hands clutch at the sword alone. Whether the magistrate upon whom the decision of this cause devolved was right in holding this to be such an occasion is not now to be discussed; it is enough to say that his decision sustained at every point the Ramsey board, and crushed in succession all the schemes of the Erie ring. The opinion was most noticeable in that it approached the inquiry in a large spirit. Its conclusion was not made to turn on the question of a second of time, or a rigid adherence to the letter of the law, or any other technicality of the pettifogger; it swept all these aside, and spoke firmly and clearly to the question of fraud and fraudulent conspiracy.

"'All the elaborate comparisons of watches, and noting of fractional parts of a minute, which marked the organization of the Erie meeting, were treated with contempt, but the meeting itself was pronounced to be organized in pursuance of a previous conspiracy, and the election held by it was "irregular, fraudulent, and void." The scandals of the law—the strange processes, injunctions, orders, and conflicts of jurisdiction—were disposed of with the same grasp, whenever they came in the path of the decision. The appointment of Fuller as receiver was declared to have been made in a "suit instituted for a fraudulent purpose," and it was pronounced in such "clear conflict with the law and settled practice of the court" as to be explicable only on a supposition that the order was "granted incautiously, and upon some mistaken oral representation or statement of the facts of the case." The order removing the regular inspectors of election was "improvidently granted" and was "entirely void;" and the keeping it back by counsel, and serving it only at the moment of the election, was "an obvious and designed surprise on the great body of stockholders." The suit under which the Barnard order of arrest was issued against Ramsey and Phelps was instituted without right; the order of arrest was unauthorized; the order to hold bail was "most extraordinary and exorbitant," and procured "in aid of fraudulent purposes." The injunction forbidding Ramsey to act as President of the Company was "entirely void." The 3,000 shares of forfeited stock reissued to Mr. Groesbeck were pronounced "valid stock," and numerous precedents were cited in which the principle had been sustained. Even the injudicious subscription for the 9,500 new shares of stock by Ramsey and his friends, on which they had not attempted to vote at the election, was declared in point of law regular, valid, and binding Upon the facts of the case the decision was equally outspoken; it was fraud and conspiracy everywhere. "The importation and crowding into a small room" of a large number of "rude, rough, and dangerous persons," and furnishing them with proxies that they might participate in the proceedings of the meeting, "was a gross perversion and abuse of the right to vote by proxy, and a clear infringement of the rights of stockholders, tending, if such proceedings are countenanced by the courts, to convert corporation meetings into places of disorder, lawlessness, and riot." Finally, costs were decreed to the Ramsey Board of Directors, and a reference was made to Samuel L. Selden, late a Judge of the Court of Appeals, to ascertain and report a proper extra allowance in the case, and to which of the defendants it was to be paid.'

"Everything being decided in favor of Ramsey, the judgment of course included a decree that he and his Board were lawfully elected, although they had received a very small minority of the votes. The scales being discarded, the majority weighed no more than the minority.* An order was

* The statements both of Mr. Adams and Mr. Curtis are obscure concerning the votes given by the respective parties at the election. The important and leading fact, however, is well established, and not denied, that the Church party owned, and held, and voted nearly two-thirds of the *bona fide* stock; and the Groesbeck stock was voted for them besides under an injunction of their opponents. Mr. Adams informs us that Ramsey did not attempt to vote any part of the 9,500

accordingly made that Ramsey and his Board 'be immediately let into possession.' The first thing they did was to put the property forever out of the owners' reach by a perpetual lease to the Hudson and Delaware Canal Company. This was not all or nearly all. Within one month after Ramsey and his Board got possession, they voted to him, at his own request and on his own dictation, two sums of money, amounting in the aggregate to $62,802.25, and 1,330 shares of stock, worth at par $133,000. If this was not a mere gratuity—a naked robbery of the stockholders—it was based on some transaction grossly corrupt; for Ramsey refused to explain the ground of it, and the Board has ever since steadily resisted all efforts to investigate it.

"This cause it took but little time to dispose of. In two months from the day when the stockholders were called into court—'two little months or ere those shoes were old'—they were turned out, despoiled of their property, and branded as fraudulent conspirators for trying to hold it. We would suppose that this could not be a very expensive operation. On a road at once so short and so rough the tolls should not be heavy. The justice which the Church party got in Judge Smith's court ought to be a cheap article, since it has no other quality to make it desirable. But costs were awarded—extra costs—not in favor of the plaintiffs, nor against the defendants in a body, but against some of the defendants in

shares. If he voted only those *bona fide* shares which he held and had a right to vote, his own return must have shown him in a very meagre minority. But the Court declared him elected. Whether this was done by throwing out of the count *all* the votes of the Church party, or by throwing out *only enough* to put them in a minority, or by *adding* to Ramsey's votes others which were *not cast at all* by either party, or by transferring votes *actually* cast for Church to Ramsey, for whom they were *not* cast, we have no information. All these modes of electing a defeated candidate are adopted when occasion requires by Philadelphia return judges, and sometimes they are very ingeniously compounded together.

favor of other some. An ex-Judge of the Court of Appeals was appointed assessor to aid in fixing the amount, and it was fixed at *ninety-two thousand dollars!* An economical nation might carry on a small war without spending more than it costs a private citizen to defend his plainest rights in a Rochester court.

"The Church party appealed to the General Term, where all the rulings of Judge Smith were reversed, through and through, except upon the validity of the election. That was affirmed on the ground that he was *competent* to pass upon it; that is to say, he had legal authority which made his determination upon the point conclusive. . . .

"Ramsey, being elated with his conquest of the Albany and Susquehanna, determined to invade the Erie, in hopes of subjugating that also. He was not a creditor nor a stockholder; but to give him nominal status, Groesbeck—the same Groesbeck—bought for him thirteen shares of stock and six bonds. With these he went to Delhi, the most secluded county town in the State, situated twenty miles from any railway line, and accessible only by mountain roads. There he found Judge Murray, one of the thirty-three, and to him he complained that he was in danger of losing the money he had invested in these bonds and this stock, by reason of certain mismanagement of its officers and Directors, the recital of which covered three hundred and forty folios. On this complaint the Judge gave him, not merely an injunction, but a great quantity of injunctions; suspended a majority of the Directors, appointed a receiver, restrained the suspended Directors from making defence in this or any other suit involving their official conduct, commanded the unsuspended Directors to see that the company was promptly represented by such counsel as they should select, ordered that no creditor but Ramsey should institute any suit to collect or secure his debt, and directed the defendants, under penalty of contempt, to bring no cross-suit which might embarrass the plaintiff in his prosecution of this one. Under these orders Ramsey managed to have the defendants *promptly* represented by a family connection of his own. When this destructive missile burst on the men of Erie at their New York office, it no doubt produced some terror. They immediately sought the ablest counsel they could find, and directed Messrs. Field and Shearman to adopt energetic measures of defence. But those gentlemen were informed that they could not appear, their clients being already represented by an attorney who had been selected for them, whom they did not know, and whose name even they were not permitted to learn. Nor could they discover who was the person appointed to take charge of their client's property, and exercise over it the unlimited control of a receiver. The alarm of the parties was greatly increased when they learned that their rights were to be in the keeping of David Groesbeck, the man who had aided Ramsey in all his previous frauds, and whose sense of moral and legal obligation may be learned from a fact stated by Mr. Adams; namely, that he defended Ramsey's fabrication of fraudulent stock and his appropriation of the Albany and Susquehanna Company's bonds, and 'declared that under the same circumstances and fighting the same men he himself would have gone as far, and further too if necessary.'

"Here was such a case as no community living under any kind of a code had ever seen before. All the property of a corporation worth sixty millions of dollars, and employing in its service the daily labor of twenty-five thousand hands, was snatched from the owners in the twinkling of an eye by an order made behind their backs, and all their rights and the rights of their employés and creditors were put at the mercy of a man who, speaking of these very owners, had openly avowed that in dealing with them he would be restrained by no moral principle; that fighting the same men he would betray the most sacred trust, clandestinely appropriate their property, make false papers to cheat them, and injure them otherwise by going still further if necessary. All these perilous notions of right and wrong were fully shared by the plaintiff, who had secured an attorney for the defence, and so made himself *dominus litis* on both sides. *Ex parte* injunctions had often before this torn men's property out of their possession without a hearing, but the Rhadamanthian justice of a subsequent trial was always conceded. Here the right to make even an *ex post facto* defence was taken out of their hands. . . .

"Messrs. Field and Shearman, after much difficulty and delay, got on the track of the unknown person who was representing their clients, wrung the case out of his hands, and gained a position where the plaintiff was compelled to face them with his proofs. He broke down utterly and his complaint was dismissed. Afterward he and his backers raised a clamor that he had been forced to trial with his hands tied. In truth his hands were as loose as need be, but they were not clean enough to be shown.

"If no counsellor can be concerned for Fisk and Gould in any case whatever without becoming infamous, it follows that no court can, without incurring a similar penalty, extend the protection of the law to their plainest rights. They are mere outlaws; they may be slandered, swindled, robbed with impunity, 'and it shall come to pass that whosoever findeth them shall slay them.'* If this be consistent with the

"* This was written, and in the hands of the printer, before the assassination of Colonel Fisk."—ED.

IN CONFIDENCE WITH JOSIE

AS ADMIRAL,

genius of our institutions, we have misapprehended those provisions of the fundamental law, which declare that the courts are open to *all* men, and that *all* shall have a fair trial, with counsel to assist them in getting justice.

"This style of attack upon Mr. Field looks to us like a very unmistakable tribute to his good fame. The character of a lawyer must be more than commonly spotless when his enemies have no material for defaming him, except what they get by raking about among the faults and follies of his clients. But that society is a very unsafe one to live in whose sense of justice will permit one man to be hunted down, merely because the wolf's head has been placed on another. The reputation of lawyers—which is the life of their lives—will be extremely precarious, however virtuous their own acts may have been, if the concentrated odium of all their clients' sins can be cast upon themselves.

"The Church party—that is to say, the proprietors of the Albany and Susquehanna Railroad—had a cause as just, legal, and fair as any court ever saw. They had been remorselessly plundered by a gang of reckless knaves, who made no secret of their intentions to repeat the robbery in the same, as well as in other, forms. Messrs. Field and Shearman accepted the retainer of these injured parties, and gave them the promise of such redress and protection as they could legally obtain for them. Now it is charged that this engagement to procure justice by legal means, in a perfectly upright case, was a prostitution by Messrs. Field and Shearman of their talents and influence, because one or two of the parties thus injured are supposed to have been previously engaged in other transactions, in which they were themselves to blame. Whether this be true or false, it furnished no reason to Messrs. Field and Shearman for rejecting the case on moral grounds. If the cause, though just, was likely to become unpopular because Fisk and Gould were in it, that was an additional reason for taking it. Mere public clamor will not deter any honorable man from the performance of a duty; on the contrary, he is excited to higher efforts when 'the heathen rage and the people imagine a vain thing.'

"That they behaved with scrupulous uprightness in the progress of the cause, and used no unfair means to reach the ends of justice, is a proposition which will not be denied, unless by some who think that it is wrong, in all circumstances, to take out an *ex parte* injunction. Certainly, the law which allows this mode of proceeding is entitled to no commendation. But, while it is in full force, it may be used for a proper purpose, with a safe conscience. Every man is justified in defending the right against the wrong, with such weapons as the law puts into his hands. Even L'Estrange's 'Honest Lawyer,' rigid as he is, 'uses the nice snapperadoes of practice, in a defensive way, to countermine the plots of knavery, though he had rather be dumb than suffer his tongue to pimp for injustice, or club his parts to bolster up a cheat with the legerdemain of law-craft.'"

## CHAPTER XXVIII.

THE Albany and Susquehanna Railroad War was, indeed, a remarkable one, and for a time it threatened very serious consequences. On two or three occasions the employés of the rival holders of the property—Fisk held possession of the Binghamton end of the road, while Ramsey maintained his position at the Albany end—came together in armed conflict; and in one fight, that at the "Tunnel," in which several hundred were engaged, a large number were wounded.

So bitter was the feeling, so determined were the leaders, and so threatening to the public peace were the movements of the contending forces, that Governor Hoffman was obliged to order out a regiment of the National Guard. Fortunately, the rioters dispersed before the military reached the scene of conflict. Fisk was twice arrested by the Albany police, and was once in danger of being shot from the balcony of the building in which were the offices of the Albany and Susquehanna Railroad Company. During all the intense excitement of this remarkable period, Jim Fisk was the same easy, jolly, rollicking creature of impulse that he ever was, and his jokes and champagne were lavishly distributed to the crowd of visitors who thronged his parlors at the Delavan House. Here he had a corps of clerks, hard at work, and his army of messengers rushing in and out all day long, and far into the night, made the celebrated Albany hostelry as lively a place as one would wish to see.

The Governor had now taken possession of the road in

dispute, at the request of the two receivers, and had appointed two members of his staff, General James McQuade and Colonel R. Lenox Banks, to hold the property, repair the damages, and run the business until further orders.

The following, on "The Lesson of Erie," was written by Horace Greeley, and printed in the *Tribune*, November 2nd, 1869, just after the temporary settlement of the Erie difficulties:

". . . . . Injunctions and counter-injunctions now became so many, and so puzzling, that the shrewdest counsel could hardly keep account of them. Judge Clerke enjoined Judge Barnard from appointing a receiver, his clerks from entering the order, if one should be appointed, and the receiver from accepting it, if it were ordered. The injunction was served upon Barnard as he sat upon the bench, and he immediately proceeded to vacate the order and appoint a receiver; the enjoined clerk made the entry; and the receiver was enjoined as soon as he could be caught. The tangle finally became so hopeless that, by a sort of agreement of parties, Judge Ingraham issued a general order, forbidding everybody from doing anything, and so the rubbish was swept away. And what had been the result? Mr. Drew had escaped to Jersey City with $7,000,000, and defied the courts. Mr. Peter B. Sweeny had been appointed receiver after there was nothing to receive, and had been allowed $150,000 by Judge Barnard for his trouble in taking care of—nothing. A few ten-dollar fines had been imposed for contempt of court; and $150,000 had been divided among the Erie counsel. This was all, so far as the cases really before the courts are involved. But, incidentally there had arisen some startling inquiries about the purity of Judge Barnard's court. In the application to Judge Gilbert for an injunction, Barnard had been described as an accomplice in Vanderbilt's operations. Then came scenes so extraordinary that no honest citizen can recall them without blushing. Judge Barnard declared from the bench that he employed spies to watch the parties who were litigating before him. The old scandal of his accessibility to certain counsel was revived, and openly made the subject of a cross-examination before him; and Mr. John B. Haskin testified that, where great interests were involved, he had sometimes undertaken to personally influence the Judge; that he 'might have' influenced his action 'as a judge'—but only, of course, on the side of right; and he would not swear that he had not used his influence to get a decision in favor of some person in litigation whose cause he had expoused.

"A truce and division of profit and loss now ensued. Vanderbilt and Drew received several millions each, and the Erie Railway was left to Messrs. Fisk and Gould, who straightway made an alliance with the Tammany Ring, and began a new series of legal scandals. We remember how, at their request, Judge Barnard issued an injunction in bed, and appointed Jay Gould receiver; how, in defiance of a law of the State, (to say nothing of orders of court,) he authorized the Company, after running down their own shares in the bear interest to 40, to buy them back at 80, in order that they might arrange the famous Erie corner; how he called upon the Grand Jury to indict the newspapers which commented upon his extraordinary orders in the interest of the Erie Ring, but let the prosecution drop when the jury complied with his suggestion; how Cardozo afterward took Barnard's place, and Judge Balcom, again at Binghamton, and Judge Peckham at Albany, besides several judges in New York, took part, altogether, in the war, until law became, more than ever, a reproach, and the processes of the court a laughing-stock. And we remember, too, that every order from the bench was defeated, either by a counter-order or by insolent and unpunished defiance. The parties to the conflict settled their differences, at last, by a corrupt compromise at Albany.

" Next came the affair of the Erie and Susquehanna roads. Here, again, the battle of injunctions raged for a while, and the swindle of receivership was revived in full force. At a critical moment, the Erie Judge happened to be in the neighborhood of the Erie Railroad offices one night at ten o'clock, just in time to sign an order appointing James Fisk, Jr., receiver of the Albany and Susquehanna Company, and start him off by a late train. But even so zealous a judiciary as this could not settle the dispute. The rival companies flew to arms, tore up tracks, sent locomotives butting against each other under a head of steam, and paralyzed the trade of a whole district, until the Governor took possession of the disputed property by force, and ran it as a military road. The latest scene in the case of Erie and the courts is the great gold speculation, which has just convulsed Wall street.

" Here again, after the bubble had burst, and the chief offenders were threatened with irremediable ruin, we find the conspirators invoking the jugglers on the bench, and begging the protection of an injunction against the consequences of their own wickedness. How far they will carry out their scheme, we cannot foresee. The result so far has been to save the gamblers from the necessity of paying their debts. To-day, the people of New York will have an opportunity of deciding whether such a judiciary as we have here sketched shall continue to afflict society, or shall be changed for a better. It is a system under which the courts can easily be made the instruments of the rich and unscrupulous, while even honest judges may fail to protect the weak. We call upon all good men to vote for reform. We may have it under the new Constitution. We should never get it under the old."

## CHAPTER XXIX.

In order to exhibit the full history of the celebrated Gold Panic, in which Fisk figured so conspicuously, it will be necessary to review briefly the movement of gold during the year previous to September, 1869.

The price of gold on the 1st of September, 1868, was 145. During the fall and winter it continued to decline, interrupted only by occasional fluctuations, till, in March, 1869, it touched 130¼, its lowest point for three years, and continued near that point until the middle of the following month.

At this time Jay Gould, President of the Erie Railway Company, bought $7,000,000 of gold, and ran up the price from 132 to 140. His example was followed by other brokers, and by the 20th of May the price had advanced to 144⅞, from which point it declined steadily, reaching 136 on the 31st of July.

The first indication of a concerted movement on the part of those who were prominent in the panic of September was an attempt to secure as assistant treasurer at New York, somebody who would act in their interest and obey their behests. The two persons most active in this attempt were Jay Gould, and A. R. Corbin, a brother-in-law of President Grant. H. H. Van Dyck had resigned from the Sub-Treasury in June, and Corbin nominated for the position his step-son-in-law, Robert B. Catherwood, Jay Gould pledging his earnest support in securing the appointment. Mr. Catherwood seems to have been an honest man, for when he discovered that the object Gould and Corbin had in view was not the financial good of the country, he promptly declined the proffered honor. In his testimony before the House Committee, in March, 1870, he said:

"After I was solicited to accept this office, and had the matter under debate, I went the next day to have a conversation with Mr. Gould and Mr. Corbin, and I found that the remark was simply this: that the parties could operate in a legitimate way and make a great deal of money, and that all could be benefited by it in a legitimate manner. Nothing underhand or illegitimate. The phrase used was 'illegitimate manner.' I satisfied myself that I could not fill the bill. . . . I did not look at it in the same light that they did, and I just declined. . . . I understood that it was buying gold and stocks and bonds on a certainty of the movements of the government in selling or not selling gold. . . . It was understood that if I took the position, Gould, Corbin, myself and others, would go into some operations such as the purchase of gold and stocks, and that we should share and share alike."

After the emphatic refusal of Catherwood to accept the position of Sub-Treasurer, Corbin and Gould secured the appointment of Daniel Butterfield, a Colonel and Brevet Major-General in the United States Army, who entered upon the discharge of his duties on the 1st of July.

Previous to Butterfield's appointment, or about the 15th of June, the first attempt was made to discover, if possible, the purposes of the President and the Secretary of the Treasury in regard to sales of gold. The President was on his way to Boston on board of one of Fisk's Fall River line of steamers, in company with Cyrus W. Field, and several other prominent citizens. At the supper-table, Fisk and Gould, both being present, the conversation turned upon the state of the country, and gradually reached the subject of gold. Jay Gould's account is as follows:

"The President was a listener; the other gentlemen were discussing. Some were in favor of Boutwell's selling gold, and some were opposed to it. After they had all interchanged their views, some one asked the President what his opinion was. He remarked that he thought there was a certain amount of fictitiousness about the prosperity of the country, and that the bubble might as well be tapped in one way as another. He then asked me what I thought about it. I gave it as my opinion that if that policy were carried out it would produce great distress, and almost lead to civil war; it would produce strikes among the workmen, and the workshops, to a great extent, would have to be closed, and the manufactories would have to stop. I took the ground that the government ought to let gold alone, and let it find its commercial level; that, as a matter of fact, it ought to facilitate an upward movement of gold in the fall. . . . We supposed, from that conversation, that the President was a contractionist."

James Fisk, in his testimony before the House Investigating Committee, was a trifle plainer. He said:

"On our passage over to Boston with General Grant, we endeavored to ascertain what his position in regard to the finance was. We went down to supper at about nine o'clock, intending, while we were there, to have this thing pretty thoroughly talked up, and, if possible, to relieve him from any idea of putting the price of gold down; for, if his policy was such as to allow gold to go down to 25, our transportation would have been snapped right up. We talked there, I guess, till about half-past twelve. When we first began to talk, I could see that he was for returning to a specie basis. I remember the remark he made, that we might as well tap the bubble at once as at any other time, saying that it had come to that. That was at the first part of the conversation. He entered into the conversation with a good deal of spirit, and I made up my mind that he was individually paying a good deal of attention to the finances, which he would to a certain extent control, so far as the action of the government was concerned."

The next morning Gould was selling out his stocks.

On their return to New York, Fisk and Gould made up their minds to bring such a pressure upon the administration as to prevent, if possible, a further decline in gold, which would interfere seriously with their speculative plans. This was to be effected by facts and arguments presented in the name of the country and its business interests; and a financial theory was agreed upon, which, on its face, would appeal to the business interests of the country, and enlist in its support many patriotic citizens, but would, if adopted, incidentally enable the conspirators to make their speculation eminently successful. That theory was, that the business interests of the country required an advance in the price of gold; that, in order to move the Fall crops, and secure the foreign market for our grain, it was necessary that gold should be put up to 145. The instrument chosen to lay these views before the President was his brother-in-law, A. R. Corbin, who soon became a willing convert to the theory. It is more than probable that the previous purchase and carriage of $2,000,000 of United States bonds by Mr. Gould, for Corbin's profit, may have aided in his conversion.

Jay Gould said in his testimony before the House Committee:

"Mr. Corbin is a very shrewd old gentleman; much more far-seeing than the newspapers give him credit for. He saw at a glance the whole case, and said that he thought it the true platform to stand on; that whatever the government could do legitimately and fairly to facilitate the exportation of breadstuffs, and to procure good prices for the products of the West, they ought to do. He was anxious that I should see the President and communicate to him my view of the subject. Being connected in my railroad business with the matter of transportation, and knowing the views of those managing the other trunk lines, he thought that I knew the substance of the concentrated views of these people, and he wanted me to see the President and talk with him. I went to Mr. Corbin's, and was introduced to the President."

Corbin testified:

"I had been out of politics for a good many years, but still a remembrance remained with me; and I was now the more interested, as I had a natural desire for the success of the administration of the brother of my wife, especially during its first year. While at home Mr. Gould used to call at my house occasionally; and as I heard that he was a Wall street operator, I always improved the opportunity to talk with him. I took advantage of every occasion to impress upon him what I thought was a vital point, and that was, to let the farmers and mechanics and manufacturers have good prices for their productions."

It appears from the testimony that in these interviews secured by Corbin, great care was taken to urge only the patriotic side of the question, and its relations to the great business interests of the country. According to Corbin's testimony, the President engaged in these conversations with reluctance, and the moment any allusion was made to the future policy of the government, he became very reticent, and on one occasion reprimanded a servant for allowing Mr. Gould such ready access.

Fisk heard that the President had gone to Newport, and immediately followed him thither. His object is made sufficiently plain in the following extract from his testimony before the Committee:

"General Grant started to go to Newport. I then went down to see him. I had seen him before, but not feeling as thoroughly acquainted as I desired to for this purpose, I took a letter of introduction from Mr. Gould, in which it was written that there were three hundred sail of vessels on the Mediterranean from the Black Sea, with grain to supply the Liverpool market. Gold was then about 34; if it continued at that price, we had very little chance of carrying forward the crop during the fall. I know that we felt very nervous about it. I talked with General Grant on the subject, and endeavored as far as I could to convince him that his policy was one that would bring destruction on us all."

This visit seemed to have been productive of no good result. When Fisk returned to New York, he found Jay Gould associated with two brokers, W. S. Woodward and Arthur Kimber. They had purchased a large amount of gold, but had not succeeded in greatly advancing the price.

All their efforts to secure any promising prospect of a rise in gold had thus far failed, and Gould still tried in vain to induce Fisk to coöperate in his purchases.

But with gamblers and stock-brokers, expedients are never lacking. The conspirators started a new scheme. They managed to get control of certain press columns, for the purpose of spreading the rumor that there would be no gold sold by the Treasury for a month or more, and came very near being successful. At this time the Hon. John Bigelow was editor-in-chief of the *New York Times*. On the 5th of August he had an interview with General Grant, during which the financial condition and prospects of the country were discussed at considerable length. On the 6th and 7th of that month two editorial articles appeared in the *Times*, which were understood to represent the views of the President, if they were not directly inspired by him. On the 19th the President passed through New York, and immediately thereafter an attempt was made by the gold conspirators to use the columns of the *Times* for the publication of an article which should appear to be a semi-official declaration of the financial policy of the administration, but which should have the effect to raise the price of gold, and thus aid their speculation.

An article for that paper was written by A. R. Corbin, at the suggestion of Jay Gould, on the 23d of August. This set forth that the policy of the administration was to advance the price of gold, and in it the transportation theory of Gould and Fisk was advocated. The title of the article was "Grant's Financial Policy," and it was agreed that it should be published as an editorial, and under the auspices of Jay Gould, who was to influence the editor of the paper through the services of the great English capitalist, James McHenry, a personal friend of Bigelow and Gould. Mr. McHenry called at the *Times* office, submitted the article, and represented it as embodying the views of the President. It was ordered in, double leaded, but when the proof came down, a more careful perusal convinced the editor that the writer "had an ax to grind." Mr. C. C. Norvel, the money editor of the paper, was requested to pass upon it, and the result he narrated in his testimony before the Investigating Committee.

"How this article reached the office, I only know from hearsay. As to whether Mr. Gould, Mr. Corbin, or who sent it, I have no knowledge. I did not see the manuscript for some time after, and not until this controversy arose. That article was represented to have come from some particular friend of the President. I have every reason to believe that it was put in type just as it was written, and double leaded, to be published as an editorial leader. I had gone home to Staten Island, and my assistant in the money department told Mr. Bigelow he had better leave it over until he could see me; that whether it was written in the interest of the administration or not, it certainly seemed to compromise the administration, and utterly stultify our position in regard to gold; especially the last paragraph, which was most illogical, and seemed to be a plausible plea for the highest possible price that the market could be brought up to. I will do Mr. Bigelow the justice to say that he could not have believed that it came from any inspired source. General Grant had left the city on the 20th. This came to me about the 23d. It was to have appeared on the morning of the 24th; and when the suggestion was made to Mr. Bigelow that it was in my department, as he had just come into the office, and had not watched our course on the subject, it was proper to leave it over, which he did, and which I am sure he would not have done if he had believed that General Grant had seen it before it came into the office. I have no doubt that it was sent under false pretences, and I do not think Mr. Bigelow had any doubt, after the occurrence of September, that it was intended to be imposed upon us as a semi-official expression by the President. . . . . .

"When Mr. Bigelow left our office a few days before the row occurred in September, I thought I would endeavor to get the facts before the public. It was a delicate business for the *Times* to publish a full statement of the facts, and I got the *Commercial Advertiser* to publish the interview with Grant on the 5th of August, the results of which appeared in our paper of the 6th, in the leader, which was looked upon as a manifestation of the views of the President on the payment of the debt, and the reduction of the expenses. On the 14th of October some of our neighbors still misrepresented us as to our responsibility for the gold panic. In the meantime there came out a statement from Mr. Gould to the reporter of the *Sun* that the article of the 25th had been reversed in its position by some editor in the office; that it was not published as set up; that the purpose was to 'bull' gold, and that some person in the office had interlarded two or three lines so as to give it a different application, and had left out the closing paragraph altogether. In this article in the *Commercial Advertiser* the precise changes which were made in the original article appeared. Mr. Bigelow handed me the article and told me to do with it as I liked. I told him the honest argument of the article, if it meant anything, meant that the President and Secretary did not mean to sell gold and lock up currency in the treasury; that they would sell no more gold than they could disburse currency for, and that further, if bonds should be very favorable, the Secretary had the right to buy bonds for the sinking fund directly with gold. This fact is inserted in the body of the article, that he might perhaps exchange gold for 5-20 bonds direct. There is where Mr. Gould said the argument had been mutilated and reversed. I did it for two purposes. In the first place, I thought if the argument meant anything, it meant that the President and Secretary did not intend to lock up currency during the busy season; and in the second place, not knowing where the article came from, yet from whatever source it originated, I suspected there might be from the statements of the last paragraph a sinister purpose to 'bull' gold, so the double lead was taken out of the article, and the tail of the article (which you will find here) stricken off and the article as it appears published on the 25th. The original article was headed 'Grant's financial policy.' Mr. Bigelow, after we had changed it to conform to our own views, and to what we believed would be of service to the administration, said: 'Suppose you head it, as Boutwell has been brought into it, "The financial policy of the administration."' That heading was given, and it so appeared in the paper the next day. I now furnish to the committee the article as it was originally set up, and as it was actually published, showing what changes were made."

| *Article as set up from manuscript, double leaded.* | *Article as reduced and otherwise changed as in italics, and published in ordinary leaded type.* |
|---|---|
| GRANT'S FINANCIAL POLICY. | FINANCIAL POLICY OF THE ADMINISTRATION. |
| Thus far in his administration of the government, President Grant has not set forth, in an official form, the policy by which he is governed when acting upon fiscal affairs. This utterance cannot reasonably be expected prior to the | Thus far in his administration of the government, President Grant has not set forth, in an official form, the policy by which he is governed when acting upon fiscal affairs. This utterance cannot reasonably be expected prior to the |

BLACK FRIDAY.

meeting of Congress, in December next. In his annual message, and in the report of the Secretary of the Treasury, we may expect to see a clear and full development of the policy of the President; and in the subsequent acts of Congress that policy will be aided, strengthened, and, perhaps, modified.

In the mean time the *acts* of the Administration enable us to form decided views of its policy and intentions. *First.* The President evidently intends to pay off the "*five-twenties*," as rapidly as he may, in gold. *Secondly.* In order to be able to make this payment *soon*, the President is laboring to largely appreciate the credit of the government; he is struggling to lift its securities into the high position occupied by those of Great Britain and France. When this end is measurably attained, the President will then be able to negotiate a loan at par, in gold, at 4 or 4½ per cent., with the proceeds of which to pay off twelve or fifteen hundred millions of the public debt; thus, by a mere saving in the rate of interest, lessening our annual payments of interest, in gold, $25,000,000 or $30,000,000. *Thirdly.* To enable him to build up the government credit, and lessen the interest upon the public debt, the President has sedulously and with success labored to collect the revenues without loss or waste, and with less expense; also to introduce a rigid economy into every branch of the public service. Great savings have been realized in the Military and Treasury branches; creditable savings in the State and Interior Departments have been effected, and considerable savings are hoped for from the Navy and Post-Office.

So far as the current movements of the Treasury are concerned, until the

meeting of Congress, in December next. In his annual message, and in the report of the Secretary of the Treasury, we may expect to see a clear and full development of the policy of the President; and in the subsequent acts of Congress that policy will be aided, strengthened and, perhaps, modified.

In the mean time the *acts* of the Administration enable us to form decided views of its policy and intentions. *First.* The President evidently intends to pay off the "five-twenties" as rapidly as he may, in gold. *Secondly.* In order to be able to make this payment soon, the President is laboring to largely appreciate the credit of the government; he is struggling to lift its securities to the level of the securities of the wealthiest European States. When this end is measurably attained, the President will be able to negotiate a loan at par, in gold, at 4 or 4½ per cent., with the proceeds of which to pay off twelve or fifteen hundred millions of the public debt; thus by a mere saving in the rate of interest, lessening our annual payments of interest, in gold, $25,000,000 or $30,000,000. *Thirdly.* To enable him to build up the government credit and lessen the interest upon the public debt, the President has sedulously and with success labored to collect the revenues without loss or waste, and with less expense; also to introduce a rigid economy into every branch of the public service. Great savings have been realized in the Military and Treasury branches; creditable savings in the State and Interior Departments have been effected, and considerable savings are hoped for from the Navy and Post-Office.

So far as the current movements of the Treasury are concerned, until the crops are moved, it is not likely Treasury gold will be sold. The entire surplus of currency in the Treasury, on the contrary, will be employed in the purchase of bonds, as heretofore, that money may be abundant and cheap at the time crops are to be paid for and moved by transporters to market. At a time of the year so critical to producers, the President will not withdraw currency from the channels of trade and commerce; he will not send gold into the market and sell it for currency to lock up in the Treasury vaults. Such a procedure would reduce the value of our entire products; to buy and lock up our currency *now*, and thus make money scarce and dear, would distress all of the producers of the country, and benefit nobody but usurers and speculators. This error will not be committed. No administration can desire a money panic, and thereby low prices for produce, upon the eve of the fall elections.

The policy of the President is, then, as revealed by his acts, to appreciate the values of all government securities preparatory to the making of an effort to lessen the rates of interest on the public debt; to honestly collect the revenues; to reduce expenditures. This policy, if successful, will enable the administration to place our finances upon a solid foundation, *and to reduce the taxes.*

Such is the financial policy of the President, as developed by his acts. It is at once simple and efficient. By strengthening our credit we carry our bonds to par in gold; by becoming able to obtain money at 4 or 4½ per cent., we can save 1½ or 2 per cent. per year upon our whole debt. Contests between government and bond-holders are likely to lessen the value of bonds,

crops are moved, it is not likely Treasury gold will be sold *for currency to be locked up.* The entire surplus of currency in the Treasury, on the contrary, will be employed in the purchase of bonds as heretofore, that money may be abundant and cheap at the time crops are to be paid for and moved by transporters to market. *And it may be that further purchases of bonds will be made directly with gold.* At a time of the year so critical to producers, the President will not withdraw currency from the channels of trade and commerce; he will not send gold into the market and sell it for currency to lock up in the Treasury vaults. Such a procedure would reduce the value of our entire products; to buy and lock up our currency now, and thus make money scarce and dear, would distress all of the producers of the country, and benefit nobody but usurers and speculators. This error will not be committed. No administration can desire a money panic, and, as a consequence, low prices for produce, upon the eve of the fall elections.

The policy of the President is, then, as revealed by his acts, to appreciate the values of all government securities preparatory to the making of an effort to lessen the rates of interest on the public debt; to honestly collect the revenues; to reduce expenditures. This policy, if successful, will enable the administration to place our finances upon a solid foundation, *and to reduce the taxes.*

Such is the financial policy of the President, as developed by his acts. It is at once simple and efficient. By strengthening our credit we carry our bonds to par in gold; by becoming able to obtain money at 4 or 4½ per cent., we can save 1½ or 2 per cent. per and destroy our hope of reducing the rate of interest from 6 to 4 per cent. per annum. The policy of the President is wisest and best. It is honest, simple and statesman-like. It will succeed if adhered to and vigorously maintained.

[It may be objected, that the disbursement of currency to the largest convenient extent, and the retention in the Treasury of unneeded gold, will cause gold to rise again to 135 or 140. Suppose it should thus result. This would secure large shipments of breadstuffs, provisions, butter, cheese, petroleum, cotton, tobacco, etc., at increased prices; and, to the amount shipped, would save to our people an equal value of gold. Hence, as gold accumulated, the less would be the premium upon it; high prices for gold *before the sale of our products* would cause lower prices of gold after the sale of exports. It is better for our country to ship produce to pay for our imports than gold or bonds. The objection to the retention of gold in the Treasury, until our productions are marketed, is unsound; for the retention of gold will make both gold and the productions dearer at the time of the sale of the productions; if gold is not needed for shipment, the premium on it would fall. Large exports of produce, stimulated by the temporary high price of gold, would soon cause gold to bear a lower price. Hence, a high price for gold, during the next three months, would be productive of great good to exporters of produce. The fall of gold at this time, to twenty-five per cent., would bring ruin upon the agricultural, mechanical, and manufacturing classes; injury to these would entail injury upon the merchants and upon laborers. If gold is made cheap, it will be ex-

year upon our whole debt. Contests between government and bond-holders are likely to lessen the value of bonds and destroy our hope of reducing the rate of interest from 6 to 4 per cent. per annum. The policy of the President is wisest and best. It is honest, simple, and statesman-like. It will succeed if adhered to and vigorously sustained.

ported; if too dear to export, then produce will be shipped in lieu of it. Hence, government will not so act as to lessen the value of this year's abundant crop, but will labor to increase its value and promote its exportation to foreign countries.]

Mr. Norvel continued.—An article was published in the *Times* on the 24th of September, on the gold movement. I have it here. Mr. Bigelow said to me, "You write an editorial about the excitement; you have been in the midst of it; write it up." There had been two days of the excitement; this was before the great panic. On one of these days there had been a great fluctuation in stocks. I wrote this article, and gave strong points of rumors that were current that Fisk had gone into the gold-room and wagered any part of $50,000 that gold would go above 145; this was the day before the panic. I said in that article:

[From the New York Times, September 24.]

"THE EXCITEMENT IN WALL STREET."

. . . . . .

"The second sensation related to the speculation and practical *corner* in gold. And here about 3 o'clock on Wednesday afternoon appeared on the scene the inevitable and irrepressible Fisk, Jr. His presence in the gold-room was signalized by the rapid rise in gold from 137½ to 141¼ per cent., and by the offer of wagers for any part of $50,000 that the price would reach 145 per cent. The other engineers of the movement were not idle, nor had they been through the earlier part of the day. They not only *bulled* gold with a will, but talked freely of the warrant which they had from Washington that the government would not interfere with them. The highest official in the land was quoted *as being with them*, and he, of course, controls the action of the Secretary of the Treasury and the New York Assistant Treasurer. Although this must have been known to be false, there were abundant rumors and suspicions insidiously spread around the street to create the belief or fear with good men that the administration would *not* interpose by further sales of gold from the Treasury, or extra purchases of United States 5-20s in exchange for gold. Among these rumors was one that the Gould-Fisk party were about to secure the services and influence of Mr. Corbin, (the brother-in-law of the President,) as president of the Tenth National Bank, which they have recently purchased, in connection with Messrs. Tweed and Sweeny. The consideration was to be $25,000 per annum, equal to President Grant's own salary. This was too monstrous for serious belief. We have reason to know it is wholly out of the chapter of probabilities with Mr. Corbin himself.

"Yesterday the Central and Hudson affair was comparatively quiet, but the gold sensation was renewed with greatly increased intensity. The Gould-Fisk brokers bid the price up to 144 per cent. The party, without demanding their gold, compelled the sellers and borrowers who had contracts with them to place five or seven per cent. additional advance in price in their own hands, or else settle at the price of the day.

"This scene may be amusing enough to our readers, as a Wall street fight between *bull* and *bear*, but it has a more serious aspect. The business of the Produce Exchange, and the conduct of the ordinary foreign exchanges of the market, are paralyzed by the heavy rise and *corner* in gold *through a sheer gambling operation.* The government is scandalized by false rumors of complicity; the public credit damaged by the fall in the funds, and the general trade of the country agitated and unduly alarmed by a panic in money coincident with, if not directly superinduced by, the lock-up in gold. When or where the trouble is to end we have no present means of telling."

In order to make his *Times* article as useful as possible, Jay Gould wrote the following letter to the Secretary of the Treasury:

"OFFICE OF THE ERIE RAILWAY COMPANY,
"*President's Office, New York, August* 30, 1869.

"MY DEAR SIR,—If the New York *Times* correctly reflects your financial policy during the next three or four months, viz: to unloose the currency balance at the treasury, or keep it at the lowest possible figure, and also to refrain during the same period from selling or putting gold on the market, thus preventing a depression of the premium at a season of the year when the bulk of our agricultural products have to be marketed, then I think the country peculiarly fortunate in having a financial head who can take a broad view of the situation, and who realizes the importance of settling the large balance of trade against us, by the extent of our agricultural and mineral products instead of bonds and gold. You no doubt fully appreciate the fact that in the export of breadstuffs to European markets, we have on our side high-priced labor and long rail transportation to compete with the cheap labor and water transportation of the great grain-producing countries of the Black and Mediterranean seas, and it is only by making gold high and scarce that the difference is equalized, and we are enabled to compete in the London and Liverpool markets. It is not merely the agricultural and producing classes all over the country, north, west and south, that are enriched by your policy of furnishing a foreign market for the surplus products of the country, at good and remunerative prices, but as well the manufacturing and commercial interest. When the former classes are prosperous they buy and consume liberally; thus bringing prosperity and wealth to the latter interest. This policy will also greatly benefit the vast railway interests—which can only prosper when the general business of the country is prosperous.

"I sincerely believe that when the fruits of your policy come to be practically realized, all classes, the poor as well as the rich, will accord your services a generous appreciation.

"With many apologies for thus troubling you, I remain yours, respectfully,

"JAY GOULD.

"HON. GEO. S. BOUTWELL,
*"Secretary of the Treasury, Washington, D. C."*

To this the Secretary gave a non-committal and formal reply.

About the date of the above letter, the President wrote to Secretary Boutwell, referring to the financial condition of the country, and suggesting that it would not be wise to sell gold in too large amounts, to force down the price while the crops were moving, as it might then embarrass the West. On receipt of this letter, September 4th, the Secretary, then at his home in Massachusetts, telegraphed to the Assistant Secretary at Washington not to sell any gold in addition to the amount required for the sinking fund. By some means the information contained in this dispatch, and the letter which prompted it, reached the "bull" clique. On the 3d and 4th of September gold began to rise rapidly, and on the

6th it touched 137⅝. Gould had been all along a heavy buyer, but his associates became alarmed, for United States bonds in Europe were becoming daily firmer and firmer, the crop prospect was good, comparatively little gold was exported, on the contrary it came pouring in from all quarters, and was even returning from Europe. Gould himself began to experience the general fear. He had bought more than he intended to buy. On his examination he said that it was not the plan of himself and associates, in their efforts to advance the price of gold for the purpose of facilitating the export of the crops, to crush the market. In other words, when asked whether he had not designed to buy all the gold in the city, and then to buy as much more as the "shorts" would agree to deliver, and then force these to buy back at his own price, he answered, "No. In the spring," said he, "I put up gold from 32 to 38 and 40, with only about $7,000,000; but all these fellows went in and sold short, so that in order to keep it up, I had to buy or else back down and show the white feather. They would sell it to you all the time. I never intended to buy more than four or five millions of gold, and I made up my mind that I would put it up to 40 at one time. I had no idea of cornering it. I always made it plenty. I had in view all the time the lightening of prices. I thought to put it up so as to start business, and then quietly to sell mine off. . . . . . I did not expect to hold gold to 40. My theory was that if gold could stay at 40 or 45 until after the 1st of January, we could export about $100,000,000 of produce, and that would turn the current of gold in our favor, and gold would flow in from Paris and London. That would create a downward tendency in gold, and it would fall like a ripe apple. That would have been a natural, legitimate commercial decline. I think that gold would have gone to 25 or 20, and business be prosperous all the time, because we should have turned the balance of trade in our favor and brought gold here from abroad. That was my theory. . . . . . I commenced selling originally at 35, and intended quietly to get out of it at 37 to 40. But what put gold up so high was that these bears got frightened, and they commenced jumping over each other's shoulders for it. The worst panics ever produced are bear panics. These people know when they go to sleep that they have been selling what they have not; and when they begin to rush in to cover, that puts up the price. Gold went from 42 to 60 that day (Black Friday) without a dollar changing hands. The bears marked it right up for themselves."

Whatever may have been Jay Gould's reasons for endeaving to force gold up, one thing is certain, that he used his tact and talent to the best advantage. Failing to gain any information from the Treasury Department at Washington, he made General Butterfield his friend by buying and carrying for him during August and September, on the General's order and for his benefit, $1,500,000 of gold, and by proposing joint action with him in the purchase of a controlling share of the Tenth National Bank of New York. He bought and carried for Corbin a million and a half of gold in two lots, in order to possess himself of Corbin's boasted knowledge of the President's views and intended policy, and, as Corbin admitted, paid him on the 6th of September $25,000 cash, the profit on the smaller lot.

In addition to the influence which he had obtained by buying Corbin, Gould asserted that the President had become a convert to his theory of advancing the price of gold to aid the business of the country; and declared that General Grant had been heard to tell his brother-in-law that the order to sell gold during September had been countermanded. Corbin swore that he never heard the President make such a statement, and Mr. Boutwell testified that the President gave no order on the subject. Yet with all his efforts to depreciate the currency, Gould was not able to hold the price of gold above 135 and 136 until the middle of September. Woodward and Kimber had deserted him, and he tried again to secure the aid and co-operation of James Fisk, Jr. But let Fisk tell the whole of the gold story as he told it to the Investigating Committee in January, 1870:

"I was associated with no one in buying, selling, or loaning gold during the gold panic week. I think all the interests I had were personal. That question, however, may admit of some explanation on my part. I could say that no one was interested with me personally, or I might convey a clearer impression to the committee of my exact position by going into an explanation. At the outset, I may say that the transactions of Mr. Gould and myself are joint, and that our usual custom is to have no one else with us. At the time he started in to purchase gold, if I recollect right, he was with some other parties, perhaps with Woodward and Kimber, in the street. They spoke to me about it, and he said, I think, something to me about buying some gold. I replied that I did not believe in it; that I believed the pressure was against us on the street. At that time I was called away for three or four days; and when I came back, he had started in with Messrs. Kimber and Woodward, as I understood, and had commenced buying at about 37 or 38. You have had Mr. Gould before this committee, and have probably ascertained that he is rather a peculiar man. Gold having settled down to 35, and I not having cared to touch it, he was a little sensitive on the subject, feeling as if he would rather take his losses without saying anything about it. It went along in that way for three or four weeks, when one day he said to me, 'Don't you think gold has got to the bottom?' I replied that I did not see the profit in buying gold unless you have got into a position where you can control the market. He then said he had bought quite a large amount of gold, and I judged from his conversation that he wanted me to go into the movement and help strengthen the market. Upon that I went into the market and bought. I should say that was about the 15th or 16th of September. I bought at that time about seven or eight millions, I think. This, I think, is the only case in which we deviated from our usual custom of making up a settlement and dividing the results. It so happened that I started out with Heath & Co. The transactions of Smith, Gould & Martin, owing to the excitement that occurred, I think have never been fully settled. At any rate Mr. Gould and I have never passed a word as to whether I was to be interested in his profits or losses, and there was no understanding that I was or was not. When the settlement is made in full, if there should be a loss, I should be very glad to help him bear it; and if there are any profits, I should not say no to a proposition to divide them with him. That is not my nature. (Laughter.) I came into this movement simply to strengthen the market. I came in individually, and placed my own margins. There was no understanding between us, any more than a general understanding that we did business together.

Q. (by Mr. Garfield).—How much did you buy, or order to be bought, during the week of the panic?

Fisk.—I should think the aggregate of gold that I bought for myself during that week was, perhaps, ten or twelve millions. . . . . . . I know Abel Corbin. He had no interest in my operations; but I know of an interest that he had in the market from information which I derived from him, and from information derived from Mr. Gould.

Q.—What occurred at an interview, in Mr. Heath's office, between you and Albert Speyers, on the 23rd of September?

Fisk.—That I can, perhaps, give more clearly by referring to memoranda which I have here. Let me say that the firm of William Belden & Co. was composed of William Belden, George Hooker, and Andrew McKinley. Mr. Hooker married a sister of mine, and I had seen a good deal of Mr. Belden on Wall street for three or four years. At one time we were in business together. . . . . On the afternoon of Thursday, the day before Black Friday, Mr. Gould and I went down to Belden's back office. We went there because it was a little more out of the way than Wall street. It is on Broadway. I there gave some orders to Mr. Heath, and to Smith, Gould and Martin, brokers, that afternoon. That was the first interview, I think, I had with Mr. Belden in regard to gold. That afternoon, when I came out, Mr. Belden said, "I will meet you at the Opera House to-night." You must bear in mind that we had no idea then of the position we were drifting into. I had an idea that it might result in a transaction of fifteen or twenty millions of gold, which was not a very large amount of gold for us to carry. I met Mr. Belden at the Opera House that night at 8 o'clock. He said to me, "Evidently you have got a corner on this gold market, and I want to buy some gold to-morrow. I can just as well carry it as not. I wish you would tell me what to do." I replied to him, "Mr. Belden, the great motto on which we have acted is to do our own business ourselves, and then, if anything happens, there are no lame ducks to take care of but ourselves. I do not see that any harm is likely to come of it if you want to buy gold, and if you want to give some orders I will attend to them." He said, "I will bring a broker to you, and you can give him the orders." I said, "If you want me to do anything for you, come to me in the morning." The next morning he gave me this order: "September 24. Dear Sir, I hereby authorize you to order the purchase and sale of gold on my account during this day, to the extent you may deem advisable, and to report the same to me as early as possible. It is to be understood that the profits of such order are to belong entirely to me, and I will, of course, bear any losses resulting. Yours, William Belden. James Fisk, Jr." In the morning, when we came down town, we went to Mr. Heath's back office. I should think, about half-past ten, Mr. Belden came into the office and said, "I want to introduce to you Mr. Speyers. Mr. Speyers will receive from you any orders for purchases or sales of gold on my account." I think there were two or three parties in the room, who heard this conversation. Two of my own parties, Kingsley and Hicks, and two or three persons whom I had taken down to keep people out of the room, were within hearing. . . . . I think gold was then about 43. I said to Mr. Speyers, while Mr. Belden stood there, that Smith, Gould and Martin had just started for the market, through Mr. Willard; that we were buying gold up to 45. He started out. I should think he was gone half an hour; he then came back, and said he did not get any at that price. By that time gold had jumped to 50. He came back and said "Smith, Gould and Martin's brokers are buying gold at 50." I said yes, and he started right down again. He came in, stating that he had bought about seven or eight millions. It was then about half-past eleven. During this time gold had been up to 63 and 64, and gone back to 50. He said he had bought gold at 60; he was in a condition of great excitement; he said he had bought gold at 60 when it was selling for 50. I said to him, "You have gone crazy." "Well," he said, "I do not know where I am." I told him he had better keep quiet. As I afterward understood, Mr. Belden, seeing the position he was in, told him to go into the market and buy gold up to 60, and hold it there. That was about the last time I saw Mr. Speyers for two or three weeks; I think he was in the office some two or three times that morning. He went back to the market, and some of our people told me he was on the curb-stone, buying at 60, when gold was selling for 34. I have been in Wall street for a long time, and been in the habit of seeing people very much excited. I have seen respectable people out in the streets with their hats off, seemingly regardless of everything; but my opinion of Speyers, that afternoon, was that he was as crazy as a loon. The excitement then had got so high that, not desiring to stay there any longer, Mr. Gould, Mr. Heath, and myself, went out by a side-door, took a carriage, and drove up to our office; and that was the whole of our transactions for this day.

Q.—What was your object in putting up gold that day?

Fisk.—We had no object at all. We had intended to put it up to 45; that was the point we had decided upon.

General Garfield.—Please state in your own way, Mr. Fisk, what your object was in pursuing the policy you did?

Fisk.—Before my starting in for the purchase of this gold, and as far back as the time when General Grant went to Boston, on the occasion of the Peace Jubilee, which was in June; he went over on one of our boats, and we went with him.

"We have employed on the Erie road some twenty thousand men, all told; a stock of eight hundred locomotives, with the other equipments of the road on a corresponding scale. I am aware of no way in which these men and equipments can be used to advantage, unless the crops come forward from the West. The actual amount of transportation due us on the moving of the crops would be about three and a half million dollars. Now, if these crops should be held over and come on late in the spring, they would come right on the transportation of the mercantile people, when we could not carry the whole of them, and they would seek other channels, canals, etc., while we would lose the benefit; or, again, if they came forward very early in the fall, it would be at a time when we were doing a large business in package goods for the merchants, which pays better remunerative prices than produce. Our policy, therefore, is to encourage the crops to move forward at a time when other trade is quiet. I have been with the Erie road now some three years, and during my connection with it in the falls of 1866, 1867, and 1868, while the crops have been coming forward, gold has ranged from 41 to 45, and our freights were full all the time. When we began to figure at the precise position in which we were in regard to these freights for the last fall, we found that, unless our Western produce moved eastward early, the foreign market would be supplied from the Mediterranean, the Black Sea, and all that section of country. We had lying upon our table advices of three hundred sail of vessels, with wheat, on its way from these waters. Our cars were at that time doing a fair package business, but we were doing none of the produce trade at all. It was of vital consequence that our large railroad stock and steamers, running from Buffalo for us, should get this trade started. If we could have this produce trade of three and a half millions, with all the facilities we had for carrying it, about a couple of millions would be clear money, which, in carrying on our road, is too large an item to let go, if we can help it.

"So, on our passage over to Boston with General Grant, we endeavored to ascertain what his position in regard to the finances was. We went down to supper about nine o'clock, intending, while we were there, to have this thing pretty thoroughly talked up, and, if possible, to relieve him from any idea of putting the price of gold down, for, if his policy was such as to permit gold to go down to 25, our transportation would have been snapped right up. We talked there until about half-past twelve. When we first began to talk, I could see that he was for returning to a specie basis; I remember the remark he made that we might as well tap the bubble at once as at any other time, saying that it had got to come to that. That was in the first part of the conversation. He entered into the conversation with a good deal of spirit, and I made up my mind that he was individually paying a good deal of attention to the finances, which he would to a certain extent control, so far as the action of the government was concerned. That being his idea, it looked as if it was the policy which we should have to work up to in the fall. I know that when we got to Boston, Mr. Gould and myself made up our minds that the prospect did not look promising.

"When we got back to New York, the next thing we did was to write to Mr. Boutwell something in regard to the matter. I think it was sometime in August that General Grant started to go to Newport. I then went down to see him; I had seen him before, but not feeling as thoroughly acquainted as I desired for this purpose, I took a letter of introduction from Mr. Gould, in which it was written that there were three hundred sail of vessels then on the Mediterranean from the

MISS MANSFIELD'S FIRST VISIT TO FISK'S OFFICE.

Black Sea, with grain to supply the Liverpool market. Gold was then about 34. If it continued at that price, we had very little chance of carrying forward the crop during the fall. I know that we felt very nervous about it; I talked with General Grant on the subject, and endeavored, as far as I could, to convince him that his policy was one that would only bring destruction on us all. He then asked me when we should have an interview, and we agreed upon the time. He said, 'During that time I will see Mr. Boutwell, or have him there.' Now, then, gold had continued to go down, until it sold for 130 or 132, though when the crops began to move forward, I knew that gold would work up again without the necessity of buying to bring it up. I did not like the looks of affairs then. It was upon that theory that Mr. Gould had commenced to purchase gold. I told him that I did not think the skies looked clear enough to go into that operation, but he started to buy gold with a firm conviction that there was a short interest in the market, and I have no other idea than that it was his conviction that he could put up gold to 45, if he felt any sort of confidence that he would not come into competition with gold sold by the government. The theory was that it was safe to buy gold for the purpose of putting up the price, to enable us to secure this transportation for our road, and in the course of the operation we would get rid of our gold without loss; but the thing began to look scary to me, and I did not go into the transaction until I considered that Mr. Gould was undertaking to carry a pretty heavy burden, when I said that, of course, my entire resources were at his disposal. There was never any understanding regarding there being any corner in gold, nor had I ever had a word with any human being, except Mr. Corbin, on this subject. Mr. Gould started in again on the 17th of

September, and, seeing his position, I said, 'I will join you.' During the week before there had been a little coldness between us, which did not often exist, for the reason that he had taken upon himself a pretty heavy load, which he did not want me to share, and, therefore, he was not in the habit of saying anything about it. I remember the morning I started in that I illustrated his position by the story of a man who goes out on a spring morning to yoke his oxen. Putting the great elm bow on the neck of Brindle, and holding the other end of the yoke, he undertakes, by main force, to carry the yoke and draw Brindle over until he can yoke Star, and I described Mr. Gould as being in pretty much the same condition. He had a very heavy load to carry. He would not have invited me to help him, but I concluded I would help him to draw Brindle over. In the first place, however, I wanted to ascertain exactly how he stood, and I said to him: 'How much gold have you got?' I said to him that it was my firm conviction that, if we bought gold up, the government would unload their gold unto us. Said he, 'That 's all fixed. I suppose you have seen nothing to convince you of the fact.' General Grant was then in the city. It has always been our policy never to mix in politics, unless it is in our business; but Gould said to me that morning, 'This matter is all fixed up; Butterfield is all right; Corbin has got Butterfield all right; and Corbin has got Grant fixed all right.' That, in his opinion, they were interested together. That was a point I had not taken into consideration; I did presume Mr. Corbin had prevailed upon General Grant to make him believe that 45 was the proper point at which to carry off this crop. Up to that time I did not believe that General Grant, or anybody connected with him, had any interest in the movement whatever; but it startled me, when it was suggested that Grant was in this movement, and I determined to go right around and see Corbin. I had known him before, through a son-in-law of his, by the name of Catherwood, whom I had met in railroading; but I said to Gould: 'You give me a letter to him, so that he will talk confidentially with me.' He did so, and I went to Mr. Corbin; when I met him, he talked very shy about the matter at first, but finally came right out, and told me that Mrs. Grant had an interest; that five hundred thousand of gold had been taken by Mr. Gould at 31 and 32, which had been sold at 37; that Mr. Corbin held for himself about two millions of gold, five hundred thousand of which was for Mrs. Grant, and five hundred thousand for Porter. . . . . . I did not ask whether it was General Porter or not. I remember the name of Porter. This was given out very slow. He let out just as fast as I did. When he found that Gould had told me about the same thing, I said: 'Now, I have had nothing to do with your transactions in one way or the other; but you can make your pathway clear and straight by emptying it all out to me, because Mr. Gould and myself stand together. We have no secrets from each other; we have embarked in a scheme that looks like one of large magnitude. Mr. Gould has lost, as the thing stands now, and it looks as if it might be pretty serious business before getting it straight again. The whole success depends upon whether the government will unload unto us or not.' He says: 'You need not have the least fear.' I said: 'I want to know if what Mr. Gould has told me is true; I want to know whether you have sent this $25,000 to Washington, as he states.' He then told me that he had sent it; that Mr. Gould had sold $500,000 of gold belonging to Mrs. Grant, which cost 33, for 37, or something in that neighborhood, leaving a balance in her favor of about $27,000, and that a check for $25,000 had been sent. Said I: 'Mr. Corbin, what can you show me that goes still further than your talk?' 'Oh, well,' the old man said, 'I cannot show you anything; but,' said he, 'it 's all right.' He talked freely, and repeated, 'I tell you it is all right.' When I went away from there, I made up my mind that Corbin had told me the truth. Whether he had taken money or not—whether he had lied about that part of it or not—I made up my mind that either through speculation, or for the good of the country in moving these crops, the sale of gold, which was to have taken place in two or three weeks, in October, was stopped for October, either upon one basis or the other; either from motives of personal interest, or for the best welfare of the country. I came out with that conclusion. In the evening, Mr. Corbin came round to the Opera House, and I had another interview with him there."

Q.—Fix that date, as near as you can?

Fisk.—I should say, if it did not occur on Sunday, that it was about the 21st of September; it was either Monday or Tuesday night. We talked that evening, and Mr. Gould went home with him that night. In the morning, when Mr. Gould came down, I was over the river, and came into the office about one o'clock in the afternoon, but had no intercourse with Mr. Gould until about four o'clock. We were then doing our business on Wall street through the telegraph from our office to Wall street. I asked Mr. Gould if he had seen Mr. Corbin that morning. He said: "Yes, everything is all right; if Butterfield gives any information, we will get it in time to get out; I am to see Corbin again to-night; I think I can give you some more information to-night, after I see him.' It seems that when he started to go home that night, he stopped in at Corbin's house, when he went up or when he came back; anyhow, he came into the office about eight o'clock in the evening. Says he to me, 'Who is the most confidential man you have got?' I said, 'It all depends upon what his mission is.' He says, 'I want a man who is a quick traveler; says nothing, but passes right along.' Said I, 'I will give you Chapin.' I sent for Chapin; I said to him, 'Chapin, I want you to-morrow morning to be at Corbin's house at half-past six; you will there receive a letter from him directed to General Grant, at Washington, Pennsylvania; I want you to leave on the eight-o'clock train, traveling as fast as you can, and not stop until you lay that letter in his hands; wait until he reads the letter; drive directly from there to the nearest telegraph office, (it seems that Washington is several miles from the railroads,) and telegraph back to me whether the letter is satisfactory, if you can do so without conveying that intelligence to anybody else.' I then told Chapin, 'You are boarding at a private house; I will send another man to call you, so that you will positively not be late.' My brother-in-law went up in the morning, saw that Chapin was called, took him in a carriage at half-past six, and went to Corbin's house; rang the bell; Corbin came down, and, as Chapin says, delivered him the letter. He took it, went over the Pennsylvania Central to Pittsburgh, left the railroad the next night and drove to Washington, arriving there about half-past seven in the morning, I should judge. He sent in his card immediately saying that he was a special messenger from Mr. Corbin. General Grant came in, opened the letter and read it, and said, as he was going out, 'You wait a few minutes.' General Grant went out, and in a few minutes returned and said, 'All right.' Chapin drove to the nearest telegraph office, according to instructions, and we got a telegram about one o'clock, 'Delivered. All right.'

"I then had, one evening, another interview with Corbin. We were feeling a little nervous about the position we were then in. I said to Corbin, I hoped everything was all for the best. But, said I, 'If we should miss—if the government should sell this gold—it would certainly be a serious matter.' Corbin then said to me, 'I want you to talk with my wife.' Mrs. Corbin came into the room. I had been introduced to Mrs. Corbin before. The thing had gone beyond the matter of mere courtesy with anybody I met there. That was the first time I had seen her in reference to this transaction. We sat down and talked the matter over quite fully. I did not cover any matters up; I took it for granted that they had bought gold, and that they had as much interest in the matter as I had. She made this remark: 'I know there will be no gold sold by the government; I am quite positive there will be no gold sold; for this is a chance of a life-time for us; you need have no uneasiness whatever.'

"I had a phantom ahead of me all the time that this real gold would come out. I was well aware that we had bought all the gold there was in New York, and had no fear of that coming back on us. The gold we were then buying in Wall street, was phantom gold, and could give us no trouble.

"I started away on the strength of that conversation, and I think it was on the morning of Thursday, we left our carriage back of the Post Office, and when we came up to get into the carriage, as I came along up street, we stopped right below Duncan & Shearman's office. Gould says to me, 'Old Corbin feels troubled and nervous about some gold; he wants a hundred thousand dollars. What do you think about it?' 'Well,' said I, 'if he wants a hundred thousand dollars to feed out to parties in interest, he had better have it.' I think this was on the afternoon of Thursday. Gould asked me if that didn't look as if there might be some blow up. I said, 'If he wants that money to deal out to people, and it will help to strengthen our position in regard to this gold, we will give him one hundred or two hundred thousand.' 'Well,' said he, 'do as you please.' I told him I would go out and get the money; so I went immediately to Smith, Gould, Martin & Co., got a check for a hundred thousand dollars, and brought it and gave it to Gould in the carriage. Gould said he would stop at Corbin's when he went home that night, and would give it to him.

"Somehow or other when I was not with Corbin, I always felt shaky about the old rascal. I had my suspicions all the time, and yet when he talked to me I thought he was as innocent and guileless as a baby. But I kept my suspicions to myself. Gould had an awful bag of gold, and I could see by the way he would keep tearing up little pieces of paper that he was in up to the handle(—that's one of Gould's peculiarities). Well, I did n't learn until the afternoon of Friday, after the blow-up, anything about that hundred thousand dollar check. So I says to Gould, when things was as wild as Bedlam in a breeze, 'I'll be damned if that old scoundrel shall have that money; I'll stop the payment of that check.' Then Gould remarked in his quiet way, 'He has n't got it. He has the $25,000 check, but the big one is in my pocket.' I told him that was bully; there was so much saved anyhow.

"I went down to the neigborhood of Wall street on Friday morning, and the history of that morning you know. When I got back to our office, you can imagine I was in no enviable state of mind, and the moment I got up street that afternoon, I started right round to old Corbin's to rake him out.

"I went into the room and sent word that Mr. Fisk wanted to see him in the dining-room. I was too mad to say anything civil, and when he came in, I said, 'You damned old scoundrel, do you know what has happened?'

"This was, of course, after everything had blown up.

"Said I, 'Do you know what you have done here, you and your people?'

"He began to wring his hands. 'Oh,' he says, 'this is a horrible position; are you ruined?' I said I did n't know whether I was or not; and I asked him again if he knew what had happened. He had been crying, and said he had just heard; that he had been sure that everything was all right, but that something had occurred different from what he had anticipated. Said I, 'That don't amount to anything; we know that gold ought not to be at 31, and that it would not be but for such performances as you have had this last week; you know damned well that it would not be if you had n't failed.' I knew that somebody had run a saw right into us, and I said, 'The whole damned thing has turned out just as I told you it would;' I considered the whole party a pack of cowards; and I expected that when we came to clear our hands they would sock it right into us. I said to him, 'I don't know whether you have lied or not, and I don't know what ought to be done with you. I suspect that the whole thing was a damned trick from beginning to end.'

"He was on the other side of the table, weeping and wailing, and I was gnashing my teeth. 'Now,' he says, 'you must quiet yourself.' I told him I didn't want to be quiet; I had no desire to ever be quiet again, and probably never should be quiet again. He says, 'But, my dear sir, you will lose your reason.' Says I, 'Speyers has already lost his reason; reason has gone out of everybody but me.' I continued, 'Now what are you going to do; you have got us into this thing, and what are you going to do to get out of it?' He says, 'I don't know; I will go and get my wife.' I said, 'Get her down here.' The soft talk was all over. He went up-stairs and they returned, 'tottling' into the room, looking older than Stephen Hopkins. His wife and he both looked like death. He was tottling just like that. (Illustrated by a trembling movement of the body.)

"Finally, I said, 'Here is the position of the matter. We are forty miles down the Delaware, and we don't know where we are. I don't know but we may be rich; but it looks devilish like as if we were poor. You have got us into this scrape, and now what is going to be done?' She said she could not think this had been done with the President's consent. She thought Boutwell had done it in violation of the strict orders of the President not to sell gold. Said I, 'That don't help matters at all. I can't tell you where we stand.' We had sold large amounts of gold, which I was afraid would not go out. 'Now, Mr. Corbin, what do you mean to do?' The old man straightened up in front of the table, and said, 'I will go down to Washington and lay it at their door; I will fathom this thing.' Said I, 'When will you go—to-night?' 'No,' he said; 'they had both been abed all day, and could not go that night; but,' said he, 'we will be in Washington Sunday morning; we will ride all night Saturday night, and go to the Executive Mansion Sunday morning. You stand right still until Monday morning, and we will stop all sales of gold. We will mend up the matter; bind up the wounds, and all will be right.'

"I had made up my mind that Corbin's influence was pretty well played out, but I thought the further off he was the happier I should be, so I recommended him to go. He came down Saturday night, as I afterward heard, and went back Sunday night, spending the day at the mansion. I have never seen him from that day to this. Of course matters took such a turn that it was no use. It was each man drag out his own corpse. Get out of it as well as you can.

"This is a statement as nearly as I can give you of this gold operation. The whole movement was based upon a desire on our part to employ our men, and work our power, getting the surplus crops moved East, and receiving for ourselves that portion of the transportation properly belonging to our road. That was the beginning of the movement, and the further operations were based upon a promise of what Corbin said the government would do. Whether Mr. Corbin has lied or not regarding Mrs. Grant's having half a million dollars of this gold, and about Porter's being interested in half a million of gold, I do not know; I have no reason to believe that he did."

Q.—What Porter do you refer to?

Fisk.—I think he said General Porter; I know it was the Porter who was with General Grant in Washington, Pennsylvania. I heard my man say that Porter had an interest in half a million of dollars of this gold. You have heard of the interest that Speyers had in this gold. We had nothing to do with Speyers that day. Whatever transactions he had were with Belden. My transactions were done through Heath & Co., and were merely to support the gold market, without any understanding that there was to be any corner; without any understanding whatever, of any name or nature, further than to assist Gould in this transaction. He had started out with the view of giving work to our men and our power during the fall and winter.

"Before I started to come to Washington yesterday morning, I asked Mr. Vanderbilt to come to our office for the purpose of seeing whether he was situated as we were. I said to him, 'We are going down to Washington, and we wish to see whether you are fixed as we are; perhaps it may have some weight upon our future position, so far as this affair is concerned. I would like to know whether, representing as you do a line as large as ours, you are employing as many men as heretofore. Our men are on three-quarter time; we are ten days short in our payments, and our side tracks are filled with empty cars. We yesterday took out one hundred and twelve cars, against three hundred and seventy-five this day one year ago; and,' said I, 'where do you stand?'

"He replied, 'I have just ordered extra side tracks to put empty cars on. Our men are on three-quarter time, and so far as our matters are concerned, they are just like yours.'

"Railroading to-day is not furnishing more money than is required to pay for the labor and the oil used. We are not situated differently from any other road in that respect. There never was such prostration as has settled over these thirty-five or forty millions of people—as rests on us all here. I am now speaking to illustrate where this man Grant has brought us to. As the representative of the largest corporation on the American continent, I say to you that we are to-day starving to death. I must ask you, gentlemen, to summon witnesses whose names I shall give you. My men are starving. When the newspapers told you we were keeping away from this committee,* I say to you that there was no man in this country who wanted to come before you as bad as Jim Fisk, Jr. I have thirty or forty thousand wives and mothers and children to feed with the money disbursed from our office. We have no money to pay them, and I know what has brought them to this condition."

. . . . . .

Q.—Did you expect to carry gold as high as 50?

Fisk.—No. Only to where we could ship the crops—say to 40 or perhaps to 47. It went up to 60 because there were in the market a hundred men short of gold. There were banking houses which had stood for fifty years and which did not know but what they were ruined. They rushed into the market to cover their shorts. I think it went from 45 to 60 without the purchase of more than $600,000 or $700,000 of gold. It went there in consequence of the frightened bear interest.

* On receipt of summons to appear before the committee, Jay Gould at once replied as follows:

"PRESIDENT'S OFFICE, ERIE RAILWAY COMPANY,
"COR. 8TH AVE. AND 23D ST., NEW YORK, *Jan.* 18, 1870.

"*Hon. J. A. Garfield, Chairman, Etc.*:

"DEAR SIR.—Your telegram of this date is received, and while assuring you in reply of the intention both of myself and Mr. Fisk to respond promptly to any summons of your committee, I wish to correct an impression which seems to be entertained, (as I learn from the journals of the day,) that we would evade or shrink from a Congressional examination.

"I most emphatically assert that there is no foundation whatever for such an impression, and were it not for some recent troubles among our mechanics at Jersey City, demanding our presence here, one or both of us would have been in Washington several days ago to confer with the members of your committee, and offer them every information in our possession bearing upon the subject they are commissioned to investigate.

"Our present intention is to leave here on Friday evening, and be in Washington on Saturday, ready to appear for examination.

" . . . . . . I remain, very respectfully,
"JAY GOULD."

Q.—What frightened the bears?

Fisk.—There was a feeling that there was no gold in the market, and that the government would not let any gold go out.

Q.—Mr. Belden has stated under oath to the grand jury that you and Mr. Gould gave him a great many orders to buy gold? State in full the orders you gave to Mr. Belden upon these two days of the panic.

Fisk.—We were buying and selling. Of course, in working a market like that we were continually buying and selling gold. I think I telegraphed two or three times on Thursday to Belden to buy a million of gold. The next morning I sold a million. I know in my conversation with Belden the first night there was no relative difference between his purchases and the sales for our account.

Q.—C. C. Allen has also stated to the grand jury that you gave him orders to buy gold; please state what orders you gave him.

Fisk.—Allen is a man whom I never saw, so far as I know. Allen claims, and has brought suit, that he has a written order to buy a million of gold for William Heath & Co. The facts of the case I will state as they were told to me. When gold was at 43, I gave a young man by the name of Crother, an order to buy $500,000 of gold. It seems he could not execute the order, and he says he gave the order to this man Allen. I then had no idea of gold going up to 60 or anything of that kind; and when he came back he said to me, "Suppose I can get a million, what shall I do?" Said I, "Take it." I remember that, and that is all I ever knew about it. Pretty soon he came back and said he did not get anything at all. This was just before the jump from 45 to 60. Then Crother comes back to me and says: "You sign right at the bottom of this paper," which he handed me, "and I will see if I cannot execute the order." In a hasty moment I tore the margin off a *New York Herald*, and wrote, "Buy a million of gold. William Belden & Co." I was going to send it to Belden, as I supposed Heath & Co. had all the gold they wanted. They said I told them to send it in to Heath. Three days afterward Crother comes to me and states that he gave the order to this man Allen, and that Allen had executed it at 60. Said I, "If he has executed it let him take it." During this time Belden had failed, and Allen then tried to put it off on to Heath.

Q.—It is in evidence before the committee that you gave large orders to William Heath & Co.; please state what orders you gave to them.

Fisk.—I think, on Friday morning, Heath bought four or five hundred thousand dollars in gold.

Q.—There was a meeting on the night of the 23d at the Opera House, in which these transactions and the situation in which you were was discussed, and in which a proposition was made to publish in the papers the next morning the names of the men who were short of gold, for the purpose of forcing them to a settlement; please state to the committee what your plan was.

Fisk.—That was never mentioned at the Opera House.

Q.—Where was this meeting held, and what occurred thereat?

Fisk.—There is a theory to which you seem to refer, a measure originating with Daniel Drew—that when parties were largely short of Erie, their names and the amounts short should be published, so that, on looking at the list, they would see they were cornered, and would come right down at such prices as they could get. My counsel told me that it was unlawful—that the law would look upon it as a conspiracy.

Q.—How much did you and your associates hold the night before the blow up?

Fisk.—Perhaps $60,000,000. Of course, we knew that there was only thirteen or fourteen millions that could come in onto us.

Q.—Was your situation such that everybody who had gold must buy of you?

Fisk.—If we called in the $13,000,000, these parties must take the gold of us. I told them that our plan was to put gold up to 45, and that we were safe then, for we could loan the gold four times over, and make as much money as if we sold it, but to wait until this excitement was over; for, I assure you, I never have made money in an excitable market. I preferred, therefore, to wait until the prices were steady at about 45; when they dropped down to 43 we would buy it over again, and so make a great deal of money without bringing on any corner in gold at all. If our plan succeeded, we had nothing to do but make money all the time. 'Twould have been as easy as rolling off a log. My associates concurred in my view so far as this; there is no fright as great as the fright in Wall street when the bears become panicky. Burnt brandy won't save 'em, for the very reason that they have sold what they have not got. There are so many orders for Gold Exchange by the English and German bankers, who we knew were short of gold, that we were afraid what might be the result of the fright they would get into. . . . . . We knew who were short, for we had a list of their contracts. About two hundred and fifty were in that pickle. Jay Cooke was one, and nearly all the big firms were tarred with the same stick. They all depended upon us.

We had called in six or eight millions, enough to make a sharp demand; the banks held about as much more. And we, therefore, substantially held all that was available. We called in that gold during Tuesday and Wednesday. Our intention was to bring in enough to make a sharp call for gold, enough to make quick loans, so that we could get it right out of the way. The prices broke down on Friday because the government unloaded gold.

Q.—How soon did you know the news?

Fisk.—I will state what I know on that subject. I never had met General Butterfield but once before this. They considered him all-important. I did not see how we could get much benefit from him. Nevertheless, I could see that if they had a claim upon him, if he got the news first, he would give it to them. On Friday morning, when I went out into the street, everybody was wild. The first thing I suppose every man did who was a friend to Boutwell was to telegraph to Washington. An article also appeared that morning in the *Times*, saying that the administration was mixed up in this movement, and that the time had come when they should break up these cliques. It was a dirty article, but I found that it would break down gold; that it would be telegraphed to Washington, and that, when the time came, these men would not stand fast. I believed it that morning, the moment I got into the street. I had three or four runners with me, and I started a man from my office right up to Butterfield's every fifteen minutes. Butterfield kept sending down word to Mr. Gould that everything was all right. This continued until about twenty minutes past eleven, when gold, which had gone up to 63, all of a sudden broke down to 40. My man had then been gone about half an hour. He reported that he could not for a good while

THE RESIDENCE OF HELEN JOSEPHINE MANSFIELD.

find Butterfield. I believe that when Butterfield got the information he gave it to Seligman, and that he withheld the information from the others as long as he could, until he could get out some of the gold he had there. That is the first knowledge I had of this order.

Q.—Why, would the sale of four millions of gold break down the market?

Fisk.—It would break our corner.

Q.—The "longs" then were not so strong but that four millions would break them?

Fisk.—It would when they knew the government had eighty or ninety millions right behind it. The theory was adopted in a moment that the government had made up its mind to break up this clique. They gave real gold that took the money to pay for it every time.

Q.—Explain to the committee what you mean by "phantom gold?"

Fisk.—I mean "short" gold. That is the common title. You are a member of the board, suppose, and you say, I will sell you gold at twenty-one, and I say I will take it. You and I exchange tickets; to-morrow you have got to give me that gold; but you come to me and buy the gold, or you borrow it and give it to me. It is nothing really but a piece of paper. Again, suppose I have a million of gold; you come to me and want to borrow a million; you loan the gold or sell it to another man, and he to another, and so on, until a million of gold would settle twenty millions of transactions, and no gold has really passed at all. In fact, millions of transactions pass through the clearing-house with never a dollar of real gold at all.

Q.—You have spoken of money having been paid; do you think money was ever paid to Mr. Corbin?

Fisk.—Yes; I know that a check of twenty-five thousand dollars was given to him, and that it was afterwards returned to the bank. It was drawn on Smith, Gould & Martin, by Jay Gould. This check was tracked up, and found to have been presented to the Bank of the Commonwealth without Corbin's signature, which, of itself, has a suspicious look. We found that it came through the bank in which Corbin keeps his account, bearing the number of Corbin's account, showing that it went to his credit. Evidently he declined to indorse it, thinking it might place him more in our power.

Q.—You know Gould to have been intimately related to nearly all you have stated?

Fisk.—I know he was in the habit of calling on Corbin twice a day for six weeks. I know that he had three or four interviews with General Grant, and therefore I do not see why he should not understand the matter as I do. The testimony I have given this afternoon regarding the connection of General Grant with this movement, has been given to you by me upon the theory that what I knew about it was told to me by Mr. Corbin and Mrs. Corbin, and I have reason to believe that what they told me is true. It is, however, for those who have judgment in the matter, to say whether Mr. and Mrs. Corbin deceived me. It is proof that I cannot doubt. I believed what they said, and acted upon that belief, and placed myself in a position that no one in this country would ever care to be placed in. That is the best reason I can give for my belief in what Mr. and Mrs. Corbin told me.

Q.—What became of the gold carried for Mrs. Grant and the other members of the President's family?

Fisk.—O, that went with the rest—to where the woodbine twineth. (Great laughter.)

Q.—Do you know whether any money was paid to Mrs. Grant?

Fisk.—I only know what that old thief Corbin told me. Corbin was paid $25,000 for Mrs. Grant in a check. I have already told you all about it.

Q.—Do you know what the letter contained which Corbin sent to the President?

Fisk.—No. There's where we made a terrible blunder. There's where we were overreached. We ought to have found out the contents of the old villain's letter. It was that which sold us body, soul, and breeches.

A number of witnesses were examined by the Committee, and after many days two reports were submitted. The majority report set forth among main points in a comprehensive summary, that "Mr. Corbin, using the opportunities which his family relationship to the President afforded, and under that worst form of hypocrisy which puts on the guise of religion and patriotism, used all his arts to learn something from the private conversations of the President which could be made profitable to him and his co-conspirators. But with this and all the efforts of his associates, the testimony has not elicited a word or an act of the President inconsistent with that patriotism and integrity which befit the Chief Executive of the nation."

Also, that it was impossible to say whether the charge that Mrs. Grant was interested in the gold speculation originated with Fisk or with Corbin. "The Committee required Mr. Corbin to produce the original check for $25,000, and required Corbin to show what use he made of it." It was shown that he had used it to pay a debt which he owed to the Bank of America. The majority exculpated President

Grant and General Horace Porter, but held that General Butterfield's course during the gold conspiracy had been questionable, to say the least. The minority Committee maintained that "unconsciously or consciously, the President in his letters to Mr. Boutwell, worked in unison with the conspirators;" and closed their report with the following significant language:

"Whatever of value this examination has for future legislation, one value it has not. It has not enabled the Committee with unanimity to speak fully of the connection of the highest government official with this extraordinary movement in gold. As the examination was in this regard partial, so must be the report.

"In conclusion, the minority respectfully decline to give any certificates of immaculateness to any parties. The resolution under which we act does not call for or compel us to do so; and, however much it may be desirable in many views, we submit our report in that reticence to which we were enforced by the conduct of the President and the act of the majority.*

"The public may draw its own inferences as well from the testimony as from its absence. We have none to draw; and by this statement we frankly say that we make no insinuation or charge. Let the friends of the Executive, if he be in any way damaged by their zeal in shielding him, be held responsible for our silence."

Thus ended the business of the Gold Panic Investigating Committee, and with the following most graphic picture of the gold-room on the ever memorable Black Friday when the storm burst and so many were plunged into utter

* The President, Mrs. Grant, and Mrs. Corbin were not called as witnesses during the investigation.

ruin, this part of our eventful history is brought to a close:

"In the spacious Exchange room of the Gold Board, crowded as it had never been crowded, even in the wildest excitement of war times, amid the strangest variations of deathlike silence and tumultuous uproar, the pallid, half conscience-stricken brokers of this gambling clique appeared, one after another, to do their dirty work.

"By the little fountain which plays in the center of the floor, and around which the principal business is transacted, first one bid arose, 145 for $100,000, and there was no response. Then another bid, 146 for $100,000, and again no answer. 146, 147, 148, 149 for $100,000, with a pause between each, all amid deathlike silence.

"The hundreds gathered there, and the thousands who read the ominous words on all the telegraphic indicators in the principal business offices in the city, and the hundreds of thousands who watched the telegraph offices throughout the country, stood appalled. Each one per cent. advance involved losses of millions; the gain was with the clique. Who could tell what would be the end? There was no resisting such power. They could advance to 200 if they chose. And the usually surging, bustling, shouting-mass of humanity crowded there was held silent, almost motionless, as by a magic spell. 150 is now bid. for $100,000, and despair suddenly gives life back to many. They rush eagerly to bid and buy. Orders come in by telegraph to buy at any price. Messengers from all parts of the city, great bankers, the merchant princes, from up-town and down-town, force their way in through the crush, and give back to the brokers the sense of reality which they seem to have lost amid the dream-like terror. The stillness is suddenly succeeded by frantic excitement. Transactions of enormous magnitude are made amid the wildest confusion and the most unearthly screaming of men, always excitable, now driven to the verge of temporary insanity by the consciousness of ruin, or the delusive dream of immense wealth. But amid all the noise and confusion the penetrating voices of the leading brokers of the clique are still heard advancing the price at each bid, and increasing the amount of their bids at each advance, until at last, with voice overtopping the bedlam below, the memorable bid burst forth, '160 for any part of five millions.' Again the noise was hushed. Terror became depicted on every countenance. Cool, sober men looked at one another, and noted the ashy paleness that spread over all. Even those who had but little or no interest at stake were seized with the infection of fear, and were conscious of a great evil approaching. And from the silence again came forth that shrieking bid, '160 for five millions,' and no answer; '161 for five millions;' '162 for five millions,' still no answer; '162 for any part of five millions.' And a quiet voice said, 'Sold one million at 162.'

"That quiet voice broke the fascination. The bid of 162 was not renewed. But 161 was again bid for a million, and the same quiet voice said, 'Sold;' and the bid of 161 was not renewed. But 160 was again bid for five millions. Then dimly it dawned upon the quicker-witted ones that for some reason or other the game was up. As if by magnetic sympathy the same thought passed through the crowd at once. A dozen men leapt furiously at the bidder, and claimed to have sold the whole five millions. To their horror the bidder stood his ground and declared he would take all. But before the words had barely passed his lips, before the terror at his action had had time to gain men's hearts, there was a rush amid the crowd. New men, wild with fresh excitement, crowded to the barriers. In an instant the rumor was abroad, the Treasury is selling. Quick as thought men realized it was not safe to sell to the clique brokers. Scarcely any one now wanted to buy. All who had bought were mad to sell at any price, but there were no buyers. In less time than it takes to write about it, the price fell from 162 to 135. The great gigantic gold bubble had burst, and half Wall street was involved in ruin."

## CHAPTER XXX.

FOR a long time the Ninth Regiment, National Guard, had been in a languishing condition. It was only about 300 strong, its treasury was empty, and those most interested in the organization feared that unless something were soon done to put it properly upon its legs, the old Ninth would become, at no distant day, a thing of the past.

Some time in March, 1870, a proposition was made to James Fisk, Jr., that he should consent to serve as Colonel of the regiment.

"Elect me first, gentlemen, and then we'll talk," said Fisk. "You know I'm no military man. I've never trained a day in my life; never shot off a gun or a pistol; and don't know even the A B C's of war, yet. Fact is, I doubt whether I could shoulder arms or file left, or make a reconnaissance in force, or do any of them things, to save my boots. And as for giving orders—why, I don't know anything about it. Elect me, though, and then we 'll talk about it."

The officers of the Ninth met on the evening of April 7th, and after going through the form of an election, chose James Fisk, Jr., as their Colonel. The result was not a surprise to anybody, and the new Colonel was close at hand to learn the news. Gen. Varian, commanding the Third Brigade, presided at the meeting, and when he had announced the result of the balloting, Lieut.-Col. Braine, Major Hitchcock, and Capts. Van Wyck and Prior, were appointed a Committee to inform Fisk of the action of the officers. In a few moments he appeared in the Board Room of the Armory, and was greeted with vociferous cheering. He at once called the officers together, and after making a short and characteristic speech of thanks, proposed that they should all join a class for thorough drill instruction, and closed by paying a graceful tribute to the worth of Lieut.-Col. Braine, who had served with distinction during the war, and who had resigned the position of Colonel (to which he had been recently elected) in order that the regiment might be placed under the command of a man of wealth.

Colonel Fisk's energy and money soon began to make themselves felt. The files of the Ninth increased rapidly, and the regiment bade fair to assume the position in the National Guard to which its old traditions entitled it.

On the night of the 13th of May, in response to an invitation extended by Manager Fisk, to the regiment commanded by Colonel Fisk, the Ninth visited the Grand Opera House in full force. Five hundred, rank and file, were present in full dress. At the hour when *Ulric*, the Lost Soul, and *Rudolph*, the Tempter, and *Kalig*, the Spirit of Evil, began to show forth the nature of the first of the "Twelve Temptations," the regiment marched in with their gorgeously-attired Colonel at their head. They filed through the broad portals and into the spacious halls of the Opera House to the music of their splendid band, and in two minutes, by the stop-watch in the hands of Adjutant Allien, were comfortably seated, some in the parquet, and some in the private boxes. They were greeted by the audience already assembled with as hearty and noisy a round of applause as if they had brought the spoils of victory from a hard-fought field. During the performance Colonel Fisk was in the lobby receiving the crowds of friends who thronged about him to offer congratulations, bearing himself with the same ease and self-possession that always characterized him, whether braving the storms of ocean on the deck of one of his numerous craft, or planning the purchase of a new railroad, or worrying the brother-in-law of a President, or arranging a *ballet*, or plotting a corner in stocks, or negotiating for the sale of a ton of gold. In an anteroom hard by a corps of attentive waiters were kept busy icing champagne and dispensing it freely to all who called.

This was the second public appearance of Fisk as the Colonel of the Ninth, and the occasion was one of the happiest and proudest of his life. His vanity was tickled by the notice of the public, and he felt proud of the love and esteem that his men had for him. On his first appearance on the 14th of April, he had felt somewhat nervous, and fearful of committing blunders that might subject him to ridicule; but the people had greeted him so cordially that he soon regained his self-possession, and never afterward manifested any sign of bashfulness.

On taking command of the Ninth, the Colonel had offered a prize of $500 to the company that should have the greatest number of names on its roll by the 1st of July. Under this and other stimulants, which he knew so well how to administer, recruiting went briskly on, and by the beginning of July the regiment mustered 700 men.

On the 20th of the following month they went into camp at Long Branch. The trip down was a delightful one, and the ten days spent at soldiering will never be forgotten by the members of the Ninth. The Colonel, although brimful of fun all the time, was vigorous in enforcing military discipline, and indeed proved to be a perfect martinet, but one of the best-natured martinets that ever buckled sword-belt. He was "a knight dubbed with unhacked rapier and on carpet consideration," to be sure; and never learned much about manœuvering a regiment; but he did his duty faithfully, and while seeming to feel his responsibility, never allowed that feeling to interrupt the keen enjoyment of the fun that grew out of his novel position and his queer method of ruling affairs up to the time of his death; although proud of his regiment, and having an abiding faith that it was the best in the National Guard, he always laughed at his own inefficiency as a commander. In fact Fisk was a man who would never be obliged to wear the *point dexter tenné*, that one of the nine abatements which, according to Guillim, "is due to him who overmuch boasteth of his martial exploits."

On the first evening at the Branch the whole band wanted to leave for an hour. They were rather frightened, and nobody cared to be spokesman, but at last one of the musicians, a stout German, mustered up courage, and approaching the Colonel, who was enjoying his *otium cum dignitate* in his shirt and drawers, said to him, deferentially:

"Gurnel, of you blease, de band hafe been plowing all day,

und deir troats is patched mid de dry. Blease, cannod we nod go oud und git some beer?"

"Throats parched, eh?"

"Gurnel, yes, sir. De horns is all ferry dry, und if de trombone do nod git someding, he cannod no longer plow any more."

"Adjutant!" yelled the Colonel. Allien was soon at hand. "Let these tooting fellows go for their beer. My God! they say their throats are parched. Let 'em go for an hour; and tell the drum corps they can go. Their throats are parched, too, I guess. They've made as much noise as the tooters. And tell the beer man to send the bill to me. Too bad, ain't it? How would you like to run around with your throat parched?"

During the night there were many escapes, and the stout Colonel amused himself until three o'clock by chasing the deserters. "How in the devil," said he, as he lay down to rest awhile before starting out after the next runaway, "how in the devil can I teach these men what I know about war, when they are scattered all along from Pleasant Bay to the West End?"

Three or four days afterward the Governor went down to the Branch, and was right royally received by the Ninth. A salute of twenty-one guns was fired in his honor. While the ten-pounder was blazing away, the Governor was escorted around the camp, but on turning the corner of the line the party came unpleasantly close to the little brass piece, and as it went off fragments of the wad whizzed right by the Governor's ear.

"God bless me, Colonel," said he, starting back, "I hope your fellows are not firing canister!"

"It's grape the Colonel fires," said General McQuade, soberly.

"So it is, General," said Colonel Fisk; "but I fire it otherwise. "Here Van (to the gunner), slew your popgun a little to the left. You've nearly put the Governor's eyes out."

## CHAPTER XXXI.

THEN there was a grand ball at the Continental Hotel, given in honor of the Ninth; and on Sunday, the 28th, they had their last dress parade at the Branch. After the parade the men were marched back to camp and formed in line. When the sunset gun was fired, the orders relative to the next morning's march were read, and the regiment formed in hollow square to listen to the Colonel's address. Stepping forward from among his staff, he said:

"*Officers and soldiers of the Ninth Regiment*:—By this time to-morrow evening there will be nothing left of Camp Gould but the ground on which our tents now stand. To-morrow we shall be on the march, and therefore I avail myself of the present opportunity to address you. This is our last night in camp, and I cannot dismiss you without expressing the pride and satisfaction I feel at your conduct. You have behaved well as soldiers, and I am proud of you. You have behaved well as citizens, and I thank you. During the ten days you have been encamped I have not received a single complaint from any quarter, from the residents of Long Branch or from the visitors; and considering that we left New York nearly seven hundred strong, and have had an average of about five hundred men per day here, this is more than I expected. I certainly anticipated a little trouble from outside, but I rejoice to say that up to this moment I have not received a single complaint. Gentlemen, this is something to be proud of, and I cannot find words to express my thanks to you one and all. The few days I have spent here have been more to me than so many months. I have learned to know you better and have realized the responsibility of my position. Gentlemen, I am proud to command such a regiment, and it shall be my study to make the Ninth the model regiment of the National Guard. Once again I thank you for the attention you have paid to your duties, and in view of the progress made I am sure none of you will regret the time spent in Camp Gould."

On the following day the Ninth embarked on board the *Plymouth Rock* for New York, where, although they were not complimented by their military brethren, they received a glorious welcome from thousands of people.

In February, 1871, the Ninth gave a ball at the Academy of Music, which was a great success in every particular save the attendance of that class of society whose presence was most desired. The Colonel's open defiance of the laws of morality had shocked the respectable element of the community; and while he had scores of warm friends among the best of New York's citizens who admired him for his energy and pluck, and who respected him for his kindness of heart, there were but few of these who would risk being thrown in public contact with the men and women who were helping to drag him down to infamy, and who ultimately brought him to his untimely death.

A few months previous to the last named date, Colonel Fisk paid a visit to the vast machine shops belonging to the

Erie Railway Company at Susquehanna, Pennsylvania, and while there made a characteristic speech to about 600 employés of the road, and a number of the country people who had crowded in to see him. The speech is given here just as it was reported by one of the Susquehanna machinists. Mounting an improvised platform the Colonel removed his jaunty velvet cap and said:

"I suppose you all read the papers. Well, you've read a great deal about Jim Fisk. One day you may have inferred from what you read in the papers that this man Fisk was an angel from heaven; and on another day you may have read some other paper, and fancied that he was a devil from hell itself. Be that as it may, here I stand before you, plain Jim Fisk, either angel or devil, just as you choose to take me. Whatever I may be called, I am a worker. I am working and have worked for the interests of the workingman and of the public. I have worked for those interests untiringly and unceasingly. What was the Erie Railway six years ago, and what is it now? You are the men who can mark the vast improvement.

"Look at the improvements in your own workshops during that time, and then judge of the time and money spent in carrying on the same improvements along the whole line of the road. Hundreds of miles of steel rails have been laid, mile upon mile of blasting through solid rock has been done, the vast workshops at Susquehanna, Port Jervis, Buffalo, Elmira, Hornellsville, and Jersey City have been enlarged to nearly double their former size, and we are smelting our own iron and making our own steel rails and engines. You know this of your own knowledge. You mark the improvement of the road hour by hour, and you know how false are the impressions sought to be created by liars in white coats, whom God, for some inscrutable purpose, suffers to edit four cent papers in New York. (Great applause.) You may not know, however, that the author of these lies has eaten at the table of Cornelius Vanderbilt, and that these attacks are made in the interest of the New York Central, and Pennsylvania Central Railroads. . . . Were it not for the outrageous assaults of a portion of the press, backed by the influence and money of the competing lines who involved the road in an interminable series of lawsuits, we should have to-day a broad-gauge double track of steel rail from New York to Chicago, with the most comfortable cars and the finest locomotives that can be made. The day is not far distant, however, when these will be accomplished facts. (Cheers.)

". . . . It may seem to you a fine thing to be able to wear a diamond and a velvet coat, and to be stared at and run over by a hungry, curious crowd, whichever way you may turn, but I can assure you it is not half so big a thing as it seems. I hope none of you will hanker after big diamonds and velvet coats, for I know you will be far happier without them. I see before me men, who, I will venture to say, are rising sixty years old, but who can't show as many grey hairs on their heads as can be found under the velvet cap that I wear. Sleepless nights and work that never ends are not your portion. Your homes may be humble, but your toil is over when you straddle the legs of your supper-table. Don't think that all the work on this road is done at the vice and the lathe, for it ain't. The man who thinks that all Jim Fisk and Jay Gould have to do is to sit in a gilded office at one end of the road, and pass the time away in writing free passes and reading telegraphic dispatches, has got a false impression. You enjoy your evenings in the presence of your little families, while Jim Fisk and the heads of the road frequently spend the greater part of the night in studying how to meet a debt of $100,000 by noon the next day, when they don't know where to turn for $20; and all this, it may be, to feed you and your fellow workmen. We have to study and work —work hard for your interests as well as our own, for our interests are combined. (Loud cheers.) The mechanic and the laborer in the United States command respect from all. You are the foundation stone of society. You are the honest sons of honest toil, and you reap the rewards of honest toil. Again I tell you those rewards are far greater than the rewards of those who work with the brain alone, and not with hardened hands. And again I say, don't hanker after kid gloves, and high stove-pipe hats, and velvet coats, and diamond pins, and gorgeous neck-ties, for they will afford you no real comfort. I know I should be far happier running one of those lathes with no other care on my mind. I have been connected with the management of this road for some years, but this is the first time that I have enjoyed the privilege of meeting you. I am glad to see you, and glad to be seen by you. (Cheers.) You have my best wishes, and shall have my best efforts for your welfare. If any of you ever come to New York, and I can assist you, I shall be most happy to see you. Good bye."

At the conclusion of the speech the Colonel was loudly cheered. The men dispersed and resumed their work, with the conviction firmly settled on their minds that Jim Fisk was the working man's friend.

THE ORANGE RIOT.

## CHAPTER XXXII.

Col. Fisk's every movement was now as regularly reported in the daily papers of New York, as if he were in reality a monarch, and they so many "Court Journals." It is more than probable that at this period he was unusually clever to the press. He was always kind to suffering Bohemians, although he held them generally in supreme contempt; and was on all occasions lavish with his cigars and wine—the Bohemian's rarest luxuries. And the grateful tribe repaid the gorgeous Colonel's hospitality, by flattering him in the public prints, by giving prominence to the record of his daily walk. A comparison between the *Court Journal's* column devoted to the movements of Her Majesty, Queen Victoria, and those of the New York papers which most industriously followed the Colonel-Admiral and Prince of Erie, will prove that the admiration of royalty is not confined to the other side of the water:

Court Journal, London.

"The Queen arose at six this morning, and after prayers, breakfasted with her Royal Highness, the Princess of Wales.

"At 10 A.M., the Queen rode to Ballymacrackenhow, accompanied by His Royal Highness, the Prince of Wales, Brigadier-General Sir Thomas Dodd Fiddlededee, K. C. B., of Her Majesty's Indian army; and Lady Arabella Adelia Appletrip, of Appletrip Manor, daughter of Lord Armitage

Court Journals, New York.

"Prince Erie was out yesterday with his magnificent four-in-hand, in Central Park. The horses are splendid animals, 16½ hands high, and fast trotters. Their names are Prince, Admiral, Colonel and Ralph. Two of them are as black as the raven's wing, and two are dappled grey. They were borrowed from Mrs. Fisk, who is now at Newport.

"Col. James Fisk, Jr., has purchased a beautiful black-and-tan terrier, which

Appletrip, now absent in the Orkney Islands, in quest of relics from the ruins of the ancient Abbey of Adighamton. The party returned at 2 P.M., when the Queen retired to the chapel, and afterward to her chamber."

he has christened 'Erie.' The dog cost $107."

"Admiral Fisk's large diamond looked like a blazing meteor yesterday."

"It is understood that Prince Erie will visit Squankum to-morrow. His barber accompanies him."

"Prince Erie's tailor is a Hungarian noble; his caterer is a Spanish count."

The Long Branch trip having proved a grand triumph, the Colonel of the Ninth determined to take the regiment to Boston, and astonish the natives of the Hub. So, two months before the anniversary of the battle of Bunker Hill, he wrote to the Mayor of Boston:

"HEAD-QUARTERS OF 9TH REGIMENT, N. G. S. N. Y.,
*April 5th*, 1871.

HON. WM. GASTON, *Mayor of Boston*:

Dear Sir: This will introduce to you Major J. R. Hitchcock, Captain A. G. Fuller, and Lieutenant A. P. Bacon, officers of my regiment, and the Committee appointed by the Board to visit your city, and confer with you in regard to a proposed trip on the 17th of June, *prox*. They are empowered to make all arrangements in behalf of the Ninth Regiment; and I would respectfully ask that the hospitality of the city be extended to the regiment.

"I am, with much respect,
"JAMES FISK, JR.,
"Colonel Commanding."

This letter was duly delivered by the Committee; but the Mayor did not deign to reply to it. He simply referred it to the Common Council, who discussed the proposition with much warmth. One of the Aldermen, replying to objections raised by others, that the expense of the reception would not be justified, said that he was authorized to state that it should not cost the city a dollar. Others ridiculed the notion that Boston should give a public reception to such a man as James Fisk, Jr.; and after more discussion, the subject was laid upon the table. The following paragraph appeared in the next issue of the *Boston Advertiser*:

"The action of the Colonel of the Ninth New York Regiment, in asking for an official reception of his corps by the City of Boston, marks a new era in the history of effrontery. Such compliments are generally supposed to be tendered by the host, rather than asked for by the guest; and when the would-be guest lets it be understood that 'it shall not cost the city a dollar,' the transition from the sublime to the ridiculous is at once reached. When the City of Boston tenders her hospitalities, she does it on no mean scale, and will be slow to enter into any arrangement which smacks of those silver-plate presentations, wherein the recipient pays for the present."

"Well," said the irrepressible Fisk, when the result of his application was made known to him; "this is what you may call an attempt to snub me; but I think I can stand it. It ain't always the same dog that's the under one in the fight, and I've knowed the sickest horse cured. I'm going to 'Bosting,' boys, as sure as Satan, and the Ninth is agoing along!"

"But, Colonel," said a friend; "don't you run the risk of being insulted again, if you make another application?"

"Look a-here, Doc," was the reply, as the speaker brought his chubby fist down upon the desk with a bang; "I've set my heart upon this trip; and I'll make it, by the Eternal, if I have to take the regiment on in citizen's clothes, and send the arms and accoutrements by express. We can ship the muskets and things in coffins, you know, and consign 'em to an undertaker. Then we can dress the men up, and tell the Common Council that we don't care a tinker's dam whether school keeps or not. I'll try a little more persuasion. May be they'll mend their old tin oven, and not put on any more airs. But I don't like to crawl, although it don't seem to make no difference whether a fellow creeps or climbs—he's got to travel on all fours."

Fisk then wrote a courteous note to the Governor of Massachusetts, relating the facts in the matter of his application, and asking for permission to parade with his regiment in Boston, on the day named. The Governor's reply was equally courteous, and the permission was granted. Whereupon Fisk immediately forwarded the following pithy letter to Boston:

"HEAD-QUARTERS NINTH REGIMENT, N.G.S.N.Y.,
"NEW YORK, *April, 27th*, 1871.

"HON. WILLIAM GASTON, *Mayor of Boston:*

"Dear Sir.—On the 5th inst. I addressed to you a letter, asking an extension of hospitality to the Ninth Regiment, New York State National Guard, which letter, I understand, was delivered to you by a Committee of the regiment, and referred by you to the Board of Aldermen. I infer, from the published proceedings, that the letter, which was simply designed to obtain your official permission for the visit of my regiment, was misconstrued into an application for special favors at the expense of your city, a perversion for which there was no warrant and no excuse. The reason of my application to you was that (as I was informed) the law of your State did not allow the entry of an armed force without the sanction of the Federal Government, or of the Chief Magistrate of the State or city to be entered. Having waited a sufficient time for your decision, and my regiment not having received from you the courtesy of a reply, I have applied, in the name of the regiment, to His Excellency, the Governor of the Commonwealth, for permission to enter your city, and he has most courteously and promptly granted the request. I beg, therefore, that you will relieve the Common Council from further consideration of the subject, as their action or inaction is a matter of perfect indifference to the gentlemen under my command.

"I have the honor to be your obdient servant,

"JAMES FISK, JR.,

"Colonel Commanding."

Colonel Fisk could now turn up his nose at the Boston City Fathers. This he and the gallant Ninth did to their hearts' content, while they busily engaged in preparations to take the Athens of America by storm. The day fixed for the start was Friday, June 16th. They would arrive at Boston on the morning of the 17th, take part in the ceremonies of the day, and remaining over Sunday, would return to New York on Monday, the 19th. Fisk knew that the appearance of his regiment, with himself at its head, marching to the music of the largest and finest band in the United States, would create a sensation; but this was not enough. Military parades were common things. He must arrange for the production of a novelty which should be the talk of the whole country. The following was thereupon written and mailed from the Regimental Head-quarters:

"NEW YORK, June 2, 1871.

"Hon. WILLIAM GASTON, *Mayor of Boston*:

"DEAR SIR,—As I am informed that your city ordinances prohibit the entry of any regiment upon Boston Common without permission from the Mayor, I respectfully request permission for the use of the Common by the Ninth Regiment, N.G.S.N.Y., on the 17th, for a dress parade, and on the 18th for public religious services.

"Very respectfully, your obedient servant,

"JAMES FISK, JR., Colonel."

"What will this man Fisk be at next?" said the Bostonians when the above letter was made public.

The Mayor laid it before the Aldermen, and the Aldermen refused to allow the Common to be desecrated and the Sabbath to be broken by the praying band from Gotham under the leadership of the notorious Colonel Fisk. Here was another snub. Again Fisk wrote:

"HEAD-QUARTERS NINTH REG., N.G.S.N.Y.,
"NEW YORK, June 13—9½ P.M.

"To his Honor the MAYOR of Charlestown, Mass.:

"I am at this moment in receipt of a telegram from Boston announcing that the Ninth Regiment are denied the privilege of holding religious services in any public place in Boston, except the street, on Sunday next. Will you allow the regiment to march on Sabbath morning to your hospitable city, and there hold religious services in such suitable place as you may designate? If Monument Square or the grounds surrounding Bunker Hill Monument are subject to your control, allow us to suggest one of those places. Please answer by telegraph at earliest moment, in order that a Committee may confer with you on Thursday.

"JAMES FISK, Jr.,
"Colonel Commanding."

This communication was also submitted to the Aldermen, and after giving it due consideration, they

"*Resolved*, That the Board esteems it a pleasure to grant any military organization all the courtesies and civilities becoming an intelligent community. But in considering the request of Colonel James Fisk, Jr., for permission to hold religious services in the open air with his regiment on Sunday the 18th instant, while we respect the object of the request, we feel that the crowd and confusion necessarily attending a parade, would certainly ill accord with the proper observance of the Sabbath. And therefore, as a matter of order and regularity, we deem it inexpedient to grant the permission required."

The Ninth reached Boston on the morning of the anniversary, and were complimented, for the first time since the election of the new Colonel, by being received with military honors by one of the best of the Boston regiments. They took part in the celebration, and throughout the day were the centre of attraction. The streets through which they marched were crowded with people who cheered the gratified Colonel lustily. In the evening the Ninth Regiment Band gave a concert on the Common, which was attended by thousands, who, although residents of a city justly proud of its musical talent and culture, had never heard anything to equal the music of the Gothamites.

On Sunday morning, Colonel Fisk having received permission to hold religious services in the open air (but not in the Common), the rain came down, and the ardent piety of the Ninth cooled wonderfully. But Fisk had determined to have a praying show, and he had it. He engaged the Boston Theatre, and taking the band and the members of the regiment from the St. James Hotel to the improvised temple in omnibuses, he prepared for business with his customary vigor. Crowds of people already thronged the house. The rank and file of the regiment took seats in the auditorium, and the Colonel, the Chaplain, and the musicians occupied the stage. The band played splendidly and were applauded to the echo. The great Levy then gave one of his wonderful solos, and then the Chaplain, after a prayer, preached a short sermon. Colonel Fisk, elaborately attired, then stepped to the edge of the stage in front of the foot-lights and said:

"*Soldiers of the Ninth Regiment and Officers of the Staff:*

"On the morrow, if God spares us, we shall get back again to our own city, or, at least, to the city where you belong, for I can scarcely say *our* city, because I belong in Boston. This is my residence. I can hardly express to you the feelings which I cherish toward you all for the manner in which you have fulfilled all your duties as soldiers on this occasion. You have again occasion to feel proud, in every sense of the word, of your entire behavior from the time you left New York until now. I can only thank you in all kindness, heartfelt kindness, that you have done now as you always have done since you have been under my command; that you have again taken a great interest in the performance of your duties, and that you have, as usual, shown your willingness to carry out every wish of your superior officers. It is always with pride, when we have been anywhere, that in after times, when I have met any with whom we have been associated, that I hear of the proud name in which the regiment is spoken of. I felt certain of our reception in Boston. I felt assured of your conduct. I knew what the result would be. But a very unfortunate mistake, or accident, has occurred with regard to the authorities of the city of Boston—a mistake I would gladly have avoided. The hospitalities we wanted extended to us were those that I felt we would be sure to get, and the only thing that has gone wrong was the occasion which has made it necessary for me to offer an apology to the Mayor of the City of Boston, in behalf of my regiment, when passing in review. We did not know that he was to review us. I saw him just in time to salute him myself, but the regiment was unable to salute him, for there was not time to pass the word down the line. It was a respect which we owed to him in his position as chief magistrate of this city, and it is right that the regiment should apologize; and, therefore, when these remarks are registered, as they will be to-morrow when we have returned to our homes, he will hear that we have apologized to him for a mistake which was not ours; we should have been notified. (Applause from the spectators.)

"I wish to speak of the kind manner in which the military of Massachusetts have received us, and to thank the citizens of Massachusetts and those of other States for the exceedingly kind welcome they have accorded us. It was the only welcome we wanted. (Applause.) The matter of our hospitalities and expenses were borne by friends. Hospitalities, in the strict sense of the term, we can carry out ourselves; but the spirit evinced by the people of Massachusetts, as we passed along its streets, could not be purchased. It must come from the heart; from the good feeling they bear toward us; and I thank them, and I know that you all thank them for it. In the future, when we have occasion, and I think we shall have, of turning from the City of New York, I shall yearn toward Boston, for I think the good feeling displayed by the citizens on this visit would bring us all back here the next season, instead of anywhere else. Therefore, when we go from Boston, I will say for myself and my regiment, that we shall carry back nothing but the kindest spirit toward this good city. There should have come up no 'ism;' there should have come up nothing to say that we should not worship God how and where we pleased. It was a mistake. Nobody meant wrong toward us, and I was sorry to see that the question was agitated at all. I do not believe that the signers of the paper said to have been sent in to the Boston city government, requesting that the Common should not be opened to us, felt any differently toward us than did the 100,000 or 150,000 people who welcomed us so warmly. We will cherish no bad feeling against them. I do not believe they cherish anything against us. Again let me thank them for all they have done for us. It speaks well for us to exhibit ourselves in full ranks to-day, after the hard labors of yesterday, and reflecting on the fact that a leave of absence was granted from 9 o'clock last night to 1 o'clock to-day. I am told that, except those who are upon the sick list, every officer and private is present here this afternoon, and I am proud of the Ninth. Because why?—whether under military rule or otherwise, they feel a pride in their organization. They take pride in its good behavior, take them where you will. You have planted another peaceful battle on your flag. Thanking you for the spirit in which you have carried out your instructions, and that you have done what is right, and discharged your duties with a degree of merit to which you always aspire, I will retire." (Applause.)

The next day the Ninth returned to New York.

## CHAPTER XXXIII.

THE 12th of July, 1871, was a memorable day in the history of New York. The Orangemen's parade had been prohibited by the Superintendent of Police, but at 1 o'clock on the morning of their anniversary, Governor Hoffman revoked Superintendent Kelso's order in the following language:

". . . . I hereby give notice that any and all bodies of men desiring to assemble and march in peaceable procession in this city to-day, the 12th inst., will be permitted to do so. They will be protected to the fullest extent possible by the military and police authorities."

Notwithstanding the proclamation of Governor Hoffman, revoking the order of Superintendent Kelso, and insuring the Orangemen full civil and military protection and escort during their annual parade, it was felt by everybody that a street conflict between the Irish Catholics and the military and police was inevitable; and the order-loving citizens of New York soon found their worst fears realized.

At two o'clock the procession formed. It was led by 250 police, after whom came the famous Seventh, then the Twenty-Second, then the Gideon Lodge of Orangemen, about 100 strong; then the Eighty-Fourth, the Sixth, and the Ninth Regiments, and another battalion of police. After many false starts the column marched about two blocks down Eighth avenue, passing Fisk's Grand Opera House, near which point stones were thrown from the roofs of tenement houses upon the Orangemen and their escort. About midway between 27th and 28th streets a temporary halt was rendered necessary by the immense throng blocking the streets. Here the mob began their attack. For a moment the soldiers were demoralized, but only for a moment. Volley after volley was fired into the crowd. Fifty people were killed outright, and more than a hundred left writhing in pain upon the blood-stained pavement. Two of the most valuable members of the Ninth had been killed—Sergeants Henry E. Page and Samuel Wyatt, and private Walter Pryor mortally wounded; and their brothers in arms were not slow to avenge them. Colonel Fisk was, during the fight the victim of a ludicrous accident, and the hero of a burlesque tragedy for ever afterward. The story is here given in his own words:

"On Tuesday night, about 12 o'clock, I called on Governor Hoffman and Mayor Hall at Police Head-quarters, and had an interview with those officials in reference to my regiment in the coming trouble. During our pow-wow I informed the Governor that in case of a riot I expected that the 23d street Ferry and the Grand Opera House would be assailed by the mob. His Excellency concluded to let the Ninth regiment protect both places. There being a rumor that a body of Orangemen intended crossing the 23d street Ferry to take part in the New York procession, it was decided that should such an attempt be made, the ferry-boats should be withdrawn, and they should not be permitted to cross. Governor Hoffman thought he should have enough to do to protect his own people, and was not willing to become responsible for the safety of those belonging to any other city or State. I then left them. I was at my armory before 8 o'clock next morning, and a few of my men having already arrived, I sent them out immediately to hurry up the stragglers. About mid-day a messenger arrived from the Grand Opera House with the information that a large number of men were crossing the 23d street Ferry. I immediately went to the Opera House and sent for Jay Gould. I wanted to know of him if the charter would be violated by stopping the ferry-boats. Not being able to find Gould, I took the responsibility upon my own shoulders and telegraphed to Mr. McIntosh, agent at Jersey City, to stop running the boats. My order was at once obeyed.

"Just then I got word from a messenger that my regiment was forming at the armory and was making ready to march. I started out and began to walk back. As I approached 24th street, the crowd on the sidewalk hooted me and yelled at me. I immediately took the middle of the street, and walked on in that way till I came in sight of the Sixth regiment just ahead. In the meantime the crowd was gathering behind me, when all of a sudden I heard a shot, and felt a bullet whiz past me. I went in the ranks of the Sixth, the crowd continuing their hooting until I got to my own regiment.

"I had left my regimental coat and sword at the armory, and was in my shirt sleeves. I took the Major's sword and assumed command, after despatching a messenger to the armory after my dry goods. In the meantime the procession began to march, and soon after we started a lot of bricks and stones were thrown at us, and in some instances shots were discharged. As for the order to fire, my men received instructions before leaving the armory not to fire off their pieces until they should be assaulted by the mob; and not to fire if only stones should be thrown. But should it become so hot that they could not stand it, and should any shots be fired, they were not to wait for any orders, but were to fire into the mob and protect themselves.

"No attention was paid to the missiles until Walter Pryor was struck by a bullet in the knee, and Harry Page was killed. I was standing within a few feet of him. At that moment discharges of musketry were heard from the head of the line, and my men becoming excited at the death of one of our best members, opened fire upon the mob. My regiment was a little distance behind the Sixth. The crowd on the east side of Eighth avenue, into which the troops were firing, now came rushing between the two regiments. I was standing in front of my regiment with Major Hitchcock's sword in my hand. The mob closed in upon me in an instant, knocked me down, and trampled upon me.

"After the crowd passed me I tried to rise, and found I was hurt about the foot. I cannot say whether I was struck by anything, or received my injuries by being trampled upon. Some of my men seeing my condition carried me into a bakery close by. I was taken to the second story and the surgeons examined my foot and found that my ankle was out of joint. They took hold of it and jerked it back into place. The surgeons then left me, and as I was looking out of the window with Captain Spencer I saw the crowd close around the two men of my regiment who had been left in charge of Page's body. I saw a man make a thrust at one of them with a sword-cane.

"The next thing I remember was hearing an Irishman, who stood in front of the bakery, cry out, 'That damned Colonel Fisk is in here. Let's go in and kill the villain.' Others said, 'Hang him.' Crowds began to gather thick and fast about the door, and fearing that the house was about to be sacked, I seized a heavy cane which had been given me, and left by the back way. I must have jumped over five fences, when I reached a house through which I went, and attempted to pass out by the front door. Looking down the street toward Eighth avenue, I saw the mob still there. Coming down Ninth avenue was another crowd—a hard looking set. For a moment I thought there was no possible chance of escape, but on glancing across the street I saw a door open and ran toward it. This house is in Twenty-Seventh street, between Eighth and Ninth avenues. I went through the hallway to the yard. Here I met a high fence. I found a barrel, mounted it, and climbed over. I climbed several more fences until I became exhausted at last, and started for a house fronting on 29th street. Some woman slammed the door in my face. Seeing a basement window open, I crawled into it, and was confronted by an Irishman, who wanted to know what it all meant. I explained my case to him, and borrowed a pair of old trousers, an old hat, and a large coat. When I left the house the crowds had disappeared from 29th street, having followed the procession down.

"My first thought was now for a carriage. Seeing none in sight I limped toward Ninth avenue, and looking down the street I espied one coming up. I hailed the driver, and looking inside saw Jay Gould. The driver stopped, but Gould, not knowing me in my disguise, ordered him to go on again. I explained who I was, and was taken in. The driver took us to the Hoffman House; but I had not been there more than fifteen minutes before a mob collected around the neighborhood. Seeing that danger still followed me, I ordered another coach, and was taken to the Pavonia Ferry, where a number of our tugs are generally stationed. I got on board of one of them and was taken to Sandy Hook. From there I went to Long Branch in the cars. I did not take off my disguise until I reached the Continental Hotel."

## CHAPTER XXXIV.

COLONEL FISK appeared for the last time at the head of his regiment on the 21st of November, 1871, the day of the Grand Duke Alexis's arrival. The military display was magnificent, and the Ninth, with its splendid band, was uproariously greeted by the thousands who thronged the streets that day. Fisk himself was warmly received by the populace, and was as happy and proud as a king, despite the fact that on passing the stand at Union Square he was hissed by a few ill-bred people who had been honored with special seats.

That evening the Grand Duke was serenaded by the band of the Ninth. Thousands of people crowded the streets in the neighborhood of the Clarendon Hotel, where Alexis was stopping, and the marvelous performance of Levy and his fellow artists evoked thunders of applause. Colonel Fisk was sent for by the Grand Duke, and for half an hour or more he chatted with the young scion of royalty with all the ease and *abandon* which ever characterized Jim Fisk, whether engaged with the fireman of his express train, with the broker who sold his stocks, or with the President whom he desired to win over to his side in gigantic speculation.

In the early days of the Union Pacific Railroad, when Cornelius S. Bushnell, of Connecticut, Mr. Oakes Ames, of Massachusetts, and others, were laying schemes for the accomplishment of one of the greatest undertakings ever inaugurated, Mr. Fisk wanted to purchase a large amount of stock

GRAND DUKE ALEXIS OF RUSSIA.

by paying only a certain per cent. of the value down (as is generally done on original subscriptions), that he might have an important voice in the councils of the road. He fully realized its importance. His intellect, whatever may be said of its education, was broad-gauge and comprehensive in its range, and he readily foresaw that the first trans-continental railway must command a traffic which would insure its profitable operation. His keen wit fully understood that, first, a scheme of so gigantic a nature would, as a matter of news, be thoroughly heralded throughout the civilized world. Would not this be a splendid advertisement, adding, gratuitously, just so much to the value of the property? Fisk was not slow to perceive this advantage, as well as the fact that from its peculiarly national character it would receive more than ordinary support in various ways. Fisk wanted to get in. But his overtures were declined, and he was permitted to have only so much stock as he paid the full face-value of at once. This offended him, and he was bent on some action which would show the Company his feelings regarding what he considered a gross violation of financial usage in similar cases. He bought a half-dozen shares of the Company's stock. Then he claimed to be true, what was current report at the time, that the Company's affairs were wrongfully managed. He brought suit against the Company to compel them to make known its affairs to him as a stockholder. Of course it was necessary to have the books of the Company for inspection. The officers of the Union Pacific declined to give them up. Fisk got an order from the Court to seize them. His operations in accomplishing that purpose constituted the chief sensation of that time. He employed twenty swarthy men, muscular mechanics, who, with sledge hammers and cold chisels, repaired to the office in

Nassau street, where the Company had locked up their books in a huge iron safe. The men began work. Mr. Fisk personally directed the movements of the men under his control, and they hammered perseveringly. Officers of the Union Pacific Company were also present, but they were powerless to interfere, for the mandate of the Court must be obeyed. Sledge hammer and chisel were incessantly plied. Financiers of all grades came and looked on. Meals were furnished the workmen on the spot, and the onslaught on the safe was continued without ceasing. Relays of men supplied the places of those exhausted by labor. At last the safe was opened, and the books brought to light. The affair at the time was looked upon as the culmination of Fisk's system of arbitrary action. While it was perhaps the most plainly visible of his many acts of force, it lacked in many ways the great results which followed many others of his schemes. But it had one immediate result: the Union Pacific Company became so fearful of further interference from the Courts of New York, that it moved its offices to Boston, opening a fine establishment on State street of that city. During the beginning of 1872 the Company returned to New York, and opened offices on Broadway.

## CHAPTER XXXV.

On the night of January 7th, 1871, Edward S. Stokes was arrested at the Hoffman House, on the charge of embezzling money from the Brooklyn Oil Refining Company, of which he was a stockholder and secretary. He lay in jail that Saturday night and all day Sunday and on Sunday night, but on Monday he was bailed out. He and Jim Fisk were partners in the Brooklyn Oil Refining Company. The examination of Stokes, previous to his release on bail, disclosed the fact that while his arrest was compassed apparently by the instigation of another man, Fisk was really the moving spirit in the matter. And, while the arrest was ostensibly on the ground of alleged fraudulent operations on the part of Stokes, it became known that the real animus in the matter was a personal one. It appeared that, instead of a desire to punish Stokes for embezzlement, it was a plan to get him out of the way of Mr. Fisk. There was a woman in the case. An old Turkish pasha said that whatever crime man committed, he cared not what it was, there was a woman at the bottom of it. So it proved in this case. It appeared that the real object of Fisk was, not to punish crime, but to gratify revenge, and inspire into the heart of Stokes sufficient terror to prevent him from paying further attention to the then central object of Fisk's desire, Miss Mansfield. It had not the desired effect. Miss Mansfield, while she had had no real love or passion for Fisk, had received him as her lover, for his money. But Stokes she really loved; or if love be too exalted a word to use in connection with a woman so worldly and designing, it is safe to say that she entertained for Stokes an ardent passion. This fact, of course, Stokes well knew, and it lent him courage in his combat with his rival.

Fisk, who thought that the favors he had done Stokes gave him some hold on Stokes's regard, asked Stokes to give up Mansfield and leave the field to him. To Fisk's great surprise, Stokes declined to do so. Fisk was astounded to find that his proposal was not only declined, but was refused contemptuously. Stokes had become so thoroughly infatuated with the voluptuous object of their mutual admiration that he found in her smiles sufficient inspiration to prompt him to open warfare with the Erie Prince. Fisk tried threats. His power had always been enough to insure regard for his orders. But in this case he found opposed to him a power which not only "laughs at locksmiths," but which he soon found was strong enough to actually set him at defiance. He found that Stokes's admiration for Mansfield was enough to make him set Fisk, or the world, for that matter, at defiance. Stokes made light of Fisk's commands. It was then that Fisk lost the feeling of kindliness for Stokes which had before characterized his associations with him, and resolved on using his power to crush him. Stokes had usurped his place in love, and then defied him. Fisk was intent on revenge.

Soon Stokes was informed that certain lucrative contracts, which he held with the Erie Railway, were rescinded. Next he was asked to sell out his share in the Brooklyn Oil Refining Company, or to buy out all the other owners. He accepted the latter alternative, and an agreement as to price was fixed between him and Fisk; but the other owners in the Company declined to assent to the arrangement made by Fisk, and it fell through. Stokes, thinking to effect some sort of compromise in the matter, sent to Fisk a note, requesting his presence at Delmonico's, thinking that by a conference the difficulty might be settled. Fisk came. On reaching the appointed rendezvous, he made a remark which, at the time, was copied into nearly every newspaper in the Union:

"I thought I could cut nearer a man's heart than any man in New York, but you go plump through it."

This interview promised little result. Of course, the only thing which would satisfy Fisk was Stokes's abdication of the throne of the house of Mansfield. Stokes, satisfied of his own ascendancy in the affections of their mutual inamorata, suggested to Fisk that they leave it to Josie herself to say which she loved best. Fisk jumped at the proposal. He thought that Josie loved him best. The wily Stokes thought, and with good reason, that Josie loved *him* best. So, the two men repaired that night to Josie's house. Josie, like the shrewd financier that she is, refused to decide. She loved Stokes, and why should she not keep him? She liked Fisk's money, and why should she not keep him, too? The conference was a long and stormy one. Of course, Josie did not openly divulge her motives in refusing to decide. She simply maintained a masterly inactivity. And as for Stokes, he knew full well the real status of the case, and was satisfied to be quiescent. It remained for Fisk to do the fighting, and he did it in his characteristic way, and with a degree of manliness which fully exhibited the better side of his nature. He said to Josie:

"It won't do, Josie. You can't run two engines on one track in contrary directions at the same time."

The interview was prolonged into the small hours of the night, and there were tears shed, criminations and recriminations were made, and an angry dispute took place. Fisk was firm. But so was the politic Josie. She refused to decide between them. It was then that Fisk resolved to abandon Josie, and wreak vengeance on his rival.

Pity it is that the infatuated man could not then

> "Remember Milo's end,
> Crushed in the oak he strove to rend."

Stokes was arrested for embezzlement, the charge was dismissed, and Fisk was bitterly chagrined.

Fisk had told Josie that she was the power behind the throne. The meaning, or the application of the term was never explained. It may have signified that Josie knew all of Fisk's secrets in connection with Erie and with the Tammany Ring. At any rate she did know his secrets, and she had divulged them to Stokes. The latter made a claim against Fisk for $200,000, threatening that if the money were not paid, all of Fisk's letters to Josie should be published. Fisk gave $15,000.

Then the heartless Mansfield sued Fisk to recover $50,000, which she claimed to have given to him to invest for her. Then she brought another suit against him for libel. She charged that Fisk had decoyed a servant from her house, and had induced him to make an affidavit, charging, falsely, that she and Stokes had plotted to levy black-mail upon Fisk. The servant's affidavit had been published; hence the suit. Fisk appeared and gave bail, on the 18th of November, 1871. Josie was not present when the case was called, so the Admiral, dressed in his full naval uniform, was obliged to go and return three or four days later. This was on the 25th.

The Mansfield was put upon the stand and subjected to a very severe examination. The scene in the court-room was very exciting. The case was again postponed till January 6th, 1872, and as it was the direct cause of the murder, her evidence is here given nearly in full:

A.—I commenced to fight at about the time the waiter, King, left me. Fisk persecuted me by taking and buying my servants from me.

Q.—Have you personal knowledge of that?

A.—Personally I was not there when he did so. I spoke from my information and belief. Mr. Courtenay, my counsel, wrote the letter to Sweeney. There was not a stenographer at my house more than once taking notes, to the best of my memory.

Mr. Beach.—I see that Mr. Stokes has taken his seat behind me. I would prefer he would leave that position.

Mr. Stokes, who was sitting near the stove, removed to another seat.

A.—I am acquainted with Miss Annie Wood; first knew her in Washington, six years ago; do not recollect meeting her at 19 Brevoort place. I never asked her to introduce me to Mr. Fisk. I did not say that my dress was the best I had in the world, and that I wanted to know Colonel Fisk, as I wanted a living. No appointment was made to meet him. George Butler, the Minister to Egypt, was not there. I was not poor, and therefore could not say I was. I boarded in Lexington avenue, but never met Miss Wood after being introduced to her at her house in Twenty-fourth street. I did not tell Miss Bishop, in Lexington avenue, that Mr. Fisk had taken a fancy for me, but had not done anything for me.

Mr. McKeon objected to this line of examination as irrelevant and unjust. These questions had been suggested for an object.

Mr. Beach admitted that the questions had been suggested to him but not by Mr. Fisk.

Mr. McKeon.—No, but by some one ready to do his dirty work.

Mr. Beach.—I did not come here to throw dirt at my opponents.

Mr. McKeon.—Let the counsel confine himself to relevant matters.

Mr. Beach.—We have a right to show that she wanted to black-mail Mr. Fisk, and that she declared she did not love him, and only wanted his money.

Mr. McKeon.—I see only amatory matters.

Mr. Beach.—Mr. McKeon is suggesting thoughts that occur to himself. (Laughter.)

The Court ruled out this line of examination.

Examination continued.—A.—Miss Wood did not reply to me, "You could have got more out of him if you had been smart." I did not say, "I do not love him, but I will get all the money out of him I can."

Mr. McKeon objected. This was only intended for the newspapers.

Mr. Beach said this was one of the facts going to show the black-mailing.

Ruled out and exception taken.

Mr. Beach under these rules did not wish to pursue an examination which might hurt the feelings of the lady.

Judge Bixby.—I don't see what these questions have to do with the case.

Mrs. Mansfield.—I have never shown a disposition to black-mail Mr. Fisk.

Mr. Beach.—Well, that is for others to judge; but I do not wish to pursue the examination further.

A.—I have met Nelly Pearce in Twenty-fourth street; Mr. Stokes may have been there; we had no conversation about making money out of Mr. Fisk; did not say to her that if she should stick by me, she should have her share; I gave the letters to Mr. Stokes, but not for any black-mailing purpose.

Mrs. Williams was called and examined by Mr. McKeon.

A.—I reside in the same house with Mrs. Mansfield; she is my cousin; King was a waiter man.

Mr. McKeon read King's affidavit, previously published.

A.—No such conversations as those charged in the affidavit took place.

Cross-examined.— A.—I was married in March, 1864, in Boston; took up my residence with my cousin, Mrs. Mansfield, years ago; met Mr. Stokes there two years ago; he came there once in a while; perhaps he came there three or four times a week for a year and a half.

Mr McKeon.—I will put Mr. Stokes on the stand.

A.—He has taken meals there once in a while; three or four times in a month; other persons have dined there; but I don't wish to drag into the case the names of innocent parties. King generally attended at the table. Besides King, there were Mary Gillhally, and Frances, the cook. No conversation took place on the subject of obtaining money from Mr. Fisk; don't think there was ever any allusion made to him at the table or in the presence of King. The difficulties with Mr. Stokes were never alluded to. Her general habits——"

Mr. Beach.—I don't mean her general habits; that would involve an extensive range of inquiry. (Laughter.)

Edward S. Stokes called, and examined by Mr. McKeon.—I reside at the Hoffman House; I know Richard E. King. [His affidavit read.] No such conversation as that alluded to by King ever took place.

Cross-examined.—I am thirty years of age; have resided at the Hoffman House since last July; I have a family; first became acquainted with Mrs. Mansfield in Philadelphia; the meeting was purely accidental; I would rather not say who else was present; first visited Mrs. Mansfield in this city in company with Mr. Fisk; it was about two years ago; I have been in the habit of occasionally visiting her; I may have visited her about ten times during a month; had no stated times of calling on her; have not called upon her every day for the last six months; have taken dinner there; that was the only meal; never went there by appointment.

Mr. Beach.—You knew what the dinner hour was. No doubt she gave elegant dinners. I should like to have been there myself. (Laughter.)

Q.—Have you not threatened to pursue Mr. Fisk?

A.—I have threatened to pursue my law-suit; I have said so, in a legal way, but not physically; I have threatened to expose the way I have been swindled by him, but no other publications; you and I have had some private conversations about settling with him; I have made propositions for an arbitration; have no recollection of making other propositions; I have remarked that I would crush him in a legal way; I said I would lay the papers before the Legislature; I thought that would injure him; Mr. Fisk lived with Mrs. Mansfield, at her house, for a year after I commenced going there; I should think it was more than a year ago; never had anything to do with the domestic department of the house; I did not discharge Steers, the coachman; I did it for Mrs. Mansfield; I know nothing about Mrs. Mansfield's establishment; I paid the coachman with her money; never made any other payments; I have slept in the house a few times, three or four times during two years; I have stayed there all night when it was very stormy; I have often stayed there late in the evening, probably after midnight; sometimes there would be a great many friends in the house; Mrs. Mansfield may have been there alone; Mrs. Williams was generally in the house; I have not spent late hours in the evening alone with Mrs. Mansfield—am positive of that; the acquaintance was an ordinary one between a lady and gentleman.

Mr. Beach.—Did any familiarity take place between you and Mrs. Mansfield inconsistent with your position as the head of a family?

District-Attorney Fellows objected to any evidence that may tend to scandalize the witness.

Mr. Beach.—I am not going to press any question of that character.

Witness.—There was nothing improper between us.

Mr. Beach.—That depends upon opinions. I repeat the question?

Witness.—No, I should say not; I answer the question without any mental evasion.

Mr. Beach.—Is that question answered in reference to your peculiar opinions as to propriety and impropriety?

Witness.—Yes, sir; I have had conversations with King; have talked of my difficulties with Fisk, but never at the table; it was a very unpleasant subject to talk about; have not talked to Mrs. Mansfield about the amount of money Mr. Fisk ought to pay, that I remember; I furnished the money for Mrs. Mansfield's stables; I know of Belle Laude.

## CHAPTER XXXV.

"Spin, spin, Clotho, spin;
Lachesis twist and Atropos sever;
For in the shadow, year out, year in,
The silent headsman waits forever."

AT the conclusion of the examination, Stokes accompanied Mrs. Mansfield to her residence, in Twenty-third street. He was seated with her in the parlor, when the door-bell rang, and a friend entered and told Stokes that he had been indicted by the Grand Jury, and that a bench warrant was out for his arrest. He sprang from his seat with an oath, and hastily donning his hat and overcoat, hurried from the house. He went direct to the Grand Opera House, and inquired for Colonel Fisk. When he was told that the Colonel was not there, he hailed a coupé, and, springing in, slammed the door, and told the driver to drive to the Grand Central Hotel. When he arrived at the hotel, he jumped out of the coupé, and bidding the driver to wait for him, went upstairs, and made a search through the parlors of the house, and was about to descend the stairs, when he encountered Fisk, who was on his way up.

John Chamberlain left Colonel Fisk in the Grand Opera House at half-past three o'clock. The Colonel was in good spirits. As Chamberlain reached Eighth avenue, he noticed Edward S. Stokes looking up at the Opera House out of a coupé which was going up the avenue. Chamberlain then went down to see a friend on Broadway, and while there, was informed—at half-past four o'clock—that Stokes had shot and killed Fisk.

The long and searching cross-examination of Stokes, on the day before, was to be followed by a more humiliating one on Saturday of the next week. Judge Beach was expected to draw out all the facts having relation to his past life; his association with prize-fighters, gamblers, jockeys, and bad women; and his motive in committing the deed of blood was plain. Add to this that he had been summoned to appear before the Providence (R. I.) Trotting Association, to answer to charges of fraud on the turf; and that the Grand Jury had indicted him for the crime of attempting to black-mail James Fisk, and the desperation of the hot-blooded and unscrupulous man may be readily understood.

Stokes, knowing that Fisk was about to visit the Morse family, at the Grand Central Hotel, drove to the private entrance, descended from his carriage, entered the door, and mounted the stairs. This was at four o'clock.

At a quarter past four, Fisk drove up to the same entrance, and stepping out of his carriage, inquired of the door-boy, John Redmond, if Mrs. Morse and her daughters were in. This Mrs. Morse is the widow of the friend of Colonel Fisk, who broke his neck while bathing in Lake Ponchartrain, near New Orleans.

The hall-boy answered that he thought Mrs. Morse and her eldest daughter had gone out, but that the younger Miss Morse was in her grandmother's room. Colonel Fisk requested the boy to show him up, and the two started, Colonel Fisk leading.

At that moment, and before Colonel Fisk had mounted more than two steps, Stokes suddenly made his appearance from some place of concealment, and a shot rang out, which struck Fisk in the abdomen, two inches to the right of the navel and three inches above it, passing downward, backward, and to the left, inflicting a terrible wound. Fisk fell, shouting "Oh!" and immediately scrambled to his feet again, when Stokes again levelled his revolver and fired another shot, the ball passing through and out of Fisk's left arm without touching the bone. Fisk turned to run, but fell a second time and slid down to the bottom of the stairs, where he was picked up by the crowd, who had gathered on hearing the report of the pistol, and carried up-stairs to rooms 214 and 215, where he was laid upon the bed, and the house physicians summoned.

Stokes meantime had passed quietly down-stairs into the office, where he made the remark that a man had been shot down-stairs. The hall-boy said, "Yes, and you are the man that did it." Stokes made no reply, but calmly awaited arrest, word having been sent to the Mercer-street Police-station, whence Captain Burns and officer McCaddon soon arrived and took the murderer into custody. Dr. Tripler was in Fisk's room within a few minutes of the shooting, and probed the wound in the abdomen, without success, for the purpose of finding the ball. He made him as comfortable as possible, and awaited the arrival of the other surgeons, who had been sent for, before proceeding further.

Soon after this Police Surgeon Beach made his appearance, quickly followed by Drs. White, Folsom and Wood. Upon the arrival of Dr. Wood a consultation immediately took place, when it was decided to hold an examination and extract the ball if possible. Jay Gould, James Irving, William M. Tweed, John Chamberlain, Jay Gould's clerk, Mrs. and the two Misses Morse, Colonel Hooper and wife, Colonel Fisk's brother-in-law and sister, and several other relatives were present, having come in response to telegrams stating the Colonel's condition. No one else—not even the reporters—were admitted into the room.

The longest probe in possession of the physicians failed to sound the ragged wound. When the probe was first inserted, Colonel Fisk complained that it hurt him. Previously he did not seem to be in any pain whatever—a bad sign—and chatted gayly with his friends and attendants. He never made any allusion to Stokes, however. The surgeons were obliged to administer chloroform before they could proceed with the examination. While under the influence, Fisk suddenly arose in a sitting position, and they were compelled to jump upon him and hold him down. Very little hemorrhage was found, and it was therefore concluded that none of the large vessels had been penetrated. It was feared, however, that the ball had gone through the liver, and the chances were thought to be against his recovery. It was finally decided that a further consultation would be held at 11 o'clock, when the question would be decided whether it would be safe to perform an operation for the purpose of finding the ball. It was deemed advisable to have Dr. Lewis A. Sayre present, as Colonel Fisk had expressed great anxiety to secure his services. Telegrams and carriages were immediately dispatched in every direction in search of Dr. Sayre, and the other physicians retired to await his arrival.

Colonel Fisk immediately after coming to, noticed that his diamond stud was missing from his shirt. He asked where it was, and on being informed that one of the ladies had found it, said, "All right!" and resumed his former good spirits. About this time—6 o'clock—David Dudley Field, his counsel, arrived, and was at once admitted to an audience. Colonel Fisk greeted him heartily, and expressed a desire to make a will. The veteran lawyer at once set about the necessary preparations, and under the Colonel's dictation drew up the document in legal form. Colonel Fisk could not tell how much his property amounted to, but he devised the whole of it, whatever it might be, to his wife, his father, and his sister. This done, it was thought best to put the Colonel under the influence of morphine, and he was soon in a sound sleep.

Previously, however, officer McCaddon took Stokes up to Fisk's room, and asked him if he would identify him as the man who shot him. Fisk positively identified Stokes as the man who shot him. Stokes said not a word. Officer McCaddon then escorted his prisoner to the Mercer-street Police Station, where he was placed in the Captain's private room. Captain Byrnes, after informing him that he could answer or not as he chose, asked him what he had to say about the shooting. Stokes replied that he had nothing to say, and would say nothing. The Captain then asked his name and address, which he also refused to give. "There is one question I must ask you," said Captain Byrnes. "What did you do with the pistol?" Stokes laughed and declined to tell. The Captain afterward found it under a lounge in one of the parlors of the hotel, where Stokes had evidently thrown it after committing the murder. It is an entirely new revolver, of Colt's latest pattern, a four-shooter, largest size, and carrying a half-ounce ball. Two chambers only had been discharged, which sets at rest the rumors current that three shots had been discharged at Fisk.

Coroner Young was summoned at once, and at half-past six had reached the hotel, where he organized a jury and

HER FATHER'S FATE.

HUSBAND AND WIFE.

proceeded to take Colonel Fisk's ante-mortem statement. This was before the morphine was administered.

## FISK'S ANTE-MORTEM DEPOSITION.

At an inquest in Grand Central Hotel, before Coroner Young and the following-named jurors, Isaac W. England, 141 East Thirty-ninth street; Charles F. Moore, 143 West Twentieth street; W. O. Chapin, 273 Eighth avenue; John L. Hall, 178 Jay street, Brooklyn; Edward C. Morse, Grand Central Hotel; E. T. T. Marsh, 41 West Ninth street, Mr. James Fisk, Jr.'s ante-mortem deposition was taken, as follows:

"James Fisk, Jr., being sworn, says: This afternoon, about half-past four o'clock, I rode up to the Grand Central Hotel. I entered by the private entrance, and when I entered the first door I met the boy, of whom I inquired if Mrs. Morse was in. He told me that Mrs. Morse and her youngest daughter had gone out, but he thought the other daughter was in her grandmother's room. I asked him to go up and tell the daughter that I was there. I came through the other door, and was going up-stairs, and had gone up about two steps when, looking up, I saw Edward S. Stokes at the head of the stairs. As soon as I saw him I noticed he had something in his hand, and a second afterward I saw the flash and heard the report and felt the ball enter my abdomen on the right side. The second shot was fired immediately afterward, which entered my left arm. When I received the first shot I staggered and ran toward the door, but noticing a crowd gathering in front, I ran back on the stairs again. I was then brought up-stairs in the hotel. I saw nothing more of Stokes until he was brought before me

20

by an officer for identification. I fully identified Edward S. Stokes as the person who shot me.

"Signed. JAMES FISK, JR."

John T. Redmond, a door-keeper, the only witness examined, testified as follows:

About 4 P. M., Mr. Stokes arrived at the Grand Central Hotel, and passing through the private entrance, ascended the stairs. Soon after, Mr. Fisk arrived in a coach, and on inquiring of the door-keeper, Redmond, if Mrs. Morse was in, was answered in the negative. He then requested Redmond to see if her daughter was in, and on his consenting they both passed up-stairs, Fisk in advance. When they arrived about half-way up-stairs, a shot was fired, and Mr. Fisk fell on the stairs, crying, "Oh!" Redmond, on looking where the shot came from, saw Stokes at the head of the stairs with a revolver in his hand, and on Fisk rising to his feet shot him again, and Fisk, falling, slid to the bottom of the stairs. Rising to his feet again, he ascended the stairs, where friends assisted him to the reception-room. Stokes then passed into the office, and word was sent to the station.

Captain Burns and Officer McCadden proceeded to the hotel, where they arrested him. Surgeon Beach, being telegraphed for, arrived, and on examining Mr. Fisk's injuries, found him to have received two wounds—one in the right arm, the ball striking just above the elbow, passing inside of the bone, and out at the back of the arm. The other ball entered the abdomen, about three inches above and two inches to the right of the umbilicus, passing downward, and inward, beyond the reach of the longest probe. The wound in the abdomen was a ghastly one.

The jury found the following verdict:

"That the said James Fisk, Jr., received his injuries by a pistol-shot at the hands of Edward S. Stokes, at the Grand Central Hotel, January 6th, 1872."

Coroner Young then arrested the following witnesses of the affray:—Thomas Hart, bell-boy, Grand Central Hotel; Benjamin C. Allen, hackman (drives house stage), Fourth avenue; John T. Redmond, hall-boy, Sixty-second street, near Tenth avenue; and Patrick McDonnell, engineer, Grand Central Hotel. The coroner took the deposition of Redmond, who was just behind Fisk at the time of the shooting, and remanded all four to the Mercer-street Station-house.

The jury were temporarily discharged, to await the result of Col. Fisk's injuries. Coroner Young then visited Stokes in the station-house, but the murderer refused to answer the the most ordinary questions. The coroner thereupon made out a commitment, consigning him to the Tombs without bail. The Hon. John McKeon, of his counsel, had meantime arrived, and cautioned him to say nothing whatever to anybody, in compliance with which caution he declined to avail himself of a formal examination. Soon afterward, the Hon. W. O. Bartlett and Willard Bartlett, Esq., Stokes's other counsel, entered the station-house, and were admitted to an interview with their client and Mr. McKeon. They agreed with the latter in the propriety of refusing to answer all questions.

At 11 o'clock on Sunday morning, January 7, 1872, James Fisk, Jr., breathed his last, surrounded by his wife, mother, father, and a number of friends.

In a few minutes the fact of the decease of the strange character who had within five years risen from poverty to affluence, and had made himself one of the wonders of the age, was known all over the city, and, indeed, all over the world. Thousands of people thronged the pavements and street in front of the hotel, and crowded the corridors and lobbies. Most of these had come, no doubt, to satisfy a morbid curiosity, but there were many lingering around the portals of the house whose feeling at poor Fisk's death was one of unalloyed sorrow.

## CHAPTER XXXVI.

AFTER the body had been prepared for burial, it was taken through the rear end of the hotel, and hastily removed in a hearse to No. 313 West Twenty-third street.

The inquest was held in the court-room of the Special Sessions, in presence of five hundred people. Stokes appeared calm and unmoved. It is needless to say that Helen Josephine Mansfield was not present. The jury was composed of some of the best citizens of New York.

John T. Redmond was the first witness examined. In reply to Coroner Young, he testified as follows:

Q. Where do you live?—A. At No. 62 Tenth avenue.

Q. What is your business?—A. Hall-boy at the Grand Central Hotel.

Q. Were you at the Grand Central Hotel on Saturday last?—A. I was, sir.

Q. What were you doing?—A. Cleaning the window.

Q. What window?—A. The window of the private door.

Q. About what time was that?—A. About 4 o'clock.

Q. Now tell the jury what took place at that time?—A. About 4 o'clock, Mr. Stokes entered; about ten minutes afterward, Mr. Fisk, in a carriage, drove up to the door; I opened the door for him; he then spoke to me, and asked me if Mrs. Morse was in; I told him Mrs. Morse and her eldest daughter were out; he then asked if the other daughter was in; I said I would see; Mr. Fisk then ascended in advance of me; when he had gone up some steps, the first shot was fired, and Mr. Fisk fell down, crying, "Oh!" He then turned round to go up again, when the second shot was fired.

Q. He asked you if Mrs. Morse was in?—A. Yes, sir.

Q. He then asked if the other daughter was in?—A. Yes, sir.

Q. Did you go up-stairs?—A. Yes, sir; Mr. Fisk was in advance of me; after the first shot he fell down, crying, "Oh!"

Q. When Mr. Fisk fell down, what did he do?—A. He got up on his feet.

Q. And after the second shot?—A. He fell down about six steps.

Q. What did Mr. Fisk do then?—A. He got up and walked to the base of the stairs; he turned round and looked up the stairs to see if Mr. Stokes was there or not; he was not, and Mr. Fisk walked up the stairs, and then some ladies were led into the reception-room by some gentlemen.

Q. Well?—A. I saw no more of the parties until Mr. Stokes was recognized by Mr. Fisk.

Q. Where was this?—A. Room No. 213, Grand Central Hotel.

Q. Were you present when he recognized him?—A. I was, sir.

Q. You say you looked up and saw Mr. Stokes?—A. Yes, sir.

Q. At what time?—A. After the first shot was fired.

Q. Where was Mr. Stokes standing?—A. At the head of the stairs, with his left arm on the balustrade.

Q. Did you notice whether Mr. Stokes had anything in his hand?—A. He had.

Q. Did you notice what it was?—A. No, sir.

Q. Did you hear any words?—A. No, sir.

Q. How long was it before Colonel Fisk came that Mr. Stokes arrived?—A. Inside of ten minutes.

Q. Did Mr. Stokes go immediately up-stairs?—A. Yes, sir.

Q. Did he ask any questions as he came in?—A. No, sir; not a word.

Q. You say that Mr. Fisk looked up the stairs to see if Mr. Stokes was there?—A. I did not say that, sir; I looked up the stairs to see if Mr. Stokes was there.

Counsel for the prisoner inquired whether he could not put questions to the witness?

The Coroner stated that all questions so submitted should be put in writing.

Counsel contended that questions could be put, and that the Coroner had discretion to receive or reject them.

The Coroner said the reason he wanted the questions in writing was that they should not be made public by being openly asked in court, as many of such questions might not be entertained. He desired to proceed regularly.

Counsel submitted that it was most important that the public should know what questions were allowed and what were disallowed, in order to restrain the spirit which seemed to have taken possession of the community. They had a right to know whether the examination was conducted as free from a spirit of restraint, as it should be.

Counsel then submitted the following questions in writing:

Q. Had you ever seen Mr. Stokes before?—A. No, sir.

Q. How was Mr. Stokes dressed on that occasion?—A. Dressed as he is now.

Q. You say that this occurrence took place at four o'clock; how do you fix the hour?—A. It was twenty minutes past three when I commenced cleaning the windows, and it was twenty-five or thirty minutes of four when Mr. Stokes came in.

Q. Was there any light in the hall or on the stairway except that from the windows?—A. There was one light at the head of the stairs and one on the left.

Counsel for the prisoner.—Were they burning?

The Coroner.—It must have been burning, or it could not have been a light.

Q. From what direction did Stokes come—up or down the stairway?—A. I don't know, sir.

Q. You did not see him until he entered the hall?—A. No, sir.

Q. Did you notice whether any person had gone up the stairway between the time Fisk and Stokes came?—A. No, sir; I did n't notice.

Q. Did Mr. Stokes go in by the private entrance?—A. Yes, sir.

By a Juror.—Q. How many shots were fired?—A. Two.

Q. Did you hear the shot fired before you heard Mr. Fisk exclaim?—A. The first shot was fired, and after I looked upstairs.

Q. Where was Mr. Stokes?—A. At the head of the stairs.

Q. In what position was he?—A. He was standing near the balustrade, like this. [Witness showed by comparison in what position the accused stood at the time referred to.] He had his left hand on the balustrade.

Q. You observed something in his hand?—A. Yes, sir.

Q. When was that?—A. After the first shot was fired, and before he fired the second shot.

Q. You saw something in his hand?—A. Yes, sir.

Q. Can you tell what he had in his hand?—A. No, sir.

Q. Did you see any light proceed from the article Mr. Stokes had in his hand?—A. Yes, sir.

Q. You say you were present when Mr. Fisk recognized Mr. Stokes?—A. Yes, sir.

Q. What was said?—A. The officer said, "Who caused this?" and Mr. Fisk said, "Mr. Stokes."

Q. Is that all he asked?—A. That's all that was asked in my presence.

A Juror.—Was there any other person standing at the head of the stairway?—A. No, sir.

By Mr. Field.—Did any person come in between the time Stokes entered and Fisk entered?—A. No, sir.

The Coroner.—Was it the same person who entered the hotel that stood at the head of the stairs?—A. Yes, sir.

Q. How long was it before any person came to the rescue?—A. I cannot say.

Q. Did you see any one?—A. I saw several gentlemen going into the reception-room.

Q. Who were those gentlemen?—A. I don't know.

Q. Were they in Mr. Fisk's room afterward?—A. They brought him into the reception-room.

Q. After the first shot was fired you say you saw Stokes

leaning against the balustrade. In what position was his arm having something in the hand?—A. He was like this, (witness showing position,) with the right hand down.

Q. Was he pointing it toward Mr. Fisk?—A. Yes, sir.

Q. After Mr. Fisk was shot, who assisted him to his room?—A. I don't know.

Q. You did n't hear Mr. Fisk say that Mr. Stokes was the man who shot him?—A. No, sir; he only said, "That 's the man."

Q. Were you in the room when Stokes was brought in?—A. Yes, sir.

Q. Were you in the room all the time Mr. Stokes was there?—A. No, sir.

Q. Then Mr. Stokes was still there when you left?—A. Yes, sir.

Q. How long were you in the room?—A. About half a minute; Mr. Crawford called me, saying he wanted me, but he did not say what he wanted me for when I went into the room.

Mr. McKeon here rose and contended that, if questions were submitted to witnesses it was right that the persons asking them should be known, that the proper responsibility should attach to them; if they were Erie Railroad people, let them come on.

The Coroner submitted that he did not recognize the Erie Railroad people in the case. He did not know but the question had been asked by the counsel for the prisoner.

Q. Was there any light in the hall stairway, except what daylight there was?—A. There was a gaslight.

Mr. McKeon insisted that it was proper to know what parties were represented. He would, therefore, ask on whose behalf Mr. Beach, Mr. Fullerton, and Mr. Spencer appeared?

Assistant District-Attorney Sullivan said he did not intend to say anything as representing the District-Attorney, except when called upon by the Court to give advice. If there were any citizens who felt that, this being a public matter, they could throw any light on the investigation, they were certainly at liberty to do so.

Mr. McKeon said he would ask the Coroner whom Mr. Beach represented.

The Coroner said he would put the question in accordance with the requisition.

Mr. Beach said that, like the counsel for the prisoner, he appeared there as a citizen deeply interested in the question. He came there at the suggestion of the surviving relatives of Mr. Fisk—not retained by the Erie Railroad. He came there influenced only by the desire to see the way in which the melancholy occurrence took place.

Counsel for the prisoner replied, and said that, once for all, he wanted to have his position understood. He had come there, not to get up a heat, but to prevent heat getting up. They had only to look at the press of that morning. The public had not got the truth of the case. He did not want the facts to go before the public in a garbled form. They were told in the papers that before thirty days Mr. Stokes would be condemned. Now, he meant to say, and he said it on his own responsibility, knowing what he was saying, that, if the facts were properly developed, in less than thirty days *the public would be strongly in Stokes's favor!* If the facts were properly spread, the sympathy for him would be as great as the feeling was now against him.

Mr. Fullerton said he intended to remain silent. The question put was suggested by himself, in order to elicit the truth of the case. In due time it would appear to be proper.

Mr. McKeon concurred in the opinion, that the public would be as much in favor of Stokes as their feelings were now against him. The people little knew what had been existing in their midst.

By the Coroner.—Had you ever seen Mr. Fisk before that day ?—A. Yes, sir.

Q. You knew him when you saw him ?—A. Yes, sir.

Q. (Submitted.) Will you say no person passed up or down the stairway between the entrance of Mr. Stokes and Mr. Fisk ?—A. There was nobody.

Q. Can you describe the gaslight you saw burning, if any ?—A. The gaslight at the head of the stairs had a single jet, it was turned on full; the other one round to the left was not turned on full; but it was burning. That's all the gas that was there.

Q. What colored pantaloons had Mr. Stokes on.—A. Light.

Q. From which way did Mr. Fisk come—which way were the horses heading ?—A. Toward Bleecker street.

By a Juror.—As the gas was situated, could the burner be seen from the head of the stairs ?—A. Yes, sir.

Q. The object of that light is to light the stairway ? — A. Yes, sir.

Testimony of Thomas Hart. Q. Where do you reside ?—A. Grand Central Hotel.

Q. What is your business ?—A. Door boy.

Q. Were you at the Grand Central Hotel on Saturday afternoon ?—A. Yes, sir.

Q. Did you notice anything unusual on Saturday afternoon ?—A. Yes, sir.

Q. About what hour ?—A. Five minutes to four o'clock.

Q. What were you doing at that time ? — A. Cleaning the globe at the head of the stairs.

By the Coroner.—How far from the head of the stairs?—A. Between five and six feet.

Q. Did you see Mr. Fisk on that day?—A. Yes, sir.

Q. Where was he?—A. He was coming up the stairs.

Q. What stairs?—A. The private stairs.

Q. Where did those stairs lead?—A. To the stairway from Broadway.

Q. Leading to the stairway on which you were standing?—A. Yes, sir.

Q. Was anybody with him?—A. I did not see anybody.

Q. Did you hear him say anything?—A. No, sir.

Q. Did you see anybody else there?—A. Yes, sir.

Q. Who?—A. Mr. Stokes.

Q. Were you acquainted with Colonel Fisk?—A. Yes, sir; I saw him coming in and out.

Q. Were you acquainted with Mr. Stokes?—A. No, sir; I might have seen him passing by.

Q. Where did you see Mr. Stokes?—A. Coming along the hall from the first parlor.

A Juror.—First parlor to the right or to the left as you go up?—A. To the left.

By the Coroner.—Was there anybody with Mr. Stokes?—A. No, sir.

Q. Was Mr. Fisk going up-stairs?—A. When I first saw Mr. Fisk he was going down to the foot of the stairs.

Q. Tell us exactly what occurred—what you saw and what you heard.—A. I was going up the stairs; the other boy was cleaning the window; I looked down and saw Mr. Fisk coming up; my attention was drawn to Mr. Stokes, a kind of stealing along; he acted like a man who had suddenly seen some one; I heard him say, "Come along, I have got you now," or something to that effect.

Q. Can you remember the exact words?—A. "I have got you now," and with that he fired two pistol shots; at that time Mr. Fisk was standing with one foot on the first step and one on the second; Mr. Fisk cried, "Oh, don't!" and the second time he slid down stairs. I saw Mr. Stokes draw his right hand toward his overcoat; Mr. Stokes afterwards said to me, "There's a man shot;" and said I, "You are the man that shot him;" he walked to the first parlor and turned to his left, and made a motion with his hand, as if he was throwing something away; I cannot say what it was; I followed him, and he went into the hall, and going up the centre, he said, "There's somebody shot, go and see him." Patrick McGowan, Benjamin and Patrick Farrell came up; Mr. Powers afterwards came into the hall, and having heard that there was a man shot, said, "Stop that man;" Mr. Stokes was then taken to the bar; Mr. Powers said, "Bring in an officer." That is all I saw or know of the case. Mr. Stokes went up-stairs with an officer, and was identified.

Q. Were you in the room at the time?—A. No, sir; I was not.

Q. Are you positive you cannot mistake as to the two gentlemen, Mr. Fisk and Mr. Stokes?—A. Yes, sir; I am positive.

Q. In what position was Stokes standing?—A. Standing at the head of the stairs.

Q. He had something in his right hand?—A. Yes, sir; but I cannot say what it was. [Witness endeavored to show the position in which Mr. Stokes stood at the head of the stairs.]

A Juror.—What was your relative position to Mr. Stokes? —A. I was about six feet beyond Mr. Stokes.

Another Juror.—Were you standing with your back to him?—A. Looking right at him.

Mr. Field.—How much time elapsed between the first shot and the time you saw Mr. Stokes concealing something in his overcoat?—A. About three seconds.

Q. The two shots were then fired without any interval?—A. Yes.

By another Juror.—Did you see the flash from the pistol?—A. I did not.

Q. Were there banisters on both sides of the stairs?—A. Yes, sir.

Q. Could you see the carriage driving up from the parlor window?—A. Yes, sir.

Mr Field.—Had you passed the parlor door before Mr. Stokes came up?—A. I had not, sir.

Another Juror.—Did you assist Mr. Fisk when he got to the head of the stairs?—A. No, sir; I followed Mr. Stokes.

Q. Did Mr. Stokes have his overcoat buttoned at the time?—A. No, sir.

Q. Was there sufficient gas-light to recognize a person?—A. Yes.

Q. How was the gas-light then?—A. It was not fully turned on.

Q. Does that light throw light upon the stairway?—A. Yes, sir.

Q. Was the light sufficiently bright to recognize a person by his dress?—A. Yes, sir.

By the Coroner.—Are you sure it was five minutes to 4 o'clock when Mr. Fisk entered?—A. Yes, sir.

By a Juror.—How did Mr. Stokes move, did you say?—A. He came along as if he was stealing away; as if somebody was coming.

Q.—Did you judge that by his expression or by his walk? —A. By his walk.

By another Juror.—Did you keep watch on him after he was arrested?—A. Yes, sir.

Q. Was he walking rapidly, or was he walking stealthily? —A. He was stealing along by the wall.

By the Coroner.—Had you seen Mr. Stokes that evening, before you saw him coming up then?—A. No, sir.

Q. Have you had any conversation with him in regard to the testimony you were to give about it?—A. No, sir.

Mr. Field.—Have you been interviewed by any reporter? —A. No, sir. I gave the same testimony at the Fifteenth Precinct, on the ante-mortem examination, as I give here.

By the Coroner.—Have any of the three gentlemen here, Mr. Fullerton, Mr. Spencer, or Mr. Beach, had any conversation with you in regard to the testimony?—A. No, sir.

Q. You don't know whether Mr. Stokes had a cane or not?—A. I did not see, sir.

Q. Do you know a man named Patrick Hart?—A. Yes, sir.

Q. What was his business?—A. He was working in the house, in the employ of the Grand Central Hotel.

Q. Did you see him there at the time of the occurrence? —A. No, sir; I did not.

Q. Do you know Mr. Spencer?—A. No, sir.

Q. Mr. Fullerton?—No, sir.

Q. Mr. Beach?—A. Yes, sir; I know Mr. Beach; I saw him in Troy.

Q. Has he conversed with you about this affair?—A. No, sir; nobody has conversed with me.

Q. Could you have failed to see a cane if Mr. Stokes had one?—A. He might have carried it in his left hand; but I watched his right.

By Mr. Opdyke.—Fisk and Stokes were the only persons there?—A. Yes, sir; except the boy.

By another Juror.—You say you only watched his right hand. Did you suspect there was something wrong by his walk?—A. Yes, sir.

By the Coroner.—Had you ever seen Fisk and Stokes together before?—A. No, sir.

Q. Did you hear any words between Stokes and Fisk?—A. No, sir.

By a Juror.—When he was going to the head of the stairs he made the remark you mentioned?—A. Yes, sir.

By the Coroner.—Could he see any person on the stairs when he began to use those words?—A. Yes, sir.

Q. Did you see any one on the stairs?—A. Nobody but the boy and Mr. Fisk.

Q. Did Stokes make any other remark?—A. No; he did not make any remark until Mr. Fisk was ascending.

Q. How far was Mr. Fisk from Mr. Stokes at the time he made the remark?—A. About six steps.

By a Juror.—How many steps are there?—A. About twenty.

Q. Then there is a landing?—A. Yes, sir.

Q. And he was six steps from the first landing?—A. Yes, sir.

Q. In what position was Mr. Stokes?—A. He kept close to the wall.

Q. How many steps separated them when you heard the first pistol shot?—A. About four.

By another Juror.—Did you notice him fall?—A. I saw him stagger.

By the Coroner.—I understood you to say you expected something wrong when you saw Stokes advancing. If you

THE LUNCH BEFORE THE MURDER.

suspected something wrong why did you not give the alarm? A. I don't know exactly; I thought Mr. Stokes was watching for a lady when I saw him stealing along.

By a Juror.—Did Mr. Stokes walk right up the stairs, or was he crouching along?—A. He was walking along the wall.

Q.—How many shots were fired?—A. Only two.

Q. That you are sure of?—Yes, sir.

Q. Are you positive Mr. Fisk entered the passage-way before Stokes reached the head of the stairs?—A. Yes, sir.

Q. By the time he had his head turned around had Mr. Fisk already entered?—Yes, sir.

By the Coroner.—Do you know that you would be guilty if you did not give the alarm in case you suspected anything wrong?—No, sir; I did not.

Q. Has Mr. Beach been present at any time when you have made any statement in reference to this occurrence?—A. No, sir; I have not seen Mr. Beach before I have seen him here.

By a Juror.—You made no effort to seize Mr. Stokes after he fired?—A. No, I thought to catch him, but he went away too quickly.

By another Juror.—You kept him in view all the time?—A. Yes, sir.

Testimony of John Chamberlain.—Q. Where do you reside?—A. No. 8 West Twenty-fifth street.

Q. What is your business?—A. A speculator.

Q. Were you acquainted with Colonel Fisk?—A. I was, sir.

Q. Did you see him on last Saturday evening?—A. Yes, sir.

Q. Where did you see him?—A. In the Erie Railway office.

Q. At what time did you see him?—A. I went there at two o'clock, and remained there until between three and half-past three; that's about the time; it was not later than that.

Q. Did you leave him at the Erie office?—A. Yes, sir.

Q. Are you acquainted with Mr. Stokes?—A. Yes, sir.

Q. Did you see Mr. Stokes on that day?—A. I did, sir.

Q. Where did you see him?—A. I saw him between three and half-past three, as I drove across Eighth avenue; just as I crossed the track, I saw him sitting on the right in a coupé, with his eyes looking toward the Erie building.

Q. At what time?—A. Near half-past three.

Q. Did you see Mr. Stokes after that day?—No, sir.

Q. Did you see Mr. Fisk?—A. Yes; I saw him when he was dead.

Q. Where was the coupé of Mr. Stokes?—A. He was driving towards the Opera House; I was going the other way; he got so far that he could see the windows of the Erie office; he was sitting close to the right-hand corner; I don't think he saw me.

Q. By a Juror.—Was the carriage in motion?—A. Yes, sir.

By the Coroner.—Where?—A. On Eighth avenue and Twenty-third street,

Q. Do you know anything of the occurrence that took place at the Grand Central?—A. On my way down I stopped at a store, and I think about five or a quarter-past five I heard of the occurrence; I didn't think it was probable, having seen Mr. Fisk so recently before.

Q. How long after you saw Mr. Stokes was it until you heard it?—A. About an hour or an hour and a half.

Q. Was Mr. Fisk's carriage in front of the building when you left?—A. I did not look.

Q. Did Mr. Fisk say anything to you about being threatened?—A. No.

Q. Do you know of any appointment he had to come down to the Grand Central?—A. I do not; when I was at the Erie office somebody called me into Mr. Gould's room; I stayed there ten or fifteen minutes; I did not see the Colonel in his office after that; when I came down Broadway somebody told me Colonel Fisk's carriage had gone down.

Q. Was Mr. Stokes in a private coupé?—A. I think it was a public coupé.

Q. Did you notice how he was dressed?—He had a light overcoat on.

By a Juror.—Did you ever hear Stokes express himself against Fisk?—A. No, sir, I don't think I have.

By Mr. Field.—Do you know whether Mr. Fisk was going armed?—A. I don't know; I have never known him to be armed.

Q. Did you know that Mr. Stokes was in the habit of carrying a pistol?—A. I think he was.

Q. Did you ever see him in the possession of a pistol?—A. I cannot say positively.

Q. What was your reason for saying that he carried a pistol?—A. Only hearing people talking about it.

Q. Has any person ever communicated to you any threats made by Stokes against Fisk?—A. No, sir.

By the Coroner.—Did you notice where Stokes' coupé went?—A. I did not look around, but just as he passed I saw him in the coupé; he was not looking toward me.

Q. Give the time you saw Stokes as near as possible?—A. It was not half-past three, but it was after three o'clock.

Q. Can you tell where Mrs. Mansfield's house is in that street?—Yes, sir.

Q. How near the place was that when you saw Mr. Stokes?—A. About half a block.

Q. How long have you been acquainted with Mr. Stokes?—A. I have known him five or six years, I should judge.

Q. Was Mr. Stokes' coupé going in the direction of Mrs. Mansfield's house?—A. It was.

Testimony of Benjamin Allen.

Q. Where do you live?—A. No. 12 Fourth avenue.

Q. What is your business?—A. I drive a stage for S. R. McClellan.

Q. Were you at the Grand Central Hotel on Saturday evening?—A. Yes, sir; I was there between three and half-past three.

Q. Do you know of any unusual occurrence having taken place?—A. I do, sir.

Q. Then tell the jury all you know about it?—A. I was sitting on the porter's bench; two shots were fired, and some of the porters ran up-stairs; some people said, "Get a doctor, there's a man shot up-stairs;" I heard a hallooing, "Stop that man;" I went through the reading-room and after the man, who went towards the telegraph office; I went to the man saying, "Here, they want you;" he turned right round; he did not say a word; Mr. Powers came up when a crowd gathered round and asked him where the pistol was; the gentleman never said a word; we sat him down on the seat and were holding him when he said, pleasantly, "Let me go and I'll sit still;" so we let him go, and in a minute or two a policeman took him up-stairs; I did n't see any more of it.

Q. Do you see him here now?—Yes, sir.

Q. Point him out. [The witness pointed to Mr. Stokes.]

Q. Had he anything in his hand?—A. He had a cane in his hand; he never said a word to anybody.

By a Juror.—When he passed out toward the barber-shop was he running or walking?—A. He was walking as if he wanted to go, and didn't seem lazy about it.

Q. Was the cane long enough to be used as a walking-stick?—A. There was no head on it, but it was long enough.

Q.—Did you ever see this gentleman before?—A. Never laid my eyes on him before.

Witness then gave evidence as to the time of the occurrence, stating that he judged the hour by the time he was going to leave, which was about four o'clock.

Testimony of Patrick McGowan.—Patrick McGowan, in reply to the Coroner, testified that he resided at the Grand Central Hotel, where he was employed as an engineer. On Saturday evening last I was down in the engine-room, when Mr. Powers rang, and I came up; I walked across toward the office, when I heard the boy say, "You are the man that shot him;" I ran for the man; he was in the reading-room; Mr. Allen and Mr. Powers brought him down as far as the office; I went for an officer, but returned, stating that I could not find one; Mr. Powers said, "There's one passing;" I went out and told the officer to come in, and he did so; that's all I know about it. Witness did not hear the firing; he did not see Colonel Fisk till next day; Hart was the boy that pointed the man out; witness was about forty feet from the engine-room at the time the shots were fired; it was about five minutes to four o'clock.

Testimony of the Hackman.—Lawrence Corr examined.—I live at 322 East Thirty-sixth street.

Q. What is your business?—A. I am a public hackman.

Q. Were you driving your coupé last Saturday?—A. Yes, sir.

Q. Are you acquainted with Mr. Stokes?—A. No, sir.

Q. Do you remember having a fare during that day that wanted to go to the Grand Central Hotel?—A. I remember driving to the Hoffman House.

Q. Did you take Mr. Stokes there?—A. Yes, sir.

Q. Would you know that gentleman if you should see him?—A. Yes, sir. (Witness here identified the accused.)

Q. How long did he remain at the Hoffman House?—A. About ten minutes.

Q. Where did you go again?—A. Down Twenty-third street, between Eighth and Ninth avenues.

Q. Do you know what house?—A. I do not know, sir.

Q. Do you know what number?—A. No, sir; I do not, sir.

Q. When you went down Twenty-third street, between Eighth and Ninth avenues, did you leave him there?—A. No, sir.

Q. How long did you wait for him at any time?—A. I did not wait for him any time; I turned around, drove down Seventh avenue, Fourteenth street into Fifth avenue, to Fourth street and to Broadway, and let the gentleman out.

By a Juror.—What time did you let him out?—A. To the best of my knowledge about 4 o'clock.

Q. Did you notice where he went to?—A. He went up Broadway.

By the Coroner.—Did he make any remark to you that he wanted to go to the Grand Central?—A. I turned around and drove towards the Grand Central.

By Mr. Field.—When he told you between Eighth and Ninth avenues, did he direct you to go to some particular number, or did he only tell you between Eighth and Ninth avenues?—A. I drove him to some number between Eighth and Ninth avenues.

Q. Did you stop on the way?—A. Yes, sir.

Q. Did you go to the house?—A. I did, sir.

Q. Did you pass the Erie building?—A. Yes, sir.

Q. Did you stop there?—A. No, sir; the gentleman did not leave the coupé.

Q. Did you stop anywhere before you got to Fourth street and Broadway?—A. No, sir.

Q. At the house did any person come out?—A. No, sir.

Q. There was no communication between the house and the coupé?—A. No, sir.

Q. Was there any person in the coupé with Mr. Stokes?—A. No, sir.

Q. Did he seem excited when he got into the coupé—A. No, sir; not very much excited.

Q. What did he say when he got out of the coupé?—A. He said nothing.

Q. Did he ask what the price was?—A. No, sir; he handed me my fare and went in an opposite direction.

Q. You saw Mr. Stokes going in the direction opposite to the way you were going; where was that from?—A. The south-west side of Broadway.

Q. Did you notice whether he had a cane?—A. He had.

Q. What time was it when he first engaged you?—A. About three o'clock.

Q. Where did he engage you?—A. Opposite the City Hall; I was standing among the other coaches.

Q. How do you fix the time that you left him at the corner of Broadway and Fourth street?—It was twenty-five minutes past three o'clock when going past the Hoffman House.

Q. How long did you stop at Twenty-third street?—A. Not two minutes.

Q. Did you see Colonel Fisk or his carriage while driving Mr. Stokes?—A. No, sir; I knew Mr. Fisk, but I don't know his carriage. While driving towards Fourth street and Broadway there was no carriage ahead of me.

Q. Was Mr. Stokes's manner more than usually excited? —A. He looked as if he was a bit put out.

Q. How long have you been in the habit of driving Mr. Stokes?—A. I don't know; about twelve months.

Q. Have you ever driven him to Twenty-third street before?—A. No, sir.

Q. Have you ever driven him to the Grand Central before?—A. No, sir.

Mr. David Dows, one of the jurors, here inquired whether they had assembled to try the case or hear the evidence. If they continued to proceed in that manner they would not get through until to-morrow morning. He wanted to know if they were trying the case or hearing the evidence. The Coroner stated that the jury had been empanelled to hear the evidence and to determine the manner in which Colonel Fisk came by his death.

The counsel for the defense, at the conclusion of Corr's testimony, stated that he hoped that no restraint would be placed upon the prisoner's counsel in eliciting testimony for this case, as there was a murderous spirit abroad in the public mind that would have to be put down by calm, reason and a desire on the behalf of the administrators of the law to see justice done to all persons in this unfortunate affair. The Coroner then adjourned the inquest until three o'clock the next afternoon.

## CHAPTER XXXVII.

THE hearing of the evidence was resumed on the afternoon of January 9th in the Court of Special Sessions. The room was crowded to excess, and the interest in the proceedings seemed unabated. The same counsel engaged on the previous day were in attendance. Owing to the absence of some of the jurors, the hearing was considerably delayed, and the Assistant District Attorney suggested the propriety of sending an officer after the absentees.

Patrick Hart examined.—Q. What is your business?—A. Hall boy, sir.

Q. Were you at the Grand Central Hotel on Saturday afternoon?—A. Yes, sir.

Q. Did anything happen there that evening?—A. Yes, sir, the death of Mr. Fisk; that's all I know.

Q. Now, tell us all you know?—A. I know nothing at all about it; I heard a hallooing, and took a man up-stairs; he was asking somebody to come to his aid.

Q. What time was that?—A. Five minutes to four o'clock.

Q. Where did you find Mr. Fisk?—A. Standing right by the door.

Q. At the foot of the stairs?—A. Yes, sir; standing right up.

Q. Did any one send you to him?—A. No, sir; I heard the noise; I heard a man hallooing who wanted somebody to go to him.

Q. Did you help him up?—A. I took him up to the reception room; he walked right up with me.

Q. Did he say anything?—A. He said he felt bad; I took him up-stairs and left him in the room; that's all I know.

Q. Did you ask him what was the matter?—A. I didn't have time; he said he had been shot twice.

Q. Did he say who shot him?—A. No, sir.

Q. When you took him up-stairs what did you do?—A. I left him sitting in the reception-room.

Q. Did you go out immediately?—A. Yes, sir, right away.

Q. What was your business in that part of the hall?—A. I was going up-stairs when I heard the noise; I looked down at the head of the stairs and saw him standing there.

Q. You know nothing more of this affair?—A. Nothing more than that I kept out of the crowd; I picked up a ball and gave it to Mr. Crocker.

Q. What kind of a ball?—A. A cartridge ball.

Q. Do you think you could recognize that ball?—A. Yes, sir; I guess I could.

Q. Is that like the ball (produced)?—A. Yes—no—no, sir; it don't seem to be it.

Q. You are not positive that that is the ball?—A. No, sir.

Q. After you picked up the ball, what did you do with it?—A. I handed it to Mr. Crocker; I never noticed the ball after I picked it up.

Q. Did you tell him where you found it?—A. Yes, sir.

Q. Did you see Colonel Fisk from the time you left him in the reception-room up to the time of his death?—A. I never saw him since.

Q. Did you know Colonel Fisk?—A. Yes; it was easy to know him; I have seen him several times.

Q. Was he a visitor at the hotel?—A. Yes, sir; I saw him out with the regiment.

Q. Are you acquainted with Mr. Stokes? No, sir; I never saw the man in all my life.

Q. And you would not know him if you saw him?—A. No, sir.

By Mr. Field.—What stairs were you coming up at the time?—A. I came up from the office in the middle stairway; I was passing by the hall when I heard the hallooing.

Q. Where had you been three or four minutes preceding the time you started to go up?—A. I came right up; I was not a minute.

Q. But where had you been preceding the time you went up?—A. I was in the office; I had just come from delivering a message, and that's all I know.

Q. Did you examine the ball immediately?—A. No, sir; I hadn't time, there was so much excitement.

Q. What makes you think it was the ball?—A. I don't know.

Q. Then you don't know whether it was the ball or not?—A. Yes, exactly.

Q. What was your reason for saying you didn't think it was the ball?—A. Because I didn't take any notice of it.

Q. You mean to say you know nothing about it?—A. I don't know anything about it.

Q. When did you see Mr. Fisk previous to Saturday last?—A. I haven't seen him for some time.

Q. Cannot you remember when you saw him before last Saturday?—A. I saw him the night of the reception at the Grand Central Hotel, and not since.

Q. How long ago is that?—A. Twenty-fifth of last March.

Q. Who did you see? Who was on the stairway when Mr. Fisk called for assistance?—A. No one that I knew of.

Q. Describe the reception-room.—A. No. 217, a little way up the stairway.

Q. Did you see any pistol in it?—A. No, sir; I saw nothing at all there.

Q. Did you hear that one had been found there?—A. No, sir; I heard nothing about it.

By Mr. Field.—Did you see a pistol in the first parlor?—A. No, sir.

By Mr. Clews.—Who was in the reception-room when you brought Mr. Fisk there?—A. There was a crowd around there.

Q. Where did they come from?—A. They came out of the hall.

Q. Were they boarders?—A. I cannot tell you; I cannot say anything about it; visitors, I suppose.

Q. Was there more than one?—A. Well, I don't know; there was a crowd there.

Q. Were there six persons?—A. Of course, there was; the excitement caused more than that many to be there.

Q. Was there a dozen persons there?—A. I don't know; I believe there was excitement enough to cause that many to be there.

By Mr. Clews.—Would you recognize any one that was there?—A. I knew Mr. Haskins; he spoke to me, and sent me to the hall to get a key.

Q. Who is Mr. Haskins?—A. Book-keeper in the house.

Q. Did you leave Mr. Fisk with Mr. Haskins?—A. No, sir.

Q. Who then?—A. I cannot tell you; I left him on the sofa.

Q. You could not have left him alone?—A. There was a crowd around him; he didn't talk to me; I tell you they were all strangers to me.

By the Coroner.—Was there a great deal of excitement in the hotel at the time?—A. Not at the time.

Q. Well, how long afterwards?—A. About half an hour.

Q. How long have you been employed in the hotel?—A. Since it opened.

Q. Since October?—A. It was opened in August, I guess.

By Mr. Clews.—Did Mr. Fisk make any remark in the reception-room?—A. He made the remark that he was shot.

Q. Did he say so to you?—A. No, sir; he mentioned nobody's name.

Q. What did he say to you, or did he address his remark to any one present?—A. Mr. Haskins was by.

Q. Did anybody speak to him?—A. The crowd asked him what the matter was.

By the Coroner.—Did he mention where he was shot?—A. He said he had been shot twice, and pointed to the wounds. (Witness pointed to his abdomen.)

By Mr. Clews.—That's all he said?—A. I didn't hear him say anything more.

By Mr. Clews.—Did anybody ask Mr. Fisk who had shot him?—A. No, sir.

By the Coroner.—Did anybody speak to him?—A. I told you twice they did.

Q. What did they say?—A. He said he had been shot twice, and pointed to the places.

Q. Are you positive he mentioned no names?—A. No, sir; he mentioned no name while I was there.

By Mr. Clews.—Where did you go after that?—A. I went to attend to my business.

Q. You did not see Mr. Stokes after that?—A. Never saw the man in all my life, and wouldn't know him if I saw him.

By the Coroner.—You say you picked up the ball on the

stairs?—A. I picked up the ball and walked away with it. (Witness here examined the ball.)

Q. You cannot describe the ball you picked up?—A. I cannot.

Q. Was it a leaden bullet?—A. It looked very much like this ball (examining it), but I cannot tell.

Counsel for the prisoner insisted that the witness should be more closely interrogated as to the ball.

By the Coroner.—What is the reason you cannot describe the ball you picked up?—A. I did not notice it when I picked it up; I walked up-stairs with it and handed it to Mr. Crocker.

Q. Did you look at it?—A. No more than a look.

Q. From the time you picked it up until you handed it to Mr. Crocker, did you look at it?—A. No, sir.

Q. Then it is impossible for you to describe the ball?—A. It is.

By Mr. Field.—Was it a round ball?—A. I tell you I can't tell you; I can't describe it.

Q. Did you carry it in your hand?—A. Yes; I carried it in my hand and handed it to Mr. Crocker on the stairs.

Q. Do you know whether it was lead or iron?—A. I know it was lead; they are all made of lead, I guess. (Laughter.)

By the Coroner.—State precisely where you picked up the ball.—A. Right opposite the second door.

Q. On the stairs?—A. At the foot of the first stair.

Q. You have looked at the ball?—A. I have not, sir.

Q. You have just looked at here?—A. Oh, just now; but I can't tell; I tell you I can't tell you anything about it.

By Mr. Field.—Was there any blood on the ball when you picked it up?—A. I don't know.

Q. Had you any blood on your hand?—A. No.

Q. Was there any blood on the stairs?—A. None at all, sir.

Q. Did you see any on the carpet?—A. No, sir.

Q. Did you see any blood on Mr. Fisk's person?—A. I saw none on any part of him at all; I often saw blood, but I didn't see any there.

By the Coroner.—Who was the first person you recognized after Mr. Fisk said he had been shot twice?—A. I saw nobody around that I could recognize.

Q. Who was the last person you remember after you heard Mr. Fisk was shot?—A. I saw Mr. Powers.

Q. Now who was the last person you remember before you heard the shot?—A. I never heard the shooting; I told you I heard a noise, a kind of hallooing.

Q. You didn't hear any shooting?—A. I didn't hear any shooting, sir.

Q. Who was the last person you remember seeing before you heard the call?—A. I cannot tell; you could not tell in a hotel where there are so many people running up and down stairs.

Q. Are you well acquainted with the attachés working in the hotel?—A. Yes, sir.

Q. Do you remember seeing them there?—A. None of them that I can tell.

By Mr. Field.—Were you going up-stairs in answer to a bell?—A. No, sir; I had an order.

Q. Was that by a guest in the house?—A. Yes, up in his room; first part of the fourth floor.

Q. What were you doing there?—A. I was going there on business.

Q. What business?—A. Waiting on a guest in the house.

Q. You went up in answer to an order from some one?—A. Yes.

Q. Whose order was it?—A. I don't know the gentleman; he was a stranger to me.

Q. Where was that whence the order came?—A. Well, the number is 474, if you want to find him out.

Q. Where were you when you received the order to go up-stairs?—A. I was in the room; I went out, and when I returned I got the order.

Q. Then it was just when you returned that you heard the noise?—A. I heard the call for assistance and looked up the stairs.

Q. What is the distance to the head of the stairs?—A. I never have measured it; I cannot tell what it is.

Q. Is it ten or fifty feet?—A. Well, it is a large house, and you have to round it. (Laughter).

The Coroner.—Officer, preserve order. This is no place for levity, and I hope the gentlemen will not indulge in any.

By the Coroner.—Do you know how many steps there are?—A. I never measured it.

Q. You have gone up and down a good many times?—A. Yes; a good many times.

Q. How long would it take you to go up?—A. Well, if I liked to loaf it would take a good while.

Q. Would it take you five minutes?—A. Oh, no; one flight of stairs would take me about a minute, I guess.

By Mr. Clews.—Have you talked with any one about this occurrence?—A. No; I didn't talk to anybody.

Q. Nobody came to see you about it?—A. No, sir.

By Mr. Field.—Have you ever talked about it?—A. Yes, I have, but to nobody except the clerks in the office.

By the Coroner.—Did you pick up the ball at the foot of the stairs?—A. Yes, at the foot of the middle stairs; I told you that four or five times.

STOKES LYING IN WAIT FOR COL. FISK.

Q. To whom did you give the ball?—A. To Mr. Crocker at the head of the stairs.

Q. How did you know it was a ball?—A. It looked like a ball when I picked it up.

Q. You say you cannot tell whether it was round or not?—A. I cannot tell; I never noticed the ball.

Q. Did you think it was square?—A. I cannot tell you.

Mr. Opdyke, one of the jurors, here suggested that the jury had obtained enough information from the witness.

By a Juror.—I just wish to ask one question—Who is Mr. Crocker?—A. A clerk in the house.

As the witness was leaving the stand the Coroner ordered an officer to detain him in court.

Captain Byrne was next sworn, and said:—I am attached to the Fifteenth Precinct Police as Captain; I first heard of the shooting about ten minutes after four o'clock; I was going up the stoop of the station-house; I was told by one of my sergeants; I went to the Grand Central Hotel, and went to the room where Colonel Fisk was lying; it is in the north-east corner of the building; I was given a ball at the Grand Central Hotel. (Ball handed to witness.) This is the same ball given to me by one of the attachés of the hotel at the foot of the private stairs; Mr. Crocker gave it to me; he told me a man named Hart found it; there was a pistol placed in my possession by Mr. Crocker; he told me that it was given to him by one of the ladies; I went to see the lady, and she said she found it lying on the sofa, on one corner of it; it was in the parlor, on the Broadway side; I searched the barber shop, the reading-room and the writing-room; Mr. Crocker was also searching for the pistol; I arrested Mr. Stokes in the reading-room, about half an hour after Mr. Crocker told me that the pistol had been found.

By Mr. Field.—The sofa was near to the door; the entrance to this parlor was on a line to the main hall.

By the Coroner.—The pistol produced is the same; two balls were discharged out of it; it is now loaded.

The witness here held the pistol in his hand, with barrel pointing toward the ceiling. He turned it about in his hand slightly careless. While doing so the Coroner said so him, "Will you discharge one of those barrels (Sensation in Court)—and let us see the ball?"

Mr. McKeon.—I object to that, Mr. Coroner. It was my practice to do differently in such cases. Let the pistol, with the balls, as they are now, be enclosed in paper and your seal affixed to it, and let it be handed over to the District Attorney.

The Coroner.—That course shall be pursued, sir.

Counsel for the Prisoner.—That had better be done, sir, for we have a Grand Jury now that will indict without evidence.

Witness resumed.—I was not present when Mr. Stokes was arrested; Officer McKeddon arrested him.

By Mr. Clews.—Mr. Crocker examined the pistol; he gave me all the information he could, and manifested no more desire to do this than a person in such circumstances would manifest; any person passing the entrance of the parlor and going to the main stair-way could readily fling anything out of his hand into the parlor; I have not heard of any reports of a pistol being found in 217, where Mr. Fisk was taken.

By Mr. Field.—Mr. Crocker did not take any more interest in the matter than a person in his position under the circumstances would be expected to show.

Mr. McKeon asked Captain Byrne to send to the prisoner a cane, which he (McKeon) thought might have been left at the station-house.

Dr. Thomas H. Tripler testified:—I reside at the Grand Central Hotel; I saw Colonel Fisk last Saturday afternoon; as near as I remember, it was twenty minutes after four o'clock; I saw him in the room 214; it is located to the north and east of the ladies' entrance fronting on Broadway; Mr. Fisk looked very pale and was agitated; I went there to offer professional aid; Colonel Fisk told me he was shot; I heard him say later that it was Mr. Stokes who shot him; Colonel Fisk was standing with his clothes on in the parlor when I saw him first; I remained with him until half-past one o'clock in the morning, and then left for a few moments; I was present when he died, at five minutes to eleven on Sunday morning.

By Mr. Field.—I assisted Mr. Fisk to undress; I did examine his clothing; there was no weapon found upon him; there were rumors that Mr. Fisk did carry a weapon—that he was armed at the time the accident occurred; I think I heard it in the hotel; if there had been a pistol around his waist I could not have failed to see it.

Q. Was the wound in the abdomen a fatal one, and, under all circumstances, must Mr. Fisk have died from the effects thereof?—A. In my opinion it was.

Q. Do you think that the probing of the wound had anything to do in either causing or accelerating death?—A. I do not.

Q. What do you think caused death?—A. The shock, causing peritonitis and the wounding of the intestines; there were four holes in the intestines, and I think this accelerated the death.

By the Coroner.—Did you probe Colonel Fisk's wound?—A. I did, sir.

By Mr. Field.—Was Mr. Fisk perfectly sensible when

you were probing the wound?—A. Yes; it was necessary to give him chloroform, but when Dr. James Wood probed the wound he showed that he was sensible of pain; it would not be excessively painful.

Q. Was Mr. Fisk sensible at the time of death?—A. No, sir.

Q. How long had he been sensible?—A. Until four o'clock in the morning.

Q. Then it is your opinion that after Colonel Fisk received the wound in the abdomen, under no circumstances could he possibly recover?—A. That is my opinion, sir; I think he died of the wound, and nothing else.

Q. Don't you consider that the length of time Mr. Fisk survived showed great vitality?—A. I think it did show great vitality.

Q. Would an ordinary person have survived so long?—A. It is impossible to say.

Q. If he had only received the wound in the arm, would he have recovered from that?—A. Yes, sir.

By Mr. Field.—If you had been successful in extracting the ball, would it have made any difference as to the result?—A. None whatever, in my opinion.

By the Coroner.—Have you seen any pistol that was said to be found on Colonel Fisk?—A. No, sir.

Q. Did Mr. Fisk complain that the probing of the wound had hurt him?—A. He complained a little of the wound in his arm—more than of the wound in the abdomen.

Q. At what time did the physicians regard the case as absolutely hopeless?—A. At eight o'clock in the morning.

Counsel for the defence suggested that witness should give a "square" answer as to the probing. Witness said that when the wounds were probed Colonel Fisk winced a little.

Q. He did not tell you that he was shot by Mr. Stokes?—A. He did not relate any of the circumstances.

Coroner Young here stated that he would rest the evidence at this point, as far as the witnesses were concerned. He wished to make a statement, however, which was, that between six and seven o'clock on Saturday evening he was sent for to take the dying statement of Colonel Fisk. He was not quite certain as to the time, but he remembered stopping at the Fifteenth Precinct Station-house about that time. When he reached the room of Colonel Fisk he was asked to take the ante-mortem statement of the Colonel, and he proposed now to read it to the jury,

Counsel for the prisoner objected to this being done, and, appealing to District-Attorney Sullivan, said that gentleman knew that it was not right that it should be read.

District-Attorney Sullivan said that, on the contrary, he knew that the Coroner was doing perfectly right, and had advised him to read it.

The Coroner said he had had a number of cases of homicide since he had been Coroner, and he had never heard an objection before to the reading of ante-mortem statements.

The ante-mortem statement and the verdict of the jury were then read by Dr. Marsh.

Dr. Marsh read the post-mortem. In reply to questions put by the Coroner and jury, Dr. Marsh confirmed the previous medical testimony as to the certainty of death and the probing of the wound.

Counsel for the defence protested at some length against the case being submitted to the jury without evidence as to the stripping of the body and the probing of the wounds.

The Coroner said he had fully decided to close the case there, and believed that he had fully performed his duty, which was not to try the case, but to find how Colonel Fisk came by his death.

The Coroner then proceeded to address the jury. He said:

"GENTLEMEN OF THE JURY,—I feel that it is unnecessary for me to refer you to the evidence that has been offered. You have listened attentively, and the positions you occupy in society, your intelligence, your reputation as good citizens, preclude the necessity of my advising you upon any point. All that I ask of you is to render a verdict in accordance with the testimony. That is all. I have no particular point to address you upon; but I would ask you only to commence with first witnesses and review the line of testimony to the close of the examination, to the end of the post-mortem. I do not know that I should say one more word to you. Gentlemen, I assure you that in the examination of the witnesses it has not been my desire to ask one improper question. I have not been animated with a prejudice against any man. I have no personal feeling. I have endeavored to discharge my duty, as I have already said to the counsel, conscientiously, fearlessly, and as I shall always continue to discharge it. With these few remarks, I leave the case in your hands. You will please retire and agree upon a verdict, if you can do so."

The Counsel for the prisoner.—Against that we protest and except.

Coroner.—With all due deference to the gentleman I decline to take any protest.

Counsel for the prisoner.—Well, we can make you hereafter.

## CHAPTER XXXVIII.

At a quarter to five o'clock the jury retired to deliberate upon the verdict. It was thought that their absence would be brief, having merely to inquire into the cause of death. Contrary to general expectation, however, they remained out nearly three hours, and, meanwhile, the crowded court became gradually thinned.

At twenty minutes to eight o'clock, the jury returned into court and resumed their seats.

The Coroner asked whether the jury had agreed to their verdict.

Mr. Opdyke replied in the affirmative.

The Coroner.—What do you find, gentlemen?

Mr. Opdyke.—Shall I read it?

The Coroner.—If you please.

### THE VERDICT.

Mr. Opdyke then read the following verdict:

"The jury find, from the testimony submitted on this inquest, that the deceased, James Fisk, Jr., came to his death at the Grand Central Hotel, in the city of New York, on the 7th day of January, 1872, at or about ten minutes before eleven o'clock, A. M., in consequence of a wound or wounds inflicted by a ball or balls from a pistol in the hands of Edward S. Stokes, discharged by him in a deliberate manner at the person of said Fisk, at the Grand Central Hotel aforesaid, on the sixth day of January, 1872, at or about four o'clock, P. M.

"Jesse Hoyt, Henry Clews, John J. Gorman, William H. Locke, Alex. McKenzie, George Opdyke, A. V. Stout, David Dows, M. B. Field, Lowell Lincoln, James R. Edwards, William M. Bliss.

"NEW YORK, *January* 9, 1872."

The announcement of the verdict created very little sensation in court; nor was any change noticed in the demeanor of the accused from that which he had previously borne during the trial.

The Coroner then requested Mr. Stokes to step up to the witness stand. Accompanied by his counsel, the accused did as requested. The Coroner continued: "Mr. Stokes, the jury having rendered their verdict, which you have heard, it now becomes my duty to ask you certain questions. You are at liberty to answer them or not, as you please."

Q. What is your name?—A. Edward S. Stokes.

Q. How old are you, Mr. Stokes?—A. I am thirty years of age.

Q. Where were you born?—A. I was born in Philadelphia.

Q. Where do you reside?—A. I reside at the Hoffman House, in the city of New York.

Q. Have you anything to say—and if so, what—relative to the charge preferred against you?

Counsel (answering for the prisoner).—By the advice of my counsel, I decline to answer any further questions at this time. I am in their hands, as my counsel, and am governed by their advice.

The prisoner then signed his name to the above in a bold hand, without any symptoms of nervousness.

The Coroner.—Mr. Stokes, the jury having rendered a verdict that James Fisk, Jr., came to his death by a pistol-shot wound at your hands, I shall commit you to the Tombs, to await the action of the Grand Jury.

The Coroner then turned to the jury present, and, having tendered his thanks for their attendance, discharged them.

Counsel for the prisoner, in a lengthened address, drew the attention of the Coroner to the statutes relative to the return of the proceedings of the Court. He dilated upon the crime that had been committed, and alluded to the fact that the public mind was unduly excited. In order to secure justice to the prisoner, he contended that it was the duty of the Coroner to comply with the terms of the statute, which set forth that the testimony of the Coroner's jury should be reduced to writing by the Coroner, and should be returned to the next Criminal Court that should be held in the county within thirty days. Counsel cited the case of McFarland to show that had he been tried within thirty days after the coroner's verdict, he must have been convicted. But when sober second thought came upon the public mind, always sure to follow in a case of that kind, he was not only acquitted by the public so incensed against him, but almost received the thanks of the jury for the act originally committed. He submitted that the prisoner was entitled to what was known in criminal proceedings as a continuance, owing to the prejudice now existing in the public mind. Under the circumstances, he trusted the Coroner would not return the proceedings until the time specified by law, and until such time as the excitement incident to the case had died away.

Mr. McKeon followed on the same side, contending that it was the duty of the Coroner to withhold the proceedings until the full extent of time required by law.

Assistant District-Attorney Sullivan intimated that the usual practice was, that where recognizances were taken by a committing magistrate and called for an appearance at the next term, it meant the term then pending. It was the well-settled practice to regard as the next term any part of the then current or unexpired term.

After some further discussion, the counsel for the prisoner read the words of the statute:

"The testimony of witnesses examined before a coroner's jury shall be reduced to writing by the coroner, and shall be returned by him, together with inquisition of the jury and all recognizances and examinations taken by such coroner, to the next criminal court of record that shall be held in the county."

Counsel then commented on the fact that the jury had not rendered a verdict that showed the prisoner had committed wilful murder, in the legal acceptation of the term, and that, although it was set forth that the shooting had been done deliberately, many a highwayman had been shot with deliberation. He also adverted to the fact that two of the witnesses produced on the day preceding had contradicted themselves. The second one, he contended, had committed perjury, while the third witness wiped out the testimony of both.

The Coroner, at the conclusion of the counsel's observations, stated that he had listened attentively to the suggestions which had been made, and would give them a careful consideration.

The accused was then removed to his cell, and the inquest was brought to a close.

On the same day the body lay at Colonel Fisk's residence in Twenty-third street, and was viewed by the friends. It was then taken in a rosewood casket to the Grand Opera House, where it was placed on a splendid catafalque. Thousands of people, numbers of whom were ladies, came in to look for the last time upon the face of the man who had for so long a time been the talk of the wonder-loving world.

The scenes at the side of the corpse were very affecting. Poor women whom Fisk had aided, bent over and kissed the cold lips, and men stood by with tears of genuine sorrow in their eyes. After the reading of the funeral service by Chaplain Flagg, of the Ninth, Mrs. Fisk and Mrs. Hooker entered the room and kissed the dead husband and brother. Then the casket was closed.

At ten the next morning the final preparations for the military funeral were made, and at noon the column was set in motion to the sound of muffled drums. Then the band played a solemn dirge, and the sad procession marched through the crowded streets to the New York and New Haven depot, where the casket was placed in the special funeral car, and the train started.

The little town of Brattleboro' was reached at half-past 12 at night. At every station along the route hundreds and thousands of people had collected to view the funeral train, with its locomotive and cars draped in the deepest mourning. At Brattleboro' the whole population were at the station, waiting to receive the remains of their deceased fellow-citizen and friend.

All that was mortal of Colonel Fisk was given back to earth on the next day, after impressive funeral services, both at the church and at the grave in the little cemetery. The last prayer was offered up, the last military honors were paid, the grave was closed, and the sorrowing multitude turned away.

The funeral sermon preached in the church by Chaplain Flagg was listened to with deep attention. The speaker was often interrupted by the sobs of his audience, and was at times himself almost too much moved to proceed. He said:

"Beloved: The conventional services of the Church have been performed over the remains of our dead friend. In spite of a recent indisposition, I have traveled into these far-away mountains to attempt to do justice to the Commander of the regiment of which I have the honor of being Chaplain. I did not travel so far either to give vent to the promptings of malice or pronounce a fulsome panegyric, but simply as an officer of the regiment commanded by him who raised it from a comparatively insignificant position to a peerage with the best and most efficient militia organization in the United States. I have known him only a short time, but in that short time I found him to be my friend, and have been led hither because I found in him that which attracts us to a man as goodness and truth always attract us. He who lies before you was no common man. He was not like the mass. As to his faults, I will not speak of them. A censorious world will do them ample justice. He had enough denunciations from those who never looked into his merits. It is but natural that a man of his strong characteristics should have had strong faults as well as strong virtues. Were he a person of mediocrity, he would probably have passed through the world without censure. When his good qualities are balanced against his bad, I venture to say that we will have at least an equipoise; we will find them at least up to the average. I will speak of those virtues which were most manifest in him. He was magnanimous by nature, and never consulted his means when he wished to do a good deed. Rich men oppress the community both privately and publicly. There is a crabbed meanness in rich men generally which is contemptible. Colonel Fisk was generous to a fault. He once remarked to me: 'I care little for money for its own sake. I wish for money in order to be enabled to do good to others.' He gave his money to the poor, to such as truly needed it. It was a noble feature of his character that he gave not to those who had, but to those who had not.

"When lying a corpse in the Grand Central Hotel, a lady holding a child by the hand attempted to force her way into his room. 'For six months,' said she, 'he has kept me and my child from starvation, and I have never seen his face. I want to look upon my noble benefactor.'

"Another peculiarity was his independence and manliness of character. Colonel Fisk knew how to say I will and I will not. He always expressed the sentiment of his soul in spite of all opposition. This is a virtue which cannot be too highly commended, There was nothing of the hypocrite about Colonel Fisk. Whatever he did was open and above board. I believe that he did everything, whether good or bad, from conviction. Those things which shock public sentiment are not to be commended, but conscientiousness is. We have a wide testimony to his work. New York is giving such testimony at this moment. No matter what the maledictions of the press may have been, and no matter what those persons whom he has beaten at their own game may have said against him, they have all had the manliness to come forth in the last few days and acknowledge his virtues.

"The crowded hotel, the immense and respectable assembly in the streets, their sad faces as we passed in procession to the depot, show that where true virtue exists, the world is ever ready to acknowledge it. We have every reason to believe that he gave testimony to his faith in Jesus. We may hope that, although not professing that name during life, his prayer has been heard and accepted at the throne of the Almighty.

"As for you who have met with so deep an affliction, there is only one consolation I can offer you, and that lies in your own consciousness; you know what he has done for you, you know his goodness, his excellence and his virtues, and the memory of this will ever be gratifying to you—will ever be a power to banish sorrow from your hearts. It is fitting that his body should be returned to the scenes of his childhood, that he should come back in death to his native hills. It is fitting that the last resting-place of citizen soldiers should be among those scenes where every footstep brings a reminder of the glorious deeds of our revolutionary forefathers. It is fitting that a man of such indomitable courage should lie in a spot which has been prolific of so much heroism, and which has furnished the world with so many courageous men.

"In conclusion, let me warn you that we tread in uncertain places. You do not know who may be the next to fall. Be you ready, soldiers of the Ninth. You especially have reason to remember the terrible time which called your swords from your scabbards so recently. This funeral is but a sequel to the funerals which followed the 12th of July. You may again be called upon to fight, perhaps to fall, in defense of your country's honor. God knows whether in the uncertain future some of you may not be reserved for a similar fate. Heed, then, I beg of you, the voice which proceeds from those mute lips. Do your duty to your regiment, to your God, to yourselves, and to your country."

## CHAPTER XXXIX.

THE letters written by Colonel Fisk to Miss Mansfield are a strange compound of love, jollity, and sorrow. Some are flippant in the extreme, many relate to money matters only, and not a few breathe a spirit of real manhood. Some of those last written, especially those written after his separation from Miss Mansfield, are replete with genuine sorrow, and, more than that, a total absence of the reckless indifference which was supposed to be the man's dominant characteristic. He even speaks tenderly of the rival who supplanted him in the affections of Josie, and not only tells her "Take him," but says that no harm shall come to him.

The letters were the source of much angry litigation before they were printed, and their publication was enjoined by the courts.

Fisk's first letter was written on a visiting card. This was when the lady bore the name of Lawlor, and before she became publicly identified with Fisk:

"MRS. JOSIE LAWLOR, 42 Lexington avenue: Come. Will you come over with Fred and dine with me? If your friends are there bring them along. Yours truly, J. F., JR.

"Have not heard from you as promised."

On the back of the card was the following:

"Come. Fred is at the door. My room, eight o'clock. After many good looks I found Mr. Chamberlain. The understanding is now that yourself and Miss Land are to go with me, say at half-past nine o'clock, and the above gentleman to come at eleven o'clock, as he has some matters to attend to which will take him until that time. Answer this if you will be ready by half-past-nine o'clock.

"Yours truly, JAMES FISK, JR."

One day in January, 1868, Mrs. Mansfield visited the Erie offices. She must have made a scene, for here is what Fisk wrote the day following:

"Strange you should make my office or the vicinity the scene for a 'personal.' You must be aware that harm came to me in such foolish vanity, and those that could do it care but little for the interest of the writer of this.

"Yours truly, JAMES FISK, JR."

Later in the same month Fisk felt better toward his inamorata, and sent this, the following curious little note. From the fact that Fisk addressed her by a pet name, it would appear that Miss Mansfield had, in a very few days, succeeded in accomplishing a wonderful change in his feelings toward her:

"5th AVE. H.

"DOLLY: Enclosed find money. Bully morning for a funeral! J. F., JR."

Mark his growing infatuation:

"DEAR JOSIE: Get ready and come to the Twenty-third street entrance of the hotel and take me down-town, and then you can come back and get the girls for the Fulton dinner to-day. Yours truly, SARDINES."

Here is a soberer one. Perhaps she had slighted him:

"MRS. MANSFIELD: The sleigh will call here for you at two P.M. Yours, J. FISK, per J. C."

His wife must have demanded his attention when the following note was written:

"My people are partaking of New York, in the shape of

THE NEGRO SERVANT'S TRIBUTE OF FLOWERS.

'White Fawn,' and two or three other different matters. I may not be able to see you again to-night. If not, will take breakfast with you—the best I could do. Yours truly, JAMES.

"*February* 5, 1868."

Which he liked best is shown by his note the next morning:

"DEAR DOLLY: Get right up now, and I will be down to take breakfast with you in about thirty minutes. We will take breakfast in the main dining-room down-stairs.

"Yours truly, JAMES FISK, JR.

"Wednesday Morning, *February* 6."

February 22, 1868, Fisk sent Josie some money and a note, saying:

"Have the kindness to acknowledge. Yours truly."

February 26, Fisk took Josie to the Opera:

"DEAR JOSIE: I have got some matters to arrange, and cannot call for you until it is about time to go. I will be there twenty minutes before eight. Be ready. Yours truly,

"*February* 26, 1868. JAMES."

There is a tinge of grossness coupled with his love, as evinced in his letter on the day following:

"DOLLY: Enclosed find $50. Sleep, Dolly, all the sleep you can to-day—every little bit! Sleep, Dolly! I feel as three cents worth of clams would help me some.

"Yours truly, J. F., JR."

Again separated from her by his family:

"MONDAY MORNING.

"I am going to the San Francisco Minstrels with my family. If Mr. L. was here I should ask him to take you. Shall see you to-morrow evening. Yours truly, J. F., Jr."

He has vexed her—he sends more money:

"DOLLY: Enclosed find ——. I am wrong, but I am bothered. It will come right. When I don't come don't wait. You shall not be placed as you was to-night again.

"Wednesday evening. Yours truly, JAMES FISK, JR."

Using her smiles to aid a railroad scheme:

"187 WEST ST., TUESDAY *Oct.* 13, 1868.

"MY DEAR JOSIE: James McHenry, the partner of Sir Morton Peto, the largest railway builder in the world, Mr. Tweed and Mr. Lane will dine with us at half-past six o'clock. I want you to provide as nice a dinner as possible. Everything went on elegantly. We are *all* safe. Will see you at six o'clock. JAMES FISK, JR."

A lapse of nine months intervenes, during which it would appear that Fisk had gone to live with Mrs. Mansfield:

"MONDAY, AUG. 2, 1869.

"DEAR JOSIE: Send my valise, with two shirts, good collars, vest, handkerchiefs, black velvet coat, nice vest, patent leather shoes, light pants. I am going to Long Branch to see about the celery. Enclosed find $25. Be back in the morning. J. F., Jr."

Still more money, and he drops the formal signature appended to his previous letters:

"ST. JAMES HOTEL, SUNDAY, *Oct.* 18, 1869.

"DEAR JOSIE: Enclosed you will find $143.

"Yours truly, JAMES."

This letter has a penitent and beseeching tone; evidently there had been a little quarrel:

"FEBRUARY 10, 1870.

"MY DEAR DOLLY: Will you see me this morning? If so, what hour? Yours truly, ever, JAMES."

Still more money:

"10TH OF MARCH.

"DEAR DOLLY: Enclosed find $75, which you need; do not wait dinner for me to-night, I cannot come.

"Yours truly, ever, JAMES."

Money again:

"MY DEAR JOSIE: Enclosed find your request. I will send to the Fifth Avenue for the things. I cannot go to the house as much as I would like to. Yours, JAMES.

"*May* 6, 1870."

Here is a letter relative to a colored man whom Fisk sent to Josie for a servant:

"COMPTROLLER'S OFFICE, ERIE RAILWAY COMPANY,
"NEW YORK, *May*, 1870.

"DOLLY: What do you think of this man? I told him you would talk to him, and then tell him to come back to me next Monday, and I will talk to you about it.

"Yours truly, JAMES."

In the following letter Fisk shows a curious change:

"C. OFFICE, MAY 31, 1870.

"Please send me the diamond brooch and necklace, my dear. JAMES."

The above letter would seem to show that Fisk had found another on whom to bestow his affections. The following looks as if the letter referred to by Fisk might be the first from Stokes, and it seems to have awakened Fisk's love for Josie:

"AUGUST 1, 1870.

"MY DEAR JOSIE: I send you letter I found to my care on my desk. I cannot come to you to-night. I shall stay in town to-night, and probably to-morrow night, and after that I must go East. On my return I shall come to see you. I am sure you will say, 'What a fool!' But you must rest, and so must I. The thread is so slender I dare not strain it more. I am sore, but God made me so, and I have not the power to change it.

"Loving you, as *none but you*, I am, yours, ever, JAMES."

In the quarrel between Josie and Fisk, Miss Nully Peiris, Mr. Rane, and Stokes seem to have been suspected by Fisk of plotting against him. He thus complains of a despatch which "Rane" sent to Stokes, who was at Saratoga or Buffalo, to come to New York:

"AUGUST 4, 1870.

"DEAR JOSIE: I found on my arrival at my office that the following despatch had passed West last night:

"'E. S. Stokes, Buffalo and Saratoga Springs:

"'Pay no attention to former despatch. Come on first train.

"'RANE.'

"Of course, *it means* nothing that *you are aware of*. But let me give you the author of it and my authority, and you will see how faithfully they have worked the case out after my departure last evening. Miss Peiris drove directly to Rane's office; from there to the corner of Twenty-second street and Broadway, where the above despatch was sent, and from there to Rulley's. A third party was with them, but who left them there. Rane and Peiris, why should they need Stokes. 'Comment is unnecessary'—a plotting house, and against me. What have 'I done' that Nully Peiris should work against my peace of mind? Yours truly, ever, JAMES.

"P. S.—Since writing the within, I understand a despatch has reached New York that he is on his way. JAMES."

Here is a letter from Josie. See how much she loved him:

"SEPTEMBER, 1870.

"JAMES FISK, JR.: That your letter had the desired effect you can well imagine. I am honest enough to admit it cut me to the quick. In all the annals of letter-writing, I may say it eclipsed them all. Your secretary made a slight error, however, in supposing that Mlle. Montaland was mentioned. The only prima donna I had referred to was 'Miss Peiris.' As you say, Mlle. has nothing whatever to do with my affairs. I have always respected her, and only thought of her as one of the noblest works of God—beautiful and talented, and *your choice*—never referring to her in my letter in thought or word. I freely admit I never expected so severe a letter from you. I, of course, feel it was unmerited; but as it is your opinion of me, I accept it with all the sting. You have *struck home*, and I may say turned the knife around. I will send you the picture you speak of at once. The one in the parlor I will also dispose of. I know of nothing else here that you would wish. I am anxious to adjust our affairs. I certainly do not wish to annoy you, and that I may be able to do so I write you this last letter.

"You have told me very often that you held some twenty or twenty-five thousand dollars of mine in your keeping. I do not know if it is so, but that I may be able to shape my affairs permanently for the future that a part of the amount would place me in a position where I would never have to appeal to you for aught. I have never *had one dollar from any one else*, and arriving here from the Branch, expecting my affairs with you to continue, I contracted bills that I would not otherwise have done. I do not ask for anything I have not been led to suppose was mine, and do not ask you to settle what is not entirely convenient for you. After a time I shall sell my house, but for the present think it best to remain in it. The money I speak of would place me where I should need the assistance of no one.

"The ring I take back as fairly as I gave it to you; the

mate to it I shall keep for company. Why you could say I obtained this house by robbery, I cannot imagine; however, you know best. I am sorry that your association with me was detrimental to you, and I would gladly with you (were it possible) obliterate the last three years of my life's history; but it is not possible, and we must struggle to outlive our past. I trust you will take the sense of this letter as it is meant, and that there can be no mistake I send this by Ella, and what you do not understand she will explain."

To this and other letters of Josie, Fisk made the following reply:

"NEW YORK, Oct. 1, 1870.

"MRS. MANSFIELD:—There can be no question as to the authority of the letter which was handed to me yesterday by your servant, in this respect differing from the epistle which you say you received from Miss Peiris, and which, in your opinion, required the united efforts of herself, Mlle. Montaland, and myself. Certainly the composition should be good if these parties had combined to produce it. But the slight mistake you make is evident from the fact that the letter referred to was never seen by me, and, I presume, Mlle. Montaland is equally ignorant of its existence, as it is not likely she troubles herself about your affairs. I can scarcely believe that she assisted Miss Peiris in composing the letter, and the credit is, therefore, due to Miss Peiris for superior talent in correspondence. As far as the great exposure you speak of is concerned, that is a dark entry upon which I have no light; and as I fail to see it, I cannot, of course, understand it. I have endeavored to put your jumbled letter together, in order to arrive at your meaning, and I presume I have some idea of what you wish to convey; but as your statements lack the important element of truth, they cannot, of course, have any weight with me. You may not be to blame for entertaining the idea that you have shown great kindness to Miss Peiris and others, and that they are under great obligations to you for favors conferred. The habit of constantly imagining that you were the real author of all the benefits bestowed upon others, would naturally affect a much better balanced brain than yours, and in time you would come to believe that you alone had the power to distribute the good things to those around you, utterly forgetful of him who was behind the scenes, entirely unnoticed. Can you blame, then, those from whose eyes the veil has fallen, and who see you in your true light, as the giver of other's charities? I would not trouble myself to answer your letters, and I do not consider it a duty I owe you, to give you a final expression of my opinion. In venting your spite on Miss Peiris, (with whose affairs, by the way, I have nothing to do,) you have written a letter, in answering which you afford me an opportunity of conveying to you my ideas respecting the theories which you have taken every opportunity to express to those around you, and which many people have considered merely the emanations of a crazy brain. I could not coincide with this view; for crazy people are not inclined to do precisely as they please, either right or wrong, and so long as they are *loose*, I consider them sane, and, therefore, I could not put that construction on your conversation.

"As for Miss Peiris 'being a snake in the grass,' I care but little about that. She can do me neither harm nor good. I have done all that has been done for her during the past year. She comes to me and says: 'Sir, you have been my friend; you have assisted me in my troubles, and I thank you from the bottom of my heart.' That is a full and sufficient recompense for me for any good I may have done her, and she can return. If she be a snake in the grass, I know full well her sting is gone, and she is harmless. But what think you of a woman who would veil my eyes first by a gentle kiss, and afterward, night and day, for weeks, months, and years, by deceit and fraud, to lead me through the dark valley of trouble, when she could have made my pathway one of roses, committing crimes which the devil incarnate would shrink from, while all this time I showed to her, as to you, nothing but kindness both in words and actions, laying at your feet a soul, a heart, a fortune, and a reputation, which had cost, by night and day, twenty-five years of perpetual struggle, and which, but for the black blot of having, in an evil hour, linked itself with you, would stand out to-day brighter than any ever seen upon earth. But the mist has fallen, and you appear in your true light. I borrow your own words to describe you, 'a snake in the grass,' and verily I have found thee out, and you have the audacity to call your sainted mother to witness your advice to me. 'A dog that bites, etc., etc.'

"You accuse her of leading you on, and of ever standing ready to make appointments for you. The tone of your letter is such that you seem willing to shoulder the load of guilt under which an ordinary criminal would stagger. I believe you have arrived at that stage when no amount of guilt will disturb your serenity or prevent your having sweet dreams, and we still shall see you crawl—'a snake in the grass.'

"How I worship the night I said: 'Get thee behind me, Satan!' The few weeks that have elapsed since that blessed hour, how I bless them for the peace of mind they have brought me! And the world looks bright, and I have a being. You imagined I would pursue you again, and you thought I would endeavor to tear down the castle you had obtained by robbery. God knows that if I am an element so lost to every feeling of decency as to be willing to link itself with you, I will assist and foster it, so that it will keep you from crawling toward me, and prevent me from looking on you as a snake, as you are, and from raising a hand in pity to assist you, should trouble again cross your path. So, I have no fears that I will again come near you. I send you back a ring, and, were I to say anything about it, the words would be only too decent for the same, were they couched in the worst of language. So, I say, take it back. Its memory is indecent, and it is the last souvenir I have that reminds me of you. I had a few pictures of you, but they have found a place among the nothings which fill the waste-basket under my table. I am aware that in your back parlor hangs the picture of the man who gave you the wall to hang it on, and rumor says you have another in your chamber. The picture up-stairs send back to me. Take the other down, for he whom it represents has no respect for you. After you read this letter, you should be ashamed to look at the picture; for you would say, 'With all thy faults I love thee still;' and what would be merely the same oft-repeated *lie*. So, take it down. Do not keep anything in that house that looks like me.

"If there are any unsettled business matters that it is proper for me to arrange, send them to me, and make the explanation as brief as possible.

"I fain would reach the point where not even the slightest necessity will exist for any intercourse between us. I am in hopes this will end it. JAMES FISK, JR."

Then Fisk wrote about the $25,000:

"NEW YORK, Oct. 4, 1870.

"After the departure of Etta to-day, I wasted time enough to read over once more the letter, of which she was the bearer, from you to me, and I determined to reply to it, for the reason that, if it remain unanswered, you might possibly think I did not really mean what I said when I wrote; and, besides, I was apprehensive that the friendly talk carried on through Etta, at second hand, between you and me, might lead you to suppose I had somewhat repented of the course I had taken, or of the words I had penned. It is to remove any such impression that I again write to you, as I would have the language of my former letter, and the sentiments therein expressed, stamped upon your heart as my deep-seated opinion of your character. No other construction must be put upon my words. I turn over the first page of your letter; I pass over the kind words you have written; have I not furnished a satisfactory mansion for others' use? Have I not fulfilled every promise I have made? Is there not a stability about your finances to-day (if not disturbed by vultures) sufficient to afford you a comfortable income for the remainder of your natural life? You say you have never received a dollar from any one but me, and you *will never* have another from me, until want and misery bring you to my door, except, of course, in fulfilment of my sacred promise, and the settlement of your bills up to three weeks ago, at five minutes to eleven o'clock.

"You need have no fear as to my sensitiveness regarding your calling on any one else for assistance, as I find the word '*assistance*' underlined in your letter, to make it more impressive on my mind. That, of all others, is the point I would have you reach; for in that you would say, "Why, man, how beautiful you are to look at, but nothing to lean on!' And you may well imagine my surprise at your selection of the element you have chosen to fill my places (Stokes). I was shown to-day his diamonds, which had been sacrificed to our people at one-half their value, and, undoubtedly, if this were not so, the money would have been turned over to you, that you might feel contented as to the permanency of your affairs. You will, therefore, excuse me if I decline your modest request for a still further disbursement of $25,000. I very naturally feel that some part of this amount might be used to release from the pound the property of others, in whose welfare the writer of this does *not* feel unbounded interest.

"You say that you hope that I will take the sense of your letter. There is but one sense to be taken out of it, and that is an 'epitaph,' to be cut on the stone at the head of the grave in which Miss Helen Josephine Mansfield has buried her pride. Had she been the same proud-spirited girl that she was when she stood side-by-side with me, she would not have humbled herself to ask a permanency of one whom she had so deeply wronged, nor would she stoop to be indebted to him for a home, which would have furnished a haven of rest, pleasure and debauchery, without cost, to those who had crossed his path and robbed him of the friendship he once felt. The length of time since I had seen her, and the kind words she spoke, left my mind ill prepared for the perusal of your letter at that time, and it was not until after her departure, when I was seated quietly alone, that I took in the full intent and meaning of your letter, and felt that it was 'robbery,' and nothing else.

"Now, pin this letter with the other,—the front of this is the back of that,—and you will have a telescopic view of yourself, and your character, as you appear to me to-day;

and then, I ask you, turn back from pages of your life's history, counting each page one week of your life, and see how I looked to thee then, and ask your own guilty heart if you had not better let me alone; and, instead of trying to answer this letter from your disorganized brain, or writing from the dictation of those around you to-day, simply take a piece of paper, and write on it the same as I do now, so far as we are now, or ever may be—'Dust to dust, ashes to ashes. Amen.'

"J. F., JR."

But Fisk could not resist the fatal influence. He pays her bills:

"(J. F., Jr.) [Monogram.]

"Oct. 19, 1870.

"MADAME:—Enclosed, I send you bill of Harris receipted, and I also beg to hand you $126.29, being the honest proportion of the Bassford bill, which belongs to me to pay. I should have made the word 'honest' more definite; for, had not Mr. Bassford to put the dates to the bill, as he had received instructions from Miss Mansfield to have the bill all under the date of June 8, 1870, although ($146.26) the amount of the goods, as bought by you or your agent, was spent at a much later date. I should not suppose you would care to place yourself in the light that this bill put you, knowing as I do the instructions that you gave Mr. Bassford. I had supposed you 'honest,' but I find that a trace of that virtue does not even cling to you.

"I am yours, J. F., JR."

"A FEARFUL DREAM."

"DEPARTMENT OF FINANCE, ERIE RAILWAY,
NEW YORK, Oct. 20, 1870.

"MADAM: You know I would not wrong you, and I would

take back all my acts when there could be a shadow of doubt that you was right and I was wrong; and let me speak of the other harsh letters I have written. I wrote them because you had wronged me positively, and because you had placed between me and my life, my hopes and my happiness, an eternal gulf, and I felt sore and revengeful, and on those I am now the same. It would be idle for me to write about them or about *us*, when I could talk to you there. You did not listen. I presume it to be the same now.

"The entire connection is like a dream to me—a fearful dream—from which I have awoke, and, while dreaming, supposed my soul had gone out; and the awakening tells me I am saved, and, from the embers of the late fire, there smoulders no spirit of revenge toward you, for you acted right, and the *wrong* only came to me from you because you did not act sooner, and I would not believe that any power on earth would make any question of money influence me or come between me and the holy feeling I once had for you. I sent John to Bassford's, and they told him what I said, or he told me so, that the dates of the bill should not be changed. But what does it matter whether it is so or not. I cannot *feel* that you would do it, and something says to me this was one of the things she was not like. So I pass it by, and if the letters of last night or to-day are not like me you can wash the bad act out from your memory, and leave but the one idea that I want to do my duty and fulfill every unsettled relic. At least in my heart rests no remorse, for the memory is too deeply seated and I would cherish all that is good about you, and forget forever the bad. Of late you have thought different from me (this may be imaginary on my part), for which I think you give me all the credit you can. We have *parted for ever*. Now, let us make the memory of the past as bright and beautiful as we can; for on my side there is so little to cherish that I cling to it with great tenacity, and hope from time to time to wear it off. You know full well how I have suffered. Once you knew me better than any one on earth. To-day you know me less. It is the proper light for you to stand in. It is all you desire on your side. It is all you deserve on mine.

"This letter should remain and be read only by you. Should you see fit to answer it, the answer will be the same way kept by me. There has been a storm. The ship, a noble steamer, has gone down. The storm is over, and the sea is smooth again.

'Little ships should keep near shore;
Greater ships can venture more.'

"'My ship is small and poorly officered.'

"I am yours ever, etc., etc., J. F., JR.

"P.S.—I would have liked to have answered your letter in full, but, as you say, I have not a well-balanced brain, and I know I could not do justice to a letter of that kind, so refrain, and content to let the sentiments of it 'know and fret me.'"

Josie called on Fisk frequently during the month of October. As much as he had resolved on separation, her presence always melted his heart. This letter explains itself:

"October 25, 1870.

"Why should I write you again? Shall I ever reach the end. There comes another and another chapter, until I get weary with the entire affair. I would forget it, and no doubt you would the same. The mistake yesterday was almost the mistake of a life-time for me. Who supposed for an instant that you would ever cross my path again in a spirit

of submission and with a contrite spirit? You have done that you should be sorry for, and I the same in permitting it. This cannot be, and I shall write you the final letter, and I shall see you no more. I told you that much yesterday evening, and shall I write it to you again. Yes, for the reason I treated you falsely last night, and I left you with a different impression, and I would put that right. You acted so differently from your nature that I forgive you, and even went so far as to bring my mind to bear how I could take you back again. First, the devil stood behind, and my better reason gave way for the moment, and I came away, telling you I would see you no more. When your better character comes in contact with mine, we are so much alike that much of what is said, like that last night, had better been unsaid. All now looks bright and beautiful, and my better nature trembles at ideas that were expressed last night. But that I should have left on your mind an idea that you could control me is erroneous. There are truths in this affair, and they must be spoken. You have gone out from one element and have taken another (Stokes), and for you to turn back, either when you are situated that way, or when even you could say that element had gone, should make no difference to me. It was you that took the step, and you should and shall suffer the consequences. Supposing the part you took last night and yesterday afternoon was one of truth, if not, and I——
Again, if you was not dealing from your heart in what took place, and I hope it was not true, then there are no consequences and no suffering for you to endure, Why, it has been many a long year since I could say to myself that I had committed such a folly. To find another like yesterday would bring me back almost to childhood. To imagine that I should have again crossed your threshold, and crossed it,

too, deliberately, knowing that the same facts existed that had given me all my trouble, and made me this sorrow—why, it is devilish. I told you that I had passed the realm where I had forgiven you all the sorrow you had made me, and that I would not murmur; I would not find fault with all that I saw. I would fain tear your image from my mind, and I will. Why, I thought all night last night, and all day to-day, of your saying, 'I would rather be a toad,' etc., etc. Was that written to apply to me? I should say so. Yes. Who knows what you would not conceive? No one but yourself. And I must weigh you carefully, for I have nothing but a great character to deal with, and I must meet things carefully. You might suppose you could love two, and perhaps more elements, and make them hover near you. Certainly you did last night, and, for shame, I was one of them. But it will *never* occur again. For once let us be honest. You went that road because it looked smooth and pleasant, and mine looked ragged and worn. Now, a mistake cannot be found out too soon. Travel further along, and you don't try to turn so soon. I can see you now as you were last night, when you talked of this man (Stokes); and do not deceive yourself—*you love him.* Yesterday there was nothing left but the breaking up of strong pride and the giving way of wilfulness. Cling to that one. Leave me alone; for in me you have *nothing* left. Why ask me to weaken yourself with him? All this you must study; but I pledge you to-night that I will not countenance even your impression on my mind until the door is closed behind him forever. For what you can gain from me you probably cannot afford to do that; so let me advise you—nourish him and be careful. Nothing is so bad for you as changes. He loves you; you love him.

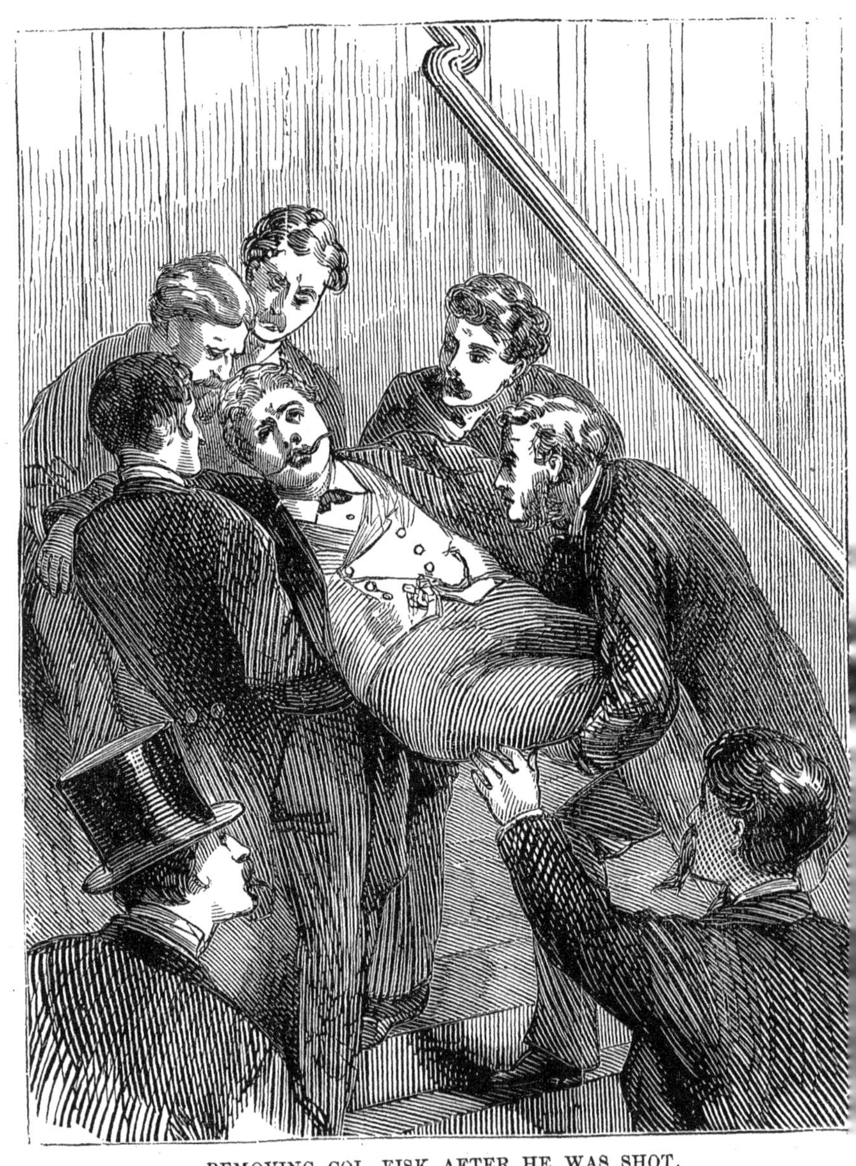

REMOVING COL. FISK AFTER HE WAS SHOT.

"You have caused me all the misery you could. Cling to him. Be careful what you do, or he will be watchful. How well he knows you *cheated me.* He will look for the same. And now I know precisely how you stand from your own lips; I will treat him differently. Although you would not protect him, I will. While he is there, and until his memory is buried forever, never approach me, for I shall send you away unseen. Ever be careful that you do not have the feeling that you can come back to me, for there is a wide gulf between you and me. I would not hold a false hope out to you. I shall not trouble you more in this letter. You have the only idea I can express to you. You know when you can see me again, if ever. The risk for you is too great. Loving and suited as you are, cling to him for the present, and when your nature grows tired of that throw him off. And so long until it is time for you to be weary and for you to be 'put in your little bed' forever, you must rest contented. Don't begin plotting to-morrow. Take to-morrow for thought, and be governed by this letter, for the writer has much of your destiny in his hands."

He addresses her formally, but his signature to the following letter shows the old yearning for her:

"NOV. 1, 1870.

"MISS MANSFIELD: I have taken the steps for the corn doctress's removal to a Southern clime, where her business should be better, as vegetables of that class thrive more rapidly there than on our bleak shores. I presume it will take from two, or say four days, before I get the passes, when they will be sent to you. Should she call on you, say to her to come back in four days and you will have them for her. I sent you a package by Maggie for what you wanted on Saturday evening, with a little surplus over for trimmings, which I hope you received. I am of your opinion regarding not only Dr. Pape, but all of the doctors. You are well, let nature take its course. You are in too good health to tamper with a constitution as good as yours. This is important for your consideration. "Yours truly, JAMES."

The following letter would indicate that they had met, and that there was prospect of a reconciliation:

"Nov. 10, 1870.

"Enclosed find $300. Please use. I am very sorry we could not have arrived at a more satisfactory conclusion last night. I did all I could, and the same feeling prevails o'er me now. With careful and watchful manner you should look at all our affairs. You should make no mistake. You told me I should hear from you when you came to a conclusion. Therefore I wait upon your early reply, and until then I must of course pursue the same course I have for the last six weeks. I hope we shall mutually understand each other, for the thing could be made, as should be made, satisfactory to you. "I am, yours, JAMES."

And yet more money. It looks as if there had been further meetings:

"Erie Railway Company. Treasurer's Office, Nov. 7, 1870, Receiving Desk—$500.

"WM. H. B.

"Erie Railway Company. Treasurer's Office, Nov. 19, 1870, Receiving desk—$500.

"WM. H. B.

"Please acknowledge receipt. JAMES."

More favors:

"NOVEMBER 11, 1870.

"Enclosed you will find the order on Miss Guthrie, which have Etta or you present, and it will be all right. Mr. Comer gave them an order not to deliver anything only on my written order to stop the 'opera bouffers;' but present this enclosed order, and it will be all right. Mrs. Reher was here this morning, and I gave her transportation for self and Michael to Charleston by steamer.

"Enclosed you will find box at theatre in order to get the same, as it was sold. I have convinced myself that I desire you and yours to come.

"Please answer the note, that I may know you are to come. Yours truly JAMES."

The following letter, written but a day after the previous one, shows Fisk in better spirits. He is evidently again basking in Josie's smiles:

"NOVEMBER 12, 1870.

"Enclosed find the letters. I was not aware Miss Jordan was to come until I saw her pass the gate-keeper; but that is nothing astonishing, as she is one of our regular customers. Of course, I did not send her the box, for she is not in a mood that I presume such civilities would be received from Fisk, Jr. I am glad you was pleased. I would have been glad to have you seen 'Le Petit Faust.' At the 'Duchesse' we used old clothes and scenery; while in 'Faust' all was new. We play 'Faust' this afternoon. Shall I send you a box? And on Monday night we give the world 'our diamond,' 'Les Brigands,' all new.

"Surely, the world is machinery. Am I keeping up with it? is the question. Yours truly, JAMES."

The next letter shows Fisk again completely in the toils, and happy:

"NOVEMBER 14, 1870.

"DEAR DOLLY,—Do you really wish to see a 'brigand' at your house to-night? If so, what hour, or from what hour and how late shall I call? for I might be able to come at eight, or, perhaps, not until ten. Say what hour, and how late is your limit after the time you first say."

Still in love:

"NOVEMBER 15, 1870.

"Enclosed find box for to-night. Should you find you cannot use it, send it back to me later. Do you feel as I said you would this morning? The box, of course, is for whoever you may invite. Yours ever, JAMES."

Utterly infatuated:

"NOVEMBER 16, 18—

"DEAR DOLLY,—Don't feel that way. Go riding, and to-night, darling, I will take you to rest. I shall go out at half-past three, and you can safely look ahead, darling, for rest. It will come, and we shall be happy again.

"Yours truly, JAMES."

The last:

"NOVEMBER 18, 1870.

"Shall go to the race to-day, and this evening I am engaged until late, and I am afraid you would get tired waiting for the ring of the bell or the ring of the door. So I will not ask you to wait my coming, unless it be your wish, in which case I will come as early as I can. Yours, etc.

"Enclosed find the Leidunnor Ball.

"Yours truly, J. F., JR.

"MONDAY MORNING.

"Not time to come up. J. F. JR."

These are the letters of a man infatuated by a siren bent on leading him to destruction. They are not what a prurient public expected.

Fisk fought hard to prevent their publication, and gave his enemy $15,000 that his shame might not be blazoned forth to the world. It is evident that he did not write them—they were penned by a better scholar.

For a long time certain of Fisk's immediate friends strove earnestly to induce him to publish the letters himself. He refused.

"You may laugh at me, but I tell you I can't put up on a sign-board some of the purest thoughts that ever stirred me, and let the world laugh at me. They may curse me for this, and damn me for that, and ridicule me for something else—but, by the Lord, this is my *heart* that you want me to make a show of, and I won't."

But, a few weeks before the publication of the letters in the *Herald* he yielded to the solicitation of his friends, and furnished his copies of the correspondence to an amanuensis with orders to prepare them for the press. When this had been done to his satisfaction, he dictated a letter to the public, in which occurred the following words:

"This will amuse a great many heartless people, but I am satisfied to let them laugh. For much that I have done, I have been justly blamed, and have been ridiculed for much more. In this correspondence, which was an insult to one of the purest women that ever lived, I have been more guilty than in anything else. I have sought and obtained the forgiveness of my wife. Now let the world laugh."

It was most unfortunate that Fisk changed his mind again, thereby losing an opportunity to present himself in a far better light than the public had yet viewed him in.

## CHAPTER XL.

FOR years past the management of the Erie Road had been a scandal in Europe. It had to some extent interfered with the negotiation abroad of other American securities, and had been pointed at as a type of the protection foreign creditors might expect in this country. Various attempts had been made by individuals to break up the Erie Ring, but, as has been already seen, it was found that the Ring absolutely controlled the judiciary of this city. The first real victory accomplished by the English stockholders, who were the parties under whose sponsorship the last great movement was made, was the dethronement of Jay Gould from his position as Receiver of the Atlantic and Great Western Railway, which was accomplished in 1871. This blow to Erie was followed by the fall of the Tammany Ring, with which Erie had been so closely allied. When Tammany fell, the representatives of the European interest determined on another struggle for their rights. They were in constant communication with counsel on this side of the water, and the plans were partially matured, when in January, 1872, it became known that General Sickles was coming to this country on leave of absence. It also became known to the representatives of Erie in London, including James McHenry. Both parties saw that General Sickles possessed in a great degree the political influence and the executive ability necessary to give efficient aid in extricating the road from the clutches of the Ring. He was visited in London before leaving; and in the interest of the stockholders, as well as of the American people, he agreed to do what he was able to aid in the restoration of the Company to its proper owners, and to bring about the election of an entirely new Board of officers. He did this from no selfish motives, but purely in the interest of his country. As our representative at a foreign court, he had ample opportunities to see how much our credit was damaged by the frauds of Erie, and he undertook to remedy the evil so far as in his power.

On General Sickles's arrival in New York, the plans were matured. It was known that many of the Directors were beginning to waver in their allegiance to Jay Gould, especially since the death of Fisk, and this was the rock upon which it was determined to break the entire Erie machine. Such Directors as were known to be hostile to the administration, were approached, and the plans boldly laid before them. They entered into the scheme heartily. Then the more doubtful ones were cautiously sounded, and one by one added to the list of malcontents. A diplomatist backed by lawyers is irresistible in some things, and in less than a month enough had been gained over to render the success of the scheme certain.

On Friday evening, March 8, a meeting was held, at which it was determined to begin active operations. Gens. Dix and McClellan were then first informed of what was to take place, and asked to accept positions in the Board. They consented. Gen. Dix also consented at that time to take Jay Gould's place as President of the Board. The entire complexion of the new Board was decided on, and the gentlemen to be elected were told to be present at the meeting when called. The next day, Saturday, Jay Gould was asked to call a meeting. He telegraphed from his downtown office that he did not see the necessity of calling a meeting. This had been foreseen, so that no time was lost.

On Saturday, March 9, Mr. Gould being in Albany, Vice-President Archer called a meeting of the Board of Directors for Monday, March 11. At 11 o'clock A. M. of that day the great movement began to take visible shape in the splendid hall of the Erie offices. As noon approached there were more signs of life. At that hour several of the Board of Directors had made their appearance. At 12 o'clock Mr. Lane walked to the head of the staircase leading to the vestibule. By that time it began to leak out that a startling change in the management of Erie was imminent. Flying rumors said that the Board contained but fifteen members, while it should be composed of seventeen. More rumors said that Mr. Lane was the prime conspirator in a new movement which was to sweep away Jay Gould and several others of the Board, and place the road under a new authority.

Soon after 12 o'clock, Gen. Dix appeared on the staircase. The tough old soldier was accompanied by a younger soldier, Gen. McClellan. This certainly looked like war, when two distinguished generals led the army which swarmed over the ramparts of Erie. Mr. Lane met them on the landing, and escorted them to the Directors' room. While Lane had been waiting outside, Mr. Shearman, the attorney for the road, had visited those Directors who had assembled inside. He flourished an injunction and declared the meeting illegal. The injunction was not good. It was instantly taken from Mr. Shearman's hands, and thrown upon the floor. Shearman was backed out of the room, which Jay Gould had not entered. Those there were Judge Hilton, Capt. M. R. Simons, Messrs. Hall, Thompson, Otis, Archer, Ramsdell and White.

Mr. Lane entered with Gens. Dix and McClellan. The room was ordered cleared, and balloting for the new directors was begun. Gens. Dix and McClellan were voted in. This made the required number. Then some of the disaffected directors, men who were against Gould, sent in their resignations. Then more men came in. There were Sam. L. M. Barlow, William R. Travers, H. G. Stebbins, Charles Day, W. W. Sherman, and Gen. Devins of Elmira. They passed into the directors' room. They were all elected members of the Board.

At this juncture Attorney Shearman again made his appearance, this time backed by forty policemen. The heavy folding doors were thrown open, and in they marched. Bedlam broke loose in an instant. All hands jumped to their feet, and howled with mingled rage and fury. Wild gesticulations were emphasized with angry words.

"Shearman, what do you want here? Get out! You don't belong here!"

"It is the custom," shouted Shearman, "for counsel to be present at meetings of the Board of Directors."

"Can't help it! Get out!"

Shearman stayed in and ordered the room cleared. The policemen did not move, nor did the directors.

"By what authority do you enter here?" cried one.

"By the authority of Jay Gould," said Shearman.

"That won't do," said Mr. Barlow. "Jay Gould is no longer an officer of this road."

The police were quiescent. "By whose orders do you come here?" said Barlow.

"Jay Gould's," said the Captain.

"Not good," said Barlow. "If you are acting for the Erie Company you must take your orders from Gen. Dix."

Mr. Shearman endeavored to have the room cleared, while men shouted and swung their fists, and there was imminent danger of blows. Shearman shouted something which could not be distinctly heard above the uproar, but it sounded like:

"I am willing for all the Erie directors to resign——place resignations in hands of Horace Greeley——protest——"

Shouts of laughter temporarily took the place of angry altercation.

"Oh, for one hour of Jim Fisk!" shouted a man outside. "He'd have a thousand men here if need be, and he'd sweep the room like a deluge!"

But the impetuous Fisk was not there. His fertile brain and dashing action were invoked in vain, and Mr. Shearman and the police were obliged to retire before the tempest.

Mr. Barlow offered a resolution that Mr. Jay Gould be dispensed with as President of the road. Carried. Then Mr. Barlow moved that the Board proceed to ballot for a President. Carried, and Gen. Dix was elected. Mr. Archer was re-elected Vice-President. Then Messrs. Field and Shearman were voted out of their positions as attorneys for the road, and Mr. Barlow was voted in, and Mr. Sherman was elected Treasurer. Then orders were telegraphed all along the Erie road to take orders from no one but Archer or Dix, and the new Board rested on its laurels.

During all that night the Erie offices were in a state of siege. Jay Gould and a gang of roughs whom he had sworn in as special officers, by virtue of a long-forgotten act of the Legislature, retained possession of a portion of the Erie office. The reformers held the remainder of the field. Gould protested without avail.

On Tuesday the Opera House was the scene of constant

excitement. The new Board was in session in the Directors' room, and Jay Gould had locked himself in his office.

At two o'clock, General Sickles went into the room where Messrs. Field and Shearman were, and was conducted into Mr. Gould's room. After a quarter of an hour he came back, this time followed by Mr. Gould. Mr. Gould had not been seen for the last twenty-four hours.

"It's a treaty for peace," said a few, while others conjectured that it was a final notification to Mr. Gould to leave the premises.

After a half-hour's waiting, Mr. Gould appeared, in company with Mr. Shearman and General Sickles, and entered the Directors' room. Instantly the news was communicated to all portions of the building, and an immense assemblage blocked up the vestibule.

"Thank God!" cried the police; "this looks like a compromise. Now, we'll get out of this."

The crowd clamored for admission to the Comptroller's room, and it was a difficult task for the police to prevent them from making a forcible entrance.

Mr. Gould was very pale, and looked hardly able to walk. He and the General went into the Directors' room.

From what followed, it would seem that the new Board had decided to acknowledge Mr. Gould's authority, and to take such action, this time, as would be undoubtedly legal. What took place was in pursuance of a compromise which General Sickles had effected at the time of the conference in Gould's room.

Around the long table in the Directors' room sat all the members of the old Board. Mr. Gould, with trembling steps—he seemed very much agitated—took the President's chair, and said:

"Gentlemen, I call this meeting to order."

In an instant one could have heard a pin drop. Then followed a repetition of Monday's meeting. One by one the Directors rose and tendered their resignations. As soon as one of the old Directors had resigned, one of the members of the new Board came in from the dining-room and took his seat. When all the new Directors had taken their seats, Jay Gould rose and said, in rather a tremulous voice:

"Gentlemen, I herewith resign the office of President of the Erie Railroad Company."

This announcement was the first received with silence. Then the resignation was accepted. General Dix was proposed to fill the vacancy, and unanimously elected. General Dix came out of the dining-room and took the chair. Messrs. Lansing, Diven, and Archer were appointed an Auditing Committee. The new members all shook hands with Mr. Gould, and said they were glad to see everything settled in so satisfactory a manner. Then, previous to taking a recess of half an hour, the following resolutions were passed by the new Board:

"*Resolved,* That public notice be given that it is the intention of this Board that the *bona fide* stockholders of this Company shall, at all times hereafter, have and be allowed to exercise their full and absolute right to control the direction of this Company, and that this Board will do all in its power to bring about such a speedy election as shall secure this result; and, in view of this determination, it is further

"*Resolved,* That this Board does heartily approve of the principles embodied in the Act recently reported to the Senate and Assembly of this State, for the repeal of the so-called Classification Act, and for other purposes, and that Messrs. Porter and McFarland, two of the counsel of this

Board, be requested to proceed to Albany to urge the passage of the Act.

"*Resolved,* That the resolution of the Executive Committee, passed last year, by which Mr. Gould was authorized to issue $22,000,000 of convertible bonds, under which authority no action has been taken by Mr. Gould, shall be and hereby is rescinded by the Board of Directors, and the Stock Exchange is notified of this decision.

"*Resolved,* That the stock transfer books are ordered to be closed by order of the Board of Directors."

The newly organized Directory is understood to be provisional only, and the members lately introduced lay great stress upon this point. Many of them were elected at a moment's notice, and accepted only on the understanding that an election by the stockholders was to follow as soon as the necessary legislation could be secured. The Provisional Administration, as this chapter goes to press, is as follows:

*President*—John A. Dix; *Vice-President*—O. H. P. Archer; *Treasurer*—W. W. Sherman; *Asst.-Treasurer*—Justin D. White; *Superintendent*—Lewis D. Rucker; *Directors*—John A. Dix, O. H. P. Archer, Jay Gould, W. W. Sherman, J. D. White, George B. McClellan, Geo. C. Hall, F. N. Drake, H. G. Stebbins, W. R. Travers, S. L. M. Barlow, Charles Day, Homer Ramsdell, Edwin Eldridge, A. S. Diven, Gen. Lansing, F. N. Drake.

Mr. John Hilton entered the service of the road in 1836, as Engineer. Since then he has filled the positions of Auditor and Treasurer. Soon after the present administration came into power he tendered his resignation as Auditor of the Company, and retired for three years, resuming his connection again five or six months ago, and remaining a Director during the interval.

Mr. Simons has been for twenty years in the management of the Narragansett Steamship Company.

Mr. Otis became connected with the Company in 1845, and was the transfer clerk when the road was resuscitated and opened in 1852. In 1859 he was elected Secretary of the old New York and Erie Railroad Co. When the road went into the hands of a receiver he was appointed Secretary of the new Company—a position he has ever since held. He claims he has retained that position through advice of counsel, who had opposed his desire to resign.

George C. Hall was elected to the Board in 1869. His election was effected, he says, without consultation with him at all, and he knew nothing of it until he saw it in the papers. He says he is anxious to have his record examined, and to that end was ready and glad to resign. He found that getting out was a much more difficult thing to manage than to get in. Twice he resigned on account of the odium which attached to any one having anything to do with the Board, and twice his resignation was sent back, and by advice of counsel he determined, he says, to remain until he could obtain justice for the corporation and for himself. He claims he has opposed Gould throughout, and has been the means of defeating some of the Ring schemes.

Henry Thompson, a relative of President Eldridge of the Boston, Hartford and Erie Road, also claims credit for having stood out firmly against Gould, and he hailed the present moment gladly as an opportunity to show what he says is a "clear record in all things."

Homer Ramsdell originally entered the directory of the road in 1844, and was elected President in 1853, serving in such capacity four years. In 1857 he went out of office, but was reëlected in 1867, and has been a director ever since.

He says his contracts with Erie are as profitable to the road as to himself, and courts investigation of the terms and his transactions.

Mr. Archer, the present Vice-President, came into the service of the Company a rich man, and says he only went into the Board with the idea of assisting by his credit and the money he should raise, to put the road on a proper basis. A number of times he has come into direct collision with Mr. Gould, in regard to the schemes of the latter, when he has told him that he could not consent to such action as Gould proposed, and should oppose him, or any other member of the Board, who did anything contrary to the interests of the road. Gould made several attempts to get rid of him, but all ultimately failed. Not long ago, when Gould attempted to get control of Mrs. Fisk's stock in the Narragansett Steamship Co., by trumping up a false claim and threatening to attach the estate, it is claimed that Archer went to Gould, and informed him plainly that he should protect Mrs. Fisk's interests in the matter. If Mr. Gould attached the stock, he would have him arrested. It appears, to state the scandalous story in detail, that in the settlement of Col. Fisk's estate, it became necessary to dispose of various stocks, and an effort was made to sell them to the best advantage. In one instance (the Elmira Rolling Mill Company), upon several offers the stock was disposed of at par; but in other cases, buyers who stood ready to purchase certain stocks at favorable rates, were deterred from so doing on an intimation from Jay Gould, that such purchase would be disagreeable to him.

A newspaper report claimed that the Hon. Horace Greeley was quite active in bringing back the change in the management. As the story ran, Mr. Greeley was approached by one of the heaviest of the English stockholders, who sought his assistance. About two weeks before the final overthrow, Mr. Greeley conferred with Mr. Thomas A. Scott, the President of the Pennsylvania Central road, at Philadelphia. The result was that the two gentlemen came to New York, where they met Mr. Gould at the Metropolitan Hotel. Mr. Gould then offered to place his resignation in the hands of Mr. Greeley. This was on March 11, 1872. It was, doubtless, at this conference, that Mr. Gould formed the determination which he carried into effect as stated above.*

As this chapter is brought to a close, it is understood that the Classification Bill has been repealed at Albany.

Jay Gould resigned his position as Director of Erie three days after throwing up the Presidency, and on the 18th of March, 1872, Erie stock was quoted at 47½.

* This report Mr. Greeley most emphatically denies.

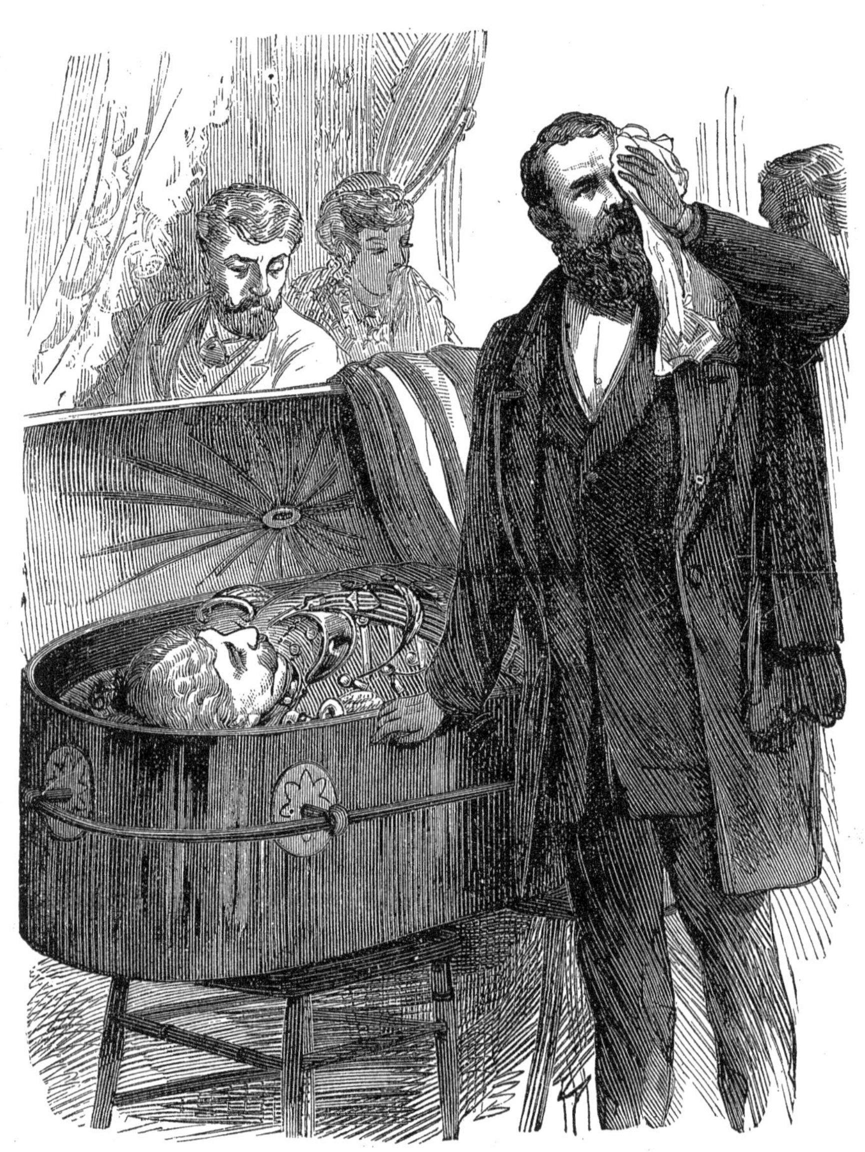

JAY GOULD WEEPING BESIDE THE COFFIN.

# ANECDOTES

OF

# COL. JAMES FISK, JR.,

## MISCELLANEOUS INCIDENTS IN HIS LIFE,

TOGETHER WITH

BIOGRAPHICAL SKETCHES OF CORNELIUS VANDERBILT, DANIEL DREW, EDWARD S. STOKES, JAY GOULD, WM. M. TWEED, AND HELEN JOSEPHINE MANSFIELD.

---

"On Saturday (the day following Black Friday) there ran through the town a wild rumor of a fresh atrocity, a rumor coming no one knew whence, but established in the mouths of a thousand self-constituted witnesses. It declared that James Fisk, stock-gambler, had been shot in the street by John Morrissey, ex-prize-fighter, proprietor of faro banks, and member of Congress. It declared furthermore that Fisk had cheated Morrissey out of large sums of money in the late gold excitement, that Morrissey had threatened to punish him publicly unless he made restitution, and that the killing was as deliberate as the threat of public chastisement had been. Two hours later the whole story proved a canard, hatched probably by some unscrupulous reporter.

"But this tale had a moral. Commonly a murderer so shocks the moral sense of the community, by the cowardice and malignity of his act, that public sentiment is disposed to defend, if not to vindicate, the victim so brutally deprived of the opportunity of self-defense. Yet when this report was at its strongest, the business world received it with a mild acquiescence in the fitness of the agent to his horrible work, if not with positive and expressed satisfaction. Nobody seemed horror-stricken, nobody cried out for retaliation in blood. No doubt this apathy or carelessness was due in part to the convocation of horrors which has so sickened, disgusted, or appalled the community, one treading upon another's heels, so fast they followed. But an explanation beyond this lies in the feeling of the public that James Fisk is a man whose hand is against every man's—in the feeling of the public that a man who made sport of common honesty, of truth, of decency, in his own life and in his dealings with men, living literally an outlaw, in some sort satisfied the claims of society upon him in dying the death of an outlaw. It is a test of the hollowness of the 'success' which this man had achieved, that nobody cared for him living, and nobody mourned him dead. It is a most startling commentary on the recklessness of public sentiment and the mockery of justice which pervade the time, that his own world was neither shocked nor surprised."—*Tribune.*

"He has a great many warm enemies, and scores of earnest friends. He is generous, social, and warm-hearted, and has a sort of winning way in his general deportment which it is impossible to describe, and almost impossible to resist. . . . . . . He is, or has been intimate with men of all classes, from the President of the United States down; and what is more remarkable, his acquaintance is sought by the very men who denounce him. His future career will be watched with great interest by the whole American people, and whether his life is spared for a longer or shorter period, he can make his exit with the proud satisfaction that he once made considerable stir in it."—*Herald, Nov.* 7, 1869.

"While I am writing, let me say something about another man mentioned in the same number of the *Tribune*, Mr. James Fisk, Jr. In commenting on the report that he had been shot, you speak of him as a man whose hand is against every man's, one whom nobody ever cared for living, or mourned when he was supposed to be dead. Now, I do not know Mr. Fisk, never held any communication with him, never even saw him. Of the nature or justifiability of his operations, I can say nothing, because I know nothing. But I was sorry to see these remarks, because I do know of at least one person whom he cared for, and who should remember him, living or dead. In the hight of the gold panic, when it might reasonably be supposed that any man who was but moderately interested in the issue would be entirely and nervously absorbed in his own affairs, Mr. Fisk found time and had the nerve and the inclination to write a letter to a friend of mine for the sole purpose of serving a woman —a woman old and poor. The fact impressed me when I learned it at the time of its occurrence, and I refer to it now, because it seems to me that a man who under such circumstances could do such an act, cannot be quite the Ishmael of his kind, or quite deserve to be held up as one whom no one should care for living, or will mourn when dead.

"Your obedient servant, R. G. W."

—*Tribune, New York, Jan.* 25, 1870.

This grateful and chivalric letter of the celebrated Shakspearian scholar, Richard Grant White, was widely copied.

The *Evening Mail* said, in referring to it, "It required no courage to say a good word in behalf of a great public benefactor,* whose magnificent gifts to the public are now justly praised on all sides; but as to Mr. Fisk, the undertaking of his defense was a different matter, and we respect Mr. White for the sense of justice which led him to write the following"—(the extract above quoted.)

"I tell you he was one of the warmest-hearted men in this big city; as I will prove by relating a little incident of his way of doing things," said one of the Colonel's friends:

"A short time ago a prominent New Yorker, whose available means were tied up, discovered on a Saturday night that unless he could raise $81,000 by Monday morning, he would become hopelessly bankrupt. He made the matter known to a few personal friends, who at once resolved to obtain the money for him, if possible. They held a meeting and adopted the plan of trying to get enough men to advance $5,000 each to raise the amount required. The case was stated to Fisk, and although he was not under the slightest obligation to the embarrassed merchant, he said,

"'Gentlemen, you can put me down for $10,000.'

"After some difficulty they succeeded in raising $51,000, still finding themselves $30,000 short.

"They again called on the Colonel, and mentioned their dilemma, at the same time saying that they would deposit deeds of land as security for $30,000 more.

"'All right, gentlemen, here is the amount,' replied the Colonel, handing them a check.

* Mr. Robert Lenox, who had presented his large and valuable private library to the City of New York, and to whom Mr. White had referred in the letter.

"'You had better examine the deeds, Colonel, to see if the land is worth the money,' suggested a prudent friend.

"'I don't care whether the land is fit to raise cauliflowers or cranberries, the man is in a tight place, and must have the money,' remarked Prince Erie, as he shoved the deeds aside. W. Y."

"When I was completing my classical education at Brattleboro'," said Fisk, "there came along one of these travelin' curiosities—a kind of a cross between a parson and a played-out schoolmaster. Well, he poked into the school-room and got to talkin' with the teacher. He was a slab-sided individual, and walked something about like old Greeley, but he hadn't half as lovely a profile, and he lacked Horace's sweetly innocent expression of countenance, and Horace's taste in dress. It was n't long before the stranger rose up and straightened the tails of his coat, and pulled up his shirt collar—about as dirty a collar as you ever see. He cleared his throat, and begun to air his eloquence. I don't remember now what he talked about, but I have a lively recollection of the fact that me and the boys had an idee that the speaker, with a little more education and better raiment, might some time or other make a tolerable circus clown. Well, now, we laughed every once in a while, and the man got pesky wroth. He stopped short in the middle of his sermon, and, says he, 'Now, boys, I want you should keep so quiet till I git through thet you could hear a feather fall.'

"'Let her fall!' said I. The whole school roared, and the man could n't finish his talk; so after a spell he left. I ketched the worst thrashing that afternoon that ever helped to make me virtuous, and I've had a good many, too."

On the night before the November election of 1871, Colonel Fisk was in his private box at the Grand Opera House, surrounded by a number of friends, among whom was Jay Gould. The Governor of the State had that day ordered the Ninth, and another regiment of the National Guard, to hold themselves in readiness to aid in preserving the peace of the city on the morrow. The President had already ordered troops to Governor's Island, under the apprehension that a terrible riot on election day was imminent; and it was feared by many good citizens that there might be a difficulty between the United States troops and the militia, arising out of the supposed disagreement between the President and Governor Hoffman, involving a conflict of authority; the opinion being that in the event of a rising of the disorderly element, and an attempt on the part of the government force to suppress the riot, the State troops would side with the people, in which case the streets of New York would be the theatre of a bloody battle.

The Colonel and his friends were listening to the music of the Grand Opera House Orchestra, when a messenger entered the box and handed a telegraphic dispatch to Mr. Gould.

"I say, Colonel!" said Gould, excitedly, as he rose hastily from his chair and passed the dispatch to Fisk, "this concerns you. Read it."

The Colonel glanced at the paper and turned pale.

It was a dispatch purporting to come from Amos J. Cummings of the *Sun*, and was thus worded:

"Have just learned that Grant has ordered the officer in command of the regulars, that in the event of any trouble between the people and the military to-morrow, he shall see that Jim Fisk is shot by the troops."

The Colonel sent for his staff. Colonel Braine, Major Hitchcock, Adjutant Allien, Surgeon Pollard, and other officers of the Ninth, were soon at his side. They all advised him not to appear at the head of his regiment on the next day.

"Gentlemen," said Fisk, "I don't know what in thunder this thing means; but I will let you and Grant and everybody else know that Jim Fisk is the Colonel of the Ninth, and that he commands it to-morrow unless there should be something the matter with his old tin oven."

He kept his word, and appeared at the head of his regiment. Fortunately there was no riot; and even had there been one, Colonel Fisk's life would have been in nowise imperilled by the regulars—for the Cummings dispatch was one of Jay Gould's tricks, over which he enjoyed many a ventriloquial chuckle afterward.

During the session of the Legislature in 1869, the various charges of bribery and corruption that had been made against members were considered. Accusations of this kind had appeared frequently in the public prints during the preceding year, in connection with the passage of the "Erie Bill," and a resolution was passed providing for a committee to make investigations, and ascertain "whether any party or parties interested in supporting or opposing any measures relating to railway companies have, either in person, or by agent, directly or indirectly, paid or offered to pay any member or members of the Senate, during that session, any money or other valuable thing, to influence their vote or action in Senate or committee."

By a subsequent resolution, this committee was authorized to sit during the recess and report at the next session. They entered into an extended investigation occupying several months, and examined as witnesses parties interested upon both sides in the alleged corrupt legislation, members of the lobby, and the editors of the papers in which the original charges appeared. Their report was made on the 11th of March, 1869, and the conclusions at which they arrived were thus summarily stated:

"1. Large sums of money were expended for corrupt purposes by parties interested in legislation concerning railroads during the session of 1868.

"2. Lobbyists were thus enriched, and in some cases received money on the false pretence that the votes of the senators were to be thereby influenced.

"3. There is no proof of actual bribery of any senator.

"4. The newspaper charges made in the instances that were brought to the notice of your committee were founded upon rumor alone, and have in no case been sustained by the evidence of the writers or other proof."

They expressed their opinion, however, that under the law as it then existed, it was almost impossible to prove the crime of bribery, because both parties to the transaction were liable to punishment.

"True," the committee said, "the testimony given by one on the trial of another cannot be used against the person testifying. But the witness well knows that such testimony necessarily gives the clue to evidence by which he himself can be convicted and punished. The result is either a refusal to testify, or remarkable forgetfulness, or something worse."

A bill had already been introduced by the chairman of the committee, Mr. M. Hale, "for the more effectual suppression and punishment of bribery," which embodied suitable provisions, and also made it an indictable offense for any officer of a company or corporation to use the money of such company or corporation for purposes of corruption. This act subsequently passed both Houses of the Legislature, and received the approval of the Governor.

In May, 1869, the society for the Advancement of Women's Rights held a convention in New York City. Miss Susan B. Anthony wished to secure from the Erie Railway passes at half fare for delegates from the West coming to New York over the Erie road. She visited the offices of the Company, which were then located in the old building at the foot of Duane street; a very different place from the magnificent structure at Eighth avenue and Twenty-third street which now contains the offices of the Company. Reaching the office, Miss Anthony saw two men; one had snapping black eyes, and coal-black moustache and beard; while the other was of florid complexion, his eyes blue, and hair and moustache curly auburn. Miss Anthony drew a copy of the *Revolution* from her pocket, and approached the dark-complexioned gentleman.

"Is this Mr. Jay Gould?" she asked.

The gentleman nodded assent, while the lady laid the copy of the *Revolution* on his desk, and stated her business. She enlarged upon the ennobling influence which the advancement of the cause she represented would have upon society; and closed by assuring Mr. Gould that she knew him to be the friend of every movement tending to purify and elevate humanity. Then she asked for reduced rates of fare to those attending the Convention.

The gentleman of the auburn locks stopped his writing, and looked as if he had heard the rumbling of an earthquake.

Mr. Gould began a lively conversation with Miss Anthony, while the light complexioned man fidgeted uneasily in his chair.

"So you are Miss Anthony, of the *Revolution?*" inquired Mr. Gould.

"I am," was the reply.

"Would it be ungallant for me to inquire who reports the Wall street gossip for the *Revolution?*" continued Mr. Gould.

"I cannot tell you," answered Miss Anthony. "Our reports have created a great sensation. The Wall street line is the only line in which we beat the other papers; and I believe that some of them are favorites with you gentlemen. I think you must acknowledge that the Wall street reports of the *Revolution* are always accurate."

Mr. Gould made no reply. The other gentleman could stand it no longer. He arose to his feet, walked to Mr. Gould's desk, looked Miss Anthony in the eye for fourteen seconds, and then strode back to his desk with a heavy step and dropped in his cushioned chair.

"I know," said Miss Anthony, "that it must worry you gentlemen mightily to have the secrets of Wall street laid bare in the *Revolution* every week; but the fact of the matter is, gentlemen, that there is so much quarreling in Wall street, and there are so many noses out of joint, that the jobbers are like a set of old women. They all tell stories about one another, and the *Revolution* gets hold of these stories. But," she continued, turning to Mr. Gould, "how about reducing the fares for the delegates to the Woman's Rights Convention? I know you have a noble heart, a kind disposition, and a generous——"

"Oh, certainly," interrupted Mr. Gould; "we will reduce the fare."

Here the auburn-haired gentleman again jumped to his feet, and walked to Mr. Gould's desk, saying:

"Mr. Gould, I wish you would remember that the *Revolution* has done us more harm than have all the rest of the New York journals put together."

Miss Anthony's gray eyes sought the mild blue eyes.

"Is this Prince Erie?" she smilingly inquired.

"I am Mr. Fisk, at your service, madam," replied the prince, gallantly lifting his hat. "Are you the Queen of the strong-minded?"

Miss Anthony blushed, fastened her eyes on Mr. Fisk's huge diamond, and answered: "I am the managing editor of the *Revolution*, and I am glad—I may say, I rejoice—to hear that it has done you so much injury. It is a sure indication that it can do the Erie road as much good, when that road is put on a sound basis."

Here Prince Erie replaced his hat, and returned to his desk. Miss Anthony again began a quiet conversation with Mr. Gould, during which she twice dropped her shawl, which Mr. Gould twice raised and hung upon her extended arm. In a few moments Miss Anthony sweetly smiled, said, "Good morning, gentlemen!" and floated from the room.

The next number of the *Revolution* contained the glad announcement that those members of the Woman's Rights Convention coming to the city on the Erie road, could procure return tickets free, on application to Miss Anthony.

When President Grant visited New York, June 18, 1869, he passed the evening at Fisk's Fifth Avenue Theatre, where he listened to the warblings of Irma and Desclauzas, and witnessed the can-can, in the opera bouffe, which the Erie Prince had placed on the stage at this cosy temple of Thespis.

The President was delighted with the entertainment, and Prince Erie was happy at the success of the company which he had brought together.

During the great Peace Jubilee in Boston, in June, 1869, President Grant visited the Hub. He left New York on the Providence, one of the superb steamers of the Narraganset line, of which Company Colonel Fisk was the president. President Grant received a military escort to the boat. He was also accompanied by Mr. Jay Gould and Vice-Commodore Simons, of the Narraganset line. At the pier the party was received by Mr. Fisk, who was clad in an Admiral's uniform, most gorgeously decorated. His moustache had paid a recent visit to his inimitable barber; his gold-trimmed uniform shone with extraordinary brilliancy, and his big diamond sparkled brighter than Venus on a frosty night. The Admiral received the party with that careless ease which always characterized him. From bow to stern, inside and out, the Providence was decked with streamers and pennants. A bridal chamber had been set apart for the President's use; and the Admiral, with his usual prodigality, offered the President the entire boat, if he wanted it. Champagne which could not be surpassed, and cigars of fabulous cost, were ordered for the delectation of the honored guest. Dodworth's band accompanied the party; and nothing, which the most lavish expenditure of money could command, was wanting to enhance the delights of the occasion. After a lively trip, in which the festive Admiral figured extensively, the party arrived in Boston.

On June 16th, the second day of the great musical festival, Grant and his suite, which included many prominent civilians and military and naval officers, (among the last-named, Admiral Fisk,) visited the Coliseum to witness the great musical festival and listen to the anvil and cannon choruses. The Admiral was dressed in his gorgeous uniform, which far exceeded in splendor that worn by any other officer in the retinue. He took a prominent position in the suite, and marched down the grand aisle, the observed of all observers. The entire chorus and orchestra gave—

"See, the conquering hero comes!"

and the President was greeted with the greatest demonstrations of welcome. While he reservedly acknowledged the cordial greeting, Admiral Fisk, in the most gracious and unaffected manner, acknowledged such portion of the applause as he deemed intended for him, and his easy and profuse style left no doubt that he thought a large share of the plaudits meant for him.

During the performance, a photographic apparatus was brought upon the stage and the vast audience had its likeness taken. Among the naval officers present were several admirals. Admiral Fisk was a prominent figure in the photographic group, and he appeared on terms of easy familiarity with his brother officers.

Fisk's splendid impudence during the entire visit to the Coliseum did not, as it has in some similar cases, where men of smaller calibre have attempted the same role, bring upon him any measure of contempt. In fact, the vast assemblage seemed rather to enjoy it. He was, very soon after, dubbed "Jubilee Jim," which title was, perhaps, more frequently applied to him thereafter than that of Prince Erie.

During the summer of 1869, the Hon. Horace Greeley had occasion to visit Boston. He went by Admiral Fisk's line of steamers. When he reached the pier, he found the Admiral, in his gorgeous uniform, superintending the loading of the steamer. Mr. Fisk spied the quaintly-attired philosopher of the *Tribune,* and recognized him in an instant. Seizing his carpet-bag, the Admiral cried out:

"Mr. Greeley, I am happy to see you; you are welcome. Come right on board. We shall be off directly."

Mr. Greeley hesitated, and, in evident alarm, clung to his carpet-bag.

"My name is Fisk," said the Admiral. "You have, probably, heard of me before, Mr. Greeley?"

"Oh, yes; I remember you now. You were an ensign in the North Atlantic blockading squadron in 1864? I remember you very well. I had occasion to use your name while compiling the 'American Conflict.'"

The Admiral drew back, apparently dumbfounded. Then he seized Mr. Greeley by the arm, and drew him on the boat, laughing heartily.

"You are much mistaken, Mr. Greeley," said he. "I am James Fisk, Jr., of the Erie Railroad; you should certainly know me, for I have been indebted to you for several compliments in the *Tribune* on the conduct of that road."

Mr. Greeley cast his eyes upon the sparkling diamonds on Mr. Fisk's bosom, then gave a fresh glance at the glittering uniform, and replied:

"Yes; it has been my opinion that the Erie road has been mismanaged. I am, and always have been a friend of the Erie. I urged the building of the road; I sank $10,000 in aid of it. The road should pay; there is no reason in the world why its stockholders should not receive a handsome yearly dividend. It runs through an agricultural section of country, and the milk-trains alone—."

Here the Admiral escorted Mr. Greeley to the cabin, and, calling the head waiter, directed him to procure a first-class state-room for his friend, the Hon. Horace Greeley. The waiter soon returned with the alarming intelligence that, with one exception, every state-room on the boat was engaged.

"What?" shouted Mr. Fisk.

"The bridal chamber is the only state-room unoccupied," was the reply.

"Well, escort Mr. Greeley to that, then," answered the Admiral.

Mr. Greeley objected to the bridal chamber, and said he had no objection to sleeping on a sofa. He finally yielded, however, and accepted the situation.

Mr. Greeley was received at the supper-table with marked attention. Every delicacy was set before him, and a bottle of Roederer was sent him, with the compliments of the Admiral. This was declined by Mr. Greeley, who would drink nothing but water.

No money was taken from Mr. Greeley. The freedom of the boat was placed at his disposal. When he offered to pay his fare, it was refused, with the remark that his money was not good. Mr. Greeley, apparently surprised, offered another greenback. This was also refused on the ground of its suspicious character. Mr. Greeley insisted that the clerk was mistaken. The clerk then told him that he was under orders from Mr. Fisk to receive no money from him. He was the guest of the company.

In the evening Mr. Greeley visited the deck. The band struck up "Hail to the Chief," which was followed by cheers from the passengers. At 11 P. M. Mr. Greeley retired to the bridal chamber, escorted by Mr. Fisk.

One of Mr. Fisk's most curious actions was his presentation of birds to Judge Barnard. While the Judge has suffered much from imputations cast upon his character by reason of his decisions in suits involving the Erie Railway, the decisions always suited Fisk. In June, 1869, Mr. Fisk sent the judge two owls. The owl is emblematic of wisdom. To send a judge one owl is to signify to him only that you consider him a grave and reverend judge. On the other hand, comparisons being odious, it is not always easy to say to a judge that you consider him superior to all other judges. But how delicate a way did Mr. Fisk discover for doing this difficult thing! He sent to the learned judge *two* owls! as much as to say, "I consider your Honor equal in wisdom to any two other judges."

Fisk's tropically luxuriant tastes, his almost grotesque desire for gaudy colors and brilliant surroundings, reached their climax in the furnishing of the Erie offices in the Grand Opera House. Over $250,000 was expended in fitting up this unequalled business palace. A flight of stairs ushers the visitor into the main hall, floored with marble of tesselated white and blue. The hall is fitted with sections of polished black walnut inlaid with other polished woods. Richly-figured ground glass is inserted in the panels, and the desks are of equal costliness. The ceiling displays the richest suggestions of Pompeian art. Blue, carmine, lilac and gold are blended in a fanciful tracery of lines and curves. Through these run intertwining flowers and vines, among which nestle naked cupids and rosy nymphs. In the center is a mythological maiden in a drapery of green and red. Other and fantastic devices in brilliant colors decorate the ceiling. In the four several corners are Morse, Franklin, Fulton and

WILLIAM M. TWEED.

Watt, in a blaze of color. Chandeliers costing $1,000 each hang from the ceiling.

At one end of the grand hall a lofty pair of $500 doors swing back, revealing what was the sanctum sanctorum of the blonde Admiral. A plushy carpet of gold and brown sinks under the feet. On a raised platform stands a $500 desk of polished walnut, inlaid with walnut root and striped with gold. Behind this a $500 chair, richly upholstered and studded with gold-headed nails. The prevailing hues of the wall-paper are brown and gold, while the ceiling is of cerulean blue blended with fawn, and bright with crimson ovals. On these latter is imprinted in letters of gold the word "Erie." In one corner stands a $1,000 wash-stand, of most delicate marble and porcelain, the bowl being tinted with rose and gold, and displaying the figures of lovely nymphs in disporting attitudes. Every other appurtenance is of the same splendid description, and the rooms of the other officers of the company display the same royal magnificence.

At the time of opening the offices a great storm was raised throughout the country over what was claimed to be a fraudulent expenditure of the Company's moneys. But public clamor proved unavailing, and the Erie Company's business is still transacted in the same superb apartments, which include besides, perfectly appointed kitchens and elegant dining and sleeping rooms.

Fisk could do nothing like other people. Whatever he did must be bigger, better or gaudier. In the summer of 1869 he placed on the North River the ferry-boat James Fisk, Jr., undoubtedly the finest of New York's ferry-boats. The vessel's extreme length is 178 feet, and her extreme breadth 63 feet. In compliance with the Admiral's characteristic love of notoriety, a portrait of himself, elaborately framed and surrounded by the national insignia was placed at either end of the boat. The panels in the cabin are painted a delicate green, with pearl stiles, while the cornices and arches are of lilac, pink and pearl. Each seat in the smoking cabin is provided with a spittoon and a match-scraper, while a gas-light similar to those seen in tobacconists' stores hangs conveniently near.

The boat is built of the best materials throughout. A large number of handsome mirrors adorn the saloons. Her life-saving apparatus is unusually complete. She runs from Twenty-third street to the Erie Railway pier.

One day in July, 1869, Admiral Fisk stood in his office getting ready to leave for the piers to see his steamers off. While the Admiral pared his nails with a fifty-dollar pocket knife, his valet got ready his uniform. Donning his jaunty cap, he was about to leave the office, when he received the following telegram:

"Save a state-room for Chief-Justice Chase. He is on train. Don't fail."

Fisk was delighted. He rushed down to pier 30 to stop the steamer *Bristol*. "Chase is coming on the Jersey road. Send a carriage for him," said Fisk.

"What Chase?" asked Simons.

"What Chase?" said Fisk. "Old Chase; Salmon—Horace Greeley's friend."

While Simons dashed off after the Chief-Justice, Fisk detained the boat; a crowd of admiring boot-blacks gathering about and watching the resplendent Admiral.

When half an hour past her sailing time, the Admiral reluctantly gave orders for the *Bristol's* departure, and went down to pier 28 to hold the Newport boat; thinking that Simons might bring the Chief-Justice there, as he (the Admiral) did not know whether Mr. Chase wanted to go by the Newport or the Fall River line.

The Newport was detained until 7:30 P.M., when half-a-dozen carriages dashed down the pier. Simons descended from one of them, but no Chase.

"Where's Chase?" shouted the Admiral.

"He's gone on the Stonington line," said Simons. "The train was delayed by an open draw-bridge, and while I was on this side of the river looking for him the Stonington fellows went across and gobbled him up."

The Admiral took off his silver-starred cap and scratched his head. Then he shouted, "Cast off!" to the Captain of the Newport, and turned and walked up the pier. As he entered his carriage he said:

"Well, shiver my mizzen mast, and rip my royal halyards! I've had a great deal to do with justices and judges in my time, but a Washington justice lays over anything of the kind I ever saw in New York City. Drive on, Tom!"

Fisk's pluck and audacity were well shown in the celebrated war between the Erie and the Albany and Susquehanna Railroads. Mr. Van Valkenburgh, of the last-named road testified on the examination that Fisk told him he would get possession of his road "if it cost millions of money and took any number of men." Mr. Van Valkenburgh also testified that Colonel Fisk offered to play Mr. Ramsey, President of the Albany and Susquehanna road, a game of seven-up for the railroad.

Fisk used often to tell of his first mistake in life.

Said the Colonel, "When I was a little boy on the Vermont

farm, my father took me up to the stable one day, where a row of cows stood in the stable."

Said he, "James, the stable window is pretty high for a boy, but do you think you could take this shovel and clean out the stable?"

"I don't know, 'Pop,'" said James, "I never *have* done it."

"Well, my boy, if you will do it this morning, I'll give you this bright silver dollar," said his father, patting him on his head, while he held the silver dollar before his eyes.

"Good," says James; "I'll try;" and away he went to work. He tugged and pulled and lifted and puffed, and, finally, it was done, and his father gave him the bright silver dollar, saying—

"That's right, James; you did it splendidly, and now, I find you can do it so nicely, I shall have you do it *every morning all winter!*" E. P.

Fisk said his second mistake occurred in maturer years—when he first became associated with Gould in the Erie office.

"How was it?" asked Colonel Rucker.

"Well," said Fisk, "Gould had some woman litigation on hand, and he came to me and said he wanted to use my name."

"What for?" said I.

"Well, Fisk," said Gould, "you know my wife is very sensitive, and you know this woman business is full of scandal. Now, you know you don't care, so just let me use your name for a week in this case."

"What was the result, Colonel?" asked Bucker.

"Result? Why, by thunder, Gould used my name one week, and there wasn't anything left of it. It was used up.

He got it so mixed up and scandalized, that I never could retain it, and I felt as if I didn't care a damn about it afterwards!" E. P.

Fisk was busy at his desk. A poor old man came to the door.

"I want to see Colonel Fisk," said the stranger.

"Here he is, Pop," said the Colonel, with a laugh; "come in, and tell us about it."

"I want your assistance in getting me to Lowell, where my wife is. I am out of money."

"Where have you been?" asked Fisk.

"I don't like to tell you, sir," said the grey-haired stranger, hanging his head.

"You'd better tell me," said Fisk. "It won't hurt you."

"I've been four years and six months in State prison. I was put in for five years; but on account of good behavior, I had six months taken off."

"What were you put in for?"

"Grand larceny."

"Hell!" said Fisk. "John,"—to his private secretary—"give this old man a pass, and some money to pay his fare to the boat; and send a man to show him how to get there. He's been so long away that he's forgotten. And, old fellow, make a good start for an honest life; and if I can help you, let me know."

The ex-convict departed with tears in his eyes, and a sob in his throat. "God bless you!" was all he could say. "You'll not be sorry for this."

Six months later Fisk received a letter from the old man. He was then a respected citizen, doing an excellent business, and brim-full of gratitude to one of the few men in the world who could say a kind word to a thief.

In the summer of 1869, when Fisk first moved into the Opera House, he received an indignant call from Daniel Drew, against whom he had recently opened suit for the recovery of certain moneys. Uncle Daniel came in, puffing his cigar in his peculiar manner, and after dodging the question for a while, blurted out, with a whine: "Now, Jeems, how kin you find it in your heart to treat an old man so?"

"Do you remember what the Nabob said to the other fellow?"

"No, I don't.

Well, he remarked quietly to him, under circumstances much like the present, 'How, if the boot were on the other leg?'"

A poor woman came in one day, with a pitiful story. Her husband, a mechanic, had broken his leg, and they were in a state of utter destitution. Fisk called a detective "Go with this woman. Learn whether her story is true."

The officer returned, with the report that affairs were even worse than the poor woman had made them.

"John," said the Colonel, "put down $25 a week for that woman, till her husband gets well." The payment was kept up regularly till March, when the mechanic, having fully recovered, came down to thank his benefactor.

"Never mind thanks, my good fellow; I find that I made a damned good investment."

Fisk's $15, received for attending each meeting of the Erie Board, he never used. He always handed the amount to his secretary, with directions to put it in an envelope and give it to the first deserving object of charity that should come in. At the last meeting that Fisk attended, he was all alone. "John," said he, "take that money and put it away. The Lord will send somebody for it."

Sure enough, on the following day a letter came from a family in distress.

"Told you so, John. The Lord will take care of these fellows. Send it on."

"My colored brother," said the Colonel to a plain, honest-looking colored gentleman, who had called to get pecuniary aid for his little church on Eighth Avenue; "if there's anything I like to boost along, it's early piety--and it's damned hard to have too much of it. Captain Williamson will go down with you and make inquiries. If he says it's all right —and I believe it is—you shall have the money."

The Captain made a favorable report, and the hearts of the colored brethren were soon made glad.

A conductor on the Erie road was detected in embezzling the Company's funds, and was discharged. He begged very hard to be taken back, restored the stolen money, and promised solemnly that he would never again betray his trust. He was a politician in a small way, and his application for reinstatement was endorsed by a number of the city's political magnates, among whom was a judge of the Supreme Court. The judge was very urgent in his demand. "All right," said Fisk; "I'll send you some papers to-night, and then we'll talk about it." He forwarded a number of affidavits to the judge, who read them carefully. On the following day Fisk met the Judge. "What do you say now? Shall I put that man back on your recommendation?"

"I guess I'll say no more about it," said the judge.

A hump-back boy, hat in hand, walked in timidly one morning.

"Are you Colonel Fisk, sir?" said he, twirling his well-worn hat around nervously.

"That's what they call me, sonny. Now, what can I do for you?"

"I'm a news-boy; and I'm trying to get a stand in some good place where I can sell more papers,"

"Got father and mother?"

"Got a mother and two little sisters, as I takes care of."

"Good boy! Now run over to the corner of Eighth Avenue and 23d street, give my compliments to the gentleman in the drug-store, and ask him to give you permission to build your stand on that corner; then come back to me."

In a few minutes the boy was back, his face wearing a look of great disappointment."

"Won't do it," said the boy.

Fisk was now changing his coat.

"Come along, Deacon, and I'll get you a stand."

They marched from place to place for an hour or more, but no stand was secured. At last, at the corner of Broadway and 29th street, the coveted site was found, and full permission given to the boy to establish himself there. The little fellow's gratitude was more than doubled when Colonel Fisk, with a pleasant word of encouragement, handed him a greenback of goodly size, with which to purchase his stock in trade. At this writing the young stationer is driving a brisk trade at the stand which Colonel Fisk procured for him; and he holds in lively remembrance the kindness of his benefactor.

When Fisk was shot by Stokes, he was calling upon Mrs. Morse and her daughters. Mr. Morse was an old friend of Fisk's. While bathing near New Orleans a year or two ago, he broke his neck by diving in shallow water. When Fisk heard of the accident, he at once sent for Mrs. Morse, her mother and her daughters, and pledged himself to support them while they lived; and the pledge was faithfully kept. A few months ago the elder Mrs. Morse became afflicted with a dangerous disease of the eyes. Fisk sent the whole family to Europe, where they remained until the patient was thoroughly cured, through the efforts of the best surgeons in the old world.

"Alighting at No. 74 Chester Square, and ascending a flight of massive granite steps, we pulled the silver bell-knob, and soon the large plate-glass doorway swung open, and a colored servant in livery ushered us into the magnificent reception room. After a few moments delay, Mrs. Fisk entered the room, She was dressed for an evening reception, which she was to have attended at Rice's, on Beacon street. We had anticipated seeing a splendid lady, but the magnificent woman who appeared before us, attired in a white velvet dress, *en train*, cut slightly *decollete*, with jewels and the flash of diamonds, quite bewildered us. Presenting our note of introduction, we received a most genial welcome, and at once felt at home in the presence of her who lives in indulgence of all the wants and wishes that wealth can secure. Presently another lady, Miss Fanny Harrod, entered the room. She is the companion of Mrs. Fisk, and the *financée* of a Broad street banker. The two ladies, whether at the opera, the theatre, or driving along the Boston boulevards, or traveling over the country, are inseparable.

Mrs. Fisk's marriage with James Fisk, Jr., took place at Ashland, Massachusetts, in the autumn of 1855. Her maiden name was Lucy D. Moore. She was an orphan, and a ward of Mr. Sanderson of Springfield. For two years previous to her marriage she attended the Brattleboro Female Seminary. There is where she first met Mr. Fisk, and became engaged to him. They resided there until 1865, when they removed to Boston, and took rooms at the Marlboro Hotel, on Washington street. They then went to the more fashionable Tremont House, remaining there until 1867, when Mrs. Fisk purchased in her own name her present splendid residence. It is valued at $75,000; and its situation is the best not only in Chester Square, but in Boston. . . . A Mansard roof crowns the structure. The basement is very deep, and divided into kitchen, laundry, and dining-room. The first floor is an extensive drawing room, the whole length of the deep house; on the floor above are the reception rooms. The third floor is divided into a library, Mrs. Fisk's suite, and chambers for guests. In the fourth story are the billiard and card rooms, and chambers for servants. The drawing-room, while one of the largest in Boston, is furnished with a splendor seldom, if ever, met with in any New England State. The furniture, chairs, settees, cases, tables, are of solid rosewood, elaborately carved. The chairs are covered with bright crimson; the curtains are costly lace, with over-curtains of crimson satin, looped to a border of gold. The carpet, which is a heavy Axminster, is a delicate pearl-color ground-work, which blends with the prevailing color of the frescoed walls. The ground-work of the carpet is relieved by flowers of various hues, of which crimson is the chief. These correspond with the tapestry of the furniture. The mantel is Parian marble. The chandeliers were imported from Paris, and are exceedingly *récherché*. The walls are dressed with rare and costly paintings. There are among them a number of porcelain-types and paintings of James Fisk, Jr. At least two dozen, possibly fifty, representations of James Fisk, Jr., hang on the walls. Some are burlesque; many are of ordinary artistic work, while a few are superior in design and execution. He is represented in quite all positions and attitudes, from a quiet seat in the drawing-room to a standing position on a flying locomotive, with Grant and Jay Gould clinging to him. The reception rooms are richly furnished and cosy. The same superior taste which we notice in the arrangement of the drawing-room, also prevails here. The carpets are Axminsters, woven solid; scarlet ground-work with central figures of flowers wreathed into an immense bouquet. The furniture is highly polished solid rosewood.

"The curtains are of the richest lace. The paintings are fine. It is here where Mrs. Fisk's domestic traits of character are observed. The rooms glow with flowers, delicate plants and shrubs. They are seen in every window, in all the corners of the rooms, in the niches of the marble mantles, and underneath the rosewood and marble tables. They are hung in tasty bead, moss, and china baskets, from different parts of the rooms. The halls on each floor contain flower-pots and vines. The carpets in the rooms of the third floor composing Mrs. Fisk's suite are Axminsters, pearl white ground-work, with chintz figures in every variety of colors. The billiard-room above, and the adjoining card-rooms, are carpeted with scarlet brussels. A linen shield extends around the billiard-table, which is one of the best. The furniture of this floor is solid mahogany and black walnut. The halls and stairs are covered with brussels carpets of a prevailing crimson color. The rugs and mats throughout the house are most costly and elegant. The dining-room is elegant. The furniture is rosewood, sideboard, tables, chairs and all. The chairs are trimmed with velvet. Lace curtains hang at the windows, and a fine brussels carpet sleeps on the floor. The ground-work of this carpet is green, of that lovely shade that almost compels the thought that one is standing on wood-mosses. The shade is relieved with tiny figures of orange. The whole effect is that of a woodland carpet. There are costlier and more magnificent carpets in the rooms above, but the prettiest in the house is that in the dining-room. The china and silver sets for Mrs. Fisk's table are probably the most complete in this country. The house has been furnished entirely regardless of expense.

"Mrs. Fisk's jewels are not only more numerous, more varied, and comprise a greater range of gems, but are the most valuable in this country. We can only mention a few of her most valuable jewels. She has several watches set in diamonds, and a number of very fine chains, both long and short. One watch, of recent importation, is perhaps the only one of the kind worn in this country. It is a miniature album, in the centre of one of the covers is a very tiny time-piece. The covers are studded with diamonds. The album contains a number of gold leaves in which small miniatures may be adjusted.

"A diamond brooch with a four carat steel white centre diamond, and sixteen two carat stones, each worth $3,000 in gold, is the most valuable diamond ornament in the United States, excepting two diamond crosses owned in New York.

Mrs. Fisk owns a set of diamond ear-rings, brooch and cross for necklace valued at thirty thousand dollars. Her various ear-rings, finger-rings, crosses and brooches containing diamonds, represent more than four hundred thousand dollars. Her pearl necklaces, one of triple rows, and another of great length, are exceedingly beautiful and very valuable. Her *trousseau* is not second to any worn by an American lady. Mrs. Fisk's splendid coach and four-in-hand, is the finest turn-out in New England, or in the United States outside of New York city. Most of the harness was made to order in London. It is black, with profuse gold-plated ornaments. The coach is high and long, with an oval glass front, and is trimmed with heavy blue silk, quilted with white thread. The panel of each door and the rear of the coach bear the monogram J. F., Jr., in raised gold-plated letters. The horses are two coal-black geldings and two superb milk-white steeds, and are arranged as follows: A coal-black nigh wheel horse, and white off wheel horse; black off leader, and white nigh leader. When this turn-out, which is driven by Albert Reed, Mrs. Fisk's coachman, appears on the Boston drives, or tears up Beacon street heights, crowds pause to admire and wonder over it. This turn-out has created a sensation in the Hub. Mrs. Fisk, however, prefers to drive out into the country and enjoy the quiet of the many beautiful drives surrounding Boston. This establishment and most of her jewels are presents from her husband.

"In her personal appearance Mrs. Fisk is unusally attractive and charming. The majority of observers would call her beautiful. She is tall, even a trifle taller than Mr. Fisk, slightly inclined of late years to *embonpoint* and with a perfect carriage, appears most stately at all times. She is 32 years old. Her complexion is blonde. Her hair is dark-brown, but long, fine and heavy. Her figure is one that commands attention wherever she goes. This excellent lady's character, her benevolence, which is unbounded and quietly bestowed, her love of home and many accomplishments, have made her of late years the cynosure of all eyes. Mrs. Fisk's fortune is among the millions, but she has not received gifts of large sums of money from Mr. Fisk, as is generally supposed. As soon as they were wedded she received a present of some property located in Main street, Brattleboro, Vermont. Since that time she has continued to purchase property there in her own name, and at present owns the majority of the business buildings and residences in Main street. Her property has so increased in value that it is now estimated to be worth $2,000,000. She is a woman of admirable business tact."

A poor young negro theological student came to Fisk.

"What's the matter with *your* tin oven, Brother Johnson?" asked the Colonel.

"I wish to go to the Howard Seminary in Washington, sir, to complete my studies for the ministry; and I am without money."

"Too bad. Now, we must always help along the cause. John, give Brother Johnson a pass to Washington.

One day Fisk was traveling to Niagara with his brother-in-law Hooker. The director's car passed a car full of calves.

"There, Colonel—there are some of your relations," said Hooker, laughing.

"Yes; relations *by marriage*," said Fisk. E. P.

The day before Fisk was shot he came into the office, and after looking over some interest account, he shouted, "Gould! Gould!"

"Well, what?" says Gould, stroking his jetty whiskers.

"I want to know how you go to work to figure this interest so that it *amounts to more than the principal?*" said the Colonel.
E. P.

Some of the trustees of a church in Brattleboro' sent to Fisk for money to build a new grave-yard fence.

"What in thunder do you want with a new fence?" exclaimed he. "Those that are in can't get out; and those that are out don't want to get in; so what's the use of it?"

This is the way a Williams College Junior dishes up the life and adventures of the Prince of Erie in the *Williams Review:*

Now lith and listen, gentylmen,
That of myrthes loveth to here,
And I wil tel to you a storye
Wil mak you monye a tere.

Syr Jimfisk hee was the noblest knyghte
In al New Yorke citee,
In hys stockyngs al hee was sixe fete tal,
And hys gyrdel was sixe fete thre.

Ful merry a chylde was Syr Jimfisk,
In drynk and al pleasaunce,
And ful ofte hee sate in the theeatyr,
To se the fayre mayds dance.

Thys mickle knyghte in hys garden walked,
Which was hys maner mete,
When hee behelde a lyttel footepage
Com runyng down the strete.

"Now tel me, tel me, thou lyttel footepage,
What mought the matere bee?"
"Syr Knyghte, the men in yon citee,
In cryance cal upon thee."

"Now, harnys me quick six horses,
And carye me to the fraye,
And I wil sucor thys faytheful towne,
That caleth on mee thys daye."

With his faytheful band of frendes treu,
To the batyl he is gon,
And there hee findeth a grieveouse stryfe,
When that hee is com anone.

For the Yrishmen had brokyn loose
And monye men had slayne,
Then did Syr Jimfisk kil them al,
And get the towne grate gayne.

"Now blesse thee, now, our lord Jimfisk!"
The peple with joie did crye;
But hee's wounded soe in hys smallest toe,
That it feres hym he must dye.

But then cam a leech and guv him quicke,
A draft of vertues grate,
That uppe hee rose from hys dying bed,
And called for a whiskye strate.

Thys doughtye wight was sore distraught,
For a vyrgin fare to se,
Hyght Josephine shee was yelept,
With eyen bryght of blee.

But thys mayden fare was fals-hearted,
A treytress foul and fel,
And shee is gone to the mayre of New Yorke,
And a fals tale shee does tel.

Now heaven thee save, thou gentyl knyght,
They plot agaynst thy hed.
And but if thou flee the morrowe mornyng,
I wot thou wilt bee ded!

Then a carlish churl of the north country,
Whom hyghte was Stoaks by name,
Rose upp and tooke a lyttel pystol,
And hee loaded the same.

And hee shot Syr Jimfisk in the hart,
As hee cam out of the dore,
And such a mournful tale as thys
I never wil tel you more. Amen.

As many statements have from time to time been made public, purporting to be correct copies of the will of James Fisk, Jr., which were, all of them, incorrect, that it is gratifying to be able at length to give a true copy of the will as admitted to probate by Surrogate Hutchings.

James Fisk, father of the decedent, named as legatee in the will with the widow, joined in the petition for the admission of the will to probate, thereby waiving all objection to its provisions. Mr. Jordan, too, named as co-executor with the widow, retired from such office, thereby constituting Mrs. Fisk sole executor of the will.

All necessary conditions and preliminaries being complied with, the Surrogate felt justified in admitting the will to probate, granting letters testamentary to Mrs. Fisk.

The estate was sworn to as not exceeding one million dollars.

THE GRAVE OF COL. JAMES FISK, Jr.

## THE WILL.

I, James Fisk, Jr., of the City of New York, being of sound mind and memory, do make, publish and declare this my last will and testament, hereby revoking all former wills by me made.

1. I give, devise and bequeath all my estate and property, real and personal, except the special legacy hereinafter mentioned, to my beloved wife, Lucy D. Fisk, subject, however, to a trust to pay to my dear father and mother jointly, or to the survivor of them, $3,000 a year for their support, during the life of them or either of them; and further to pay to Minnie F. Morse and Rosie C. Morse each $2,000 a year, during their lives respectively until marriage, when the annuity of the one marrying shall cease. The property and estate aforesaid to vest absolutely in the said Lucy and her heirs, forever, subject only as aforesaid; and the said trust shall not effect her right freely to dispose of and transfer any such property.

2. I give and bequeath to my sister, Mrs. Mary G. Hooker, stock in the Narragansett Steamship Company of the par value of $100,000, for her sole and separate use for ever.

3. I appoint my said wife and my friend Eben D. Jordan, of Boston, executors of this my last will and testament.

In witness whereof I have hereunto set my hand and seal this 6th day of January, 1872.

JAMES FISK, JR.

Signed, sealed, published and declared by the testator to be his last will and testament, in the presence of us, who have hereto subscribed our names as witnesses, at his request and in his presence, and in the presence of each other.

THOMAS G. SHEARMAN, 316 West 22nd st., N. Y.
JAY GOULD, 578 Fifth Avenue, New York.
F. WILLIS FISHER, M. D., Grand Central Hotel.

Fisk was always fond of birds. His houses and his steamers were always kept alive with them. A month or two after his death, the little songsters belonging to the Narragansett were sold at auction. There were 250 of them, and a large crowd had assembled at the Art Rooms, 587 Broadway, to take part in the sale, or to gratify curiosity. Nearly all the birds had been named by their owner. They were numbered from 1 to 250, and sold in regular order. No. 3, Crazy Bill, brought $7; Charlie Williams, $5.50; Humpty Dumpty, $6.50; Old Billy, $6.50; Beauty, $5.75; Col. Braine, $6.50; Robinson Crusoe, $6.00; Charlie McGowan, $6.50; Ben Wood, $6; Jeff Davis, $6.25; Mrs. Scudder, $6.25; Col. Fisk, Jr., $16.25; Jay Gould, $8.50; Charles Macintyre, $7.50; Hamilton Fish, $6.25; Major Hitchcock, $6.75; Daniel S. Dickinson, $6; A. T. Stewart, $6; Commodore Vanderbilt, $6.50; August Belmont, $6.25; Captain Leslie, $6.00; "Gus" Fuller (named after the President of the New York and Boston Express Company), $7.50; Charles Kimball, $7; Commodore Tilton, $10.50; Sampson, $6.50 (a very strong singer); M. R. Simons, $8; Ben Butler, $7.50; Gen. McClellan, $6.50; Dr. Helmbold, $6; Wm. M. Tweed, $6; Col. Murphy, $6; Robert Bonner, $6.25; Stokes, $7.50; Gen. Sheridan, $7.25; Gen. Hammond, $6: Dr. Tyng, $9.50; Gen. Scott, $6.75; Commodore Ringgold, $6.50; Admiral Farragut, $6; Top-Knot, $7.50; Blind Tom,

$4.75; Schuyler Colfax, $6.50; Senator Revels, $6.25; and Gen. Grant, $7.50.

A number of birds were sold at $14, $12, $11, $10, $9, and $8, the finest singers bringing usually the highest prices.

At 12:45 the music box, with a working model of the steamer Providence attached, made to order, and wrought in solid silver and gold, and costing $2,500, was put up. The first bid was $4, decidedly a small figure, taking into consideration the original cost. This was raised to $500. Other bids followed until $800 was reached. Then the sale rested.

At 3 o'clock bidding was resumed, and the splendid trinket was finally knocked down to Miss Nullie Pierris, an actress and singer at the Grand Opera House, for $1,500.

The cages containing the birds were of gilt brass, very handsome, and worth at least $5 each. The prices realized for birds and cages ranged from $4.75 to $16.25. The net proceeds of the sale were $3,000.

"Pinion," the New York correspondent of the Boston *Mechanics' Advertiser*, thus wrote to his paper a day or two after Fisk's death:

"I went to Boston with the Ninth Regiment, last year. As near as I could judge, the people of Boston thought that Fisk was doing the thing as a mere act of bravado; but it is my belief that they were greatly mistaken. Fisk's first recognition in regular commercial circles was in Boston, with Jordan, Marsh & Co., and he always cherished as one of the bright spots of his life this partnership in a heavy and respectable house. Then Boston, pre-eminently pious, aristocratic Boston, had turned up its nose at Fisk, and voted him a vulgar *parvenu*. Fisk (than whom there was no better judge of human nature) knew that much of this verdict was based on the opinion of men as low in moral status as himself. There is no doubt that he wanted to snub these men, but, seriously, I believe that he felt a longing to be recognized of society and his fellows, a desire to be regarded as Jim Fisk the man, rather than Jim Fisk the monstrosity, and I think he desired such recognition more in Boston than anywhere else. I really believe that his speech in the Boston Theatre was from the heart, and it spoke the yearning of a man who felt himself barred out from men, but who wanted to open a heart which he still had within him, and take all the world into fellowship.

"Well—you remember the advent of the Ninth. In this city their reputation is not second to that of the 'Seventh.' The Ninth fairly compelled the admiration of Boston, and Fisk was delighted. But his greatest triumph was on the night when the superb band of the Ninth played on the Common. Of course you remember the vast assemblage which congregated, and you remember the music which the red-coated musicians made. I don't believe there was a man in the band who did not share the desire of Fisk to impress Boston favorably, and they all played splendidly. Levy blew his cornet as he never did before, and there is no disguising the fact that the people who crowded on the Common were delighted. Jim was happy over their repeated manifestations of approval. He cared far more for them than for the so-called upper classes who had tabooed him. When Levy gave the final blast on his bugle, a Boston man who stood near the stand (you remember the fight over whether the Ninth could worship on Sunday) cried out: 'Jim, you can have the Common to-morrow.'

"Fisk was delighted. He turned to me with pleasure

beaming on his face, and said, 'I really think the people of this town would vote against their Council if they had the chance.'

"I thought (and still think) the same way, and I told him so. When we got back to the St. James, I guess Jim was the happiest man in Boston; not because he had *spited* Boston, but because he thought he had won some share of honest esteem from its people."

Fisk heard, two or three winters before his death, that a young man whom he had befriended was lying ill at his boarding-house. He went to see the sufferer and found that he was not properly cared for. "I can't see a Brattleboro boy treated this way," said Fisk. He sent his carriage and a nurse to the young man's lodgings, and had him brought to his own residence, where he was tenderly cared for until he had thoroughly recovered his health and strength.

A friend met Fisk one Saturday afternoon and said to him, "I am afraid the National Savings Bank will go by the board."

"How much do they want to float 'em?" said Fisk.

"I think about $40,000."

"Too bad," said Fisk, "to let that bank break. Why, if it should burst up, what in thunder would the poor policemen do? You know them poor fellows deposit their money in the National. Tell Hank Smith I'm ready with $5,000."

The next day Fisk saw Henry Smith, President of the Bank. He was accompanied by the venerable Thurlow Weed. The three walked into the Metropolitan Hotel. Mr. Smith was in great distress.

"Here Hank," said the impulsive Prince of Erie, "dry up, now, and tell me what you want."

"$40,000, and by ten o'clock to-morrow morning," was the answer.

"You shall have it."

He sent for Mr. Bingham, the attorney of the Erie Company. "Bingham," said he, "go and find Comer. Get a good accountant, and you three come back here.

After Mr. Bingham had gone, Fisk asked Smith, "Can I get into the bank to-day?"

"Yes," said Smith.

The accountant, accompanied by Messrs. Bingham and Comer, were soon at hand.

"Go to the bank," said Fisk, "Get the securities, and bring them here. Comer, you and the accountant stay there and examine the books and report to me."

When the securities were brought, Fisk sat down, rolled up his sleeves, and gave them a rapid examination.

"Some of these ain't worth a damn, Hank," said he; "but I guess we'll fix things. Don't worry. To-morrow morning you shall have the money."

Thurlow Weed rose from his chair, and putting his arms around the stout body of the young millionaire, said with a choking voice.

"Mr. Fisk, this is a noble act. If I ever hear a man speak ill of you, I shall feel it incumbent upon me, old as I am, to knock him down on the spot."

The next morning Fisk sent to the bank by the hands of his trusty friend and secretary, Mr. Comer, $40,000 in greenbacks, and the bank was saved.

Mr. Borrowes, of the Everett House, New York, and the

Continental, Long Branch, had purchased the Maison Doré, on Fourteenth street, and was fitting it up at great expense. Fisk heard that Borrowes was in pecuniary trouble. One morning he went to Borrowes.

"I have come, Mr. Borrowes, to make reparation for an injury I did you down at the Branch. My presence at your hotel drove away some of your best customers. I hear you are in trouble. Now tell me all about it."

The hearer was taken by surprise, but recovering from his astonishment, and feeling assured by the manner and tone of the man before him that he was in earnest, he made a brief statement of his trouble.

"Send that mortgage to me," said Fisk," and I'll have it transferred on Monday. Don't worry yourself."

This was Friday, the 5th of January, 1872. On Saturday evening he was assassinated.

One day he took the Police Captain of his precinct into his office, and said to him: "Captain, I want to be charitable, and I don't want anybody to know it. I want what I do in this way kept out of the newspapers. I know there are a large number of poor widows and helpless orphans in this ward, and no one ought to know their circumstances better than you. Whenever you come across any that are really needy send them to me, and each family can have either a ton of coal or a barrel of flour. Yes, they can have both the coal and the flour too, if they're very poor." The captain thanked him for his kind offer, and promised him to attend to it. As he was taking his leave, the Colonel called him back and said: "And, Captain, if you hear of any poor people who want to go West and have no money, you can have a ticket for them at any time. Come yourself and get it." Captain Killalee informed a reporter that he sent over twenty poor widows to Colonel Fisk, to each of whom he gave an order for coal or flour, and, in many instances, both.

A great deal of comment was made by papers inimical to Fisk in relation to his having gone to Brooklyn to obtain an injunction from Judge Pratt forbidding Stokes, Mrs. Mansfield, and Mr. James Pooton, a well known journalist, to furnish for publication the letters of Fisk to Josie. It was stated that Mr. Pooton, who lived in Brooklyn, had been joined as a defendant simply to get the case over there, and that there was no good reason why he should be made a defendant. The fact is that Mr. Pooton had negotiated to furnish the letters for publication, and was in the very act of carrying out his agreement when he was served with the injunction order, he having been entirely ignorant in the meantime that Fisk's counsel had discovered his intention or had applied for an injunction against him.

[From the Chicago Times.]

A reporter of the *Times* interviewed Mr. Frank Lawlor, a popular and talented actor of this city, with regard to a very cruel slander which has been published. We saw the article on its rounds; but knowing Mr. Lawlor to be no such man as it represented, refrained from publishing it. The writer of this boarded for several months at the Kirkwood House, Washington, with Mr. Lawlor and his then wife, now known as Josephine Mansfield, Josephine being a relative of the writer's wife's family. We frequently sat at the same table with them. We are fully prepared to indorse Mr. Lawlor's statement with regard to his character, and to Josephine

Mansfield's, at that time. They were both looked upon as most respectable and reputable people, and Miss Mansfield was not only without reproach, morally, but when we subsequently heard of her connection with Fisk, we could not believe it possible, for we had previously looked upon her as not only a strictly virtuous character, but an exceedingly retiring and modest woman, as respected her manner and disposition.

Reporter.—Have you any objection, Mr. Lawlor, to give the *Times* a statement of your California experience for publication?

Mr. Lawlor.—None in the least, now that I have been so shamefully slandered and stigmatized as a blackmailer. I had intended to say nothing about it, and have refused several newspaper men before, as I did not want my name mixed up with the Fisk affair, and wanted to say nothing to injure Josephine, but it is no more than right that I protect my own character now that it has been assailed, and I shall do so in a court of justice.

R.—The story of your elopement with Josephine was not true?

Mr. L.—No, sir. In the first place I was never in San José, where the elopement is said to have occurred, in my life. I first met the girl about 1863. She was young pleasing, and attractive, and at that time good. I liked her very well, but had no engagement with her, and no desire to marry. Some time in 1864 I went over to Virginia City, Nevada, to play an engagement, and it was while I was there that Warren and his wife undertook the blackmailing operation on the man Perley. I was not in the State of California at the time, and can prove it. Moreover, I never saw Perley in my life to know him. When I returned to San Francisco, Josie told me all about it, and said she relied on me for protection; that she did not know her step-father and mother would try to make money off Perley by using her. I told her I didn't know how I was going to protect her without marrying her, and that I was unable to do. She insisted, and finally I did marry her to save her from the evil influences of her own parents.

R.—Then you did not reside with her mother after marriage?

Mr. L.—No. From that day to this I have never spoken to Warren, nor did I allow Josie to, and she never saw her mother but once after that, and that was just before she left California for New York. I tried to keep her good and pure, and for two years, I will say this in her behalf, no wife ever conducted herself more properly toward her husband than she did to me. Before we married I told her that she might find some one richer than me, and, indeed, she might have married almost whom she pleased in San Francisco at that time, but she declared she had rather live in a cottage with me than in a palace with any person else. I was fond of her, but never cared for her so much but that I could give her up easily when I found that she was going astray.

R.—When was that?

Mr. L.—It was after we had arrived and were living in New York; I had some reason to suspect her, and told her one day if she did wrong I should have nothing more to do with her; I saw that she was determined to do wrong, and that I could not stay with her longer without becoming the laughing-stock for everybody that knew us, so I left.

R.—When was that?

Mr. L.—Sometime in 1868.

R.—How long did you livc apart before you were divorced?

Mr. L.—Several months. After I left her I continued to send her thirty dollars a week for her support, until I had positive proof that she had gone astray, and then I stopped. I told her as long as she would live a virtuous life I would send her money for her support, and should have been doing so until now, probably, if she had behaved herself.

R.—Have you seen her since your divorce?

Mr. L.—I have not, and I have always wanted to forget her, and not have my name connected with hers any longer. It was the mistake of my life marrying her, but any person might have done the same. But I have no ill feelings toward her. and do not wish to say anything that will injure her more than she is hurt already.

R.—Have you been "interviewed" concerning this matter before?

Mr. L.—Never before. At the time of the "black Friday" the *Herald* sent a man to Albany to interview me, but I knew nothing about it, and told him so. Since Fisk was assassinated, the Associated Press wished to interview me. They received orders from New York to that effect, but I did not wish my name connected with hers, and I have tried all I could to keep out of the affair.

R.—One question more, Mr. Lawlor. Concerning your leaving California?

Mr. L.—Yes, it is published that Perley ordered me out of the State within thirty days, on penalty of death, and that Mr. Maguire discharged me from his company. Both of those are the basest falsehoods. As I said, I never saw Perley to know him, and never knew that he ordered me out of the State, if he did. As to Mr. Maguire, it is a sufficient denial of the statement that he discharged me, to say that he tendered me his opera-house, just before I started, for a benefit, and that all his company volunteered their assistance. It was the largest benefit ever given in that city, and it gave me $3,500 in gold clear of expenses. Besides, when I came away, Mr. Maguire and the whole theatre company accompanied me to the depot. My character stands as high in San Francisco to-day as in Albany, my native city, or anywhere else I have ever lived, and there is not a public man in the State that I do not know, and by whom I am not respected. Then to be branded as a blackmailer, is too much. I believe Josie was entirely innocent of the blackmailing affair. Had I not believed so, I should not have married her. To show you how I am regarded by the people of Albany, where I was born and raised, I will say that right after the fire, which pretty nearly ruined me financially, I went there and was given a $2,800 benefit.

# BIOGRAPHICAL SKETCHES.

## COMMODORE VANDERBILT.

CORNELIUS VANDERBILT, the Railroad King, is now in his 76th year, although he has the appearance of a man of 55. He is over six feet in height, is strong and lusty, and bids fair to leave his hundredth birthday many years behind him.

The "Commodore," as he is now known all over the world, was born on Staten Island in 1797. His father was a waterman and was engaged in running a little sail-boat between Staten Island and New York, making his landing at the Battery (Whitehall). When Cornelius was a child he made frequent trips with his father, and, as his size and strength increased, he became very useful to Vanderbilt, Sr. Cornelius took naturally to the water, and at the age of fifteen began life on his own account as a Whitehall boatman. During the war of 1812 he made himself very useful to the government by carrying despatches to and from the forts and ships in the harbor, and became celebrated for his boldness and utter insensibility to fear. No storm could deter him from making a trip that he had promised to make, and he was never known to disappoint those who employed him.

Just after the repulse of the British in September, 1813, in their attempt to run up the channel, Vanderbilt was approached by the commandant of one of the harbor forts. It was a very stormy day, and young Cornelius was resting at the Fort, having only a short time before come down with despatches from New York.

"I want to go to the city at once," said the officer. "Will you risk the trip?"

"I'm ready as soon as you are, Major," said Cornelius. "You must expect rough times, but I guess we can make Coffee-House Slip all right."

The little craft was soon on her way. The Major's fellow-officers had begged him to delay a few hours until the storm should subside, and Vanderbilt's friends, the boatmen, had tried hard to convince him that this would be his last run, but remonstrances and predictions were alike unavailing. The two adventurous men—or rather the man and the boy, for Cornelius was now only sixteen years old—were not to be detained. The Major wished to hurry to New York for reinforcements for his garrison—this was before the days of the telegraph—and the young boatman wished to keep his word. They made the voyage in safety. Cornelius was liberally rewarded, and during the continuance of the war was always the first boatman called for by the officers in want of transportation to and from the city and the forts.

As soon as steamboats began to ply regularly on the Hudson, Vanderbilt, after having married, sold his sailing vessels and entered the service of Thomas Gibbons, who owned a steamer running between New York and New Brunswick. He advanced rapidly in a knowledge of his new business, and was soon put in command of the steamer. While he was occupied on the water his thrifty wife managed a profitable hotel at New Brunswick, and by the exercise of that prudence and economy which always characterized the pair, their few thousands were before many years turned over, until the Vanderbilts were known far and wide as comfortably rich.

For twelve years Captain Vanderbilt remained with Thomas Gibbons. During this period occurred that remarkable contest between Gibbons and the millionaire Stevens for supremacy in the waters of New York. Many flattering inducements were held out to Captain Vanderbilt by the Stevenses, but he would not desert his old friend and employer, and in the end had the satisfaction of seeing him come out of the fight with flying colors.

About 1828 or 1830, he built the little steamer Caroline, which was afterwards seized at Ogdensburg by a party of Canadian raiders and driven over Niagara Falls. This act gave rise to extensive diplomatic correspondence between Great Britain and the United States and well-nigh created a war between the two countries.

Steamboat after steamboat was built, until in 1840 he was acknowledged as the "Steamboat King" of the world. He had already built two or three steamships, but as the commerce between Europe and the United States increased, and there was a consequent demand for increased means of transportation, he paid more attention to sea-going vessels and became in time the proud owner of a fleet. In 1861, after having presented a steamship to the government, his floating stock consisted of 33 first-class steamboats and 17 magnificent steamships, worth in the aggregate millions of dollars. At this time he began to turn his attention to railroads, of which he now owns four, the Harlem, the Hudson River, the New York Central and the New Jersey Central, besides having a leading voice in the management of several others. By the legitimate earnings of these roads his fortune has been swollen to a fabulous amount, but when it is considered that he has manipulated the stock in Wall street so as frequently to make millions in an hour, it may be readily inferred that it would be difficult for even the Commodore himself to give an estimate of his wealth which should approximate the truth. It is probable that he is worth between $60,000,000 and $80,000,000, although many shrewd business men do not hesitate to assert that $100,000,000 would be nearer the mark.

Commodore Vanderbilt is a man of great natural intelligence. He is very abrupt in his manner, and except to personal friends is generally intensely selfish. He never acts without due deliberation, and rarely makes a mistake. In his dealings with the world on a large scale, he has met with only three men whom he feared—Daniel Drew, Jay Gould, and James Fisk, Jr. When Fisk's name began to be heard in Wall street, the Commodore said to one of his many agents:

"Who is this Fisk?"

"I understand that he is one of Drew's pets."

"Then we must kill him off," said the Commodore. "He's too sharp for a greenhorn, and too bold for an old hand. I don't know what to make of him."

The effort to "kill Fisk off" was a disgraceful failure. The young adventurer was a match for the veteran, and on more than one occasion his *élan* and dash sent him far in advance of the Commodore in his assaults on the money changers of Wall street.

Although the Commodore is indebted to Wall street for millions of his capital, he holds it in slight esteem, but believes that the dealers in that busy mart are nearly all scoundrels.

"Keep out of Wall street," was his advice to one of his young relatives who proposed to purchase a certain amount of stock for a rise.

COMMODORE VANDERBILT.

"But, this is a dead sure thing. I'll put up $25,000, and I want you to match me. We can clear $20,000 right off."

"Keep out of Wall street," said the Commodore.

The young man invested his $25,000 and cleared $10,000.

He came again: "Now, Commodore, I'm going to put up $50,000 and try it again. Will you go in?"

"No!" thundered the Commodore. "I tell you, *keep out of Wall street*, or you 'll be burnt."

Again the young man ventured, and again he won. He was elated with his success. Once more he called upon the Commodore and urged him to coöperate with him.

"For the last time," said the old gentleman, with a snap and a scowl; "for the last time, I tell you to keep out of Wall street. Invest your money in some legitimate business, and you 'll have enough to keep you comfortable for life. Invest in Wall street, and those thieves will strip you naked, you d——d fool."

If there is one thing the Commodore dislikes worse than another, it is to have his advice disregarded, and he rarely fails to punish the unhappy wight who thus flouts him. As his young relative left him on this occasion, the angry old gentleman sent for one of his brokers.

"Look here, Smith," said he, "Sam is going into the street to put up every cent he has in the world on Salt Island. What is the stock to-day?"

"Thirty," said Smith.

"Then go right down, buy all you can get at 30, and before night see that you have run it down to 20. If the d——d fool won't be advised, let him suffer."

Sam went home that night a ruined man, although in order to ruin him the Commodore spent a little fortune, all of which he recovered, of course, in a few days.

Six or seven years ago, Commodore Vanderbilt celebrated his golden wedding. No fewer than one hundred and forty of his descendants surrounded him on that happy occasion. Eight daughters and five sons, with a little regiment of their children, formed the party. One year afterward, he lost his youngest son, a young man of extraordinary promise, who died of disease contracted while serving in the army, during the Rebellion.

The Commodore is fond of whist, and extravagantly fond of horses. His stables contain many of the finest animals in the country, his "Mountain Boy" occupying such quarters as only a prince is supposed to provide for the favorite of his stud.

He is not at all ostentatious. His servants wear no livery. He drives himself down town every day from his plain residence, on Washington square, to his plainer office, near the Bowling Green, where he transacts an immense amount of business. He talks but little in regard to his affairs, and has a supreme contempt for what he calls "gabblers."

Mrs. Vanderbilt died about five years ago, after the loss of her youngest son. The Commodore remained a widower until the spring of 1869, when he married a beautiful and talented young lady of Mobile, Alabama. At her suggestion, he himself rarely taking any interest in religious affairs, he purchased a church in Winthrop place, which he gave in trust to the Rev. Dr. Deems, pastor of the Church of the Strangers, by which name the church is now known.

A few years ago, he purchased for $1,000,000 what was once known as St. John's Park, on which he erected the largest freight depot in the world, forming the city terminus of his Hudson River Railroad. In 1868, the celebrated "Vanderbilt bronzes" on the Hudson street front of the building, were unvailed in presence of thousands of people. The statue of the Commodore and the accompanying figures, all symbolical of the Railroad King's occupations in life, the whole telling the story of his career from youth to old age, from poverty to affluence, were designed by Albert Degroot and executed under his immediate supervision. The same artist designed and cast the statue of Franklin, in Printing House square, and presented it to the city of New York on Franklin's birthday, January 17th, 1872.

Toward the close of 1871, Vanderbilt opened the great Union Depot of the Harlem, Hudson River, and New York Central Railroads, on Fourth avenue, the largest passenger depot in the world. The ground and the building cost between $3,000,000 and $4,000,000.

## DANIEL DREW.

THIS shrewd, cunning, crafty, yet devotedly pious, financier was born at Carmel, Putnam County, New York, on the night of July 29th, 1797. Carmel has for nearly a century been considered the paradise of showmen. From very early times its male inhabitants were, to a greater or less extent, engaged in the circus and menagerie business. When, after their many seasons of travel with horse, lion, monkey, elephant, bear, dancing woman, clown, and gymnast, they had made the fortune which was the grand ambition of the Carmelite, they almost invariably came back to the banks of Lake Glenida, and pitched their tents for life. There are dozens of old showmen in and around Carmel to-day—men who have traveled through every populous district of this country and Europe, and who can tell more about the wild beasts of the world than all the Du Chaillus and Livingstones that ever shot gorilla or stuffed chimpanzee.

Daniel Drew began life a poor boy. He went to school a little while, but spent most of his younger days in gambolling with the monkeys of the menagerie, and in riding circus horses to water.

At the early age of sixteen, Daniel went for a soldier. This was during our war of 1812–14, with Great Britain. No sooner was Daniel appointed to the command of a flint-lock musket, carrying one ball and three buckshot, than he proceeded by forced marches to Fort Gansevoort, on the Hudson, where he served until peace was declared. At the close of the war he tramped back to Carmel, where he bought a few head of cattle. Having made a little money, he began the cattle business on a larger scale, and loves to tell how proud he was when overreaching the sharp drovers, who congregated at the yard where the Bowery Theatre stands now. In 1829, having made the acquaintance of Henry Astor, a brother of John Jacob, and known everywhere as Butcher Astor, he borrowed a few thousands, and entered still more extensively into the cattle trade. He made his head-quarters at the old Bull's Head Tavern, on the corner of Fourth avenue and Twenty-fourth street, where he sold thousands of cattle and made thousands of dollars. He was spoken of as an excellent landlord and as one of the shrewdest dealers within the limits of old Gotham.

In 1835, meeting with Isaac Newton, who wanted a partner in the steamboat business on the Hudson, he struck hands with that famous pioneer, and the two founded a line of steamers between New York and Albany, in opposition to Cornelius Vanderbilt, then plain Captain Vanderbilt, but nevertheless a strong man to oppose. Vanderbilt was charging three dollars fare from New York to Albany. Drew added five fine boats to his fleet in rapid succession, and put down the fare to one dollar. Vanderbilt saw that he had a determined man to deal with, so he made a proposition that they should combine their interests. Out of the compromise that resulted grew the celebrated "People's Line," of which Drew, Vanderbilt, Newton, and Eli Kelley, were the principal owners.

Drew next glided from steamboats to railroads, and then into Wall street, where he soon became known as the King of the Bears. In his stock speculations, he was ever one of the most unscrupulous men on the street, and he seemed to glory in the fact. When detected in a trick, he would whine and repent; but it would not be long before his victim would discover that the wily trickster was busily plotting to overthrow him again. Many a stock gambler has been brought to grief by Daniel Drew; but into his cold heart has never yet crept one sentiment of pity for the victim of his duplicity. Of course, such a man must be a coward.

"Where is that damned hoary-headed old hypocrite?" thundered Commodore Vanderbilt, as he stalked into Drew's office one day, after having been badly sold by his quondam partner. "Where is the ——"

But it is not necessary to repeat all that the Commodore said. Uncle Daniel was hiding under his counter. His clerks were trembling in their boots. The Commodore stormed at a terrible rate, but at last there came a lull.

"Did you mean me, Commodore?" asked a meek voice, as Daniel Drew's head appeared from beneath the counter. "I wish you would n't use such awful language. You had n't ought to do it, Commodore. It is n't right, by no means."

In 1850, in conjunction with Vanderbilt, Drew bought the

Stonington and Boston Railroad. Selling out his interest therein, in 1856, he became interested in the Erie Railway Company, then in great pecuniary difficulty, and advanced several millions to help them out. The story of what resulted from this seeming kindness of Mr. Drew has been fully told in another part of this volume. Subsequently he and the Commodore got nearly all the stock into their hands, and Drew was said for a long time to "carry Erie in his breeches pocket."

In 1857, Drew and Vanderbilt got possession of the Harlem River Railroad; but, in 1864, the Commodore "cornered Drew on Harlem," and took about $1,000,000 from him during the week. Some time afterward, Drew had his revenge. He secured an over-issue of Erie stock, and, with the aid of James Fisk, Jr., punished the Commodore by taking from his well-filled coffers no less than $8,000,000 by his celebrated "bear" movement.

Great as Daniel Drew is in stock-gambling, cattle dealing, steamboating, and railroading, he is greater far as a religionist of the intense type. When in this city he attends church at St. Paul's, on Fourth avenue, where he may be seen every Sunday, handing the plate around for the pennies of the pious. He built a monumental church at Carmel, which he named after himself, and which is under the charge of the Rev. Mr. Clapp, his son-in-law. He also endowed a Young Ladies' Seminary at Carmel, and this institution, by the terms of his donation, must be conducted on the most pious principles. His greatest work in behalf of religion, however, was the endowment of the Drew Theological Seminary, at Madison, New Jersey, which has already cost him more than half a million.

Mr. Drew is about six feet high, thin and stoop-shouldered.

He has been married since 1821, and his wife, a most estimable lady, is still living at the country seat at Carmel. He has two children, a son and a daughter, the former his land agent, the latter the wife of the Rev. Mr. Clapp.

Daniel Drew's property is variously valued at from $15,000,000 to $40,000,000.

## JAY GOULD.

JAY GOULD'S name has for some years been inseparable from that of Fisk. The men were totally different in their natures. While Fisk was extremely impetuous, and relied for guidance on his intuition, Gould is preëminently a man of reason. He is always cool and deliberate in his action, and whatever he does is the result of carefully considered and well-matured plans. As a financier he was well known long before Fisk entered the arena. His cool, concentrated powers were considered by the general public as a fitting balance to the dashing qualities of Fisk; but later events tend to show that he deliberately planned to allow Fisk to become the notorious man in order that, should events go against them, he (Gould) might escape the odium which might attach to their transactions. He was a man of wonderful ability, the keenest powers of analysis, and superb judgment and skill in manipulation, but in nowise a man of great executive ability. His connection with the Erie Road is fully explained in another part of this book. Mr. Gould is a man about five feet five inches in height, straight and slender. His hair is coal-black, as are his long beard and moustaches. He has very keen black eyes, and his whole expression is of a Jewish cast. He has a quiet, deliberate speech, and never outwardly shows signs of excitement. When irritated or excited, the only visible manifestation of his mood is in his tearing paper into little bits, which he scatters on the floor. He wholly lacks that manliness which was undoubtedly the underlying stratum of Fisk's character, and the best exemplification of this fact is shown in the following statement of how, at the last, he served a friend who had for years stood by him through thick and thin, and suffered all manner of reproach in his behalf.

Two weeks before his death, Colonel Fisk resigned his position as Vice-President of the Erie Railway Company, and for a reason very little dreamed of. He was not, as is generally supposed, the leader of the Erie Ring, although he was always ready to stand in the forefront and take the responsibility for anything that was done. It has leaked out that his share of the Ring spoils was very small. He was favorably disposed toward a compromise with the English stockholders, but his first duty, he thought, was to those whom he considered his friends, and at their instance he never hesitated to act as the scapegoat of the Ring and take all the obloquy to himself which his fellows should have divided on account of his actions at law.

About a month before the assassination of Colonel Fisk, Jay Gould and another director who had garnered the greater part of the money crop harvested by the Erie Ring, feeling that the overthrow of Tammany must inevitably result in their own destruction, together with that of all their confederates, unless some one of their number could be induced to shoulder the weight of their crimes, resolved that Fisk should be approached and induced to resign. His resignation, they knew, would have the effect of breaking the force of the storm of indignation which was certain, sooner or later, to burst upon them; and, once out of the Ring, on his own volition, he would be powerless, and the whole guilt of their nefarious actions would be fastened upon him.

At first, Gould, although Fisk's most intimate friend, and of all men, best acquainted with his moods, best able to work upon his easy nature, was afraid to approach him. He prevailed upon Frederick A. Lane to risk a meeting with the impetuous Colonel. Lane called upon Fisk and opened the subject. He had hardly advanced beyond the threshold of his introduction before Fisk started to his feet in a rage.

"Look here, Lane! If Gould sent you to me, go back to him and say that I will never talk to anybody else on a subject in which he is concerned. Go back to him and tell him that when Jim Fisk is to hear anything from Jay Gould, Jay Gould must come and say it in person."

The message was delivered and Gould entered the Vice-President's room. As he advanced toward the desk at which Fisk sat in his shirt sleeves, be began hastily tearing up paper into small bits and scattering them upon the floor—an operation, which, as Fisk well knew, betokened a stirring contest in the mind of his associate.

"Fisk," said Gould, as he took a seat near the desk; "I've come to talk to you on a more delicate and painful subject than I have ever been called upon to broach to you since we have had dealings together."

"Gould," said Fisk, as he turned and looked the other full in the eye, while his cheek blanched and his heart throbbed with emotion hard to suppress, "blurt it out. Don't be afraid of hurting my feelings. Blurt it out!"

"The time has come," said Gould, still tearing the bits of paper in his hand, "when we must begin to set our house in order. We are on the eve of a great trouble; and the only thing that can prevent utter annihilation for the whole of us is your resignation as Vice-President of the Company."

Fisk looked his old companion in the face for several moments.

"If you have the heart to ask this after all I have done for you," said Fisk, with a sob rising to his throat, "I'll show you that I have the pluck to do it."

As he spoke he put his head down upon the desk and cried like a child.

Suddenly rising from his seat with a flushed face, and bringing his fist down upon the desk, he exclaimed:

"You have asked for my resignation. If you have the heart to write it, give it to me and I will sign it."

The document had been already prepared. It lay upon Gould's desk in the next room. Gould stepped in and brought it to the Colonel, who, seizing a pen, affixed his signature to it. Then putting on his coat and hat, he left the room without a word. He had braved public opinion, and suffered disgrace for the sake of his friends. They had repaid him by striking him a harder blow than he had ever received from an enemy.

Fisk's resignation is now on file in the office of the Erie Railway Company. That which covers it to-day, before the snow has melted from his grave, bears the signature of Jay Gould. On the 17th of March, 1872, he resigned as Director.

## WILLIAM M. TWEED.

WILLIAM M. TWEED was born April 3, 1816, in the "Bloody Sixth" ward of the city of New York. His father was a chairmaker. The son was apprenticed to his father, but he never showed any inclination for work. He much preferred the company of dissolute companions, and he did not serve out his apprenticeship; though he subsequently entered the business and failed. He took naturally to political life, and at an early age was on terms of friendship with the politicians of his ward. He was popular with his fellows and was soon elected foreman of Six Engine Company, which was known as "Big Six," which title was subsequently applied to Tweed. Big Six was the terror of the ward, and in the days of hand engines, Tweed and his boys bore off the palm in the bloody fights which were of frequent occurrence. His popularity constantly increased and he was elected to the Board of Aldermen, and then to the Board of Supervisors. He graduated from the Columbia Law School, and for a short time practiced law; but politics was more to his liking, and he soon became practically the chief of the Democratic party in New York City. He was elected to the Legislature and soon after became known for his superior executive abilities. He planned political campaigns in the city, and by the aid of other men as unscrupulous as himself, inaugurated that system of "repeating" for the purpose of carrying doubtful wards, which earned for him the foul name he deserved. He was appointed a member of the Street Opening Commission, in which capacity he developed fully his utter disregard for honesty, and perpetrated some of the most unblushing frauds which ever disgraced the party. But he was popular and powerful, and he was sent to the State Senate from the Fourth District of the city. Soon after, he founded the Americus Club, of which he was, and is, the President. This club located itself at Greenwich, Conn., where it has an extensive establishment of regal splendor. Its members were politicians, and the club was the real power which controlled New York City. While many of its members were men of the most inferior grade, still they could command votes, and that was enough. The money so prodigally spent by the club and by its members individually, was plundered from the people, either by the aid of bills engineered through the Legislature by Tweed, or received as bribes from parties interested in the passage of bills. In the spring of 1869, Tweed made his *coup d'etat.* It was the passage of the new charter for the city of New York, dividing its government into *bureaux*, and giving each head of a bureau actual and full control. Tweed took the Department of Public Works, and then began that unprecedented era of plundering which brought disgrace upon the city, and ultimately resulted in the downfall of Tweed.

Tweed is five feet ten inches in height, broad-shouldered and very strongly built. His hair is a mixed sandy and gray, and he is somewhat bald. His full beard is nearly gray. His eyes are of the same color. His nose is the most prominent feature of his face, being very large and long. His forehead is broad, and exceptionally high, giving him the appearance of a "long-headed man." His whole face indicates great strength. He is very much averse to speech-making, but is a marvellous presiding officer, displaying great tact in handling a meeting, and marvellous speed and accuracy in his decisions. His executive ability is of the very highest order, and this has been his tower of strength.

He was for a long time a Director in the Erie Railway Company, from which he was ousted because of the impression that then existed, that the "Boss" of Tammany, who had been kicked from his throne on the discovery of his giant frauds in the City government, must have had a hand in swindling the stockholders of Erie.

Tweed is very intense in his likes and dislikes, and while he never forgets an enemy, he never failed to reward a friend. He has troops of friends and thousands of enemies

—among the latter none more bitter than a little fellow named Tom Nast, of *Harper's Weekly*, whose inimitable caricatures have made the world as familiar with the face as they are with the frauds of the greatest thief of the period.

## EDWARD S. STOKES.

THE assassin, Edward S. Stokes, was born in Philadelphia, in 1841. His parents were people of the highest respectability, and possessed of ample means. They were very faithful in the duty of educating and training their son, and up to a few years ago had no reason to feel ashamed of their offspring, although his almost ungovernable temper more than once gave them cause to tremble for his future.

Stokes, after having passed creditably through the different grades of one of the best of the Quaker City public schools, was admitted to the Philadelphia High School, then under the principalship of Professor John S. Hart. Here the boy displayed more than usual aptness in his studies, and gave very general satisfaction to his teachers in the matter of deportment. He did not remain long enough at the High School to graduate, as, in 1851, his parents removed to New York, where his father established himself as a provision merchant. Young Stokes began his business career as his father's clerk, and while thus employed, developed most excellent talent. About 1863, he married the beautiful and accomplished daughter of Mr. John W. Southwick, then a furniture dealer, but now a retired gentleman of great wealth, residing in Fifth Avenue. Mrs. Stokes went to Europe for her health in the spring of 1871, taking with her her only child, a lovely little girl of seven or eight years.

Stokes became acquainted with Fisk some time in 1869.

A seemingly strong friendship sprung up between the two men, and they engaged together in a number of business enterprises and speculations, in all of which Stokes is said to have secured the lion's share of the profits. Their last joint business enterprise was the Brooklyn Oil Refinery, the history of which is given in another part of this book.

Stokes' connection with Helen Josephine Mansfield began shortly after the establishment of the notorious woman in her mansion in Twenty-third street, which Fisk had provided for her. In an evil hour he introduced his friend "Ned" to the *odalisque*, and from that time James Fisk was a doomed man.

Stokes is now the occupant of a cell in the Tombs. Several attempts have been made to proceed with his trial for murder; but, with the usual trickery of counsel on either side—who in these days seem to think that the law was made for the defence of the guilty, and not for the protection of the innocent—the case has been again and again postponed, and it is exceedingly doubtful whether, in the event of a *bona-fide* trial, the murderer will receive punishment. His counsel have played a bold game, but, with John Graham at their head, whose resources were never known to fail, there is little question that the next move will be bolder still. It is said that the attempt will be made to prove that Stokes killed Fisk in self-defence.

## HELEN JOSEPHINE MANSFIELD.

THE heroine of the tragedy that sent James Fisk, Jr. into eternity in the full flush of vigorous manhood, is a woman of about 25. She was born in Boston, and has had a very checkered career. When she was sixteen years old, her

REMORSE.

mother, a widow, Mansfield by name, took Helen to California, where, on the 1st of September, 1864, she married Frank Lawlor, from whom she was divorced two years afterward. Her own story as given before Judge Bixby at the trial which preceded the assassination may be thus epitomized:

After parting finally with Lawlor, whom she accompanied to New York, she went to Boston to secure a divorce. She then removed to Philadelphia, and resided there for a short time, at 1312 Chestnut street, near the corner of 13th. It was here, as she says, that Lawlor left her "and went to live with another lady." She next went to New York, where, according to her own testimony, she must have lived a loose life from the beginning. She first met Fisk at the house of a notorious woman named Annie Wood, then residing in 34th street. Fisk became attached to her and secured for her a splendid suite of rooms in the American Club House, where she dwelt with him until the flight of the Erie Directors to Jersey City, she occupying rooms with him at Taylor's Hotel. Next with Fisk to Boston, making a stay of two weeks; next to the Clarendon Hotel, New York; and then to her beautiful residence in West 23d street, after having spent a few months at the Sherman House, and at No. 18 West 24th street. She made the acquaintance of Stokes in Philadelphia.

Her intimacy with Stokes and Fisk since that time, and its results, require no further mention here.

An incident or two in her Western life, however, deserve mention.

Her mother married a man named Warren, in San Francisco. One D. W. Perley began to pay attention to Helen at an early date, and was warned away by Warren, who on two occasions pointed a loaded pistol to his head, and forced him to take to his heels—once with very little clothing upon him. A few months after this Helen met Frank Lawlor, and asked him to protect her against Warren, who was trying to ruin her character. Lawlor is said to have replied that it would not be proper for him to assume the position of her protector, unless she were his wife, whereupon she proposed that he should marry her. This he did without hesitation, as he had been infatuated with her at first sight.

Not long afterward he had reason to suspect that his wife was not a chaste woman. He warned her not to deceive him, and she promised. A few months elapsed, and his suspicions were realized. He then sent her away from him, but provided liberally for her on receiving her pledge that she would not throw herself away. On discovering that she had forfeited her pledge, he withheld his bounty, and there has been no communication between the two since that time.

Helen Mansfield is of full, dashing figure, not at all gross. Her eyes are large, deep and bright, and inclined to Chinese in type. Her purple black hair, worn in massive coils over a well-shaped head is a wonder in its luxuriance and native gloss; and her well-cut lips, full but not large, her magnificent teeth, her clear pearl complexion suffused at times with a soft pink flush—make her altogether just such a creature as would soonest captivate and enchain an impulsive, sensual, and affectionate nature like Fisk's. Her voice is very soft and sweet, but her smile that of a woman who grants it only after measuring its width and depth, and calculating its results to a nicety before bestowing it. Perhaps a colder disgrace to her sex has never helped to ruin man since the world began.